ENGLISH DRAMA
Select Bibliographical Guides

Other Select Bibliographical Guides

ENGLISH POETRY
edited by A. E. Dyson

THE ENGLISH NOVEL
edited by A. E. Dyson

SHAKESPEARE
edited by Stanley Wells

ENGLISH DRAMA
(excluding Shakespeare)

Select Bibliographical Guides

Edited by STANLEY WELLS

OXFORD UNIVERSITY PRESS
1975

Oxford University Press, Ely House, London, W.1

GLASGOW   NEW YORK   TORONTO   MELBOURNE   WELLINGTON
CAPE TOWN   IBADAN   NAIROBI   DAR ES SALAAM   LUSAKA   ADDIS ABABA
DELHI   BOMBAY   CALCUTTA   MADRAS   KARACHI   LAHORE   DACCA
KUALA LUMPUR   SINGAPORE   HONG KONG   TOKYO

PAPERBACK ISBN 0 19 8710283
CASEBOUND ISBN 0 19 8710348

© OXFORD UNIVERSITY PRESS 1975

PRINTED IN GREAT BRITAIN
BY RICHARD CLAY (THE CHAUCER PRESS), LTD
BUNGAY, SUFFOLK

CONTENTS

Introduction   vii

Abbreviations   ix

1. The Study of Drama *by Peter Thomson*   1

2. Medieval Drama *by John Leyerle*   19

3. Tudor and Early Elizabethan Drama *by T. W. Craik*   29

4. Marlowe *by D. J. Palmer*   42

5. Jonson and Chapman *by J. B. Bamborough*   54

6. Marston, Middleton, and Massinger *by S. Schoenbaum*   69

7. Beaumont and Fletcher, Heywood, and Dekker
   by Michael Taylor   100

8. Webster, Tourneur, and Ford *by Inga-Stina Ewbank*   113

9. The Court Masque *by K. M. Lea*   134

10. Davenant, Dryden, Lee, and Otway *by H. Neville Davies*   150

11. Etherege, Shadwell, Wycherley, Congreve, Vanbrugh, and
    Farquhar *by John Barnard*   173

12. Gay, Goldsmith, Sheridan, and Other Eighteenth-century
    Dramatists *by Cecil Price*   199

13. Nineteenth-century Drama *by Michael R. Booth*   213

14. Shaw *by Margery M. Morgan*   231

15. The Irish School *by Ann Saddlemyer*   248

16. English Drama 1900–1945 *by Allardyce Nicoll*   268

17. English Drama since 1945 *by John Russell Brown*   290

Notes on the Contributors   299

Index   301

INTRODUCTION

Two of this series of four volumes, both edited by A. E. Dyson, deal respectively with English poetry and the English novel. In them, each chapter is devoted to a single, major author. Drama seemed to require a different treatment. Shakespeare is so dominant that he has been given a volume to himself. The remainder of English drama forms an uneven terrain. In some periods, especially the Elizabethan and Jacobean and the late-seventeenth century, major figures stand out, but there are other periods in which interest is much more evenly distributed among a number of less individually important writers. It would not be easy, for instance, to claim a single major dramatist between Sheridan and Shaw. Yet the interim includes much fascinating theatrical activity. The distinctive school of Irish drama which emerged in the late-nineteenth century would be inadequately represented by a single dramatist, yet the members of the school do not individually demand chapter-length discussion.

As a result, this volume follows a different pattern from its predecessors. The opening chapter offers a survey of writings on dramatic theory, of reference books, and of studies of theatre history and practice. Many of the works recommended here are of value to students of the drama of any period. Of the chapters that follow, some are devoted to individual dramatists, some to small groups of dramatists, some to broader surveys of the drama of particular periods, and one to that sub-species of drama, the masque. Not every English dramatist of merit is included; but the attempt has been made to provide adequate guidance to the major playwrights, and to the overall achievements of those periods in which major talent is less easy to discern. The grouping of dramatists is not intended to imply any special affinity.

The aim of the contributors has been to provide selective guides to study: to recommend good editions, biographies, background studies, and critical writings; to describe and distinguish between the varied aims and qualities of the works they recommend; and, where necessary, to suggest reservations or to advise rejection. The References section to each chapter lists the writings there recommended, giving bibliographical information. The lists are subdivided where necessary, and are arranged in alphabetical order. Editions of books later than the first are cited when these are substantially revised. Many of the books are available in paperback reprints, listed in the catalogues *Paperbacks in Print* (U.K.) and *Paperbound Books in Print* (U.S.A.). In the earlier chapters it has usually been possible to recommend collected editions of a dramatist's work, along with individually edited texts of his more important plays. For the relatively compact Irish school, extensive bibliographies are given. Elsewhere, dramatists' work has had to be selectively represented; no attempt is made to list the constantly increasing output of plays from the living dramatists mentioned in the final chapter. Fuller lists of both primary and secondary material are given in, for example, the *New Cambridge Bibliography of English Literature*, edited by George Watson (vol. 1, *600–1660*, Cambridge, 1974; vol. 2, *1660–1800*, Cambridge, 1971; vol. 3, *1800–1900*, Cambridge, 1969; vol. 4, *1900–1950*, Cambridge, 1972).

Readers of this volume will probably not need to be reminded that theatrical experience is fundamental to the study of drama.

S.W.W.

ABBREVIATIONS

The following abbreviations are used in the References:

AUMLA	*AUMLA: Journal of the Australasian Universities' Language and Literature Association*
EETS	Early English Text Society
ELH	*ELH: A Journal of English Literary History*
ES	*English Studies*
HLQ	*Huntington Library Quarterly*
JEGP	*Journal of English and Germanic Philology*
MLN	*Modern Language Notes*
MLQ	*Modern Language Quarterly*
MLR	*Modern Language Review*
MP	*Modern Philology*
N & Q	*Notes and Queries*
PMLA	*Publications of the Modern Language Association of America*
PQ	*Philological Quarterly*
RES	*Review of English Studies*
Ren. Dr.	*Renaissance Drama*
SEL	*Studies in English Literature, 1500–1900*
SP	*Studies in Philology*
TLS	*Times Literary Supplement*

1. THE STUDY OF DRAMA

PETER THOMSON

DRAMATIC THEORY

Drama and Theatre

For most students of English Literature, a curiosity about drama
begins with the *reading* of plays. They are already unwittingly involved in a dilemma. What, after all, is a play? Is it, like a novel,
complete on the page? Or is it, like a musical score, inadequate until
realized in performance? Stanley Wells confronts the question with
useful directness in *Literature and Drama*. His conclusion, that 'however intangible, the potential theatrical effect of a play is part of its
significance', is cautious; more cautious, certainly, than George
Hauger's in an essay on 'Theatre in General'. Hauger distinguishes
between the performed *play* and the written *script*, affirming that 'a
script is written in order that it may result in a play, hence it must
be realisable in theatrical terms, it must be playable.' The essay,
written with concealed craft, is calculated to offend those who group
plays exclusively with other literary kinds. Hauger is prepared to
group them rather with operas and ballets. S. W. Dawson, the
author of *Drama and the Dramatic*, would be among the offended. 'No
one', he imagines, 'would be disposed to question that the novel has
been, at least for the last hundred years, the major literary form;
there might be protests at the claim that it has been the major
dramatic form, though this conclusion is difficult to avoid.' The
conclusion, on the contrary, is easily avoidable, but Dawson's short
book is an original and lucid product of a literary approach to
plays. Literary scholars like Dawson look often to poems and novels
for a clearer definition of dramatic terms. J. L. Styan has tried, in
The Dramatic Experience, to describe ways of reading a play that will
take into account the missing theatrical experience. This is an erratic
book, rather patronizingly illustrated by David Gentleman, and
marred by Styan's extravagant trust in dramatic structure ('Like a
good car, a good play matches the shape of the vehicle to the power
of the engine'), but it is enlivened by an obvious delight in drama, by
a bold attempt to present its ideas pictorially, and by the provision
of a suggested notation for dramatic speech.

General Studies

Styan is sensitive to the significance of *time* in plays. A play, unlike
a novel, is always imminent, never complete. Susanne Langer makes
the point brilliantly in a remarkable chapter of *Feeling and Form*.

It has been said repeatedly that the theater creates a perpetual present
moment, but it is only a present filled with its own future that is really
dramatic. A sheer immediacy, an imperishable direct experience without
the ominous forward movement of consequential action, would not be so.
As literature creates a virtual past, drama creates a virtual future. The
literary mode is the mode of Memory; the dramatic is the mode of Destiny.

Mrs. Langer is primarily concerned with the nature of dramatic
illusion, but her explorations contribute economically to an understanding of the whole dramatic mode. Ronald Peacock's *The Art of
Drama* also seeks to distinguish the drama from other art forms. This
is a methodical book, more successful in establishing the affinities of
drama and other arts than in illuminating the essentially dramatic.
It seems to me dangerously remote from the theatre, but in this too
it is representative of aesthetic studies of the drama.

Several books, accepting the separateness of drama as a form,
analyse its component parts. Allardyce Nicoll's *The Theatre and
Dramatic Theory* includes a provocative chapter on dramatic dialogue, but his discussion of the genres is disappointingly ponderous,
particularly by comparison with their treatment in Eric Bentley's
The Life of the Drama. The second part of Bentley's stylish book
revitalizes the critical relationship of melodrama to tragedy and of
farce to comedy, and the concluding chapter emphasizes the growing significance of tragi-comedy. 'Comedy now,' he concludes, 'when
serious, tends in general towards the tragi-comic'—a thesis intelligently strengthened by J. L. Styan's study of *The Dark Comedy*. The
first part of Bentley's book treats of particular aspects of a play;
plot, character, dialogue, thought, and enactment. The selection of
a play's aspects for detailed treatment also characterizes J. L.
Styan's lively analysis of *The Elements of Drama*, but where Bentley
probes the organism Styan is content to expose the mechanism. Both
writers are at ease in the theatre, and these two books together provide an excellent theoretical background to the study of plays.

Certain more specialized studies contain implicit theories of the
drama. The view that drama aspires essentially to the accurate
representation of 'real' life had a long run, and was at its height in
1923 when William Archer could not believe 'that Robertsonian
realism, as it has been perfected by his successors, will ever be

entirely ousted from the position it now holds'. Archer's confidence survived Strindberg and the triumphant phase of German Expressionism, largely as a result of his careful misreading of Ibsen and Shaw, but his theory did not. The widening of dramatic concepts to accommodate the predominantly European developments in the writing of plays can be seen in a number of modern studies. The first essay in Eric Bentley's early work *The Playwright as Thinker* (retitled in England, perhaps because thinking in the theatre was felt here to be unpopular or impolite, *The Modern Theatre*) identifies two traditions in twentieth-century drama, one wedded to the 'slice-of-life' theory and the other explicitly opposed to it. Raymond Williams, in *Drama from Ibsen to Brecht* and in the less fruitful *Modern Tragedy*, sets about defining the new conventions and 'structures of feeling' that followed the revolutionary determination 'to confront the human drama in its immediate setting, without reference to "outside" forces and powers'. This critical awareness of a crucial shift in the fortunes of drama coincident with and partly dependent on the plays of Ibsen was given its first important airing in Shaw's *The Quintessence of Ibsenism* (1891). Since then it has bolstered most accounts of the development of the drama. One of the most interesting, Robert Brustein's *The Theatre of Revolt*, begins, like *The Playwright as Thinker*, with an antithesis:

By theatre of communion, I mean the theatre of the past, dominated by Sophocles, Shakespeare, and Racine, where traditional myths were enacted before an audience of believers against the background of a shifting but still coherent universe. By theatre of revolt, I mean the theatre of the great insurgent modern dramatists, where myths of rebellion are enacted before a dwindling number of spectators in a flux of vacancy, bafflement, and accident.

A similar antithesis underlies a fluently contentious book by George Steiner, for whom the passing of a theatre of communion constitutes *The Death of Tragedy*. Steiner ranges round world drama like a major shareholder in the gift of tongues, and the thesis is triter than the accomplishments of the writing lead one to expect. Brustein seems, by contrast, single-minded, although *The Theatre of Revolt* is in fact composed of separate essays on eight dramatists from Ibsen to Genet, and the book's semblance of unity something of a contrivance. However, Brustein is less likely than Steiner and Williams to drown the playwright's own voice, which can be heard more directly in Toby Cole's well-managed anthology of *Playwrights on Playwriting*. There is of course a good deal of special pleading in the dramatic theories of practising dramatists, and only a few can be accounted major contributors. Granville-Barker (in *On Dramatic Method*) is one, and T. S. Eliot another. John Whiting's occasional pieces, conveniently collected in *John Whiting on Theatre* and *The Art of the Dramatist*, are an evident response to the plight of the dramatist amid emptying theatres, a dilemma which also affects the sharp, scattered prefaces to the published plays of John Arden and Edward Bond.

The Origins of Drama

At the beginning of the twentieth century the work of the Cambridge Anthropologists was giving new currency to the idea that drama is an antecedent as well as a branch of the arts. The debt of Greek drama to ancient ritual and its subsequent implication in the whole of Greek culture are a theme of, for example, Jane Harrison's *Ancient Art and Ritual*. Later critics have sometimes been prepared naïvely to assume a smooth and gradual passage from ancient ritual to the spoken drama, but the general lines of development are fairly well established. Hunningher presents them in *The Origin of the Theatre*, and Francis Fergusson, in his influential book *The Idea of a Theater*, develops from them an argument for the centrality of the drama. Fergusson is in search of 'that dramatic art which, in all real plays, underlies the more highly evolved arts of language'. He finds it through a very complex deployment of the Aristotelean term, *action*, not the whole plot nor the individual events, but 'the focus or aim of psychic life from which the events, in that situation, result'. It is Fergusson's view that through the histrionic sensibility a great dramatist or a sensitive audience will perceive the play's action directly ('before all predication'), even when that action is incapable of precise definition. He illustrates the argument by analysing two outstanding successes, *Oedipus Rex* and *Hamlet*, and two outstanding failures, *Bérénice* and *Tristan und Isolde*. It is a defect of *The Idea of a Theater* that some of its explanations need to be explained. The same is true of Lionel Abel's almost equally ambitious *Metatheatre*, which is, in a sense, an extended application of Fergusson's comments on the histrionic sensibility. Abel and Fergusson are immensely talented critics who lack an ample anxiety to be lucid.

Dramatic Genres

The Idea of a Theater offers a reappraisal of some of the principles of dramatic composition proposed in Aristotle's *Poetics*. There is no ignoring Aristotle, whose shadow covered France even before it spilt over England. English translations should be read with the relentless

John Jones's *On Aristotle and Greek Tragedy* as a ready gloss. The *Poetics* as we have it is in obvious need of authorial revision, but its ambiguities have increased its employability. It is the first of countless genre studies, the majority of them ingrown and thesis-ridden. Pickard-Cambridge's *Dithyramb, Tragedy and Comedy* links the development of the kinds of drama to the origins of the theatre. For the rest, E. H. Mikhail's list of writings on *Comedy and Tragedy* will give an idea of the size of the field. W. M. Dixon's summarizing book on *Tragedy* is unusually helpful, and Northrop Frye's *A Natural Perspective*, despite its basically Shakespearian theme, is a stimulating commentary on contrasting techniques of comedy. The Michel and Sewall anthology of modern essays on *Tragedy* is well chosen, as is Paul Lauter's collection of *Theories of Comedy*. Such gatherings are made in the knowledge that literary departments throughout the world are committed to genre study. One of the reasons for this is that genre study gives the appearance of exclusiveness without actually rejecting anything; and it is, in fact, the very permissiveness of genre study, and its openness to the idiosyncrasies of particular teachers or critics, that cause student confusion. It is the normal conclusion of scholars that definitions of comedy or tragedy have to be modified in the light of each new comedy or tragedy. The search, then, is for areas of lasting agreement, not for eventual definition; and this search is properly conducted in two books in the Critical Idiom series, Clifford Leech's *Tragedy* and W. Moelwyn Merchant's *Comedy*, both cautious, both containing selective bibliographies, and both short.

Reference books generally explain themselves in their titles. Encyclopedias form one group. Phyllis Hartnoll's *The Oxford Companion to the Theatre* is invaluable. Beside it, Gassner and Quinn's excellent *Reader's Encyclopedia of World Drama* looks ready-made, and the superbly illustrated *Enciclopedia dello spettacolo* almost gaudy. This Italian work is, in fact, a massive scholarly work. Any of these volumes will serve to demonstrate how slight and London-based a book is John Russell Taylor's over-used *Penguin Dictionary of the Theatre*.

Among primarily biographical works, the eighteenth-century Baker's *Biographia Dramatica* holds its own. As finally revised in 1812, its first volume is divided into two parts giving an alphabetical list and critical account of all known (and several by now entirely unknown) British and Irish dramatists, while the last two volumes give brief comments on their plays. Thus: 'CYMBELINE, KING OF GREAT BRITAIN. A Tragedy, written by Shakespeare, with some alterations by Charles Marsh. 8vo. 1755. Though Mr. Marsh was not at that time a magistrate, the dulness he displayed in the present undertaking, afforded strong presumptions of his future rise to a seat on the bench at Guildhall, Westminster.' The entry on Shakespeare's own *Cymbeline*, burdened with 'absurdities in point of time and place, which the rigid rules of dramatic law do not now admit with so much impunity as at the time when the original author of *Cymbeline* was living', is typical in its prime concern to identify the play's sources. In two modern works of reference, actors take pride of place. Edwin Nungezer's *A Dictionary of Actors* gives full contemporary references for all known English actors until the closing of the theatres in 1642. It is to be supplemented by *A Bio- graphical Dictionary of Actors, Actresses, Musicians, Dancers, Managers and Other Stage Personnel in London, 1660–1800*, edited by P. Highfill and others. Last in this group are John Parker's volumes *Who's Who in the Theatre*, primarily valuable for their biographical references, but useful guides also to playhouses and places of performance in London and New York and to the casts of plays performed in those cities.

Among bibliographies listing writings about the theatre, none is more detailed than *English Theatrical Literature 1559–1900*, in which Arnott and Robinson have incorporated the earlier work of the fine theatrical scholar, R. W. Lowe. *A Bibliography of Theatre Arts Publications in English*, by B. F. Dukore, is more strictly utilitarian, as are the lists published in each issue of *Theatre Quarterly*. (Simon Trussler, who compiles these lists, explains and defends his new classification system for a comprehensive Bibliography of Theatre Studies in *Theatre Quarterly*, 2, no. 6 (April–June 1972).) The more specialized aims of C. J. Stratman's *Bibliography of British Dramatic Periodicals, 1720–1960* and R. B. Vowles's *Dramatic Theory: a Biblio- graphy* declare themselves.

Stratman was a tireless theatrical bibliographer. His *Bibliography of English Printed Tragedy, 1565–1900* supplements W. W. Greg's monumental *Bibliography of the English Printed Drama to the Restoration*. Alfred Harbage's *Annals of English Drama, 975–1700* arranges chronologically the known performances of plays, gives the dates of their first and last editions, and lists the companies under whose auspices they were first performed. Also useful in tracking down the texts of plays is G. W. Bergquist's index to the microprint collection of *Three Centuries of English and American Plays*, which deals with

English drama between 1500 and 1800. The various volumes of *The London Stage 1660–1800* add detail to accuracy, and the checklist of plays that occupies the final volume of Allardyce Nicoll's revised *History of English Drama 1660–1900* is a basic reference, and one that takes into account performance as well as publication of plays.

Finally, two anthologies that are virtually works of reference— A. M. Nagler's collection of *Sources of Theatrical History*, admirably illustrated, and Barrett H. Clark's gathering of *European Theories of the Drama*, which includes a remarkable proportion of the seminal work since Aristotle.

THEATRE HISTORY AND PRACTICE
Theatre History

James Arnott ends a resourceful essay on 'Theatre History' with a timely reminder: 'Drama uses not only words but also a second language of theatrical conventions and social modes, the dictionary of which is history.' That history is not, of course, merely English, and no student of drama can afford to be insular. Four large works, all copiously illustrated, attempt an account of the whole development of the theatre. For readers of Italian, Silvio d'Amico's four-volume *Storia del teatro drammatico* is certainly the best. Heinz Kindermann's *Theatergeschichte Europas* is more laborious and much longer, the kind of scholarship to which the adjective 'German' has been half-admiringly attached. The two English works, Allardyce Nicoll's *The Development of the Theatre* and Bamber Gascoigne's *World Theatre*, are restricted to a single volume, and have to rely heavily on illustration to extend their reference. They are, nevertheless, sound and useful. So, more modestly still, is Richard Southern's *The Seven Ages of the Theatre*, in which seven crucial phases in the history of the theatre are scrutinized with a stage-manager's eye for inconsistencies. The dramatic and historical judgements of Hugh Hunt's *The Live Theatre* are too simple, and it is a pity that there are not more chapters in which Hunt discusses the staging of the plays of the past in the modern theatre. It is here that he does his best writing.

Attempts to write a comprehensive history of the drama have been less successful. Despite the fact that he is possibly the only Englishman with a right to have written it, Allardyce Nicoll's *World Drama from Aeschylus to Anouilh* is not a masterwork. Even the general histories of the English drama, like Nicoll's own *British Drama*, are critically unadventurous. G. Wilson Knight's *The Golden Labyrinth* is an exception. Much too quirky to count among his major work, it has the characteristic relishing of opinion and gleeful riding of hobby-horses (Dionysus, Byron, and bisexuality are favourites here). The seminal studies of the English stage and its drama have restricted themselves historically, E. K. Chambers and Glynne Wickham to the medieval and Tudor period, G. E. Bentley to the Jacobean and Caroline, the volumes of *The London Stage* (edited by E. L. Avery and others) to the period from 1660 to 1800, and Allardyce Nicoll to that and a hundred and thirty years more. Their most important antecedent was the work of a little-known clergyman named John Genest who in 1832 provided *Some Account of the English Stage, from the Restoration in 1660 to 1830*, a ten-volume monument to the energy of amateur enthusiasm. Strangely perhaps, one intriguing minor aspect of theatre history, censorship, has not yet received comprehensive treatment. Until it does, Richard Findlater's *Banned!* is a convenient summary.

Stage Design

The increasing prominence of scenery on the English stage has been well documented by Glynne Wickham (in the volumes mentioned above), Lily B. Campbell, Allardyce Nicoll, and Richard Southern. But scenery is only part of a larger subject. The American designer Robert Edmond Jones, writing in 1941, anticipates the time when the designer can 'turn his attention away from the problem of creating stage settings to the larger and far more engrossing problem of creating stages'. Gordon Craig was carrying the same idea around with him forty years earlier. It is the gospel of the writings collected in *On the Art of the Theatre*. Craig was an immoderate man whose articulate self-esteem divided the theatrical world into disciples and enemies. His vision of theatre, though, was splendid and prophetic. There is an old debate about his debt to the Swiss artist Adolphe Appia. Lee Simonson, in his turbulent critique of stage design *The Stage is Set*, is in no doubt. He dismisses Craig as a day-dreamer and plagiarist, and calls the first 120 pages of Appia's *Music and the Art of the Theatre* 'nothing less than the text-book of modern stage-craft that gave it both a new method of approaching its problems and a new solution'. In a later essay, *The Work of Living Art*, Appia makes a clear statement of a recurrent twentieth-century theme. 'It is characteristic of theatre reform', he writes, 'that all serious effort is instinctively directed towards the *mise en scène*.' From Appia and Craig, through Yeats and Stanislavsky with both of whom Craig worked, through Meyerhold, Brecht, and Artaud, and on to the

Living Theatre, Brook, and Grotowski, the instinctive concern with the *mise en scène* gathers new dimensions. Its documentation would be necessarily incomplete without the extensive illustration in such studies as Bablet's *Esthétique générale du décor de théâtre de 1870 à 1914*, Macgowan and Jones's *Continental Stagecraft*, Hume and Fuerst's *Twentieth Century Stage Decoration*, Moussinac's *The New Movement in the Theatre*, Haineaux's two volumes *Stage Design throughout the World since 1935* and *Stage Design throughout the World since 1950*, the first volume of *Les Voies de la création théâtrale* (edited by Jean Jacquot), in which Grotowski's version of *The Constant Prince* is presented in astonishing visual detail, and James Roose-Evans's *Experimental Theatre*, whose disappointing text is rescued by its provocative illustration. The talk of scenic revolution in the twentieth century has often depended on an underrating of the nineteenth century's achievements. The work particularly but not uniquely of Grotowski brings home to me how much has been effected, rather, by the displacement of the audience.

Theatres

Audiences are normally very obedient. They go where they are put. Where that is will depend on the shape and dimensions of the place of performance. Ritual, we can be sure, preceded plays, and plays preceded playhouses. The first purpose-built English theatre was erected in 1576, and the eager search for documentary evidence about this building and its immediate successors has produced a number of special studies. A pioneer among these was T. F. Ordish's pleasantly antiquarian *Early London Theatres*. Later work includes G. F. Reynolds's inquiry into *The Staging of Elizabethan Plays at the Red Bull Theatre, 1605–25*, and an unavoidably but intelligently speculative attempt by C. Walter Hodges to describe Shakespeare's more famous playhouse, *The Globe Restored*. Hodges may usefully be complemented by Bernard Beckerman's resourceful application of available evidence in *Shakespeare at the Globe, 1599–1609*, and by three more general studies, A. M. Nagler's *Shakespeare's Stage*, Andrew Gurr's *The Shakespearean Stage*, and T. J. King's iconoclastic *Shakespearean Staging, 1599–1642*. The fortunes of the playhouse in other periods have not been studied so intensely. There is not even a detailed scholarly account of the whole history of Drury Lane or Covent Garden to stand in place of Nicoll or the volumes of *The London Stage*. Mander and Mitchenson provide a lot of information in *The Theatres of London* and *London's Lost Theatres*, and Diana Howard's *London Theatres and Music Halls, 1850–1950* is excellently documented. Less scholarly, but full of insights, is Errol Sherson's *London's Lost Theatres of the Nineteenth Century*.

The whole history of London's various theatres until 1900 is surveyed by Barton Baker in *The London Stage*, a cautious book that is unfortunate to share its title with the massive American work. Stephen Joseph's *The Story of the Playhouse in England* is the best short general survey, a less superficial book than it may seem. Joseph is rare among theatre historians in the possession of a lively and practical knowledge of architecture. It has taken a long time to interest architects in the careful documentation of the English playhouse. D. C. Mullin's survey of theatre architecture from the Renaissance to the present is an encouraging portent, as are some of the better essays in the important French collection edited by Jean Jacquot, *Le Lieu théâtral à la Renaissance*. In *Theatre of the World* Frances Yates is more concerned with the conceptual linking of the Elizabethan theatres to the Vitruvian classical theatre and to patterns of Renaissance thought. But whether the approach is architectural or philosophical, all roads lead through Italy by way of the proscenium arch.

Places of performance inter-react with styles of performance, and the middle decades of the twentieth century have seen notable shifts in both. Some of these are described in Mordecai Gorelik's *New Theatres for Old*, Stephen Joseph's *New Theatre Forms*, and the collected essays, edited by Bablet and Jacquot, of *Le Lieu théâtral dans la société moderne*. The proscenium arch, if not dead, is restless.

Directors and Directing

Kalman Burnim boldly calls his book on Garrick *David Garrick, Director*, since he is primarily concerned to show the extent of Garrick's control over the performances in which he starred; and certainly the 'director' did not emerge suddenly in the person of the Duke of Saxe-Meiningen, Stanislavsky, or even the Mr. Barrymore who was credited on the playbill with the invention and *production* of the Drury Lane pantomime in 1828. E. B. Watson's *Sheridan to Robertson* is a pioneering and original exposition of the English background to the director's rise, and Norman Marshall's *The Producer and the Play* a tolerable description of its consequences. Marshall is primarily concerned with England, but he cannot afford to neglect the vast influence of Stanislavsky on twentieth-century directors. Stanislavsky's ideas are usefully summarized in David Magarshack's introduction to *Stanislavsky on the Art of the Stage*, and partly illustrated in the translated production 'scores' of *The Seagull* and *Othello*.

Stanislavskian concern with the detail of the *mise en scène* was fervent in the first half of the twentieth century. There was a sense of mission in, for example, Granville-Barker's Shakespearian productions which gives body to his famous *Prefaces* and to the comparatively neglected *The Exemplary Theatre*. As modified by English theatrical practice, the ideas of Stanislavsky became the sound basis of English direc-torial techniques, a new orthodoxy which can be perceived in Hugh Hunt's *Old Vic Prefaces* and John Fernald's *Sense of Direction*, though it is more easily recognized in the representative productions of the major English theatrical companies. Michel Saint-Denis proposes a 'rediscovery of style' as the key to twentieth-century reform, and behind this reform stands Stanislavsky. Other major directors have worked and written in conscious reaction. *Meyerhold on Theatre* and *Brecht on Theatre* present a compilation of the ideas of two of these, usefully introduced and glossed by the translators but without the advantage of authorial synthesis and refinement. Even so they are more lucid than any of Artaud's inspirational but oracular writings. His *The Theatre and its Double* is the chief theatrical product of the age of the manifesto. English directors, having on the whole less to shout about, have been generally more reticent than the Europeans. Peter Brook is rare in having participated fully in Continentally derived movements. *The Empty Space* expresses his sense of a threat-ened theatre, evolving even as it decays. I find it a profoundly provocative book. Less profound but almost equally provocative is Tyrone Guthrie's *A Life in the Theatre*, which grandly scatters auto-biography and opinion. Guthrie, like Brook, has been prominent in the debates about stage shape and actor–audience relationships, perhaps the major common concerns of the modern director.

Actors and Acting

The literature of acting inevitably overlaps that of directing and design. It provides a sometimes fascinating and never negligible commentary on the plays to which it relates. The views of the per-formers themselves are collected by Cole and Chinoy in *Actors on Acting*. In addition, Colley Cibber's *Apology* and Macready's *Diaries* have already earned themselves a special place in literary and dramatic studies. Almost unsung, Walter Donaldson's *Recollections of an Actor* gives an uncommonly accurate picture of the provincial stock companies and the life of the lesser actor. Donaldson made his stage début in 1807, but his book sheds light on provincial conditions from the mid-eighteenth century to the rise of the repertory move-ment. He is less garrulous and self-involved than Tate Wilkinson whose *Memoirs* present possibly the best-known of all English provincial managers, and he is more reliable than Wilkinson. Most theatrical biographies are marred by overstatement (that, splendidly, is the basis of Craig's depiction of *Henry Irving*, but then Irving overstated too), by the acceptance of approximation as a lively alternative to accuracy, and by that deceptive cosiness of mutual admiration which affects everything in show-business except the rehearsal. They can be read with pleasure and used with caution. The general picture that emerges is often more trustworthy than the detailed brush-work. The exceptions, scholarly work like Appleton's on Macklin or Downer's on Macready, declare themselves as clearly as the others betray themselves.

Of the many textbooks on acting, none has been as influential as Stanislavsky's. The ideas that went to form his famous 'system' (or 'method') reached England in something like their original form piecemeal, first through *An Actor Prepares* (translated in 1936), then in *Building a Character* (1949), and finally in *Creating a Role* (1961). The curious effects of this time-lag, particularly in America, are described in Robert Lewis's *Method or Madness*. Jerzy Grotowski's *Towards a Poor Theatre* is a confused but important attempt to describe the first coherent alternative to the Stanislavskian approach to acting. English work, even *Tyrone Guthrie on Acting*, is by comparison deferential, although Bertram Joseph's *Elizabethan Acting* is a particularly bold attempt to write what amounts almost to being a book of instruction for the long-dead. Joseph undermines any attempt to look at Shakespeare's actors through Stanislavskian spectacles, but I remain uncertain about the detail of his findings.

Few theatre critics have come nearer to writing a textbook than G. H. Lewes in the essays collected in *On Actors and the Art of Acting*. The nineteenth century possessed an unrivalled number of sharp-eyed and articulate reviewers whose descriptions of the great actors of the period provide one main source for the scholarly historian. Most of the best are represented in George Rowell's collection of *Victorian Dramatic Criticism*, and briefer excerpts from many more in Russell's *Representative Actors*. A second main source of information is the promptbook. Considerable scholarly use has been made especially of the promptbooks of Shakespearian performances. Charles Shattuck has provided an invaluable list of those extant, and Jane Williamson has made exemplary use of them in her description of Charles Kemble's most famous roles. Shattuck has also edited the Macready promptbooks of *King John* and *As You Like It*, and there is a modern reprint of James Hackett's detailed record of Edmund

Kean's 1826 performances as Richard III. The more general documentation of acting styles has often relied on Shakespearian performance. G. C. D. Odell's *Shakespeare—from Betterton to Irving* records the
various fortunes of the texts as they have been doctored to suit tastes
and actors; A. C. Sprague has vividly recorded, in a number of
studies, the high points in the stage history of Shakespeare's plays,
concentrating particularly on stage business and its usefulness in an
understanding of the texts; J. C. Trewin has followed Sprague's lead
in bringing the account of *Shakespeare on the English Stage* as far as
1964; Bertram Joseph has based his scrupulous pursuit of definitive
styles in *The Tragic Actor* on a series of Shakespearian performances;
and Richard Findlater, more popularly and more attractively than
Joseph, has similarly arranged his account of *The Player Kings*. Of
broadly based historical accounts of acting, these are the best I
know. It is, notoriously, a subject on which it is difficult to write
well—Edwin Duerr, for instance, fails bravely in his world survey
of *The Length and Depth of Acting*—but it is the essential theatrical
subject. Serious students of the drama will not be content to read
only the best books on acting and actors.

REFERENCES

DRAMATIC THEORY
Drama and Theatre

S. W. Dawson, *Drama and the Dramatic* (The Critical Idiom, London, 1970).
G. Hauger, 'Theatre in General' in his *Theatre—General and Particular*
    (London, 1966).
J. L. Styan, *The Dramatic Experience* (Cambridge, 1965).
S. Wells, *Literature and Drama* (Concepts of Literature, London, 1970).

General Studies

W. Archer, *The Old Drama and the New* (London, 1923).
E. Bentley, *The Life of the Drama* (New York, 1964).
——, *The Playwright as Thinker* (New York, 1946); pub. in England as
    The Modern Theatre (London, 1948).
R. Brustein, *The Theatre of Revolt* (Boston, Mass., 1964).
ed. T. Cole, *Playwrights on Playwriting* (New York, 1960).
T. S. Eliot, *Poetry and Drama* (London, 1951).
——, *Selected Essays 1917–32* (London, 1932).
H. Granville-Barker, *On Dramatic Method* (London, 1931).
S. Langer, *Feeling and Form* (New York, 1953).
A. Nicoll, *The Theatre and Dramatic Theory* (London, 1962).

R. Peacock, *The Art of Drama* (London, 1957).

G. B. Shaw, *The Quintessence of Ibsenism* (London, 1891).

G. Steiner, *The Death of Tragedy* (London, 1961).

J. L. Styan, *The Dark Comedy* (Cambridge, 1968).

——, *The Elements of Drama* (Cambridge, 1960).

J. Whiting, *The Art of the Dramatist* (London Magazine Editions, London, 1970).

——, *John Whiting on Theatre* (London Magazine Editions, London, 1966).

R. Williams, *Drama from Ibsen to Brecht* (London, 1968).

——, *Modern Tragedy* (London, 1966).

The Origins of Drama

L. Abel, *Metatheatre* (New York, 1963).

F. Fergusson, *The Idea of a Theater* (Princeton, N.J., 1949).

J. Harrison, *Ancient Art and Ritual* (London, 1913).

B. Hunningher, *The Origin of the Theatre* (The Hague, 1955; American edn., New York, 1961).

Dramatic Genres

Aristotle, *Poetics*. The historically important translation by T. Twining (London, 1789) has been superseded by those of S. H. Butcher (London, 1895), I. Bywater (Oxford, 1905), and T. S. Dorsch in *Classical Literary Criticism* (Harmondsworth, 1965).

W. M. Dixon, *Tragedy* (London, 1924).

N. Frye, *A Natural Perspective* (New York, 1965).

J. Jones, *On Aristotle and Greek Tragedy* (London, 1962).

ed. P. Lauter, *Theories of Comedy* (New York, 1964).

C. Leech, *Tragedy* (The Critical Idiom, London, 1969).

W. M. Merchant, *Comedy* (The Critical Idiom, London, 1972).

ed. L. Michel and R. B. Sewall, *Tragedy: Modern Essays in Criticism* (Englewood Cliffs, N.J., 1963).

E. H. Mikhail, *Comedy and Tragedy: a bibliography of critical studies* (New York, 1972).

A. W. Pickard-Cambridge, *Dithyramb, Tragedy and Comedy* (London, 1927).

REFERENCE BOOKS

J. F. Arnott and J. W. Robinson, *English Theatrical Literature 1559–1900*; incorporating R. W. Lowe, *A Bibliographical Account of English Theatrical Literature*, published in 1888 (Society for Theatre Research, London, 1970).

D. E. Baker, *Biographia Dramatica*, 2 vols. (London, 1764; 2nd edn., rev. I. Reed, 1782; 4th edn., 3 vols. in 4 (vol. 1 in 2 pts.), rev. S. Jones, 1812 and repr. Graz (Austria), 1967).

G. W. Bergquist, *Three Centuries of English and American Plays: a Checklist. England 1500–1800, United States 1714–1830* (New York, 1963).

ed. B. H. Clark, *European Theories of the Drama* (New York, 1918; 3rd edn., rev. H. Popkin, 1965).

B. F. Dukore, *A Bibliography of Theatre Arts Publications in English* (AETA, Washington, D.C., 1965).

Enciclopedia dello spettacolo, 9 vols. (Rome, 1954–62, with supplements).

ed. J. Gassner and E. Quinn, *The Reader's Encyclopedia of World Drama* (New York, 1969).

W. W. Greg, *A Bibliography of the English Printed Drama to the Restoration*, 4 vols. (London, 1939–59).

A. Harbage, *Annals of English Drama, 975–1700* (Philadelphia, Pa., 1940; 2nd edn., rev. S. Schoenbaum, 1964).

ed. P. Hartnoll, *The Oxford Companion to the Theatre* (London, 1951; 3rd edn., 1967).

P. Highfill and others, *A Biographical Dictionary of Actors, Actresses, Musicians, Dancers, Managers, and Other Stage Personnel in London, 1660–1800* (Carbondale, Ill., 1973–).

ed. A. M. Nagler, *Sources of Theatrical History* (New York, 1952).

E. Nungezer, *A Dictionary of Actors, and of other persons associated with the public representation of plays in England before 1642* (New Haven, Conn., 1929).

ed. J. Parker, *Who's Who in the Theatre* (London, 1912; 15th edn., 1972).

C. J. Stratman, *A Bibliography of British Dramatic Periodicals, 1720–1960* (New York, 1962); rev. as *Britain's Theatrical Periodicals, 1720–1967* (1972).

——, *Bibliography of English Printed Tragedy, 1565–1900* (Carbondale, Ill., 1966).

J. R. Taylor, *The Penguin Dictionary of the Theatre* (Harmondsworth, 1966).

R. B. Vowles, *Dramatic Theory: a Bibliography* (New York, 1956).

THEATRE HISTORY AND PRACTICE

Theatre History

S. d'Amico, *Storia del teatro drammatico*, 4 vols. (Milan, 1939–40; 5th edn., 1968).

J. F. Arnott, 'Theatre History', in *Drama and the Theatre*, ed. J. R. Brown (London, 1971).

E. L. Avery and others, *The London Stage 1660–1800*, 11 vols. (Carbondale, Ill., 1960–9).

G. E. Bentley, *The Jacobean and Caroline Stage*, 7 vols. (Oxford, 1941–68).

E. K. Chambers, *The Mediaeval Stage*, 2 vols. (Oxford, 1903).

——, *The Elizabethan Stage*, 4 vols. (Oxford, 1923).

R. Findlater, *Banned!* (London, 1967).

B. Gascoigne, *World Theatre* (London, 1968).

J. Genest, *Some Account of the English Stage, from the Restoration in 1660 to 1830*, 10 vols. (Bath, 1832).

H. Hunt, *The Live Theatre* (London, 1962).

H. Kindermann, *Theatergeschichte Europas*, 9 vols. (Salzburg, 1957–70. The 10th, and last, vol. is in preparation.).

G. W. Knight, *The Golden Labyrinth* (London, 1962).
A. Nicoll, *British Drama* (London, 1925; 5th edn., 1962).
——, *The Development of the Theatre* (London, 1927; 4th edn., 1958).
——, *English Drama, 1900–1930: The Beginnings of the Modern Period* (Cambridge, 1973).
——, *A History of English Drama 1660–1900*, 6 vols. (Cambridge, 1952–9).
——, *World Drama from Aeschylus to Anouilh* (London, 1949).
R. Southern, *The Seven Ages of the Theatre* (London, 1961).
G. Wickham, *Early English Stages 1300–1660*, 2 vols. in 3 (vol. 2 in 2 pts.) (London, 1959–72. Vol. 3 is in preparation).

Stage Design

A. Appia, *Music and the Art of the Theatre* (trans. R. W. Corrigan and M. D. Dirks, Coral Gables, Fla., 1962; first published as *Die Musik und die Inscenierung*, Munich, 1899).
——, *The Work of Living Art* (trans. H. D. Albright, Coral Gables, Fla., 1960; first published as *L'œuvre d'art vivant*, Geneva, 1921).
D. Bablet, *Esthétique générale du décor de théâtre de 1870 à 1914* (Paris, 1965).
L. B. Campbell, *Scenes and Machines on the English Stage during the Renaissance* (Cambridge, 1923; repr. New York, 1960).
E. G. Craig, *On the Art of the Theatre* (London, 1911; repr. New York, 1956).
R. Haineaux, *Stage Design throughout the World since 1935* (London, 1956).
——, *Stage Design throughout the World since 1950* (London, 1964).
S. J. Hume and W. R. Fuerst, *Twentieth Century Stage Decoration*, 2 vols. (London, 1928).
ed. J. Jacquot, *Les Voies de la création théâtrale*, vol. 1 (Paris, 1970).
R. E. Jones, *The Dramatic Imagination* (New York, 1941).
K. Macgowan and R. E. Jones, *Continental Stagecraft* (New York, 1922).
L. Moussinac, *The New Movement in the Theatre* (London, 1931).
A. Nicoll, *Stuart Masques and the Renaissance Stage* (New York, 1938).
J. Roose-Evans, *Experimental Theatre* (London, 1970).
L. Simonson, *The Stage is Set* (New York, 1932; repr. 1964).
R. Southern, *Changeable Scenery. Its Origin and Development in the British Theatre* (London, 1952).

Theatres

ed. D. Bablet and J. Jacquot, *Le Lieu théâtral dans la société moderne* (Paris, 1963).
H. B. Baker, *The London Stage*, 2 vols. (London, 1889; 2nd edn., 1904 and repr. New York, 1969).
B. Beckerman, *Shakespeare at the Globe, 1599–1609* (New York, 1962).
M. Gorelik, *New Theatres for Old* (New York, 1940; 2nd edn., 1962).
A. Gurr, *The Shakespearean Stage* (Cambridge, 1970).
C. W. Hodges, *The Globe Restored* (London, 1953; 2nd edn., 1968).
D. Howard, *London Theatres and Music Halls, 1850–1950* (London, 1970).
ed. J. Jacquot, *Le Lieu théâtral à la Renaissance* (Paris, 1964).

S. Joseph, *New Theatre Forms* (London, 1968).
——, *The Story of the Playhouse in England* (London, 1963).
T. J. King, *Shakespearean Staging, 1599–1642* (Cambridge, Mass., 1971).
R. Mander and J. Mitchenson, *London's Lost Theatres* (London, 1968).
——, *The Theatres of London* (London, 1963).
D. C. Mullin, *The Development of the Playhouse: A Survey of Theatre Architecture from the Renaissance to the Present* (Berkeley, Calif., 1970).
A. M. Nagler, *Shakespeare's Stage* (New Haven, Conn., 1958).
T. F. Ordish, *Early London Theatres* (London, 1894; repr. New York, 1971).
G. F. Reynolds, *The Staging of Elizabethan Plays at the Red Bull Theatre, 1605–25* (London, 1940).
E. Sherson, *London's Lost Theatres of the Nineteenth Century* (London, 1925).
F. Yates, *Theatre of the World* (Chicago, Ill., 1969).

Directors and Directing

A. Artaud, *The Theatre and its Double* (trans. V. Corti, London, 1970).
B. Brecht, *Brecht on Theatre* (trans. J. Willett, London, 1964).
P. Brook, *The Empty Space* (London, 1968).
K. A. Burnim, *David Garrick, Director* (Pittsburgh, Pa., 1961).
ed. T. Cole and H. K. Chinoy, *Directors on Directing* (Indianapolis, Ind., 1963; first published as *Directing the Play*, 1953).
J. Fernald, *Sense of Direction: the Director and his Actors* (London, 1969).
H. Granville-Barker, *The Exemplary Theatre* (London, 1922; repr. New York, 1970).
T. Guthrie, *A Life in the Theatre* (New York, 1959).
H. Hunt, *Old Vic Prefaces* (London, 1954).
N. Marshall, *The Producer and the Play* (London, 1957; 2nd edn., 1962).
V. Meyerhold, *Meyerhold on Theatre* (trans. E. Braun, London, 1969).
M. Saint-Denis, *Theatre: the Rediscovery of Style* (London, 1960).
C. Stanislavsky, *The Seagull Produced by Stanislavsky* (trans. D. Magarshack, London, 1952).
——, *Stanislavsky on the Art of the Stage* (trans. D. Magarshack, London, 1950).
——, *Stanislavsky Produces Othello* (trans. H. Nowak, London, 1948).
E. B. Watson, *Sheridan to Robertson* (Cambridge, Mass., 1926; repr. New York, 1963).

Actors and Acting

W. W. Appleton, *Charles Macklin: an Actor's Life* (Cambridge, Mass., 1960).
C. Cibber, *An Apology for the Life of Mr. Colley Cibber, Comedian* (London, 1740; ed. in 2 vols. with notes and supplement by R. W. Lowe, London, 1889; Everyman edn., London, 1914; ed. B.R.S. Fone, Ann Arbor, Mich., 1968).
ed. T. Cole and H. K. Chinoy, *Actors on Acting* (New York, 1949; 2nd edn., 1970).
E. G. Craig, *Henry Irving* (London, 1930; repr. New York, 1970).
W. Donaldson, *Recollections of an Actor* (London, 1865).

A. S. Downer, *The Eminent Tragedian, William Charles Macready* (Cambridge, Mass., 1966).

———, ed., *Oxberry's 1822 Edition of 'King Richard III', with the descriptive notes recording Edmund Kean's performance made by James H. Hackett* (Society for Theatre Research, London, 1959).

E. Duerr, *The Length and Depth of Acting* (New York, 1963).

R. Findlater, *The Player Kings* (London, 1971).

J. Grotowski, *Towards a Poor Theatre* (London, 1969).

T. Guthrie, *Tyrone Guthrie on Acting* (London, 1971).

B. L. Joseph, *Elizabethan Acting* (London, 1951; 2nd edn., 1964).

———, *The Tragic Actor* (London, 1959).

G. H. Lewes, *On Actors and the Art of Acting* (London, 1875; repr. New York, 1957).

R. Lewis, *Method or Madness* (New York, 1958).

W. C. Macready, *Diaries of William Charles Macready, 1833–1851*, ed. W. Toynbee, 2 vols. (London, 1912; repr. New York, 1970).

G. C. D. Odell, *Shakespeare—from Betterton to Irving*, 2 vols. (New York, 1920; repr. 1963).

ed. G. Rowell, *Victorian Dramatic Criticism* (London, 1971).

W. C. Russell, *Representative Actors* (London, n.d.).

C. H. Shattuck, *The Shakespeare Promptbooks: a Descriptive Catalogue* (Urbana, Ill., 1965).

———, ed., *Mr. Macready Produces 'As You Like It'* (Urbana, Ill., 1962).

———, ed., *William Charles Macready's 'King John'* (Urbana, Ill., 1962).

A. C. Sprague, *Shakespeare and the Actors: the Stage Business in his Plays, 1660–1905* (Cambridge, Mass., 1945).

———, *Shakespearian Players and Performances* (London, 1954).

———, *Shakespeare's Histories: Plays for the Stage* (Society for Theatre Research, London, 1964).

C. Stanislavsky, *An Actor Prepares* (trans. E. R. Hapgood, New York, 1936).

———, *Building a Character* (trans. E. R. Hapgood, New York, 1949).

———, *Creating a Role* (trans. E. R. Hapgood, New York, 1961).

J. C. Trewin, *Shakespeare on the English Stage, 1900–1964* (London, 1964).

T. Wilkinson, *Memoirs of his Own Life*, 4 vols. (York, 1790).

J. Williamson, *Charles Kemble, Man of the Theatre* (Lincoln, Nebr., 1970).

2. MEDIEVAL DRAMA

JOHN LEYERLE

EVER since early English drama became the subject of concerted research in the middle of the nineteenth century there has been interest in studying its origins and growth as if early drama were an organism that developed along a pattern of Darwinian evolution. A theory gradually developed that the drama grew from the seed of the *quem quaeritis* trope in the liturgy for Easter, became a sturdy plant in the form of Latin liturgical drama within the Church, was transplanted outside to the city squares and streets where it was secularized into vernacular mystery cycles, then branched out into morality plays, interludes, and Tudor farce, and finally, like a hardy, mature tree, flowered in the age of the great Elizabethans. The foundation for this theory was established in the last quarter of the nineteenth century by what now seems to be an over-simplified reading of work of Continental scholars, particularly Marius Sepet, in *Los Prophètos du Christ* (1878), and Carl Lange, in *Die lateinischen Osterfeiern* (1887). E. Catherine Dunn, in her essay 'Voice Structure in the Liturgical Drama: Sepet Reconsidered' (1972), shows that Sepet's position has been over-simplified by some of his followers and that his later work, *Origines catholiques du théâtre moderne* (1904), has been neglected by nearly all. In it Sepet investigated 'the voice patterns in the liturgical chant of the Carolingian era for their dramatic potential' and took the origins of liturgical drama, in effect, back to the Carolingian era. The full theory was articulated by E. K. Chambers in volume two of his monumental work, *The Mediaeval Stage* (1903), still of great value for a study of the subject, and consolidated in another monumental work by Karl Young, *The Drama of the Medieval Church* (1933). The materials and texts printed in Chambers's appendices are of particular value. A feature of Young's work is the incorporation into his study of many of the Latin texts in full. This intellectually satisfying structure was widely accepted and its over-simplifications were ignored or even reinforced as it found its way into classroom and textbook where it was presented, with little or no question, as an accurate history of the subject. The tradition culminates in a book by Hardin Craig, *English Religious Drama* (1955), which is probably the most accessible work for anyone to see the theory presented whole and in full statement.

Weaving in and out of the work on the liturgical origins and development of early drama was an interest in folk art, some of it looking back to pagan origins. Chambers devoted all of his first volume to minstrelsy and folk drama, an indication of the importance he attached to these contributive elements. They are often taken as the explanation for the early drama's undoubted connection with the common man and the solid earth of the English countryside. The surviving cycles juxtapose a transcendental and noble other-worldliness beside a boisterous, even grotesque, presentation of day-to-day life, a confrontation of Christian teaching and all-too-human men and women. This clash of divine and secular elements was the subject of an influential short study by A. P. Rossiter, *English Drama from Early Times to the Elizabethans* (1950), a book that did much to reawaken interest in the study of early English drama, an interest that has produced important new work on the subject with the result that the traditional model of the growth and development of early drama has undergone some basic changes.

Among the early contributions to this new look at the subject was a book by Harold C. Gardiner, S.J., called *Mysteries' End* (1946). In this book, which has been curiously neglected, Father Gardiner shows that the vernacular cycles in England were not secularized but remained under the control of the Roman Church throughout their history. This control accounts for their end because they were viewed by the Protestant reformers in the sixteenth century as part of the idolatrous trappings of popery and consequently suppressed by the same iconoclastic spirit that led to the destruction of church sculpture and stained glass in the same period. One consequence of this realization is that the mystery cycles are not an uneasy yoking of divine history to a secular setting far removed from the events portrayed. Quite the contrary, late medieval English society is introduced for doctrinal purposes as an example of the way man, of whatever time and condition, rebels against God's commandments and teachings. The ongoing confrontation of the divine and the human thereby serves to reinforce one of the main precepts of the cycles and of the doctrine they present; Christianity, like Judaism from which it developed, is a religion of covenants between God and man, but God's rule, no matter though it is given with love, is disobeyed by man, an ongoing disobedience that repeats the Fall and leads, if persevered in, to loss of God's grace. Most of the Old Testament plays have obedience as a major theme; the New Testament plays emphasize the obedience of Christ, in His human manifestation, to His role of atonement by sacrifice. The recurrent unruliness of the human beings, especially the figures often described as comic, is another aspect of the same theme. The comic element often becomes grotesque when its evil propensity is revealed, as is true for such humble figures as the torturers of Christ as well as the exalted humans, such as Herod or Pilate.

New work was not limited to late-medieval vernacular cycles, however. A basic revaluation was also under way on the perennially fascinating question of the point of origin of liturgical drama. Chambers and Young argue that the origin took place about 950 at the monastery of St. Gall in Switzerland in the form of the introit trope of the Easter Mass. An argument for its origin at St. Martial at Limoges was put forward by both Edith Wright, in *The Dissemination of the Liturgical Drama in France* (1936), and Grace Frank, in *The Medieval French Drama* (1954). Origin in Northern Italy is argued by Maria Sofia de Vito in *L'origine del dramma liturgico* (1938) and by Helmut A. W. de Boor in *Die Textgeschichte der lateinischen Osterfeiern* (1967). De Boor, in fact, abandons evolution as a means of analysis. The introit trope is identified by the words of the angel guarding the empty tomb to the three Marys, 'quem quaeritis in sepulchro?' ('whom do you seek in the tomb?'). The word trope refers to a phrase interpolated into a liturgical text to embellish it, usually with sustained elaboration of chant. Such troping was thought to have spread rapidly across Europe. A version is found in the *concordia regularis* attributed to Æþelwold, bishop of Winchester, and dated about 965–75; it is one of the earliest extant texts of religious drama from England.

In 1958 Richard Donovan published his influential study, *The Liturgical Drama in Medieval Spain*. He discovered texts unknown to Karl Young indicating that influence on liturgical drama moved from Spain to France, not the reverse as Young had thought. The analysis was a reminder that the Chambers–Young model—long accepted as fixed and proved—of the origin of liturgical drama was vulnerable to data from manuscripts relevant to the issue and unknown to them. Recent work indicates that liturgical drama may have begun before the tenth century. David Dumville has published a paper (1972) on liturgical drama found in the Book of Cerne on the subject of the Harrowing of Hell. The manuscript is dated about 820, but Dumville thinks the composition is a century earlier and associates it with Æþilwald who was bishop of Lindisfarne from about 721 or 724 to 740. Another interesting development is the

work of Clifford Flanigan who, in a paper published in 1974, argues
that liturgical drama received a major impetus as a carry-over of
dramatic elements from the emotive Gallic Rite when it was replaced by the relatively more austere Roman Rite. These two studies
are not to be thought of as establishing the origins of liturgical
drama; they do indicate that the origins are before the tenth century
and are too complex and too lightly recorded in surviving manuscripts for any theory of origin to be more than a conjectural hypothesis. The Chambers–Young model shows the dangers of allowing
a hypothesis to solidify into doctrine which inhibits others from examining the data objectively, not in the context of an accepted view.

The Chambers–Young model has been found wanting not only
from the point of view of origins but also from that of evolutionary
development. In 1965 O. B. Hardison, Jr., published his book,
Christian Rite and Christian Drama in the Middle Ages, and demonstrated
that the Chambers–Young model of the development of liturgical
drama disregards the chronology of the manuscripts. To illustrate
the supposed development from the St. Gall introit of about 950 to
the text of the *concordia regularis* of only twenty years later, Young
mentions or quotes forty manuscripts, but only four are tenth
century and no less than fifteen are from the thirteenth to fifteenth
centuries, including several that are supposed to show early stages
of the evolution. The pattern that Young detected exists only if the
texts are arranged without regard to their dates to fit the design.
Such rearrangement is, of course, dead counter to any evolutionary
development. Consequently the evolutionary model must be dis-
carded; it is an interesting example of the influence of Darwinian
thought on literary historians, but it does not appear to pertain to
medieval drama.

Although the origins of liturgical drama are apt to remain controversial because there is a lack of manuscript material bearing on the
matter, indications are clear that a fairly complex type of such
drama existed by the late tenth century and had developed from
close connections with the liturgy. The annual cycle of the liturgy is
organized about Christ's life and incorporates Old Testament
material long associated with Christ's life because of the typological
connections made between the two. The influence of typology on the
drama is discussed by Theo. Stemmler in *Liturgische Feiern und
geistliche Spiele* (1970). Jean Daniélou's *From Shadows to Reality* (1960)
is also useful. Two examples will suffice: Noah building the ark was
interpreted as a type of Christ building the church and the sacrifice
of Isaac was understood as a prefigurement of the sacrifice of Christ.

No theory of evolution is needed to explain the accretion of these
dramatic episodes into a cycle because the accretion had long since
taken shape in the form of the cycle of the liturgy. As such it was
commonplace and central to Christian visual art. One typical way
of representing the episodes was in panels with typological connection shown by juxtaposing panels of figural relevance. Examples,
among many, are the well-known Klosterneuberg Altarpiece made
about 1181 by Nicholas of Verdun and the slightly earlier west doors
of San Zeno church in Verona where one door shows scenes from
the Old Testament and the other those from the New Testament.
Taken as a whole, the panels of the two doors present what amounts
to a remarkably complete mystery cycle. These doors should not be
thought of as influencing drama or of being influenced by it so much
as both being visual presentations of the Biblical elements long incorporated into the liturgical cycle because of their importance as
events in the life of Christ or as prefigurations of His life. A work on
medieval religious art particularly useful to a student of drama is
The Gothic Image by Émile Mâle, who was himself influenced by
Marius Sepet's *Les Prophètes du Christ*. A related work is M. D.
Anderson's *Drama and Imagery in English Medieval Churches* (1963). Her
argument that drama influenced art seems doubtful.

The work of the last twenty years thus has brought about a fundamental change in our understanding of liturgical and cycle drama,
a change so radical that relatively few people outside those chiefly
concerned with the material have apprehended the extent or import
of these developments. A basic revaluation is under way and the
once-standard histories of the liturgical drama are in need of replacement. This revaluation also applies to the secular mystery cycles
although the impact of the new findings is reduced because the
English texts are much later. F. M. Salter, in *Mediaeval Drama in
Chester* (1955), shows that the Chester Plays, usually taken to be the
oldest of the four surviving cycles, cannot be much earlier than about
1370. The cycle is preserved in five manuscripts, the only one with
this richness of exemplars. It has a total of twenty-four plays and is
preceded, in two of the manuscripts, by banns, an advance proclama-
tion of the cycle. It starts with the fall of Lucifer and ends with a
Judgement play. Several passages in French are included, but do
not present clear evidence for dependence on a French source. It
was staged on pageant wagons. The standard edition, by Hermann
Deimling and G. W. Matthews (1892–1916), is badly out of date.
A new one is in preparation for the E.E.T.S. by R. M. Lumiansky
and David Mills.

The next-oldest cycle is probably the York plays, which survive in one manuscript. The cycle has forty-eight plays; it begins, as usual, with a Creation play and ends with a Judgement Day play. This cycle is not only longer than Chester, it is also more complex in presentation of character and motivation; like Chester, the York cycle was staged on pageant wagons. The language of the cycle is vigorous, especially the passages attributed to an anonymous author called the York realist. Lucy Toulmin Smith's edition (1885) is badly out of date. There is an uneven translation of part of the cycle by J. S. Purvis which is used for the York Festival performances staged every three years since 1951.

The York cycle is closely connected to the Towneley cycle from near-by Wakefield which shares five pageants with it. The Towneley cycle is probably from the early fifteenth century; it survives in one manuscript which is incomplete at several places. In the numbering of the editor, the cycle has thirty plays plus two later additions, one on Lazarus and the other on Judas. The cycle contains six pageants, the Slaying of Abel, Noah, Two Shepherd Plays, Herod, and a Buffeting which are the work of a gifted unknown playwright known as the Wakefield Master. The standard edition is by George England and Alfred W. Pollard. A new edition of the complete cycle is being prepared by A. C. Cawley, whose valuable edition of the six pageants by the Wakefield Master provides a good point of entry to English mystery plays. Martial Rose's translation of *The Wakefield Mystery Plays* has staging notes which should be used with caution.

The fourth cycle, also of the early fifteenth century, was long known as the Coventry Plays, but has no connection with that city. Now it is known as the N-town Plays, or Hegge cycle, and is attributed, with no certainty, to Lincoln. It, too, survives in but one manuscript and is unlike the other extant cycles in the prominence given to material on Mary and in the replication of the Passion sequence. It has been edited by K. S. Block (1922), in whose numbering there are forty plays. A new edition is being prepared by Stanley J. Kahrl. It shows considerable evidence for staging in the round rather than on pageant wagons. As in no other cycle the theme of chastity, a concern particularly suitable to Mary, is prominent. Embedded in the cycle is what amounts to a sequence on the life and death of Herod, a unit that foreshadows the mode of Christopher Marlowe.

Apart from these four cycles a number of other play texts survive, the small remnant of what once was a flourishing tradition of the theatre in many of the major cities and towns of England. Two plays survive from Coventry and evidently once belonged to a cycle; they have been edited by Hardin Craig. The first, *The Pageant of the Shearmen and Taylors*, is the most moving of all the English mystery cycle treatments of the Nativity and Slaughter of the Innocents. The other surviving texts are conveniently gathered together by Norman Davis, whose edition (1970) is careful and accurate, and has a much fuller introduction than was customary with early play editions published by the E.E.T.S. This collection includes the well-known Abraham and Isaac play from a manuscript formerly at Brome Hall in Suffolk. Several editions of texts drawn from various cycles and prepared for undergraduate readers are also available. A. W. Pollard's *English Miracle Plays, Moralities and Interludes* (1890) is still useful, and R. George Thomas has edited *Ten Miracle Plays* (1966). Editions in modernized English include '*Everyman*' *and Medieval Miracle Plays*, edited by A. C. Cawley (1956), and *Seven Miracle Plays*, edited by Alexander Franklin (1963).

Extended discussion of these mystery plays is not possible here but is available in several recent studies that are another result of the reawakening of interest in early English drama since about 1950. Two particularly valuable studies have appeared recently. V. A. Kolve's book, *The Play Called Corpus Christi* (1966), treats the idea of theatre as a form of divine play and has interesting suggestions about the function of laughter in the cycles and about their structure. The work is readily accessible to readers unfamiliar with the material and makes a useful entry point in criticism of the early drama. Rosemary Woolf's *The English Mystery Plays* (1972) is well informed and balanced. It provides a useful survey of previous work on the material and has a good short bibliography. Plays from various cycles on the same subject are discussed together; this provides a valuable comparative analysis but tends to fragment the cycles into parts with the result that the reader does not have the sense of wholeness and historical progression that are among the cycles' principal characteristics. The bibliography on the early drama is very extensive, but these two volumes, along with the historically oriented studies mentioned at the outset, are a sound guide to the subject. Father Carl J. Stratman's *Bibliography of Medieval Drama* (1954) should be used with caution; it has many errors and significant omissions. The Medieval Supplements of *Research Opportunities in Renaissance Drama* provide a guide to recent work. Volume 13–14 (1970–1) of this publication includes Brownell Salomon's 'Early English Drama 975–1585: A Select, Annotated Bibliography of Full-Length Studies'. The Medieval Supplements also provide information about modern productions of the cycle plays, to which Fletcher Collins's *The Production of Medieval Church Music-Drama* is relevant.

This discussion can be ended with three observations. The first is that the name of not one playwright from the period covered by this chapter survives. The mystery cycles were part of the religious life of the times and are probably composite texts derived from several hands and modified in production. The idea of individual authorship, never strong in the Middle Ages, was hardly relevant and the lack of author's names is not surprising. The second point is that these texts are for production; to read them instead of experiencing them as theatre is a serious distortion because a reader unfamiliar with their dramatic power may think them childish, even crude. This mistaken inference is reinforced by a tendency to read individual plays, not whole cycles. The importance of apprehending the cycles in their whole design is the third point. Like the liturgy which is their pattern, the cycles have, in dramatic form as ritual drama, enormous power to move and engage the mind and feelings of a modern audience for whom faith in the sacred events portrayed is not strong. The impact of these cycles in an age of belief, such as fifteenth-century England, must have been profound. The cycles do not imitate an action or hold up a mirror to the fall of illustrious men as a means to entertain and instruct their audience; they are ritual and, as such, recreate what they present, the central aspects of Christianity in which the age believed, the creation, the Fall, Christ's incarnation, death, resurrection, and the Last Judgement which all should fear because all must face. The cycle plays have the same force as the liturgy in all its complexity because they developed from it, stayed close to it, and so shared the power of what has not unjustly been seen as the supreme literary achievement of medieval man.

REFERENCES

TEXTS
Anthologies

ed. A. C. Cawley, '*Everyman*' *and Medieval Miracle Plays* (Everyman's Library, London, 1956).

ed. N. Davis, *Non-Cycle Plays and Fragments*, EETS, Supplementary Text 1 (London, 1970).

ed. A. Franklin, *Seven Miracle Plays* (London, 1963).

ed. A. W. Pollard, *English Miracle Plays, Moralities and Interludes* (Oxford, 1890).

ed. R. G. Thomas, *Ten Miracle Plays* (London, 1966).

Chester Plays

ed. H. Deimling, *The Chester Plays, Part I*, EETS, extra series 62 (London, 1892).

ed. G. W. Matthews, *The Chester Plays, Part II*, EETS, extra series 115 (London, 1916).

Coventry Plays

ed. K. S. Block, *Ludus Coventriae or the Plaie Called Corpus Christi*, EETS, extra series 120 (London, 1922).

ed. H. Craig, *Two Coventry Corpus Christi Plays*, EETS, extra series 87 (first pub. London, 1902; 2nd edn., 1957).

Towneley Plays

ed. A. C. Cawley, *The Wakefield Pageants in the Towneley Cycle* (Manchester, 1958).

ed. G. England and A. W. Pollard, *The Towneley Plays*, EETS, extra series 71 (London, 1897).

trans. and ed. M. Rose, *The Wakefield Mystery Plays* (London, 1961).

York Plays

trans. and ed. J. S. Purvis, *The York Cycle of Mystery Plays* (London, 1953).

ed. L. Toulmin Smith, *York Plays* (Oxford, 1885).

CRITICAL STUDIES AND COMMENTARY

M. D. Anderson, *Drama and Imagery in English Medieval Churches* (Cambridge, 1963).

H. A. W. de Boor, *Die Textgeschichte der lateinischen Osterfeiern* (Tübingen, 1967).

E. K. Chambers, *The Mediaeval Stage*, 2 vols. (Oxford, 1903).

F. Collins, Jr., *The Production of Medieval Church Music-Drama* (Charlottesville, Va., 1972).

H. Craig, *English Religious Drama* (Oxford, 1955).

J. Daniélou, *From Shadows to Reality, Studies in the Biblical Typology of the Fathers,* trans. Dom. W. Hibberd (London, 1960).

R. Donovan, *The Liturgical Drama in Medieval Spain* (Toronto, 1958).

D. Dumville, 'Liturgical Drama and Panegyric Responsory from the Eighth Century? A Re-examination of the Origin and Contents of the Ninth-Century Section of the Book of Cerne', *Journal of Theological Studies,* N.S. 23 (1972).

E. C. Dunn, 'Voice Structure in the Liturgical Drama: Sepet Reconsidered', in *Medieval English Drama,* ed. J. Taylor and A. H. Nelson (Chicago, Ill., and London, 1972).

C. Flanigan, 'The Roman Rite and the Origins of the Liturgical Drama', *University of Toronto Quarterly* 43 (1974).

G. Frank, *The Medieval French Drama* (London, 1954).

H. C. Gardiner, *Mysteries' End. An Investigation of the Last Days of the Medieval Religious Stage,* Yale Studies in English 103 (New Haven, Conn., and London, 1946).

O. B. Hardison, Jr., *Christian Rite and Christian Drama in the Middle Ages* (Baltimore, Md., 1965).

V. A. Kolve, *The Play Called Corpus Christi* (Stanford, Calif., 1966).

C. Lange, *Die lateinischen Osterfeiern. Untersuchungen über den Ursprung und die Entwickelung der liturgischdramatischen Auferstehungsfeier mit Zugrundelegung eines umfangreichen, neuaufgefundenen Quellenmaterials* (Munich, 1887).

É. Mâle, *The Gothic Image* (originally pub. as *L'Art religieux du XIIIᵉ siècle en France,* Paris, 1902; English translation as *Religious Art in France of the Thirteenth Century,* London, 1913; repr. as *The Gothic Image,* London, 1961).

A. P. Rossiter, *English Drama from Early Times to the Elizabethans* (London, 1950).

B. Salomon, 'Early English Drama 975–1585: A Select, Annotated Bibliography of Full-Length Studies', *Research Opportunities in Renaissance Drama* 13–14 (1970–1).

F. M. Salter, *Mediaeval Drama in Chester* (Toronto, 1955).

M. C. A. Sepet, *Origines catholiques du théâtre moderne* (Paris, 1904).

——, *Les Prophètes du Christ: Étude sur les origines du théâtre au moyen âge* (Paris, 1878) (first published as four papers in the *Bibliothèque de l'École des Chartes,* 1867–8).

T. Stemmler, *Liturgische Feiern und geistliche Spiele* (Tübingen, 1970).

C. J. Stratman, *Bibliography of Medieval Drama* (Berkeley and Los Angeles, Calif., 1954).

M. S. de Vito, *L'origine del dramma liturgico,* Biblioteca della 'Rassegna' 21 (Milan, etc., 1938).

R. Woolf, *The English Mystery Plays* (London, 1972).

E. Wright, *The Dissemination of the Liturgical Drama in France* (Bryn Mawr, Penn., 1936).

K. Young, *The Drama of the Medieval Church,* 2 vols. (Oxford, 1933).

3. TUDOR AND EARLY ELIZABETHAN DRAMA

T. W. CRAIK

THE PERIOD; DRAMATIC TYPES; SPECIAL THEMES

There are surveys of Tudor drama by Brooke, Boas, and F. P. Wilson. Some important plays have come to light since Brooke's history was published in 1912 (notably Medwall's *Fulgens and Lucrece*, which has modified the earlier view of the interlude, of the growth of comedy, and of the use of the sub-plot), but it is still useful. Boas's is a convenient pocket introduction. Wilson's should be read before, during, and after research: it is both a clear guide for the beginner and a wise reminder for the specialist; its bibliography (added by Hunter) gives much more detailed information than can be given in this chapter. Apart from these three stands Rossiter's survey, since it is more tendentious (he stresses, in Tudor as in medieval drama, the element of 'ambivalence', and is noticeably anticlerical); though inaccurate in many details of the Tudor plays, it is provocative and should be read.

A feature of Tudor drama is its fluidity. The whole period is one of development and transition, not of sharply differentiated types. The gulf between critical theory and dramatic practice is wide. Madeleine Doran's *Endeavors of Art*, which relates the two without artificially tidying up the situation, is a valuable study of the Elizabethan playwrights' gradual discovery of dramatic form. Its emphasis is on the later dramatists, especially Shakespeare and Jonson, but it also deals with the plays of Lyly, Kyd, Greene, and Peele, and with earlier plays like *Gorboduc*.

Moralities and interludes are the plays which show most clearly the transition from 'medieval' to 'Renaissance' drama. Chambers (in *English Literature at the Close of the Middle Ages*) connects them with the medieval tradition and discusses the earliest of them, including *Everyman*; the history continues in F. P. Wilson's survey. Mackenzie painstakingly analyses the allegorical element of the moral plays, and Thompson's concise and accurate account of them is worth consulting, though both these books were written before the discovery of Wager's important moral interlude *Enough is as Good as a Feast*. In discussing the dramatists of 'the Sir Thomas More Circle' —Medwall, Heywood, Rastell, and Redford—especially with regard to their ideas, Pearl Hogrefe has carried on the pioneer work of Reed. The social and political ideas of the later Tudor moralities have been examined in an important article by Wright. Peter's book on complaint and satire, Bevington's on Tudor drama and politics, and Anglo's on the social and political occasions of early Tudor shows, are also relevant to the study of leading themes, as are (to bring into focus the background) Wright's substantial account of Elizabethan middle-class culture, and Chew's stimulating bringing-together of ideas, art, and literature in the Renaissance treatment of the 'pilgrimage of life' theme. The relationship between idea and visual image is also stressed in Craik's book on the staging of inter-ludes, and there is still work to be done on Tudor drama and the emblem books. The transition from medieval drama, by way of early Tudor, to Marlowe and Shakespeare, discussed in the historical sur-veys, has been studied in connection with 'auspices' (that is, by whom and for whom the plays were performed) by Bevington in *From 'Mankind' to Marlowe*. Bevington's work can be profitably read alongside Madeleine Doran's, since he begins from the theatrical practice and she from the critical theory. Craik has a short essay on the transition, and several by Wickham also bear on Shakespeare's medieval heritage, as do a number of the accounts of comedy and tragedy to follow: Margeson's may be mentioned here for its stress on the continuity from medieval themes and character-types. The morality vice has been found by J. Dover Wilson in Falstaff, and by Spivack in Iago and other villains. Needless to say, this tracing of relationships is not without danger, and requires continual vigilance from critic and reader.

The development of comedy as a dramatic form has received sound treatment in Gayley's introduction to his collection of comedies (though, as with Brooke, Mackenzie, and Thompson, one should bear in mind its age), and in the first part of a book by M. C. Bradbrook mainly devoted to Shakespearian and contemporary comedy (her *Shakespeare and Elizabethan Poetry* also gives insights into his precursors in romantic drama). An essay on romantic narrative plays by Patricia Russell explores unfamiliar pre-Shakespearian territory; as background reading, Pettet's book on the romance tradition behind Shakespeare is useful. Classical and Renaissance theory and practice of comedy (including tragicomedy), and their effects on English drama, can be studied in two books by Herrick and an essay by Hosley (see also Bond's introduction to *Early Plays from the Italian*), while Boas's *University Drama* treats of college plays in Latin as well as in English (he also covers tragedy).

Tragedy has had more attention than comedy. As with comedy, much of the discussion has been concerned with origins and with 'native' and 'classical' elements. A particularly well-balanced account of pre-Shakespearian tragedy and its basis in earlier literature and thought is Farnham's *Medieval Heritage*; Spencer's *Death and Elizabethan Tragedy* is another excellent starting-point. In following the detailed debate on Seneca's influence, it is best to begin with the contributions of Cunliffe (introduction to his *Early English Classical Tragedies*), Charlton, Baker, and Hunter, not forgetting Madeleine Doran. Clemen's book, and Prior's on the language of tragedy, contain the fullest discussion of pre-Shakespearian tragic style. Revenge tragedy is the subject of a special study by Bowers, and domestic tragedy of one by Adams, both mainly concerned with the later Elizabethan drama but taking account of the earlier.

Plays on religious subjects are discussed in books by Lily B. Campbell and Roston, history plays by Tillyard and Ribner; these special studies also bear directly on Tudor ideas and indirectly on the dramatic types.

STAGE PERFORMANCE AND CONNECTED ASPECTS

Chambers's *Mediaeval Stage* (1903) and *Elizabethan Stage* (1923) are still the fundamental reference books, continually related to the primary sources, and indispensable: comprehensive, economical, lucid, and judicious, they are models of critical scholarship. They cover much more than stage presentation, and, with their appendices, are the first place to which to turn for the answers to queries on dates, authorship, circumstances of publication, governmental control of plays, organization of court entertainment, personnel of dramatic companies, and comparable topics. The medieval study has inevitably dated somewhat, the Elizabethan very little.

The physical structure of Elizabethan public and private theatres, and of earlier English forms of stage, has been much debated, and much is still unknown. Full discussion does not belong to this chapter; the items which follow are specially relevant to the Tudor period. Withington examines pageantry, Kernodle the influence of the visual arts and of *tableaux vivants* upon Elizabethan theatre construction, Lily B. Campbell the evidence for stage scenery and machinery under Italian influence (her argument for perspective scenery is resisted by McDowell); essays in *Shakespeare Survey 12* (1959), in a collection edited by Prouty in 1961, and in one edited by Jacquot and others in 1964, deal with various special features of staging. An important, detailed, and well-illustrated account by Wickham of *Early English Stages* includes, besides the physical conditions of performance, many of the aspects treated by Chambers (in conjunction with whose books it should be read, since it supplements without superseding them).

The staging of interludes is discussed by Craik (setting, performers, costume, action), by Bevington in *From 'Mankind' to Marlowe* with particular reference to the actors and audiences, and by Southern, who charts the course of Tudor staging from the simplicity of the unadapted hall to the relative elaboration of setting found in plays written towards the end of the sixteenth century. On the named companies performing in this period Chambers should of course be consulted, and also J. T. Murray, who gives lists of their itineraries. On the boys' companies there is a detailed book by Hillebrand, and there is a more general one on school drama by Motter. M. C. Bradbrook's social study of the rise of the common player takes the early Tudor period into consideration.

Music in plays is the subject of the last part of a study of Tudor court music and poetry by Stevens, and an essay by Dent and Sternfeld.

TEXTS: GENERAL

Anyone studying Tudor plays should at least look at facsimiles of the earliest printed copies, partly for aesthetic reasons and partly because (with a little practice) it soon becomes actually easier to interpret them in their original spelling, punctuation, and format. These early texts, of course, all contain errors, but this is a further reason for consulting them, because there is still work to be done in elucidating them, and happy emendations may occur to any intelligent and sympathetic reader.

The advantage of photographic facsimiles, provided by J. S. Farmer's Tudor Facsimile Texts or the publications of the Scolar Press, is that one gets the plays exactly as they were published; but since they carry no numbering but page signatures, they are inconvenient for reference purposes. The Malone Society's reprints are as nearly infallible as the most careful scrutiny can make them; they have introductions (mainly bibliographical) and line-numbering, but the sharp modern fount makes their black-letter very hard on the eyes. Old-spelling collections, some of them with fuller editorial matter, have been made by Brandl, Manly, Gayley, Bond, Cunliffe, Adams, and Happé; single plays have been so edited for the Early

English Text Society and the Scottish Text Society, and in *Shakespeare Jahrbuch*, Bang's *Materialien*, and the Fountainwell Drama Texts. Bibliographies appended to F. P. Wilson's *The English Drama, 1485–1585* (see above) and to Harbage's *Annals of English Drama* will help in locating particular plays in the above collections and series (and in the modernized text collections and series which follow), as well as those which have been published outside any such collection or series. Of individual dramatists, old-spelling collected editions begin with Boas's Kyd, Bond's Lyly, and Collins's Greene; the Yale University Press's Peele (various editors) has since joined them.

The assembling of old plays in modernized texts began in the eighteenth century with Dodsley the publisher: his collection was reissued, with omissions (as famous plays were reprinted in the works of Marlowe and others) and additions (as fresh old plays turned up), down to Hazlitt's 1874 version (reprinted). This is textually unreliable but handy for a quick general impression of any play which is not to be studied with care. The same may be said of Farmer's modernized collections of 1905–8 (reprinted), which have, however, useful glossaries and annotation; Farmer collected Heywood in one volume and Bale in another. There are a number of smaller anthologies, some including the earlier part of the period (Boas, McIlwraith, Armstrong, Schell and Schuchter) and many beginning with the latter part of it (needless to specify here). Individual plays are edited with introductions and notes in the Revels Plays, the New Mermaids, and the Regents Renaissance Drama Series.

TEXTS OF INDIVIDUAL DRAMATISTS

Skelton's *Magnificence* has a long introduction (of general relevance to moralities) in Ramsay's edition, and is also the subject of a book by Harris, who challenges Ramsay's belief that the play is based on secular rather than religious ethics and that it is a satire on Wolsey. Heywood, besides appearing in the books of Reed and Pearl Hogrefe, has had his debt to French farce examined by Maxwell (the French source of *Johan Johan* came to light later: see Craik's essay). There is a full-length portrait of Bale, setting the plays in the context of his whole propagandist work, by Thora Blatt, and one of Udall (author of *Roister Doister* and possibly of other extant anonymous plays) by Edgerton. Hamer's editorial commentary on Lyndsay's *Satire of the Three Estates* is of great importance. William Wager's two signed plays have been edited with a useful introduction by Benbow.

The most comprehensive account of Lyly is Hunter's, with three chapters on the plays, relating them to his whole career and to the dramatic tradition before and after him. Violet M. Jeffery maintains that Lyly was much influenced by Italian writers, but the resemblances (as Hunter suggests) may merely show a common tradition. Saccio, writing on Lyly's dramatic allegory, issues a sane warning (by analogy with Spenser's allegory) against limiting it too strictly to particular historical and philosophical correspondences: he reviews the work of those who have done this, and examines Lyly's dramatic technique, as does Best in an essay. The 'public-theatre' account of Lyly's staging given in Bond's edition is wrong (corrected in Chambers). In her edition of *Gallathea* and *Midas* Anne B. Lancashire treats with caution a hypothesis that the latter is either a revision or a conflation of an earlier work or works by Lyly. This writer's idiosyncratic style has been analysed by Barish and by Tillotson in relation to his plays. Powell sees the plays as pastimes designed to develop their audiences' faculties pleasantly.

On Kyd's life and work Freeman's book is well documented, cogent, and reliable: besides dealing conservatively with such matters as dates and the authorship of works conjecturally attributed to Kyd, it includes two chapters on *The Spanish Tragedy*. P. B. Murray's is wholly concerned with *The Spanish Tragedy*, and provides (through six of its eight chapters) a detailed scene-by-scene analysis of the play. (Incidentally, Freeman and Murray both maintain that the stage audience in the last scene is above, not on the apron as Edwards has argued.) Carrère (writing in French) dwells particularly on structure and characterization: he also, like Freeman, discusses the attribution of other plays. Whether *The First Part of Hieronimo* is Kyd's is controversial (Cairncross, who prints it in his edition of *The Spanish Tragedy*, is alone among modern editors in upholding its claim), and so is nearly everything about *The Spanish Tragedy* itself except the authorship—date, authorship of additions, theme, attitude to the hero. The morality of revenge has been the chief preoccupation of critics. Bowers's argument (in *Elizabethan Revenge Tragedy*), that Hieronimo is to blame for not leaving justice to heaven, is now generally repudiated, notably by Edwards on grounds of dramatic effect and emotional response and by Johnson on grounds of Elizabethan Biblical interpretation; see also Murray's appended critical bibliography for other contributions to the debate. The relevance of the early Portugal scenes has also been debated, their defenders (in particular Hunter and Jensen) urging that the play's leading theme is not revenge but justice. Harbage touches on the element of 'comitragedy' in Lorenzo's removal of Pedringano (further discussed by Cole in his essay on the comic accomplice, and, in its more general implications, by Rossiter and Spivack in works already noted). The most substantial modern critical introductions are by Edwards, Cairncross, and Mulryne (the latter's edition replacing an earlier New Mermaid); Edwards has also written a pamphlet on Kyd and his precursors in tragedy. The language of the play has been discussed in the books on tragedy by Baker, Prior, and Clemen, and in an essay by Barish, who shows how Kyd adapts the techniques of non-dramatic Elizabethan poetry to his special dramatic ends.

Peele and Greene have had less attention: they neither left a distinctive and coherent body of work (like Lyly and Marlowe) nor wrote a single play (like Kyd's) which profoundly influenced the course of drama. Senn has produced a careful and detailed examination of the dramatic construction of the plays of both dramatists. On Peele, the Yale introductions (which refer to such critical work as exists) are commendable: in that to *The Old Wives Tale*, F. S. Hook kills the persistent but unfounded notion that Huanebango is Gabriel Harvey (compare, under Skelton and Lyly, similar doubt cast on topical identifications of personages and events in their plays) and he writes well on the play's general character, which is not satirical burlesque. Inga-Stina Ewbank examines *David and Bethsabe* as a drama of sin and expiation, and argues that its moral structure reveals a better dramatic construction than it is usually thought to have.

Whether *Friar Bacon and Friar Bungay* was written before or after *Doctor Faustus* is still undecided. U. M. Ellis-Fermor traces the growth of Greene's technique and style and his gradual emancipation from Marlowe's overwhelming influence, Sanders compares his approach to romantic comedy with Shakespeare's, and Muir considers his merit as lying in liveliness and variety rather than in characterization. His debts to his own prose fictions are discussed by Maclain. Both his most famous plays exist in modern editions, *James the Fourth* by Lavin (who makes important restorations to the order of the text) and by Sanders (who incorporates them), and *Friar Bacon* by Lavin and by Seltzer.

REFERENCES

THE PERIOD; DRAMATIC TYPES; SPECIAL THEMES

H. H. Adams, *English Domestic or Homiletic Tragedy, 1575–1642* (New York, 1943; repr. New York, 1965).

S. Anglo, *Spectacle, Pageantry, and Early Tudor Policy* (Oxford, 1969).

H. Baker, *Induction to Tragedy: A Study of the Development of Form in 'Gorboduc', 'The Spanish Tragedy', and 'Titus Andronicus'* (Baton Rouge, La., 1939; repr. New York, 1965).

D. M. Bevington, *From 'Mankind' to Marlowe: Growth of Structure in the Popular Drama of Tudor England* (Cambridge, Mass., 1962).

——, *Tudor Drama and Politics: A Critical Approach to Topical Meaning* (Cambridge, Mass., 1968).

F. S. Boas, *An Introduction to Tudor Drama* (Oxford, 1933).

——, *University Drama in the Tudor Age* (Oxford, 1914; repr. New York, 1966).

ed. R. W. Bond, *Early Plays from the Italian* (Oxford, 1911; repr. New York, 1965).

F. T. Bowers, *Elizabethan Revenge Tragedy, 1587–1642* (Princeton, N.J., 1940; repr. 1966).

M. C. Bradbrook, *The Growth and Structure of Elizabethan Comedy* (London, 1955).

——, *Shakespeare and Elizabethan Poetry: A Study of his Earlier Work in Relation to the Poetry of his Time* (London, 1951).

C. F. T. Brooke, *The Tudor Drama* (London, 1912; repr. New York, 1964).

L. B. Campbell, *Divine Poetry and Drama in Sixteenth Century England* (Cambridge, 1959).

E. K. Chambers, *English Literature at the Close of the Middle Ages* (Oxford History of English Literature, Oxford, 1945).

H. B. Charlton, *The Senecan Tradition in Renaissance Tragedy* (Manchester, 1946; first published as introduction to Sir William Alexander, *Poetical Works* (Manchester, 1921)).

S. C. Chew, *The Pilgrimage of Life* (New Haven, Conn., 1962).

W. H. Clemen, *English Tragedy before Shakespeare: the Development of Dramatic Speech* (London, 1961; previously published in German, Heidelberg, 1955).

T. W. Craik, *The Tudor Interlude: Stage, Costume, and Acting* (Leicester, 1958).

——, 'The Tudor Interlude and Later Elizabethan Drama', in *Elizabethan Theatre* (Stratford-upon-Avon Studies 9, ed. J. R. Brown and B. Harris, London, 1966).

J. W. Cunliffe, *Early English Classical Tragedies* (Oxford, 1912).

M. Doran, *Endeavors of Art: A Study of Form in Elizabethan Drama* (Madison, Wis., 1954).

W. E. Farnham, *The Medieval Heritage of Elizabethan Tragedy* (Berkeley, Calif., 1936).

ed. C. M. Gayley, *Representative English Comedies*, vol. 1 (London and New York, 1903; repr. New York, 1969).

M. T. Herrick, *Comic Theory in the Sixteenth Century* (Urbana, Ill., 1950).

——, *Tragicomedy, its Origin and Development in Italy, France, and England* (Urbana, Ill., 1955).

P. Hogrefe, *The Sir Thomas More Circle: a Program of Ideas and their Impact on Secular Drama* (Urbana, Ill., 1959).

R. Hosley, 'The Formal Influence of Plautus and Terence', in *Elizabethan Theatre* (Stratford-upon-Avon Studies 9, ed. J. R. Brown and B. Harris, London, 1966).

G. K. Hunter, 'Seneca and the Elizabethans: a Case-Study in "Influence" ', *Shakespeare Survey 20* (1967).

W. R. Mackenzie, *The English Moralities from the Point of View of Allegory* (Boston, Mass., 1914; repr. New York, 1966, 1969).

J. M. R. Margeson, *The Origins of English Tragedy* (Oxford, 1967).

J. D. Peter, *Complaint and Satire in Early English Literature* (Oxford, 1956).

E. C. Pettet, *Shakespeare and the Romance Tradition* (London, 1949).

M. E. Prior, *The Language of Tragedy* (New York, 1947; repr. Bloomington, Ind., 1966).

A. W. Reed, *Early Tudor Drama: Medwall, the Rastells, Heywood, and the More Circle* (London, 1926; repr. New York, 1969).

I. Ribner, *The English History Play in the Age of Shakespeare* (Princeton, N.J., 1957).

A. P. Rossiter, *English Drama from Early Times to the Elizabethans* (London, 1950).

M. Roston, *Biblical Drama in England from the Middle Ages to the Present Day* (London, 1968).

P. Russell, 'Romantic Narrative Plays, 1570–1590', in *Elizabethan Theatre* (Stratford-upon-Avon Studies 9, ed. J. R. Brown and B. Harris, London, 1966).

T. Spencer, *Death and Elizabethan Tragedy: a Study of Convention and Opinion in the Elizabethan Drama* (Cambridge, Mass., 1936).

B. Spivack, *Shakespeare and the Allegory of Evil: the History of a Metaphor in Relation to his Major Villains* (New York, 1958).

E. N. S. Thompson, *The English Moral Plays* (New Haven, Conn., 1910; repr. New York, 1970).

E. M. W. Tillyard, *Shakespeare's History Plays* (London, 1944).

G. W. G. Wickham, *Shakespeare's Dramatic Heritage: Collected Studies in Mediaeval, Tudor, and Shakespearean Drama* (London, 1969).

F. P. Wilson, *The English Drama, 1485–1585*, ed. with a bibliography by G. K. Hunter (Oxford History of English Literature, Oxford, 1969).

J. D. Wilson, *The Fortunes of Falstaff* (Cambridge, 1943).

L. B. Wright, *Middle-Class Culture in Elizabethan England* (Chapel Hill, N.C., 1935; repr. Ithaca, N.Y., 1958).

——, 'Social Aspects of Some Belated Moralities', *Anglia* 54 (1930).

STAGE PERFORMANCE AND CONNECTED ASPECTS

D. M. Bevington, *From 'Mankind' to Marlowe: Growth of Structure in the Popular Drama of Tudor England* (Cambridge, Mass., 1962).

M. C. Bradbrook, *The Rise of the Common Player: a Study of Actors and Society in Shakespeare's England* (London, 1962).

L. B. Campbell, *Scenes and Machines on the English Stage during the Renaissance: a Classical Revival* (Cambridge, 1923).

E. K. Chambers, *The Elizabethan Stage*, 4 vols. (Oxford, 1923).

——, *The Mediaeval Stage*, 2 vols. (Oxford, 1903).

T. W. Craik, *The Tudor Interlude: Stage, Costume, and Acting* (Leicester, 1958).

E. J. Dent and F. W. Sternfeld, 'Music and Drama', in *The New Oxford History of Music, vol. 4. The Age of Humanism, 1540–1630* (Oxford, 1968).

H. N. Hillebrand, *The Child Actors: a Chapter in Elizabethan Stage History* (Urbana, Ill., 1926; repr. New York, 1964).

ed. J. Jacquot and others, *Le Lieu théâtral à la Renaissance* (Paris, 1964).

G. R. Kernodle, *From Art to Theatre; Form and Convention in the Renaissance* (Chicago, Ill., 1944).

J. H. McDowell, 'Tudor Court Staging: a Study in Perspective', *JEGP* 44 (1945).

T. H. V. Motter, *The School Drama in England* (London, 1929; repr. Port Washington, N.Y., 1968).

J. T. Murray, *English Dramatic Companies, 1558–1642*, 2 vols. (London, 1910; repr. New York, 1963).

ed. A. Nicoll, *Shakespeare Survey 12* (Cambridge, 1959).

ed. C. T. Prouty, *Studies in the Elizabethan Theatre* (Hamden, Conn., 1961).

R. Southern, *The Staging of Plays before Shakespeare* (London, 1973).

J. E. Stevens, *Music and Poetry in the Early Tudor Court* (London, 1961).

G. W. G. Wickham, *Early English Stages, 1300–1660*, vol. 1, vol. 2, Part 1 (London, 1959, 1963).

R. Withington, *English Pageantry: an Historical Outline*, 2 vols. (Cambridge, Mass., 1918–20; repr. New York, 1964).

TEXTS: GENERAL

ed. J. Q. Adams, *Chief Pre-Shakespearean Dramas* (London, 1924).

ed. W. A. Armstrong, *Elizabethan History Plays* (London, 1965).

ed. W. Bang and H. de Vocht, *Materialien zur Kunde des älteren englischen Dramas* (Louvain, 1902–).

ed. F. S. Boas, *Five Pre-Shakespearean Comedies* (London, 1934).

ed. R. W. Bond, *Early Plays from the Italian* (Oxford, 1911; repr. New York, 1965).

ed. A. Brandl, *Quellen des Weltlichen Dramas* (Strassburg, 1898).

ed. J. W. Cunliffe, *Early English Classical Tragedies* (Oxford, 1912).

Dodsley's Old English Plays, ed. W. C. Hazlitt, 15 vols. (London, 1874; repr. New York, 1964).

ed. J. S. Farmer, *Early English Dramatists*, 12 vols. (London, 1905–8; repr., 13 vols., New York, 1966).

——, Tudor Facsimile Texts, 143 vols. (London, 1907–14).
ed. C. M. Gayley, *Representative English Comedies*, vol. 1 (London and New York, 1903; repr. New York, 1969).
ed. H. R. Happé, *Tudor Interludes* (Harmondsworth, 1972).
A. Harbage, *Annals of English Drama, 975–1700*, rev. S. Schoenbaum (London, 1962; supplements, 1966–).
ed. A. K. McIlwraith, *Five Elizabethan Tragedies* (London, 1938).
Malone Society Reprints, General Editors W. W. Greg, F. P. Wilson, A. Brown, G. R. Proudfoot (Oxford, 1907–).
ed. J. M. Manly, *Specimens of the Pre-Shaksperean Drama*, 2 vols. (Boston, Mass., 1897–8; repr. New York, 1967).
ed. E. T. Schell and J. D. Schuchter, *English Morality Plays and Moral Interludes* (New York, 1969).

INDIVIDUAL DRAMATISTS

JOHN SKELTON (1460?–1529)

Magnificence, ed. R. L. Ramsay (EETS, London, 1908).
W. O. Harris, *Skelton's 'Magnyfycence' and the Cardinal Virtue Tradition* (Chapel Hill, N.C., 1965).

JOHN HEYWOOD (1497?–1580?)

T. W. Craik, 'The True Source of John Heywood's *Johan Johan*', *MLR* 45 (1950).
I. Maxwell, *French Farce and John Heywood* (Melbourne, 1946).

JOHN BALE (1495–1563)

T. B. Blatt, *The Plays of John Bale: a Study of Ideas, Techniques, and Style* (Copenhagen, 1968).

NICHOLAS UDALL (1506–56)

W. L. Edgerton, *Nicholas Udall* (Twayne's English Authors Series, New York, 1965).

SIR DAVID LYNDSAY (1490–1555)

A Satire of the Three Estates, ed. D. Hamer (*The Works of Sir David Lyndsay*: vol. 2, text; vol. 4, notes: Scottish Text Society, Edinburgh, 1931, 1936).

WILLIAM WAGER (*fl.* 1566)

The Longer thou Livest, the More Fool thou Art; *Enough is as Good as a Feast*, ed. R. M. Benbow (Regents Renaissance Drama Series, Lincoln, Nebr., 1968).

JOHN LYLY (1554?–1606)

The Complete Works of John Lyly, ed. R. W. Bond, 3 vols. (Oxford, 1902).
Gallathea; *Midas*, ed. A. B. Lancashire (Regents Renaissance Drama Series, Lincoln, Nebr., 1970).
J. A. Barish, 'The Prose Style of John Lyly', *ELH* 23 (1956).
M. R. Best, 'Lyly's Static Drama', *Ren.Dr.*, N.S. 1 (1968).
G. K. Hunter, *John Lyly; the Humanist as Courtier* (London, 1962).
——, *Lyly and Peele* (Writers and their Work, No. 206, London, 1968).

V. M. Jeffery, *John Lyly and the Italian Renaissance* (Paris, 1928; repr. New York, 1969).

J. Powell, 'John Lyly and the Language of Play', in *Elizabethan Theatre* (Stratford-upon-Avon Studies 9, ed. J. R. Brown and B. Harris, London, 1966).

P. Saccio, *The Court Comedies of John Lyly; a Study in Allegorical Dramaturgy* (Princeton, N.J., 1969).

G. Tillotson, 'The Prose of Lyly's Comedies', in his *Essays in Criticism and Research* (Cambridge, 1943).

THOMAS KYD (1557?–95?)

The Works of Thomas Kyd, ed. F. S. Boas (Oxford, 1901).

The Spanish Comedy, or *The First Part of Hieronimo*; *The Spanish Tragedy*, ed. A. S. Cairncross (Regents Renaissance Drama Series, Lincoln, Nebr., 1967).

The Spanish Tragedy, ed. P. W. Edwards (The Revels Plays, London, 1959).

——, ed. J. R. Mulryne (New Mermaids, London, 1970).

J. A. Barish, '*The Spanish Tragedy*, or the Pleasures and Perils of Rhetoric', in *Elizabethan Theatre* (Stratford-upon-Avon Studies 9, ed. J. R. Brown and B. Harris, London, 1966).

F. Carrère, *Le Théâtre de Thomas Kyd* (Toulouse, 1951).

D. Cole, 'The Comic Accomplice in Elizabethan Tragedy', *Ren.Dr.* 9 (1966).

P. W. Edwards, *Thomas Kyd and Early Elizabethan Tragedy* (Writers and their Work, No. 192, London, 1966).

A. Freeman, *Thomas Kyd, Facts and Problems* (Oxford, 1967).

A. Harbage, 'Intrigue in Elizabethan Tragedy', in *Essays on Shakespeare and Elizabethan Drama in Honor of Hardin Craig*, ed. R. Hosley (Columbia, Mo., 1962; London, 1963).

G. K. Hunter, 'Ironies of Justice in *The Spanish Tragedy*', *Ren.Dr.* 8 (1965).

E. Jensen, 'Kyd's *Spanish Tragedy*: the Play Explains Itself', *JEGP* 64 (1965).

S. F. Johnson, 'The Spanish Tragedy, or Babylon Revisited', in *Essays on Shakespeare and Elizabethan Drama in Honor of Hardin Craig*, ed. R. Hosley (Columbia, Mo., 1962; London, 1963).

P. B. Murray, *Thomas Kyd* (Twayne's English Authors Series, New York, 1969).

GEORGE PEELE (1558?–97?)

The Life and Works of George Peele, gen. ed. C. T. Prouty, 3 vols. (New Haven, Conn., 1952–70).

I.-S. Ewbank, 'The House of David in Renaissance Drama', *Ren.Dr.* 8 (1965).

ROBERT GREENE (1560?–92)

The Plays and Poems of Robert Greene, ed. J. C. Collins, 2 vols. (Oxford, 1905).

Friar Bacon and Friar Bungay, ed. J. A. Lavin (New Mermaids, London, 1969).

——, ed. D. Seltzer (Regents Renaissance Drama Series, Lincoln, Nebr., 1963).

James the Fourth, ed. J. A. Lavin (New Mermaids, London, 1967).
——, ed. N. Sanders (The Revels Plays, London, 1970).
U. M. Ellis-Fermor, 'Marlowe and Greene: a Note on their Relations as Dramatic Artists', in *Studies in Honor of T. W. Baldwin*, ed. D. C. Allen (Urbana, Ill., 1958).
A. H. Maclain, 'Greene's Borrowings from his own Prose Fiction in *Friar Bacon and Friar Bungay* and *James the Fourth*', *PQ* 30 (1951).
K. Muir, 'Robert Greene as Dramatist', in *Essays on Shakespeare and Elizabethan Drama in Honor of Hardin Craig*, ed. R. Hosley (Columbia, Mo., 1962; London, 1963).
N. Sanders, 'The Comedy of Greene and Shakespeare', in *Early Shakespeare* (Stratford-upon-Avon Studies 3, ed. J. R. Brown and B. Harris, London, 1961).
W. Senn, *Studies in the Dramatic Construction of Robert Greene and George Peele* (Berne, 1973).

4. MARLOWE

D. J. PALMER

TEXTS

Although in times of less exact scholarship Christopher Marlowe (1564–93) was accredited with a number of anonymous Elizabethan plays and even with much of Shakespeare's early work, there are now just six plays generally accepted as his (or seven, if the two parts of *Tamburlaine* are reckoned separately). Yet of these plays, whose chronology remains quite uncertain, only *Tamburlaine* and *Edward II* have been preserved in texts relatively free from problems of collaboration and contamination. Thus the title-page of the 1594 quarto of *Dido, Queen of Carthage* names Thomas Nashe as co-author; *The Jew of Malta* is known to us only through the quarto of 1633, in which Thomas Heywood has added a Prologue and Epilogue and may also have taken other liberties with the text of a play then forty years old; *Doctor Faustus* exists in two different versions, printed in 1604 and 1616 respectively, and if it is possible to decide which of them better represents Marlowe, there remains the further complication of a collaborator who was responsible for some or all of the comic scenes in prose; and finally, *The Massacre at Paris* may never have been a masterpiece, but the mangled state of the text as we have it must mitigate censure. Since the critical judgement of Marlowe's dramatic achievement is so dependent on the nature of the texts, no serious student of his work can ignore the problems that are explored, if not always resolved, by good modern editions of the plays.

Until the publication in 1973 of F. T. Bowers's two-volume edition, the only old-spelling text of the plays available was that edited by C. F. Tucker Brooke (1910), an edition preserved more by convention and convenience of reference than by absolute textual authority. It is still in print, however, unlike the six-volume modern-spelling edition produced under the general editorship of R. H. Case (1930–3); yet where it can be found this undertaking provides a wealth of information and insight in its generous commentaries. For the text of *Doctor Faustus*, both these editions have been superseded by the work of W. W. Greg, whose parallel-text edition of the play (1950) is a monument of bibliographical scholarship which establishes the authority of the 1616 quarto over that of the shorter 1604 version to which most previous scholars had given their allegiance. Among later editions, in modern spelling and separate volumes, *Doctor Faustus* (1962) and '*Dido, Queen of Carthage*' and '*The Massacre at Paris*' (1968) have so far been published in the excellent series of Revels Plays, furnished with comprehensive introductions and ample notes; with briefer commentary and apparatus, reliable texts of *Doctor Faustus* (1965), *Edward II* (1967), *The Jew of Malta* (1967) and *Tamburlaine* (1971) have appeared in the New Mermaid series, and editions of *The Jew of Malta* (1965) and *Tamburlaine* (1967) are included in the Regents Renaissance Drama series. Of the collected single-volume texts, Roma Gill's edition (1971) is more reliable than J. B. Steane's (1968), while those by Kirschbaum (1962) and Ribner (1963) are more readily available in the United States than in Great Britain. A major old-spelling edition is being prepared by Roma Gill.

CRITICAL STUDIES AND COMMENTARY

Broadly speaking, three very different images of Marlowe emerge from the criticism of the last fifty years. The first image is a romantic portrait of the youthful and rebellious free-thinker, the embodiment of Renaissance individualism; it derives from nineteenth-century conceptions of the artistic temperament and of the Elizabethan age, and it rests upon an identification of the figures of Tamburlaine and Faustus in particular with a somewhat glamorized and sentimental impression of Marlowe's personality. The second image is that of an orthodox Christian moralist; it develops in reaction to the first image, as the biographical approach to interpretation gives way to an emphasis on the background of the plays in the traditional thought and doctrine current in Marlowe's lifetime. The third image presents an ambivalent, disillusioned ironist, sceptical of the conventional attitudes and beliefs of his day; it restores the iconoclastic Marlowe but considerably darkens the confident self-assertion of the first image. These three images successively reflect the progression of Marlowe criticism, but they also coexist as basic positions in the continuing critical debate. There is a truth in each of them, largely dependent on which plays are under discussion, and many critics, undeterred by our ignorance of the order of their composition, have discerned in the plays a development, or else a falling-off, from the drama of titanic aspiration to a deepening sense of human limitation and failure.

Una Ellis-Fermor's book is representative of its generation in treating the plays as vehicles for the heroic figures through whom Marlowe expressed his own outlook on life: 'the limitless desire, the unbridled passion for the infinite, a certain reckless, high confidence in the will and spirit of man'. According to this school of interpretation, the plays reflect the spirit of Renaissance man, proclaiming his emancipation from the circumscribed, divinely appointed order of the Middle Ages, and Marlowe's reputation among his contemporaries as an atheist and libertine, as well as the violent and untimely end to his brilliant poetic career, invited a ready identification of the dramatist with his heroes. If Marlowe's life and work were regarded as inseparable at this time, however, interest in Marlowe the man produced, alongside the more extravagant effusions of literary criticism, the valuable biographical research of such investigators as Leslie Hotson (1925) and Mark Eccles (1934), culminating in the admirably judicious and dependable study by F. S. Boas (1940) and in the compendious but rather indigestible volumes of John Bakeless (1942). Boas's work remains the standard biography, though subsequent research by William Urry (1964) has added to our knowledge of Marlowe's family background.

The work of the biographers and source-hunters divested Marlowe's image of some of its more fanciful glamour, and Paul Kocher's important study (1946) of his learning and intellectual interests drew attention to the mind of the dramatist rather than his personality, as well as clarifying the significance of 'atheism' in Elizabethan terms. But Kocher's emphasis upon Marlowe's relationship to the more heterodox and advanced thought of his day, while it demonstrates the sophistication and maturity of Marlowe's studies in theology, politics, cosmology, and natural science, still maintains the romantic view that Marlowe endorsed the iconoclastic attitudes of his dramatic heroes. Another notable exponent of this view is Harry Levin, whose approach to the plays (1952) as tragedies of aspiration finds its central image and its title in the myth of Icarus. Levin follows the traditional line of interpretation when he writes: 'The unholy trinity of Marlowe's heresies [i.e. "concupiscence, curiosity, and vainglory"], violating the taboos of medieval orthodoxy, was an affirmation of the strongest drives that animated the Renaissance and have shaped our modern outlook.' Yet Levin is not concerned with the plays as a revelation of Marlowe's personal interests and inclinations; for him their chief significance lies in the much broader context of the development and continuity of European culture, as Marlowe created from his heritage a form of tragedy answerable to man's changing sense of his place in the world. And in his concern with dramatic form, Levin attends not only to the moral and philosophical themes of the plays, but to their style and structure as well.

Levin's urbane and sensitive study was perhaps the final consummation of the romantic conception of the plays as Renaissance celebrations of expansive and egotistic worldliness. For already the assumption that Marlowe invited admiration of his aspiring heroes had been challenged. A spate of essays on *Doctor Faustus*, including those by James Smith (1939), Leo Kirschbaum (1943), W. W. Greg (1946), and Lily B. Campbell (1952), argued that Faustus is to be regarded from an orthodox Christian standpoint, not as a Promethean hero, but as a sinner who falls through pride into despair. And Roy Battenhouse's interpretation of *Tamburlaine* (1941) drew upon a formidable array of Elizabethan theological and moral doctrine to buttress the view that, far from glorifying his hero's career of conquest and lamenting his death, Marlowe intended a perfectly traditional condemnation of worldly ambition. (Marlowe's reputation as an atheist is accounted for, not by discrediting the nature of the evidence as other scholars have tried to do, but by accepting it as a subterfuge which Marlowe assumed in the course of his duties as a secret agent.) Battenhouse's thesis has not won much assent, but it has certainly provoked further questions about Marlowe's use of learning and contributed to a more complex awareness of the moral issues and attitudes involved in the plays. *Doctor Faustus*, of course, is the more obvious play on which to base the claim for Marlowe's religious orthodoxy, and its theological subtlety has been further explored by T. McAlindon (1966), in an essay that relates the mythological and magical concerns of the play to patristic conceptions of the diabolic, and by Michael Hattaway (1970), who finds that 'the great scenes re-enact and reassert the emblems of Christian learning, the saint in his study, Solomon's conviction of vanity, the moralizations of the Helen story, the saving wisdom of Christ, and the apocalypse that will destroy all monuments to man's knowledge.' The accretion of learned commentary on *Doctor Faustus*, which is as voluminous as that on the rest of Marlowe's plays put together, has been usefully surveyed and listed by Max Bluestone (1969).

To many critics, however, there is no simple alternative between

an atheistic and a Christian Marlowe. Thus, for instance, F. P. Wilson
(1953) warns against the tendency 'to make his plays out to be more
unorthodox than they are', while he acknowledges that in the case of
Tamburlaine Part II, 'the dramatist's attitude is, to say the least,
ambiguous'. And to Miss Mahood (1950), 'the view that his dramas
represent the protest of traditional ethics against Renaissance individualism seems to me no more tenable than the view that they are
so many self-portraits.' Both she and J. C. Maxwell (1955) emphasize the quality of ironic detachment, rather than explicit moral
comment, by means of which Marlowe controls the dramatic perspective and often diminishes the heroic scale of soaring aspiration.
The case for conceiving Tamburlaine as inspiring admiration rather
than inviting moral judgement, however, was persuasively reasserted
from a new angle by Eugene M. Waith (1962), who sees in Marlowe's
figure of the demi-god the influence of Seneca's Hercules; yet in the
same year came Douglas Cole's major contribution to the Christian
interpretation of the plays, a study whose insistence on a rigorous
scheme of divine retribution for misdeeds does not always avoid the
danger of reducing complex works of art to didactic *exempla*. The
debate about the moral basis of Marlowe's tragic universe has yet to
be resolved.

While the question of Marlowe's orthodoxy, with its implications
for critical interpretation, arose from the biographical and 'background' investigations into his learning and intellectual pursuits, set
in the context of Elizabethan doctrine and controversy, our understanding of his dramatic methods has also developed since the days
when he was regarded simply as a brilliant poet with little sense of
dramatic unity or skill in plotting. As Nicholas Brooke observes
(1966), 'Marlowe was not a poet who lacked dramatic talent, he was
the reverse; a dramatist who had the resources of a great poet at his
command, when required.' *Tamburlaine*, in particular, once commonly treated as though it were little more than a vehicle for the
brilliant but monotonous rhetoric of its central figure, has been
shown in successive studies by Helen Gardner (1942), G. I. Duthie
(1948), and Clifford Leech (1964) to possess both dramatic conflict
and progression within each of its two parts, while the second part,
in which Marlowe was less dependent on narrative sources, is re-
deemed by these critics from the status of an inferior sequel to be
recognized as a completely different kind of structural achievement.
The poet and the dramatist have also been brought closer to each
other through a growing interest in the imagery of the plays. M. C.
Bradbrook (1935) was one of the earliest critics to relate poetic

imagery to the symbolism of stage-spectacle in *Tamburlaine*, the formal conventions of which make it 'more like a pageant than the modern idea of a play', and W. A. Armstrong takes this approach further in his monograph (1966) on the emblematic motifs in the same play. Marlowe's ironic use of traditional Christian typology in the language and stage-action of *The Jew of Malta* is thoroughly documented in a substantial essay by G. K. Hunter (1964), and there is a provocative discussion by C. L. Barber (1964) of the images of gluttony in *Doctor Faustus*, in which he finds an allusion to the sacrament of Holy Communion, deprived by Tudor Protestantism of its miraculous significance. Barber relates the ambivalence of spiritual and physical planes of meaning in Marlowe's use of imagery to 'the tension involved in the Protestant world's denying itself miracles in a central area of experience', and, recalling drama's ancient association with ritual, he connects 'the restriction of the impulse for physical embodiment in the new Protestant worship with a contemporary fascination in the drama with magical possibilities and the incarnation of meaning in physical gesture and ceremony'. But it is possible to argue that instead of affirming the power of ritual and ceremony, *Doctor Faustus* merely parodies them in line with the Protestant denial of their efficacy, and my own essay (1964) attempts to relate the illusory nature of magic to the make-believe world of the stage.

The importance of seeing Marlowe, not merely as the innovating predecessor of Shakespeare (an aspect reconsidered by Harold Brooks in the volume of essays edited by Brian Morris), but as the inheritor of a dramatic tradition whose conventions he adapted to his own purposes, is reflected in the work of most modern critics, including the comprehensive treatment of the subject by David Bevington (1962). In this respect, the comic elements in Marlowe's art and their relationship to tradition have considerable critical importance, as the essays of M. C. Bradbrook and Clifford Leech in the Hardin Craig *festschrift* (1962) point out. The middle scenes of *Doctor Faustus*, for instance, whose buffoonery obviously derives from the conventions of the popular stage rather than from classical notions of tragic decorum, have been both deplored and defended. Thus F. P. Wilson represents one point of view when he writes that 'the middle of the play always was disfigured by comic and clownish scenes not only feeble in invention but grossly out of harmony with the tragic theme', while Robert Ornstein (1955) voices the equally familiar critical justification that these scenes, like the medieval comedy of evil, dramatize the folly of Faustus's rebellion against

God, and so are integral to the play: 'We are always aware that Faustus the aspiring Titan is also the self-deluded fool of Lucifer.' The prevailing tone of the villainy in *The Jew of Malta*, which T. S. Eliot (1918) characterized, in a phrase often repeated since, as 'farce . . . terribly serious even savage comic humour', has similarly been related to the irreverent antics of the morality Vice, though most critics have found in the play's lack of tragic dignity not only a more constricted dramatic world than those of *Tamburlaine* and *Doctor Faustus* but also an inferior artistic achievement. For some, however, Marlowe's humour is not simply another aspect of his art, it is almost the keynote, at least as characteristic and individual as the 'mighty line' of his heroic style. Thus Nicholas Brooke, arguing that Marlowe conceived his plays in theatrical rather than literary terms, declares that *The Jew of Malta* in particular is neither strictly comic nor tragic, but 'a curiously ambiguous sort of drama, in which some scenes are simply funny, some simply painful, but many more exist in a sort of limbo where you may laugh, or may not, but you will be pained as well, either way . . . the more you laugh, the more the play bites.' Brooke extends his discussion of this black humour to include the horrific comedy of the baiting of Bajazeth in *Tamburlaine* and the sadistic wit of the murderer Lightborn in *Edward II*, and in addition to reconsidering the traditional forms used by Marlowe, he draws analogies with the modern theatre of the absurd.

A less sympathetic view of Marlowe's sense of the comic is taken by J. B. Steane (1964), who ascribes its harsh sardonic quality to the dramatist's quirks of temperament rather than to dramatic tradition. Of the slapstick scenes in *Doctor Faustus* he remarks severely that 'there are better ways of presenting boredom than by being boring, or triviality than by being trivial', and, unlike T. S. Eliot, Steane finds nothing 'terribly serious' in the farce of *The Jew of Malta*. Instead, he sees in the plays evidence of a divided and disturbed sensibility: 'destructiveness and cruelty are never far absent in Marlowe.' Steane is a very acute critic of poetic style, and his book corrects the tendency of much modern commentary to read the plays for their ideological content rather than their artistic achievement, but his approach is at times too literary, with little sense of the plays in terms of the stage. Nevertheless, his presentation of 'this passionate and unstable poet' is a major study, comparable in importance with those by Levin and Cole, but sharing little in common with either of them in its view of Marlowe.

The theatrical approach to the plays is well represented by the special issue of *Tulane Drama Review* (1964), in which no fewer than five contributors deal with aspects of interpretation raised in stage-performance. Other essays in this volume include those by Leech and Barber referred to above, and E. M. Waith's reappraisal of *Edward II*, a play once commonly regarded as Marlowe's least characteristic work in the weakness and limitation of its central figure. *Edward II* in fact found relatively little favour with critics before Clifford Leech's admiration of its dramatic 'objectivity' (1959); while J. C. Maxwell, for instance, dismissed the play as 'relatively lifeless and derivative', without 'a single unifying theme', Leech applauded the absence of moral or political doctrine from its treatment of character and action: 'There is no theory here which Marlowe illustrates, no warning or programme for reform, no affirmation even of a faith in man. . . . Here the suffering . . . is the major fact.' As Leech found in *Edward II* evidence of Marlowe's development, rather than his decline, from *Tamburlaine*, so Waith argues that 'only *Tamburlaine* is more completely an artistic success', and he traces the sense of dramatic progression in the play through 'a gradual though not steady intensification of feeling' which emphasizes 'the pathos and horror of predicaments in which man is inextricably caught'. Going even further in the evaluation of *Edward II*, Gāmini Salgādo (1971) describes it as 'in some ways Marlowe's most ambitious play'.

Nicholas Brooke's remark that *Edward II* 'totally excludes the moral' suggests that perhaps one reason for its rise in critical esteem has been a reaction against the school of interpretation which, chiefly on the basis of *Doctor Faustus*, presents Marlowe as an orthodox though sophisticated traditionalist. Certainly Brian Morris finds in the collection of essays which he edited (1968) that *Edward II* is 'almost an obsessive focus of interest', while the volume does not contain a single essay on *Doctor Faustus*. In this volume, Marlowe's ironic use of traditional emblematic devices, and the relationship of his dramatic effects and techniques to the modern theatre of Brecht and the playwrights of the absurd, are the subjects of essays by Michael Hattaway and by J. R. Mulryne and Stephen Fender in collaboration, while the divergence of view between my own contribution and that of W. Moelwyn Merchant reflects the apparent inability of modern criticism to resolve the basic question of Marlowe's moral and religious commitment: perhaps, as is sometimes suggested, our own division of opinion derives from a deep-seated ambivalence in Marlowe himself.

Finally, there are several critical anthologies which reprint in collected form many of the essays and extracts from the books mentioned in this survey. Clifford Leech (1964) and Judith O'Neill (1969) have edited general collections, which do not overlap in their choice of material; there is also surprisingly little duplication between the two anthologies on *Doctor Faustus*, edited by John Jump (1969) and by Willard Farnham (1969).

REFERENCES

TEXTS

ed. F. T. Bowers, *The Complete Works of Christopher Marlowe*, 2 vols. (Cambridge, 1973).

ed. C. F. Tucker Brooke, *The Works of Christopher Marlowe* (Oxford, 1910).

ed. R. H. Case (General Editor), *The Works and Life of Christopher Marlowe*:
1. *The Life of Marlowe and 'The Tragedy of Dido Queen of Carthage'*, ed. C. F. Tucker Brooke (London, 1930).
2. *Tamburlaine the Great, I and II*, ed. U. M. Ellis-Fermor (London, 1930).
3. *'The Jew of Malta' and 'The Massacre at Paris'*, ed. H. S. Bennett (London, 1931).
4. *Doctor Faustus*, ed. F. S. Boas (London, 1932).
5. *Edward II*, ed. H. B. Charlton and R. D. Waller (London, 1933; rev. F. N. Lees, 1955).

ed. R. Gill, *The Plays of Christopher Marlowe* (London, 1971).

ed. L. Kirschbaum, *The Plays of Christopher Marlowe* (Cleveland, Ohio, and New York, 1962).

ed. H. J. Oliver, *'Dido, Queen of Carthage' and 'The Massacre at Paris'* (The Revels Plays, London, 1968).

ed. I. Ribner, *The Complete Plays of Christopher Marlowe* (New York, 1963).

ed. J. B. Steane, *Christopher Marlowe: Complete Plays* (Harmondsworth, 1968).

Doctor Faustus

ed. R. Gill (The New Mermaids, London, 1965).
ed. W. W. Greg (Oxford, 1950).
ed. J. D. Jump (The Revels Plays, London, 1962).

Edward II

ed. W. Moelwyn Merchant (The New Mermaids, London, 1967).

The Jew of Malta
ed. T. W. Craik (The New Mermaids, London, 1967).
ed. R. W. Van Fossen (Regents Renaissance Drama Series, Lincoln, Nebr., 1964; London, 1965).

Tamburlaine
ed. J. W. Harper (The New Mermaids, London, 1971).
ed. J. D. Jump (Regents Renaissance Drama Series, Lincoln, Nebr., and London, 1967).

CRITICAL STUDIES AND COMMENTARY

W. A. Armstrong, *Marlowe's 'Tamburlaine': The Image and the Stage* (Hull, 1966).
J. Bakeless, *The Tragicall History of Christopher Marlowe*, 2 vols. (Cambridge, Mass., 1942).
C. L. Barber, ' "The Form of Faustus' Fortunes Good or Bad" ', *Tulane Drama Review* 8 (1964).
R. W. Battenhouse, *Marlowe's 'Tamburlaine': A Study in Renaissance Moral Philosophy* (Nashville, Tenn., 1941).
D. M. Bevington, *From 'Mankind' to Marlowe: Growth of Structure in the Popular Drama of Tudor England* (Cambridge, Mass., 1962).
M. Bluestone, *'Libido Speculandi*: Doctrine and Dramaturgy in Contemporary Interpretations of Marlowe's *Doctor Faustus*', in *Reinterpretations of Elizabethan Drama*, ed. N. Rabkin (Selected Papers from the English Institute, New York, 1969).
F. S. Boas, *Christopher Marlowe: A Biographical and Critical Study* (Oxford, 1940; rev. 1964).
M. C. Bradbrook, 'Marlowe's *Doctor Faustus* and the Eldritch Tradition', in *Essays on Shakespeare and Elizabethan Drama in Honor of Hardin Craig*, ed. R. Hosley (Columbia, Mo., 1962; London, 1963).
——, *Themes and Conventions of Elizabethan Tragedy* (Cambridge, 1935).
N. Brooke, 'Marlowe the Dramatist', in *Elizabethan Theatre* (Stratford-upon-Avon Studies 9, ed. J. R. Brown and B. Harris, London, 1966).
H. F. Brooks, 'Marlowe and Early Shakespeare', in *Christopher Marlowe*, ed. B. Morris (Mermaid Critical Commentaries, London, 1968).
L. B. Campbell, 'Doctor Faustus: A Case of Conscience', *PMLA* 67 (1952).
D. Cole, *Suffering and Evil in the Plays of Christopher Marlowe* (Princeton, N.J., 1962).
G. I. Duthie, 'The Dramatic Structure of *Tamburlaine the Great*, Parts I and II', in *English Studies* (i.e. *Essays and Studies*, N.S.) 1 (1948).
M. Eccles, *Marlowe in London* (Cambridge, Mass., 1934).
T. S. Eliot, 'Christopher Marlowe' (1918), in *Selected Essays* (London, 1932).
U. M. Ellis-Fermor, *Christopher Marlowe* (London, 1927).
ed. W. Farnham, *Twentieth Century Interpretations of 'Doctor Faustus': A Collection of Critical Essays* (Twentieth Century Interpretations, Englewood Cliffs, N.J., 1969).
H. Gardner, 'The Second Part of *Tamburlaine the Great*', *MLR* 37 (1942).
W. W. Greg, 'The Damnation of Faustus', *MLR* 41 (1946).

M. Hattaway, 'Marlowe and Brecht', in *Christopher Marlowe*, ed. B. Morris (Mermaid Critical Commentaries, London, 1968).

——, 'The Theology of Marlowe's *Doctor Faustus*', *Ren. Dr.*, N.S. 3 (1970).

J. L. Hotson, *The Death of Christopher Marlowe* (London, 1925).

G. K. Hunter, 'The Theology of Marlowe's *The Jew of Malta*', *Journal of the Warburg and Courtauld Institutes* 27 (1964).

ed. J. Jump, *Marlowe: 'Doctor Faustus': A Casebook* (Casebook Series, London, 1969).

L. Kirschbaum, 'Marlowe's *Faustus*: A Reconsideration', *RES* 19 (1943).

P. H. Kocher, *Christopher Marlowe: A Study of His Thought, Learning and Character* (Chapel Hill, N.C., 1946).

C. Leech, 'Marlowe's *Edward II*: Power and Suffering', *Critical Quarterly* 1 (1959).

——, 'Marlowe's Humor', in *Essays on Shakespeare and Elizabethan Drama in Honor of Hardin Craig*, ed. R. Hosley (Columbia, Mo., 1962; London, 1963).

——, 'The Structure of *Tamburlaine*', *Tulane Drama Review* 8 (1964).

——, ed., *Marlowe: A Collection of Critical Essays* (Twentieth Century Views, Englewood Cliffs, N.J., 1964).

H. Levin, *The Overreacher: A Study of Christopher Marlowe* (Cambridge, Mass., 1952).

T. McAlindon, 'Classical Mythology and Christian Tradition in Marlowe's *Doctor Faustus*', *PMLA* 81 (1966).

M. M. Mahood, 'Marlowe's Heroes', in her *Poetry and Humanism* (London, 1950).

J. C. Maxwell, 'The Plays of Christopher Marlowe', in *The Age of Shakespeare*, ed. B. Ford (*The Pelican Guide to English Literature*, vol. 2, Harmondsworth, 1955).

W. Moelwyn Merchant, 'Marlowe the Orthodox', in *Christopher Marlowe*, ed. B. Morris (Mermaid Critical Commentaries, London, 1968).

ed. B. Morris, *Christopher Marlowe* (Mermaid Critical Commentaries, London, 1968).

J. R. Mulryne and S. Fender, 'Marlowe and the "Comic Distance"', in *Christopher Marlowe*, ed. B. Morris (Mermaid Critical Commentaries, London, 1968).

ed. J. O'Neill, *Critics on Marlowe* (Readings in Literary Criticism 4, London, 1969).

R. Ornstein, 'The Comic Synthesis in *Doctor Faustus*', *ELH* 22 (1955).

D. J. Palmer, 'Magic and Poetry in *Doctor Faustus*', *Critical Quarterly* 6 (1964).

——, 'Marlowe's Naturalism', in *Christopher Marlowe*, ed. B. Morris (Mermaid Critical Commentaries, London, 1968).

G. Salgādo, 'Christopher Marlowe', in *English Drama to 1710*, ed. C. Ricks (*Sphere History of Literature in the English Language*, vol. 3, London, 1971).

J. Smith, 'Marlowe's *Dr. Faustus*', *Scrutiny* 8 (1939).

J. B. Steane, *Marlowe: A Critical Study* (Cambridge, 1964).

Tulane Drama Review 8 (1964).

W. Urry, 'Marlowe and Canterbury', *TLS* (13 February 1964).

E. M. Waith, '*Edward II*: The Shadow of Action', *Tulane Drama Review* 8 (1964).

——, *The Herculean Hero in Marlowe, Chapman, Shakespeare and Dryden* (London, 1962).

F. P. Wilson, *Marlowe and the Early Shakespeare* (Oxford, 1953).

5. JONSON and CHAPMAN

J. B. BAMBOROUGH

Ben Jonson

TEXTS

THE definitive edition of Jonson's complete works is that edited by C. H. Herford and Percy and Evelyn Simpson, and published in eleven volumes by the Clarendon Press (usually referred to as 'Herford and Simpson'). It contains, in addition to all the plays, masques, poems, and prose works, a Life (in vol. 1, with some additional biographical material scattered in later volumes), critical introductions (in vols. 1 and 2), and textual introductions prefaced to the individual works. The last three volumes contain a general survey of the text, a note on the stage history of the plays, copious explanatory notes, a 'literary record' (i.e. a collection of early references to Jonson), the elegies written on his death, and a selection of 'later criticism', which ranges from one 'G.C.' in 1640 to Carlyle and Swinburne. Altogether this is a massive work of scholarship; it will never be replaced, and there is no modern editor or critic who is not in debt to it to some extent. It has some drawbacks. Since it was in preparation for over a quarter of a century, some of the information contained in the earlier volumes was superseded, and had to be corrected in later volumes. Neither the presentation of the text nor the notes make any concession to the reader. The text is 'old spelling' and reproduces Jonson's idiosyncratic punctuation; also copied are Jonson's own act and scene divisions, but since these are given once only, in the text, and are not put anywhere else, looking up a reference can be tedious. The commentary contains a vast mass of information—sometimes more than the reader may want—and assumes a knowledge of the classical languages greater than many readers possess. Here, too, it may be difficult to find a reference quickly. Some of the critical views are a little eccentric, and some now look (reasonably enough) old-fashioned; not all the editors' views—e.g. about the dating of *The Tale of a Tub*—are generally agreed. Above all, this is the 'library edition'—invaluable, irreplaceable, but too bulky (and too expensive) for the ordinary reader.

There is no other modern edition of the complete works, and the only twentieth-century edition of the complete plays is the Every-

man's Library edition by F. E. Schelling, first published 1910. This
has a modernized text—unfortunately not very reliable—and a
rather exiguous glossary; it is very unattractive typographically.
Several of the plays have appeared in individual editions, some of
them many times. The Yale edition will eventually provide separate
editions of all the plays, in a standard format, although not with an
absolutely consistent editorial policy. Those volumes so far published
provide an easy-to-read text with light explanatory notes; the reader
is referred to Herford and Simpson for detailed examination of
classical sources, etc. The various series of Elizabethan–Jacobean
dramatic texts—the Revels Plays, the New Mermaids, and the
Regents Renaissance Drama Series—have produced single editions
of some of the plays, and there are a number of editions of the most
popular set texts (*Volpone*, *The Alchemist*, *Epicoene*) for use in schools.
The Yale editions are the easiest to use, but most of the others are
acceptable provided they are checked against Herford and Simpson
for quotations and where difficult cruces are involved. But for the
less popular plays it is Herford and Simpson or nothing.

BIOGRAPHY AND BACKGROUND STUDIES

Apart from a connected account of Jonson's life, Herford and
Simpson print all the relevant documents (including the 'Conversations' with Drummond of Hawthornden). Marchette Chute's *Ben
Jonson of Westminster* provides a brighter, chattier life, with some
reference to contemporary social and political history. The best and
most influential 'background study' is L. C. Knights's *Drama and
Society in the Age of Jonson*. This is primarily concerned with relating
the theme of acquisitiveness in the social comedy of the late sixteenth
and earlier seventeenth century, as it was written not only by Jonson
but by others (notably Middleton and Massinger), to the economic
conditions of the period. This aspect of Jonson is touched on again
rather briefly in M. C. Bradbrook's *The Growth and Structure of
Elizabethan Comedy*, and is treated more fully in B. Gibbons's *Jacobean
City Comedy*. Equally important in Knights's book is his chapter
entitled 'Tradition and Ben Jonson' (originally published in *Scrutiny*
in 1935). This essay is directed against the view of Jonson as en-
slaved to the prescriptions of the classical authorities, and strongly
emphasizes his native roots. The battle between the 'classical' and
the 'English' view of Jonson is largely a sham one, but it is still
sometimes fought in the lecture room. A quarter of a century before
Knights, C. R. Baskervill had provided an exhaustive study of
English Elements in Jonson's Early Comedy (1911), and various scholars

had followed suit in articles (Herford and Simpson give most of the references). Altogether Jonson's debt to earlier stage drama has been very well covered; attempts to relate his comedies to the traditions of 'festive comedy'—folk plays and so on—have generally not been so successful (but see the chapters in Ian Donaldson's *The World Upside-Down*). Oddly enough there is no comprehensive study of Jonson's debt to the classics comparable to Baldwin's *William Shakspere's Small Latine and Less Greeke*; perhaps the task is too formidable. Herford and Simpson give much information; E. W. Talbert has demonstrated that some, at least, of Jonson's learning was not first-hand. F. E. Schelling provides a straightforward statement of Jonson's position as heir of the ancients and forerunner of the Augustans; this is still worth reading. One particular—and obviously very important—aspect of this debate is the discussion of Jonson's models in the construction of comedy. Earlier writers tend to emphasize his debt to Roman New Comedy and the 'linear' construction of his plots, an approach of which the first example is Dryden's famous 'Examen' of *The Silent Woman* in the *Essay of Dramatick Poesie*. F. L. Townsend in *Apologie for Bartholomew Fayre*, an important book, opposes this view, and points to the multiplicity of actions and episodes even in *Epicoene*, and the presence of a unifying force other than the plot in many plays. Critics since Townsend have tended to stress the influence of *Vetus Comoedia*—i.e. of Aristophanes —as against that of Plautus and Terence (see, e.g., C. G. Thayer). M. T. Herrick's *Comic Theory in the Sixteenth Century* provides a useful general perspective for these studies of Jonson. A. Kernan's *The Cankered Muse* is very helpful in relating him to the contemporary conception of the satirist; O. J. Campbell's *Comicall Satyre and Shakespeare's 'Troilus and Cressida'*, although its main argument has been questioned, should also be read as an approach to the 'humour plays'.

GENERAL CRITICAL STUDIES

Modern criticism of Jonson begins with Dryden in 1668: the two comments in the *Essay of Dramatick Poesie*, 'I think him the most learned and judicious writer any theatre ever had' and 'I admire him, but I love Shakespeare' effectively set the lines along which nearly all commentary since has developed. Less well known, but equally seminal, are the remarks on Jonson's comedy in the Preface to *An Evening's Love* (1671) and the Epilogue and the Defence of the Epilogue ('An Essay on the Dramatique Poetry of the Last Age') to the Second Part of *The Conquest of Granada* (1672): Dryden's denial of wit to Jonson and his attack on the coarseness of Jonson and his contemporaries have found many echoes. Equally scattered, and equally valuable, are Coleridge's observations on the man he called 'this surly, robust, surly and observing dramatist': a whole stemma of critical commentary derives from his remark that Jonson's characters resemble 'the hopeless patients of a Mad-doctor'; equally important is his emphasis on the singularity and originality of Jonson, and the fallaciousness of judging him as if he were trying (and failing) to emulate Shakespeare. There are also some stimulating remarks about individual plays.

Swinburne's is the first full-length study of Jonson by a major critic. It is bound to strike the present-day reader as badly overwritten in places; here, for example, is his reference to Jonson's period as a hack-writer for Henslowe: 'he was engaged as a dramatic apprentice ... in the dim back workshop of the slave-dealer and slave-driver whose diary records the grinding toil and the scanty wages of his lean and laborious bondsmen' (p. 11). Nevertheless Swinburne succeeds in conveying an infectious enthusiasm for and enjoyment of a writer whom everyone agrees there have been not many to praise and very few indeed to love. Not that Swinburne ever loses his sense of proportion: the very first sentence, indeed, of his *Study* draws a distinction among poets between the 'gods of harmony and creation' and 'the giants of energy and invention'; Shakespeare is supreme among the 'gods' of English verse as Jonson is among the 'giants'—although 'no giant ever came so near to the ranks of the gods.' While giving full praise to Jonson's seriousness of purpose, his 'noble uprightness of mind', Swinburne repeatedly notes the sometimes deadening effect of his relentless control over and elaboration of his material—what Swinburne calls (apropos *Cynthia's Revels*) his 'heavy-handed perversity' and 'Cyclopean ponderosity of perseverance'. Naturally enough Swinburne finds the element of the willed in Jonson, the lack of grace, the absence of the apparent 'happy accident', most disabling in the poetry; the equivalent limitation in both the comedies and the tragedies is Jonson's lack of sympathy with his own characters. Some of Swinburne's judgements are unusual: he praises *The Case is Altered*, for example, and — unlike more recent critics — thinks it a pity that Jonson did not remain longer under the influence of Plautus, writing more light, fanciful comedies. Even more surprising is his liking for *The Staple of News*, which he places as fourth in order of merit among the comedies, after *Every Man in his Humour*, *Volpone*, and *The Alchemist*, but before *Epicoene* (Swinburne disliked the sneering tone of *Epicoene*, although he admitted it was 'perhaps the only play of Jonson's which will keep the reader or spectator for whole scenes together in an inward riot or an open passion of subdued or unrepressed laughter'). In *The Staple of News*, Swinburne notes, Jonson achieved, as he did not in *The Devil is an Ass*, a fusion of realistic satire with Aristophanic allegory; here, as in his remark that *Catiline* is 'a tragedy of humours', he offered important hints to later critics. There is no doubt that *A Study of Ben Jonson* (which has chapters on the poetry and the prose works as well as on the plays and masques), despite its occasional 'old-fashionedness', is far from superseded.

The last great poet and critic to write on Jonson is T. S. Eliot. His essay on Jonson (originally published in 1919) starts from the pre-miss—which has been echoed by many subsequent critics—that while Jonson has been universally accepted as a major writer, he has been virtually unread except by 'historians and antiquaries'; no critic has succeeded in making him appear 'pleasant or even interesting', largely because since Dryden no poet has found stimulus in his poetry. Eliot's own response to Jonson produced criticism which—as so often with him—manages to sound sharp and pointed, but tends to dissolve into ambiguity and imprecision when considered closely. His most influential point has been his comparison of Jonson and Marlowe ('if Marlowe is a poet, Jonson is also'); this started a new line of approach to some of Jonson's greatest figures, both comic and tragic, as 'over-reachers', embodiments of *Superbia* or Pride (see, e.g., D. J. Enright). But Eliot's emphasis, which is more profound (and recurs throughout his essay), on the essential *unity* of Jonson's creative activity, both in terms of individual works and of his *œuvre* as a whole, and on its origins in an impulse deeper in Jonson's personality even than his love of learning and his sense of style, has stimulated a number of later critics, although it has still perhaps not been fully assimilated into the ordinary reader's response.

There have not been many studies of Jonson's work as a whole since Swinburne's. M. Castelain's exhaustive (and exhausting) *Ben Jonson: l'homme et l'œuvre* contains much information, but can best be used as a quarry. G. G. Smith's 'English Men of Letters' *Ben Jonson* (the publication of which occasioned Eliot's essay) has in some ways dated more than Swinburne's *Study*, but is still a useful brief account. J. B. Bamborough's *Ben Jonson* is intended as a general introduction for sixth-formers and first-year undergraduates: the same author's essay in the British Council's Writers and their Work series is meant primarily for foreign readers. There are three useful short introductory essays. First in time and in importance is H. Levin's introduction to his *Selected Works of Ben Jonson*. This is rather too closely packed and allusive—faults which have been handed on to some American scholars who have come under Professor Levin's influence—but it has some useful insights. Levin tackles the question of Jonson's 'vernacular classicism', which is the prime concern also of L. C. Knights's essay in the *Pelican Guide to English Literature*. Different ground is covered by Ian Donaldson's general account of Jonson in the *Sphere History of Literature in the English Language*, which is very stimulating.

One final short essay must be mentioned: Edmund Wilson's 'Morose Ben Jonson'. This infuriating piece expresses forcibly and entertainingly the instinctive dislike of Jonson's personality and his writing felt by very many readers: in essence it develops the charges made by Hazlitt in his *Lectures on the English Comic Writers* and *Lectures on the Age of Elizabeth*, and the brief references to Jonson by G. B. Shaw, whose characterization of Jonson as a 'brutish pedant' is quoted by Wilson. The top-dressing of Freudianism is irritating (Jonson as an 'anal erotic'), but the comparisons with Gogol and Joyce are valuable. All students of Jonson should read this, if only because it will comfort them if they cannot stomach the plays they are expected to read; it does at the same time pay tribute to some of Jonson's good qualities.

THE COMEDIES

Discussion of Jonson as a comic writer, when it proceeds further than criticism and interpretation of individual plays, tends to focus on two topics: his dramatic construction, and the moral basis of his satire. Sometimes the two are combined, as they are in J. J. Enck's *Jonson and the Comic Truth*. This is difficult to read, quirky, and rather given to showy and over-brisk generalization, but it contains many brilliant insights, and is worth persevering with. Particularly valuable is Enck's insistence on the experimental nature of Jonson's art throughout his career; earlier critics tended to assume that Jonson had established the canons of the 'Comedy of Humours' at least by *Every Man Out*, and to try to force all the later plays into a model based on this play and its predecessor, together with selected quotations from *Discoveries*. This mode of approach is obviously unsatisfactory, and it is important to grasp that Jonson continued to evolve his ideas throughout his career, and that, as Enck emphasizes, the form of his plays has an organic connection with the moral example they were intended to embody. H. W. Baum's *The Satiric and the Didactic in Ben Jonson's Comedy* is a useful general account of Jonson as a moralist; so, from a different standpoint, is G. B. Jackson's *Vision and Judgement in Ben Jonson's Drama*. The latter is another unnecessarily opaque book, but it rightly expounds the intellectual basis of Jonson's view of the role of the poet (a briefer insight into this, in relation to *Poetaster*, is offered by E. Waith). A fuller account of the background of Jonson's ethical thought, for those who want it, is provided by C. B. Hilberry.

Critics have sought to find the unity of inspiration postulated by Eliot partly in theme (as distinct from plot), and also in image and symbol (these being ideally the outward expression of the theme). Two very valuable studies here are E. B. Partridge's *The Broken Compass* and R. L. Heffner's 'Unifying Symbols in the Comedy of Ben Jonson'. The title of Heffner's essay could well be the sub-title of Partridge's book (the two do in fact overlap in places), and is sufficiently descriptive of the approach of both. The influence of F. C. Townsend is visible, particularly in Heffner's essay, and these critics have been followed by a number of others seeking thematic or symbolic unity in the plays, not always with great success. (Another interesting and influential article of this type is J. A. Barish's 'The Double Plot in *Volpone*'.) There is a certain element of vogue in this approach, a spread-over to Jonson of techniques first, and much more convincingly, used in the examination of Shakespeare's plays; it may go out of fashion, but not before it has added a new dimension to the consideration of Jonsonian comedy.

Consideration of the symbols in Jonson leads on to—is, indeed, sometimes the same thing as—consideration of his style. Detailed studies of Jonson's language are provided by A. C. Partridge, on the accidence and syntax of his plays, etc.; E. V. Pennanen gives an equally technical account of his vocabulary. Although in some ways more limited, A. H. Sackton's *Rhetoric as a Dramatic Language in Ben Jonson* has more general interest as an account of the *dramatic* function of speech in the plays; the most valuable and stimulating of these studies, however, is J. A. Barish's *Ben Jonson and the Language of Prose Comedy*. This is a very valuable book, ranging wider than its title suggests: along with Partridge's *The Broken Compass* it must be read by everyone interested in Jonson.

THE TRAGEDIES

No one has ever found much that was good to say of the tragedies—not even Hazlitt, who preferred them to the comedies (but Hazlitt found Jonson altogether unsympathetic). Swinburne found them undramatic, and describes the verse of *Catiline* as more proper for 'an epic satire cast in the form of dialogue'—a perfectly possible way of approaching the play. Eliot always seems to be trembling on the brink of a definitive revelation, which never arrives. Many earlier commentators found it easiest to dwell on the borrowings from the Roman historians, for which Herford and Simpson provide massive evidence. More recently attention has been focused, to good effect, on the relations of Jonson's moral and political ideas to contemporary thought and contemporary problems. K. M. Burton's 'The Political Tragedies of Chapman and Ben Jonson' (1952) began this trend, and its thesis, that the two poets were 'concerned with the tragic flaw *within the social order*, not within the individual', actually applies very much better to Jonson than it does to Chapman. Two articles by J. A. Bryant continue this approach; a third, by G. Hill, is very good on the relation of Jonson's tragedies to Jacobean ideas about liberty, legitimacy, and so on. D. C. Boughner gives a very useful account of *Sejanus* in relation to Machiavellism. Unfortunately this way of approaching Jonson frees him from the traditional comparison with Shakespeare only to put him at almost as great a disadvantage in a comparison with Chapman: see, for example, the verdict of R. Ornstein in *The Moral Vision of Jacobean Tragedy*: attempts to follow up Eliot's suggestion of a Marlovian Jonson have very much the same result.

George Chapman

TEXTS

The standard complete edition of Chapman's comedies and tragedies is T. M. Parrott's in two volumes (originally projected as a three-volume edition, to include the poems). This is a modern-spelling edition, with introductions to the various plays and useful notes: it includes some plays (*The Ball, Alphonsus*, and *Revenge for Honour*) not now thought to be by Chapman. A critical edition of the comedies has been published by the University of Illinois Press; this is, of course, in old spelling and has textual notes only. *Bussy D'Ambois* is the only individual play to attract the attention of the Revels and New Mermaids series, but the Regents Renaissance Drama series has some of the comedies in addition to *Bussy*. Parrott is quite satisfactory for most purposes.

BIOGRAPHY AND GENERAL STUDIES

Chapman did not fare particularly well at the hands of the older critics. Dryden in a well-known passage in the 'Dedication' to *The Spanish Friar* (1681) describes how his earlier admiration turned to

disgust on rereading *Bussy D'Ambois*. (Dryden might have been expected to praise Chapman, who after all came close to inaugurating
heroic tragedy in English, but found it convenient to use him as a
stalking-horse for an attack on the language of the older dramatists.)
Swinburne's *Critical Essay*, although it should still be read, is less
good than his *Study* of Ben Jonson, and seems to be written rather
against the grain, without real sympathy for the subject. Finding
Chapman both obscure and uneven (as he undoubtedly is), Swinburne praises him as a poet well suited to selection, as in Lamb's
Specimens: 'there are few poets from whose remains a more copious
and noble anthology of detailed beauties might be selected' (p. 2).
Some recent critics seem to have reached very much the same position, although they have not dared to say so. T. S. Eliot's influence
on the criticism of Chapman has been very strange. In the famous
essay on 'The Metaphysical Poets' (1921) he brings Jonson and
Chapman together as poets 'notably erudite' who 'incorporated
their erudition into their sensibility', and goes on, in a much-quoted
phrase, to speak of a 'direct sensuous apprehension of thought' in
Chapman. Since no one has ever been quite sure what this means it
has proved an uncertain guide to subsequent writers on Chapman,
and one or two have been bold enough to say it is nonsense; most
have agreed that, if Chapman is properly to be regarded as a
'metaphysical poet', he is closer to Fulke Greville than to Donne.

The best general study of Chapman is certainly J. Jacquot's
(Chapman has often attracted the attention of French scholars,
perhaps because he went so often to French history for the material
of his tragedies). Jacquot goes into the life in some detail—perhaps
more than is really wanted; and he finds it necessary to give selected
scenes from the plays in French translation (these can easily be
skipped). But his book is not difficult to read, and is particularly
good on the comedies. M. MacLure's critical study has the advantage of being in English, and of making use of some specialized
studies which were published after Jacquot's, but it does not supersede Jacquot. There is a shorter study, later still, by Charlotte
Spivack which covers the ground adequately, if to no great depth;
the second chapter is a useful summary of Chapman's theory of
poetry, which is directly relevant to his drama.

THE PLAYS

It is unfortunate that the only study devoted entirely to Chapman's
comedies, that of Kreider, is really, as its title makes plain, a general
examination of Elizabethan conventions in comedy, with Chapman

as central feature. Kreider's justification of this—that Chapman
'exercised so little originality that he cannot be considered more than
a purely conventional Elizabethan' (p. 4)—is hardly likely to inspire
a reader, although the book is certainly useful. On the whole, the
comedies have received surprisingly little attention: D. J. Enright,
for example, dismisses them in a sentence in his essay on 'Elizabethan
and Jacobean Comedy' in the Pelican *Guide*. Many writers have
been satisfied to point out Chapman's historical importance, noting
that the *An Humorous Day's Mirth* is the first 'Comedy of Humours',
All Fools the most successful English adaptation of Terence, and *The
Gentleman Usher* and *Monsieur D'Olive* forerunners of tragicomedy as
practised by Beaumont and Fletcher. Even Jacquot bleakly acknowledges that 'Chapman est un auteur comique de second plan', but
his commentary has much to offer; MacLure also makes some useful
points.

The tragedies have received far more critical attention than the
comedies in this century, but nothing which could be called a critical
consensus has been reached. One reason for this is that they divide
so obviously into the 'Marlovian' plays—*Bussy D'Ambois* and the two
Byron plays (Ellis-Fermor is very good, though brief, on Chapman's
relation to Marlowe)—and the 'Stoic' plays, culminating in *The
Tragedy of Chabot* and *Caesar and Pompey*. Swinburne, as might be
expected, responded more naturally to the mood of *Bussy D'Ambois*,
identifying its 'bright and fiery energy' and 'vigour of ambitious
aspiration' with Chapman's own spirit. A very good essay on the
same lines is Edwin Muir's 'Royal Man'. Since *Bussy D'Ambois* is
universally agreed to be Chapman's finest tragedy, this view will
never be extinguished. There is, however, no doubt that the later
plays contradict what seem at first sight to be the values held up for
admiration in the earlier—and, indeed, there are contradictory
elements in *Bussy* itself. Study of Chapman's political and ethical
ideas, and their sources, has swung several critics the other way. The
most extreme example, which should be read, is Rees's *The Tragedies
of George Chapman*. Developing the work of earlier scholars, particularly Schoell and Wieler (whose books, though important, are rather
too detailed for undergraduate use), Rees synthesizes a coherent
system from Chapman's works, and relates the tragedies to it.
Chapman emerges as essentially a Christian humanist, with a tinc-
ture of Stoicism; it follows that Bussy and Byron are intended by
Chapman to be taken as examples of wrong, indeed positively evil,
attitudes and action. Rees has been much criticized (particularly by
MacLure) for over-simplifying the complexities of Chapman's

thought in the interest of neatness, and there is no doubt that his version of Chapman does not really satisfy. Another way of resolving the contradictions is to postulate a development in Chapman from an early confidence in man to a stoic resignation in the face of disillusion: so Irving Ribner, who sees Chapman in the general context of 'Jacobean pessimism'. Ribner's book is a useful antidote to Rees's. One difficulty here is the uncertainty of the order of the plays. Cato, in *Caesar and Pompey*, is the most Stoic of Chapman's heroes, and the thesis of Chapman's development towards Stoicism is only tenable if *Caesar and Pompey* is indeed Chapman's last play, as it is commonly taken to be; there is, however, evidence to suggest that it is an early play (see Parrott's Introduction).

Another way out is to follow K. M. Burton's thesis that Chapman, like Jonson, was not interested in individuals at all, but in the ills of society. This is difficult to accept; moreover, attempts to arrive at Chapman's political beliefs have produced widely differing results, from the statement that he was 'a classical republican' to an emphasis on his belief in legitimacy. Many critics end up admitting that Chapman was not only obscure in the verbalization of his ideas, but actually confused, and that he failed to find adequate dramatic expression of his vision (that is, he wrote bad plays). Ornstein makes the interesting observation that 'Chapman came to tragedy twenty years too late'—a remark that neatly sums up the unease everyone feels at the forcing of a Senecan hero into the Revenge mode in *The Revenge of Bussy D'Ambois*; Ornstein's chapter in *The Moral Vision of Jacobean Tragedy* is a useful one. Those who refuse to accept the notion of Chapman's incompetence may find comfort in the concept of different levels of meaning in his tragedies, adumbrated by P. Ure and followed up by Ribner, and in the defence of his dramatic poetry provided by J. Smith. The dilemma may never be fully resolved, but an understanding of Chapman's conception of the hero is very much helped by an approach through Eliot's essay 'Shakespeare and the Stoicism of Seneca' (1927), Schücking's British Academy lecture, and above all E. M. Waith's *The Herculean Hero*.

REFERENCES

Ben Jonson (1573?–1637)

TEXTS

ed. C. H. Herford and P. and E. Simpson, 11 vols. (Oxford, 1925–52).
ed. F. E. Schelling, *The Complete Plays of Ben Jonson*, 2 vols. (Everyman's Library, London, 1910).

The Alchemist

ed. D. Brown (The New Mermaids, London, 1966).
ed. A. B. Kernan (Yale Edition, New Haven, Conn., and London, 1974).
ed. F. H. Mares (The Revels Plays, London, 1967).

Bartholomew Fair

ed. E. A. Horsman (The Revels Plays, London, 1960).
ed. F. M. Waith (Yale Edition, New Haven, Conn., and London, 1963).
ed. E. B. Partridge (Regents Renaissance Drama Series, London, 1964).
ed. M. Hussey (The New Mermaids, London, 1964).

Catiline

ed. W. F. Bolton and J. F. Gardner (Regents Renaissance Drama Series, London, 1973).

Epicoene

ed. L. Beaurline (Regents Renaissance Drama Series, London, 1967).
ed. E. B. Partridge (Yale Edition, New Haven, Conn., and London, 1971).

Every Man in his Humour

ed. M. Seymour-Smith (The New Mermaids, London, 1966).
ed. G. B. Jackson (Yale Edition, New Haven, Conn., and London, 1969).
ed. J. W. Lever (Regents Renaissance Drama Series, London, 1972).

Sejanus

ed. J. A. Barish (Yale Edition, New Haven, Conn., and London, 1965).
ed. W. F. Bolton (The New Mermaids, London, 1966).

Volpone

ed. P. Brockbank (The New Mermaids, London, 1968).
ed. A. B. Kernan (Yale Edition, New Haven, Conn., and London, 1968).

BIOGRAPHY AND BACKGROUND STUDIES

C. R. Baskervill, *English Elements in Jonson's Early Comedy* (Austin, Tex., 1911).
M. C. Bradbrook, *The Growth and Structure of Elizabethan Comedy* (London, 1955).

O. J. Campbell, *Comicall Satyre and Shakespeare's 'Troilus and Cressida'* (San Marino, Calif., 1938).

M. Chute, *Ben Jonson of Westminster* (New York, 1953).

I. Donaldson, *The World Upside-Down* (Oxford, 1970).

B. Gibbons, *Jacobean City Comedy* (London, 1968).

M. T. Herrick, *Comic Theory in the Sixteenth Century* (Urbana, Ill., 1950).

A. B. Kernan, *The Cankered Muse* (New Haven, Conn., 1959).

L. C. Knights, *Drama and Society in the Age of Jonson* (London, 1937).

F. E. Schelling, *Ben Jonson and the Classical School* (Baltimore, Md., 1898).

E. W. Talbert, 'New Light on Ben Jonson's Workmanship', *SP* 40 (1943).

C. G. Thayer, *Ben Jonson: Studies in the Plays* (Norman, Okla., 1963).

F. L. Townsend, *Apologie for Bartholomew Fayre* (New York and London, 1947).

GENERAL CRITICAL STUDIES

J. B. Bamborough, *Ben Jonson* (Writers and their Work, London, 1959).

——, *Ben Jonson* (London, 1970).

M. Castelain, *Ben Jonson: l'homme et l'œuvre* (Paris, 1907).

I. Donaldson, 'Ben Jonson', in *English Drama to 1710*, ed. C. Ricks (*Sphere History of Literature in the English Language*, vol. 3, London, 1971).

J. Dryden, *'Of Dramatic Poesy' and Other Critical Essays*, ed. G. Watson, 2 vols. (Everyman's Library, London, 1962).

T. S. Eliot, 'Ben Jonson', in *Selected Essays* (London, 1932).

D. J. Enright, 'Crime and Punishment in Ben Jonson', *Scrutiny* 9 (1940–1).

W. Hazlitt, *Lectures on the English Comic Writers* and *Lectures Chiefly on the Dramatic Literature of the Age of Elizabeth*, in *Complete Works*, ed. P. P. Howe, 21 vols. (London, 1930–4), vol. 6 (1931).

L. C. Knights, 'Ben Jonson, Dramatist', in *The Age of Shakespeare*, vol. 2 of the *Pelican Guide to English Literature*, ed. B. Ford (Harmondsworth, 1955).

H. Levin, Introduction to *Selected Works of Ben Jonson* (New York, 1938; repr. in *Ben Jonson: A Collection of Critical Essays* (Twentieth Century Views), ed. J. A. Barish, Englewood Cliffs, N.J., 1963).

G. G. Smith, *Ben Jonson* (English Men of Letters, London, 1919).

A. C. Swinburne, *A Study of Ben Jonson* (London, 1889).

E. Wilson, 'Morose Ben Jonson', in *The Triple Thinkers* (rev. edn., New York, 1948; repr. in *Ben Jonson: A Collection of Critical Essays* (Twentieth Century Views), ed. J. A. Barish, Englewood Cliffs, N.J., 1963).

THE COMEDIES

J. A. Barish, 'The Double Plot in *Volpone*', *MP* 51 (1953) (repr. in *Ben Jonson: A Collection of Critical Essays* (Twentieth Century Views), ed. J. A. Barish, Englewood Cliffs, N.J., 1963).

——, *Ben Jonson and the Language of Prose Comedy* (Cambridge, Mass., 1960).

H. W. Baum, *The Satiric and the Didactic in Ben Jonson's Comedy* (Chapel Hill, N.C., 1947).

J. J. Enck, *Jonson and the Comic Truth* (Madison, Wis., 1957).
R. L. Heffner, 'Unifying Symbols in the Comedy of Ben Jonson', in *English Stage Comedy*, ed. W. K. Wimsatt (New York, 1955).
C. B. Hilberry, *Ben Jonson's Ethics in Relation to Stoic and Humanist Ethical Thought* (Chicago, Ill., 1933).
G. B. Jackson, *Vision and Judgement in Ben Jonson's Drama* (New Haven, Conn., and London, 1968).
A. C. Partridge, *The Accidence of Ben Jonson's Plays, Masques and Entertainments* (Cambridge, 1953).
——, *Studies in the Syntax of Ben Jonson's Plays* (Cambridge, 1953).
E. B. Partridge, *The Broken Compass* (London, 1958).
E. V. Pennanen, *Chapters on the Language of Ben Jonson's Dramatic Works* (Turku, 1951).
A. H. Sackton, *Rhetoric as a Dramatic Language in Ben Jonson* (New York, 1948).
E. M. Waith, 'The Poet's Morals in Jonson's *Poetaster*', *MLQ* 12 (1951).

THE TRAGEDIES

D. C. Boughner, *The Devil's Disciple* (New York, 1968).
J. A. Bryant, Jr., 'The Significance of Ben Jonson's First Requirement for Tragedy: "Truth of Argument" ', *SP* 49 (1952).
——, '*Catiline* and the Nature of Jonson's Tragic Fable', *PMLA* 69 (1954).
K. M. Burton, 'The Political Tragedies of Chapman and Ben Jonson', *Essays in Criticism* 2 (1952).
G. Hill, ' "The World's Proportion": Jonson's Dramatic Poetry in *Sejanus* and *Catiline*', in *Jacobean Theatre* (Stratford-upon-Avon Studies 1, ed. J. R. Brown and B. Harris, London, 1960).
R. Ornstein, *The Moral Vision of Jacobean Tragedy* (Madison, Wis., 1960).

George Chapman (1559?–1634)

TEXTS
ed. A. Holaday and others, *The Plays of George Chapman: The Comedies* (Urbana, Ill., Chicago, Ill., and London, 1970).
ed. T. M. Parrott, *The Comedies of George Chapman* (London, 1914).
ed. T. M. Parrott, *The Tragedies of George Chapman* (London, 1910).

Bussy D'Ambois

ed. N. Brooke (The Revels Plays, London, 1964).
ed. R. J. Lordi (Regents Renaissance Drama Series, London, 1965).
ed. M. Evans (The New Mermaids, London, 1965).

All Fools

ed. F. Manley (Regents Renaissance Drama Series, London, 1968).

The Gentleman Usher

ed. J. H. Smith (Regents Renaissance Drama Series, London, 1970).

68   J. B. BAMBOROUGH

The Widow's Tears
ed. E. Smeak (Regents Renaissance Drama Series, London, 1967).

BIOGRAPHY AND GENERAL STUDIES

T. S. Eliot, 'The Metaphysical Poets', in *Selected Essays* (London, 1932).
J. Jacquot, *George Chapman: sa vie, sa poésie, son théâtre, sa pensée* (Paris, 1951).
M. MacLure, *George Chapman, a Critical Study* (Toronto, 1966).
C. Spivack, *George Chapman* (New York, 1967).
A. C. Swinburne, *George Chapman: A Critical Essay* (London, 1875).

THE PLAYS

K. M. Burton, 'The Political Tragedies of Chapman and Ben Jonson', *Essays in Criticism* 2 (1952).
T. S. Eliot, 'Shakespeare and the Stoicism of Seneca', in *Selected Essays* (London, 1932).
U. M. Ellis-Fermor, *The Jacobean Drama* (London, 1936).
P. V. Kreider, *Elizabethan Comic Character Conventions as revealed in the Comedies of George Chapman* (Ann Arbor, Mich., 1935).
E. Muir, ' "Royal Man": Notes on the Tragedies of George Chapman', in *Essays on Literature and Society* (London, 1949).
R. Ornstein, *The Moral Vision of Jacobean Tragedy* (Madison, Wis., 1960).
E. S. Rees, *The Tragedies of George Chapman* (Cambridge, Mass., 1954).
I. Ribner, *Jacobean Tragedy: The Quest for Moral Order* (London, 1962).
F. L. Schoell, *Études sur l'humanisme continental en Angleterre à la fin de la Renaissance* (Paris, 1926).
L. L. Schücking, 'The Baroque Character of the Elizabethan Tragic Hero', British Academy Annual Shakespeare Lecture (1938).
J. Smith, 'George Chapman', *Scrutiny* 3 (1934–5), 4 (1935–6).
P. Ure, 'Chapman as Translator and Tragic Playwright', in *The Age of Shakespeare*, vol. 2 of the *Pelican Guide to English Literature*, ed. B. Ford (Harmondsworth, 1955).
——, 'Chapman's Tragedies', in *Jacobean Theatre* (Stratford-upon-Avon Studies 1, ed. J. R. Brown and B. Harris, London, 1960).
E. M. Waith, *The Herculean Hero in Marlowe, Chapman, Shakespeare and Dryden* (London, 1962).
J. M. Wieler, *George Chapman, the Effect of Stoicism upon his Tragedies* (New York, 1949).

6. MARSTON, MIDDLETON, and MASSINGER

S. SCHOENBAUM

THE three dramatists treated in this chapter were born within a few years of one another, and, as is to be expected, their playwriting careers overlap; indeed the names of Thomas Middleton and Philip Massinger come together (along with that of William Rowley) on the title-page of one early quarto, the 1656 edition of *The Old Law*. But chronology can mislead. When John Marston exchanged the playhouse for the pulpit in 1609, Middleton had not yet written his masterpiece of City Comedy, *A Chaste Maid in Cheapside*, and all his tragicomedies and tragedies (with the possible exception of *The Witch*) lay ahead; Massinger, who did not make his début as a writer for Henslowe until 1613, outlived Middleton by a dozen years, during which time he produced some of his major work. In artistic temperament these men differ: Marston, flamboyant, idio-syncratic, Italianate; Middleton, reticent, seemingly detached, the inveterate ironist; Massinger, the sober professional, capable of sub-merging his own identity in collaborative play-crafting. Nor do the three belong to a shared theatrical tradition. Marston wrote for the children's troupes, mainly the Queen's Revels; Middleton worked for a variety of adult and juvenile companies (Paul's boys, the Lady Elizabeth's men, the King's men); Massinger became, after the death of Fletcher in 1625, the 'ordinary [i.e. regular] poet' for the King's men, a post in which he continued until his own death. Two of these dramatists—Marston and Middleton—have stimulated an impressive resurgence of critical and scholarly interest since World War II, but Massinger has not attracted anything like as much notice. It is tempting to conclude that what the three playwrights have principally in common is the fact that their surnames begin with the same letter. As alphabetical consanguinity may be reckoned not substantive but accidental, they are best treated individually rather than yoked together by forced comparison.

John Marston

TEXTS

In 1633 the printer William Sheares gathered together six of Marston's plays and published them, in the author's absence, as *The Workes of Mr. John Marston*. Then a priest, Marston took exception to the republication of these vanities of his youth, for when the collection was reissued, later in the same year, as *Tragedies and Comedies*, it did not bear his name. Marston's plays were next brought together two centuries later, in 1856, when J. O. Halliwell (later Halliwell-Phillipps) issued the *Works* in three volumes. Halliwell seems to have done little more than supply the printers with copies of the early editions (including, apparently, the 1633 Sheares collection, which has no authority, for the six plays contained therein), and instructions to modernize *i–j* and *u–v*. He provided a scattering of notes, some of which draw attention to gross errors preserved in the text; also an introduction, factual rather than critical, and notable chiefly for reproducing a letter in which Marston offers 'Mr. Henslowe, at the rose in Bankside' his 'play of Columbus'. The letter was forged by J. Payne Collier, and planted by him in Dulwich College library; a play on Columbus, by Marston or anyone else, is not otherwise known.

In 1887 a new *Works of John Marston* in three volumes was published by the dedicated gentleman-amateur A. H. Bullen. Like most of Bullen's editions of the Elizabethans, this one offers modern spelling and punctuation and some useful notes. For the reader's convenience he includes brief plot summaries. Although inadequate by modern standards, this edition represents a vast improvement upon Halliwell. It was reprinted by Olm in 1970.

Bullen's *Marston* is not superseded by H. Harvey Wood's *The Plays of John Marston* (1934–9) for the Blackfriars Playwrights, which aimed at furnishing 'accurate and inexpensive texts' of the Elizabethan dramatists. Wood is not accurate, nor does he have the technical expertise required of a modern editor. A destructive but just review of the first volume by the foremost bibliographer of the day, W. W. Greg, concluded: 'Altogether a slovenly piece of work, unredeemed by either judgment or taste.' Wood announced a forthcoming rebuttal, to be included in his second volume, but he prudently desisted. Students interested in the evidence on which Greg based his verdict may consult his notice (*MLR* 30 (1935), 90–4); also the review, similarly adverse, by R. E. Brettle (*RES* 11 (1935), 221–8). In the preface to the last volume Wood complains of his

'thankless task', and acknowledges deficiencies. With this edition the
Blackfriars Playwrights series abruptly ceased. The Wood edition is
still sometimes used, *faute de mieux*, for quotation. An adequate
complete edition remains a major desideratum of Elizabethan
scholarship.

Meanwhile we have been given a scholarly edition of the poems
by Arnold Davenport (published posthumously in 1961), and a number of individual plays have been soundly edited for the several
paperback series. The Regents Renaissance Drama series has made
available modern-spelling texts, based on fresh collations of all
sixteenth- and seventeenth-century editions, of *Antonio and Mellida*
and *Antonio's Revenge*, edited by G. K. Hunter (1965), and *The
Malcontent* and *The Dutch Courtesan*, both edited by M. L. Wine
(1964, 1965). *The Dutch Courtesan* has also appeared in an old-
spelling edition prepared by Peter Davison for Fountainwell Drama
Texts, and another modern-spelling edition of *The Malcontent*, by
Bernard Harris, is to be had in the New Mermaid series. The introductions to these semi-popular editions are sometimes important for
the interpretative criticism they contain.

The Malone Society has published type-facsimile reprints of
Antonio and Mellida and *Antonio's Revenge*, from the editions of 1602
(in one volume, 1921). *Eastward Ho*, in which Chapman and Jonson
collaborated, is included in editions of those dramatists, and also in
anthologies. The most frequently anthologized of Marston's plays,
The Malcontent, has been reprinted too often for enumeration here.

CRITICAL STUDIES AND COMMENTARY

From early on, Marston criticism has struggled with the personality
revealed in the *œuvre*, which has struck readers as odd, turbulent, and
sometimes unsavoury. The 1824 revised edition of Thomas Warton's
History of English Poetry struck a prophetic note in seeing Marston
as an instance of the satirist who defeats his design by too freely
indulging his own taste for licentiousness (sec. LXV). The necessity
of distinguishing between the man and the masks—the character
of the writer and the characteristics of the writing—raises large
theoretical issues which have only recently challenged Marston
criticism.

The question had been passed over by Lamb. In his *Specimens of
English Dramatic Poets* (1808), which did so much to spark the revival
of interest in the Elizabethan dramatists, he includes half a dozen or
so extracts selected for their eloquence or gravity, but his comments
are sparing (the banished Andrugio in *Antonio and Mellida* reminds

him of Lear). Hazlitt admired Marston as a satirist whose forte was 'an impatient scorn and bitter indignation against the vices and follies of men'; in his *Lectures on the Dramatic Literature of the Age of Elizabeth* (1820), he judges *Parasitaster* and *The Malcontent* to be the dramatist's masterpieces.

The Victorians were less favourably impressed. Significantly, Marston did not find his niche in the wide-ranging Mermaid series. Bullen's cool introduction should be read as representative of the Establishment opinion of his day. He finds much of Marston uncouth, exaggerated, or tedious, although *The Dutch Courtesan* is praised for its vivacity; what finally fascinates Bullen is the personality of 'a scornful spirit, at strife with himself and the world; a man convinced of the hollowness of present life, and yet not looking forward hopefully to any future sphere of activity; only anxious to drop into the jaws of that oblivion which he invoked in his verse and courted even on his gravestone' (I.lviii). The extreme of Victorian enthusiasm for Marston is expectedly to be found in Swinburne, who made him the vehicle for one of the ten rhapsodies comprising *The Age of Shakespeare* (1908). But even Swinburne is defensive—he grants the strenuousness and crudity—and extravagantly derisive of that 'abortion of letters', *Histriomastix*, 'begotten by malice on idiocy'.

Histriomastix, as well as *Jack Drum's Entertainment*, figures largely in two monographs expressive of Victorian biography-mongering, Josiah H. Penniman's *The War of the Theatres* (1897) and Roscoe Addison Small's *The Stage Quarrel between Ben Jonson and the So-called Poetasters* (1899). The latter is the more critical, but both leave something to be desired methodologically. They have not yet been supplanted; modern scholars find the 'poetomachia' less absorbing than did their predecessors. However, the linguistic abuses attacked by Jonson in *Poetaster*, in which Crispinus the affected satirist presumably represents Marston, are analysed in detail by Arthur H. King in *The Language of Satirized Characters in 'Poëtaster'* (1941).

Morse Allen's *The Satire of John Marston* (1920), a Princeton dissertation, endorses the then-prevailing low estimate of Marston, here seen as a playwright who in another age might have had better success with the looser form of the novel. The modern revival of interest in Marston stems properly from the appearance of Wood's first volume. Along with an edition of *The Malcontent* by G. B. Harrison, it is the occasion for T. S. Eliot's essay, 'John Marston', published in 1934, and hence too late to be included in the first edition of his enormously influential *Selected Essays*. If Eliot takes a conventionally personalist view of Marston—he sees the *Antonio* plays as the work of a man who 'deliberately wrote worse than he could have written, in order to relieve his feelings'—he is unconventional in praising *Sophonisba* as Marston's best play, and he puts his finger on the Marston problem: 'for both scholars and critics he remains a territory of unexplored riches and risks. The position of most of his contemporaries is pretty well settled . . . but about Marston a wide divergence of opinion is still possible. His greater defects are such as anyone can see; his merits are still a matter for controversy.' Marston's riches remain unexplored in Theodore Spencer's urbane essay, 'John Marston', published the same year by Eliot in his *Criterion*. Spencer praises *The Dutch Courtesan* as the most sensitive treatment, Shakespeare always excepted, of the theme of lust, but the tone is mostly depreciatory: 'Marston's style might be described as a kind of growing pain which language was bound to suffer as it passed from the manner of Spenser to the manner of Donne.' Thus Marston emerges as a failed Metaphysical as well as a failed Shakespeare. Like his predecessors, Spencer is mainly concerned with the personality of the 'twisted, unhappy figure', who, it turns out, is our old friend the disillusioned idealist. 'When the facts hit him in the face the blow was severe, and in order to conceal how much he was hurt, he pretended that he had known about them all along, that he enjoyed them.' This is too easy. A few more years would pass before criticism confronted the task posed for it by Eliot.

For all his deficiencies as an editor, Wood seems to be the first to break new ground by considering Marston's plays on their own merits as dramatic experiments. In his introduction to the third volume of the *Plays*, 'Marston as a Dramatic Author', Wood challenges the view (held by Eliot) that in his heart Marston despised the stage; rather he sees him as a theorist with canny notions of what would take with his public, and a commitment to his medium self-evident from the elaborate stage-directions and musical instructions included in the texts. Even the idiosyncrasies of the dialogue are defended as echoing the rhythms and irregularities of the spoken language. A theatrical context of a different kind, broadly social, is provided by Alfred Harbage in his influential *Shakespeare and the Rival Traditions* (1952). Marston's plays reflect the attitudes towards sexual behaviour, literature, the divine plan, etc., of the coterie, i.e. affluent, audiences of the small enclosed private playhouses, Paul's and Blackfriars. In every respect this drama contrasts with the popular tradition represented pre-eminently by Shakespeare. Harbage's book usefully considers Marston's plays as belonging to a repertory, and not merely as thinly disguised personal revelation—even if one does not wholly accept Harbage's view of Elizabethan drama as a sort of grand morality play, in which the various dramatists appear as Virtues and Vices, Marston being one of the latter. In *The Cankered Muse* (1959), Alvin Kernan considers another context, that of Renaissance satire. Marston's eight plays (Kernan excludes the collaborate *Eastward Ho*) all contain 'a satirist of some sort', and in their variety of genre these works reflect the playwright's 'restless search . . . for a suitable vehicle for his satirist'. Thus in *The Malcontent* Malevole, in his bitter anatomization of men and manners, exercises the conventional prerogatives of the satirical *persona*. This is a liberating approach.

The directions indicated by Harbage and Kernan are usefully pursued by Anthony Caputi in *John Marston, Satirist* (1961), the first book in English to offer a systematic treatment of all of Marston's writings. (A. José Axelrad's *Un Malcontent élisabéthain: John Marston (1576–1634)*, 1955, is comprehensive in the manner of French theses, with chapters on the life, satire, influences, dramatic technique, language and style, etc., but does not on the whole challenge received opinion.) Caputi discusses the 'orphan [i.e. innovative] poet', 'sharp-fanged satirist', and Neostoic philosopher; then goes on to demonstrate how Marston assimilated these aspects of his literary personality to the demands of the stage, and in particular of the boy actors, whose special aptitude (Caputi argues) was for burlesque. The author's analysis of Marston's serio-comic mode, his 'peculiar union of levity and seriousness', brings its interpretative rewards, although in his effort to suit the action to his thesis Caputi makes cheerier romps of *The Malcontent* and *The Dutch Courtesan* than some readers will be prepared to accept. Although at least one reviewer (John Peter in *MLR*) singled out for commendation the chapter on Neostoicism, Caputi's argument is not without vulnerability, and is searchingly questioned by Philip Finkelpearl in the latest and best book on Marston, *John Marston of the Middle Temple* (1969). This is an examination, as the subtitle puts it, of 'An Elizabethan Dramatist in his Social Setting'. That setting was the Middle Temple, where Marston resided throughout most of his writing career. Finkelpearl explores the special ambience—literary, theatrical, political—of the Inns of Court in the late sixteenth century. He offers the suggestive hypothesis that *Histriomastix*, which boasts a cast of one hundred and twenty, was designed for revels at one of the inns. (He has put this case more fully in an earlier article, '*Histrio-Mastix* as an Inns of Court Play: A Hypothesis', 1964). In *What You Will*

Marston dramatizes 'the world of his verse satires without recourse to an intrusive representation of his own point of view'. *Antonio's Revenge* foreshadows the 'central concern' of most of his later work, the 'moral cost of immersion in the destructive element'. The chapter on *Parasitaster* elaborates provocatively on a suggestion by Upton that Gonzago in this play caricatures James. The whole book repays close reading.

Since the 1950s Marston has also figured as the subject of a number of comprehensive essays or chapters of books. In 'The Precarious Balance of John Marston' (1952) S. Schoenbaum sees the dramatist as a turbulent and divided spirit, at once attracted and repelled by the body and its functions, and ambivalent even in his attitude towards his own literary achievement. This essay was written too early for the author to profit from the salutary new direction in Marston criticism, with its focus on genre, conventions, and *personae*. The role of the body, and especially of sexuality, in Marston also occupies Paul M. Zall in 'John Marston, Satirist' (1953). Zall sees Marston as an anti-Stoic, intrigued by 'the problem of the normality of concupiscence', and analysing love and lust in terms of the faculty psychology of his day. Similarly, in 'The Retrograde Genius of John Marston' (1961), Gustav Cross seeks to demonstrate 'the depth and seriousness of Marston's concern with moral and philosophical problems': a concern evident in his treatment of sexuality ('both a symptom and a symbol of the disruptive power of the passions') and handling of Stoic ideas, which are debated in *The Dutch Courtesan* and embraced in the austerely didactic *Sophonisba*. Cross briskly canters through the whole corpus in eight pages, and in so doing fails to escape the pitfalls of superficiality. All three critics take an unnecessarily solemn view of their hero; a refreshing corrective here is Robert Ornstein's section on Marston in *The Moral Vision of Jacobean Tragedy* (1960). To Ornstein, Marston is an 'original': exuberant, naïvely gross, modish in his exploitation of ideas, especially Montaigne's ideas; 'an "artist" first, a moralist second'. In her few terse pages on Marston in *The Growth and Structure of Elizabethan Comedy* (1955), M. C. Bradbrook, while finding him unpleasant, acknowledges that 'the very oddity, violence and rankness of his style freed comedy from traditional limitations.' An important and balanced treatment of Marston is to be found in G. K. Hunter's 'English Folly and Italian Vice: The Moral Landscape of John Marston'. Hunter penetratingly explores Marston's choice of the Guicciardini period of Italian history as backdrop for dramas of courtly *Realpolitik*; in these plays, from *Antonio and Mellida* to *The*

Malcontent, Italy is less a geographical entity than 'a mode of human experience'. Marston's comedies, source of the counterbalancing folly of Hunter's title, provide a coda to the essay; he views *The Dutch Courtesan* as also depicting a fallen world, 'where depravity may be checked but cannot be forgotten'. Altogether slighter are the portions, one whole chapter and part of another, that Brian Gibbons devotes to Marston in *Jacobean City Comedy* (1968). Gibbons sees the plays as importantly influenced by Jonson's comical satires, as well as by Middleton's *Phoenix*, yet distinctive in the 'ambiguities of motive and personality' they dramatize; for him, although not for Hunter, *The Dutch Courtesan* teeters on the edge of tragedy. At the extreme of objective study of Marston stands Cross's 'Some Notes on the Vocabulary of John Marston', published in twenty-four instalments in *Notes and Queries* from 1954 up to 1963. As Cross observes, the *O.E.D.* cites Marston more often than any other writer, Shakespeare excepted, as a coiner of words or user of words in new senses at the turn of the seventeenth century. The compiler supplements *O.E.D.* by listing even earlier Marston neologisms. Although admittedly marred by reliance on Halliwell-Phillipps for the poems, these notes put the student of Elizabethan English as well as the critic of Marston's style in Cross's debt.

Of Marston's plays *The Malcontent* and *The Dutch Courtesan* have most powerfully appealed to the modern critical sensibility, but they are not alone in eliciting interpretative essays devoted to the single work. The more notable among these include Kernan, 'John Marston's Play *Histriomastix*'; Cross, 'Marston, Montaigne and Morality: *The Dutch Courtesan* Reconsidered'; Egner Jensen, 'Theme and Imagery in *The Malcontent*'; Ellen Berland, 'The Function of Imagery in Marston's *Antonio and Mellida*'; Joel Kaplan, 'John Marston's *Fawn*: A Saturnalian Satire'; and Philip J. Ayres, 'Marston's *Antonio's Revenge*: The Morality of the Revenging Hero'. These studies, as well as the books and editions that have appeared since Eliot's essay in 1934, show that the Marston territory is at last being explored, although it cannot be said that 'a wide divergence of opinion' about him is no longer possible.

Thomas Middleton

TEXTS

On the whole Middleton has been better served than Marston, as regards the number and quality of editions. A fair number of plays—including *A Mad World, My Masters*, *The Widow*, and *Women Beware*

Women—found places in the collections of old plays edited by
Dodsley (1744) and Dilke (1815–16); Isaac Reed first printed *The
Witch* in 1778. Alexander Dyce's edition of *The Works of Thomas
Middleton* in five volumes in 1840 was an ambitious undertaking.
Possessed of a deep and wide-ranging knowledge of Elizabethan
literature, Dyce was by the standards of his day an excellent editor.
Those standards are not our own. Dyce did not scruple to smooth
away metrical irregularities. In the first volume and part of the
second, he recorded with some minuteness his departures from
the old editions; but this practice he afterwards abandoned as
'unnecessary'. Still, his edition represents pioneering scholarship—
for *A Game at Chess* he examined five texts, and collated the two
manuscripts of which he knew—and has not been properly superseded, despite the appearance in 1885–6 of Bullen's edition of the
works in eight volumes. The latter sensibly excluded both parts of
The Honest Whore as more appropriate to a collected *Dekker*; he added
a few minor items missed by Dyce (e.g. *The Triumphs of Honour and
Virtue*, already edited by James L. Pearson for the Shakespeare
Society in 1845); and for his text of *A Game at Chess* 'looked through'
—his own phrase—the Trinity College manuscript, unknown to
Dyce. But mostly Bullen took over his predecessor's text, and freely
availed himself (as he acknowledged) of the earlier editor's notes.
Nevertheless the Bullen edition, rather than Dyce, is usually
described as 'standard', and preferred for citation—presumably because it is later, more easily accessible, and offers the convenience
of line numbering.

For the two volumes of Middleton plays, ten in all, in the
Mermaid series (1887, 1890), the editor, Havelock Ellis, claims to
have made 'a careful collation' of the 'two admirable editions' by
Dyce and Bullen. The Swinburne introduction reprints, with revisions, an essay that had first appeared in the *Nineteenth Century* in
1886. Although of negligible importance textually, the Mermaid
volumes made available to a wider public a few of Middleton's
lesser-known plays, including *A Chaste Maid in Cheapside* and *The
Mayor of Queenborough*. In 1915 Martin W. Sampson edited four
plays, including *A Fair Quarrel*, for a similar but less ambitious
American series, Masterpieces of English Drama, of which Felix E.
Schelling was General Editor. Martin follows Dyce's text, 're-
enforced by a number of quarto readings'. Edgar C. Morris edited
The Spanish Gypsy, along with Rowley's *All's Lost by Lust*, in old
spelling for the Belles-Lettres series in 1908. *The Spanish Gypsy* was
also chosen as the single Middleton play in *Representative English*

Comedies (vol. 3, 1914), under the general editorship of Charles Mills Gayley; this too is in old spelling.

The present century has yet to give us a complete Middleton, but a number of editions, some excellent, of individual titles have appeared. Here the greatest contribution has been made by R. C. Bald. For his edition of *A Game at Chess* (1929) Bald collated four contemporary manuscripts (two others, now in the Folger Shakespeare Library, came to light too late for him), as well as the three early quartos; his text is based on the Trinity College holograph, with omissions supplied where possible from the Huntington manuscript. The introduction gives an account of the fascinating historical background to this topical *tour de force*. In 1938 Bald edited *Hengist, King of Kent; or The Mayor of Queenborough* from the Folger Lambarde manuscript, which affords a better and fuller text (including a different ending!) than the 1661 quarto, the basis of the Dyce and Bullen editions. Bald also prepared the Malone Society reprint (1953) of Middleton's *Honourable Entertainments* from the unique copy in the Huntington Library. These entertainments, ephemeral pieces designed for civic occasions between Easter 1620 and Easter 1621, were not known to Middleton's nineteenth-century editors. Lastly, Bald edited *The Inner Temple Masque, or Masque of Heroes* for *A Book of Masques in Honour of Allardyce Nicoll* (1967).

Recovered in 1920, *The Ghost of Lucrece*, Middleton's early narrative poem in the popular complaint form, was edited in modern spelling by Joseph Quincy Adams in 1937; the volume also included a facsimile of the copy of the original octavo in the Folger. Of the more familiar pieces, *The Changeling* and *A Chaste Maid in Cheapside* have appeared in excellent editions, by N. W. Bawcutt (1958) and R. B. Parker (1969) respectively, in the Revels Plays series. These editions offer carefully edited texts in modernized spelling, with full annotation and comprehensive introductions. Parker is able to date *A Chaste Maid in Cheapside* more precisely than was previously possible, and he has an especially valuable section on the original staging of the only play known definitely to have been performed at the Swan Theatre. J. R. Mulryne is preparing an edition of *Women Beware Women* for the same series. In 1945 L. Drees and H. De Vocht provided, in the Louvain series Materials for the Study of the Old English Drama, the most accurate text of *The Witch* that had yet appeared, but this was shortly superseded by the authoritative Malone Society transcript prepared by Sir Walter Greg and F. P. Wilson (1950, for 1948). The collaborate *Roaring Girl* is definitively edited in the Bowers *Dekker* (vol. 3, 1958). The Regents Renaissance

Drama Series has furnished editions, somewhat uneven in quality, of *A Mad World, My Masters* (ed. Standish Henning, 1965), *Michaelmas Term* (ed. Richard Levin, 1966), and *The Changeling* (ed. George W. Williams, 1966). The last-mentioned play has also been edited, 1966, in a popular modern-spelling edition by Matthew W. Black. Available in old spelling in the Fountainwell Drama Texts are *A Trick to Catch the Old One* (1968), *A Chaste Maid in Cheapside* (1969), and *Women Beware Women* (1969), all three edited by Charles Barber; the New Mermaids offer, in modern spelling, *The Changeling* (ed. Patricia Thomson, 1964), *A Game at Chess* (ed. J. W. Harper, 1966), *Women Beware Women* (ed. Roma Gill, 1968), and *A Chaste Maid in Cheapside* (ed. Alan Brissenden, 1968). These are conscientious, inexpensively produced editions based on fresh collations of the seventeenth-century originals. For *A Game at Chess* Harper has advantageously consulted the Folger Archdale manuscript, which apparently represents an earlier version of the play.

A Trick to Catch the Old One and *The Changeling* have been the most frequently anthologized of Middleton's plays. Brook and Paradise however selected *A Game at Chess* for their *Elizabethan Drama 1580–1642* (1933).

While ungratefully questioning whether the world cries out for four new editions of *The Changeling*, one can only welcome the recent editorial interest in Middleton. Still a number of interesting plays by this prolific dramatist—among them *The Phoenix, More Dissemblers Besides Women,* and *The Old Law*—remain unavailable in any modern edition, let alone one satisfying the demands of the post-Greg era. It is no exaggeration to claim that Middleton is the pre-eminent writer of his day for whom we yet await an authoritative collected edition.

CRITICAL STUDIES AND COMMENTARY

From the Romantic age onward, Middleton has not gone unnoticed, nor has he failed to receive his meed of praise, although the modern estimate of his importance does not begin to emerge until late in the Victorian era. Lamb, always handy as a starting-point, furnished a number of extracts in his *Specimens*, including *More Dissemblers Besides Women* (still not very well known) and *No Wit, No Help like a Woman's*; also, rather surprisingly, Allwit's soliloquy on the rewards of cuckoldom from *A Chaste Maid in Cheapside*. Lamb praises the moral sensitivity of *The Old Law* and *A Fair Quarrel*. Oddly he prints nothing from *The Changeling*. That play, and in particular the character of De Flores, powerfully impressed Leigh Hunt; but Hunt too gives no extract in *Imagination and Fancy; or Selections from the English*

Poets (1844). Hazlitt (*Lectures*, 1820) is cool to Middleton, whose style he finds nondescript. *The Witch*, lauded by Hazlitt as Middleton's 'most remarkable performance', tends to get disproportionate attention in this period because of the *Macbeth* connection. Hazlitt recognizes the human insight shown in *Women Beware Women*, and the 'cool cutting irony of expression'; but the play falls apart. To an anonymous critic in the *Retrospective Review* in 1823, *Women Beware Women* is 'on the whole . . . Middleton's finest play'. The article consists mainly of illustrative passages from that piece, as well as from *The Witch* and *The Changeling*; but the author shrewdly remarks Middleton's interest in morally deformed women. Dyce's introduction to his edition crystallizes mid-century opinion. He praises *Women Beware Women*, and sees *The Changeling* as (while on the whole inferior) having in several places 'a depth of passion unequalled' elsewhere in Middleton. *A Game at Chess* is 'original and ingenious', the comedies 'faithfully reflect the manners and customs of the age'; but Dyce ends by assigning Middleton to the third rank, below Webster and Ford, and on a par with Dekker and his compeers—including Marston.

A half-century later, a different critical wind wafts through the introduction to Bullen's edition. He cites the praise of Middleton in the ninth *Encyclopaedia Britannica* ('he of all the dramatists of that time is the disciple that comes nearest to the master'), echoes Lamb on *A Fair Quarrel*, and bluntly asserts that '*The Changeling*, *Women Beware Women*, and *The Spanish Gypsy* are among the highest achievements of the English Drama.' On *A Chaste Maid in Cheapside* he is refreshingly free from Victorian sanctimony. Swinburne, to whom Bullen dedicated his edition, translated commendation into the language of enthusiasm in his essay, which ultimately found a place in *The Age of Shakespeare*: but despite characteristic rhetorical excesses, he does not yield to undiscriminating eulogy. Swinburne has harsh words for *The Family of Love* ('very coarse, very dull') and for the underplot and denouement of *Women Beware Women*. It is *The Changeling*, especially the 'horribly human' De Flores, that moves him to rapture. That play also represents the pinnacle of Middleton's achievement to Arthur Symons in his chapter on Middleton and Rowley for the Cambridge History. Middleton is seen as achieving with Rowley heights beyond him when working alone. For the most part Middleton's work is flawed; he excels in the single scene, he lacks lyricism. Although Symons's chapter was published in 1910, it does not yet give us a Middleton for the twentieth century.

Nor do the first monographs on Middleton transcend their origin as post-graduate theses. Pauline Wiggins's *Inquiry into the Authorship of the Middleton–Rowley Plays*, an early (1897) Radcliffe dissertation, offers scene-by-scene allocations between the two dramatists of *A Fair Quarrel* and *The Changeling*, and although the assignments have more or less stood the test of time, the method on which they are based has not. In *The Dramatic Technique of Thomas Middleton in his Comedies of London Life* (1925), a University of Chicago dissertation, Wilbur Dwight Dunkel furnishes charts of plots, verse distribution, etc., and such critical revelations as, 'In these comedies the comic is frequently derived from frankness about sexual relationships.'

If Lamb provided a *locus classicus* for criticism in the last century, Eliot performs a similar function in our own. The views he expresses in his 'Thomas Middleton' (1927) are sometimes conventional, as in his endorsement of the 'usual opinion' that *The Changeling* marks Middleton's highest achievement, and at times eccentric, as when he declares of *The Roaring Girl* that 'It is typical of the comedies of Middleton, and it is the best.' But in Eliot's pages on *The Changeling* insight and appreciation operate on a high level, and the assertion of Middleton's greatness (despite critical misgivings about his long-windedness) is made in terms which, unlike Swinburne's, are acceptable to modern taste. Not everybody has whole-heartedly endorsed Eliot's verdict—a distinguished historian of criticism is disconcerted 'to find the adjective "great" applied to Middleton eight times in four successive sentences'[1]—but Middleton's present high position in the hierarchy of Elizabethan dramatists undoubtedly owes much to Eliot's influence.

The personality or impersonality of the artist, the pattern of his development as revealed in the *œuvre* (in Henry James's phrase, the 'figure in the carpet'), are preoccupations of Eliot which sometimes reveal more about the critic than about his subject. Middleton, Eliot insists, has no personality, he is solitary, inscrutable, 'merely a great recorder'. This challenge to the critic concerned with the whole corpus rather than with the individual work is taken up by Richard Hindry Barker in his *Thomas Middleton*, the first general book on the dramatist. Barker finds 'peculiar to Middleton . . . his persistent concern with the irony that invests the sinner's career', and which leads him to set in motion the forces that result in eventual disaster. This pattern, which Barker traces in a heterogeneous and voluminous body of writings written over a period of many years, is critically serviceable as far as it goes; but of course irony is not peculiar to Middleton, nor is the idea that the sinner destroys himself. Published

[1] René Wellek, 'The Criticism of T.S. Eliot', *Sewanee Review* 54 (1956), 437.

in 1958, Barker's *Middleton*, as the preface notes, was written around 1943, and its approach—impressionistic rather than systematically analytical—now seems somewhat old-fashioned and superficial. But the book is compendious and lucid; Barker provides a useful run-down of the facts of Middleton's life, and through adroit summary and judicious quotation conveys the flavour of the individual pieces. This introduction to Middleton might be especially recommended to the beginning student were it not for Barker's treatment of questions of authorship attribution, the special vexation of Middleton studies. Scholarship in this century has questioned the dramatist's responsi-bility for certain plays (e.g. *Blurt, Master Constable, The Spanish Gypsy*); others, most notably the anonymous *Revenger's Tragedy*, are now thought by some to be his. Barker's methodology is not up to his task. As regards *The Revenger's Tragedy*, he claims to have adduced 'new evidence that will, I think, settle the controversy about author-ship once and for all', but he has not settled the controversy once and for all. The play is discussed in this volume in the section on Tour-neur. On problems of ascription generally, the reader may consult Schoenbaum, *Internal Evidence and Elizabethan Dramatic Authorship: An Essay in Literary History and Method* (1966). In *The Art of Thomas Middleton: A Critical Study* (1970), David M. Holmes finds rather a different figure in the carpet. If Barker sees Middleton as moral, to Holmes he is a moralist prone to delivering dramatized sermons on such themes as appearance versus reality, the contest in man be-tween the human and the animal, and 'self-development through creditable response to experience'. Holmes makes *Blurt, Master Constable* a touchstone of Middleton's art; he thinks Middleton's the dominant hand in *The Roaring Girl*, and interprets *Hengist* as a de-liberate travesty. These are positions some would question. Middleton emerges as oddly humourless, if edifying. (R. B. Parker comes closer to the complex critical truth when he discerns in Middleton's world a tension between 'satiric observation and determined moralizing'; a tension that the playwright attempts to resolve by his 'strange mixture of realism, irony, and exaggeration'. Parker's excellent essay, 'Middleton's Experiments with Comedy and Judgement' (1960), focuses on the comedies, as the title would lead us to expect, but includes several illuminating pages on *Women Beware Women*. To Dorothy M. Farr, in *Thomas Middleton and the Drama of Realism* (1973), Middleton was 'too good an artist to be obtrusively moralist', although 'moral assumptions are firmly worked into the background of his characteristic work.' The author limits herself to seven repre-sentative plays, from the City comedies (here chief emphasis falls properly on *A Chaste Maid in Cheapside*), through the transitional *Fair Quarrel*, to the two great tragedies, with a concluding chapter on *A Game at Chess*. There is occasional evidence of careless proof-reading (Middleton, we are told, was born 'about 1680'), and Miss Farr shows a shaky grasp of chronology when, having tentatively dated *The Widow* between 1604 and 1608, she proceeds to discern in it the influence of Fletcher; but this attractively modest and unpolemical study yields its share of insights. Still, a comprehensive book on Middleton, so accessible yet so extraordinarily complex a subject, remains a goal rather than an achievement of criticism.

Meanwhile Arthur Kirsch, in *Jacobean Dramatic Perspectives* (1972), has devoted a sensitive chapter to psychomachic patterns and theatrical self-consciousness in Middleton's plays; and the tragedies have received considerable attention. Schoenbaum's *Middleton's Tragedies: A Critical Study* (1955), although published before Barker's book, was written under the latter's inspiration and tutelage, and has the limitations of youthful discipleship. Schoenbaum devotes considerable space to sources and to authorship questions; as regards interpretation, perhaps his most interesting pages are those on *Hengist*, where the dramatist's sexual preoccupation is seen as resulting 'in a total shift of emphasis as the play progresses: an historical drama becomes a melodrama of amorous intrigue, a study of ambition becomes a study of lust.' An anomalous work, *Hengist* is little noticed in subsequent work on the tragedies. Important discussions of the two major plays figure in books that cast a wider net. The passage in William Empson's *Some Versions of Pastoral* (1935) on the integration of the tragic main action with the farcical underplot of *The Changeling* represents pioneering criticism, which was carried farther by M. C. Bradbrook in her chapter on Middleton in *Themes and Conventions of Elizabethan Tragedy* (1935). She explores connections between plot and underplot in *The Changeling* and *Women Beware Women* (regarded by her as the 'slighter play'), and also dominating imagery: food and poison in the former play, food and wealth in the latter. In *The Moral Vision of Jacobean Tragedy* Ornstein probes the ironic inversions of romantic themes in *The Changeling* (compared with *The Maid's Tragedy*) and *Women Beware Women*. The same works provide matter for a chapter, more broadly based but somewhat reductive, of Irving Ribner's *Jacobean Tragedy: The Quest for Moral Order* (1962). Ribner sees Middleton's tragedies as 'conditioned by a Calvinistic bias which leaves little room for the redemption of sinners'. The assertion of generalities, e.g. Middleton's tragedies are statements about man's relation to evil in the world, does little to enhance the persuasiveness of the argument, but Ribner writes penetratingly on how imagery drawn from commercial exchange relates to the sordid moral choices made in *Women Beware Women*. The commercial ethos in this play also interests T. B. Tomlinson in *A Study of Elizabethan and Jacobean Tragedy* (1964). His chapters on *Women Beware Women* (linked with the City comedies, especially *A Chaste Maid in Cheapside*) and *The Changeling*, regarded as a triumph of poetic naturalism although Tomlinson himself questions the propriety of the term 'naturalism', are pleasantly informal in tone if rather slight in substance; the discussion of *The Changeling* is not free from symbol-mongering.

The tragedies have inspired several noteworthy essays. It is difficult to understand how some critics can continue to regard condescendingly the underplot of *The Changeling* after Karl J. Holzknecht's demonstration of its structural functions in 'The Dramatic Structure of *The Changeling*' (1954). Christopher Ricks, in 'The Moral and Poetic Structure of *The Changeling*' (1960), sees the underplot as contributing to the play a tone of sexual innuendo; but mainly he considers the presence of certain words—*blood, will, act, deed*, and (most importantly) *service*—which establish mood and poetic themes. 'Word-play in *Women Beware Women*' (1961), by the same author, shows how such words as 'business' express the play's central meaning, how money corrupts life, degrading love into mercenary lust. This useful, if limited, approach is incorporated into a larger discussion of symbols, imagery, and conventions in Ricks's contribution to the volume he has edited (*English Drama to 1710*) for the *Sphere History of Literature in the English Language* (1971). Ricks illuminatingly compares Middleton in these respects with Webster, Tourneur, and Shakespeare. *The Changeling* is compared with *Dr. Faustus* and *Macbeth* in a brilliant passage of Helen Gardner's essay, 'Milton's "Satan" and the Theme of Damnation in Elizabethan Tragedy' (1948). In 'Myth and Psychology in *The Changeling*' (1970), Robert Jordan, picking up where Ornstein leaves off, finds echoes in the play of the motif of the wild man and the maiden, as well as of the myth of beauty and the beast. Lastly one may note an earlier study by G. R. Hibbard, 'The Tragedies of Thomas Middleton and the Decadence of the Drama' (1957). In Hibbard's view, Middleton betrayed his intuition regarding the tragic experience by making concessions to audience expectation; hence the final blood bath that 'ruins' *Women Beware Women*. The finale has however been defended, for example by Ribner, as employing a legitimate ritual technique, and Schoenbaum has questioned the utility of the term decadence in 'Peut-on parler d'une "décadence" du théâtre au temps des premiers Stuarts?'

If comedy in general has stimulated less critical enterprise than tragedy, that is certainly the case specifically with Middleton; the tragicomedies, belonging as they do to a bastard genre, are even more neglected. L. C. Knights, in *Drama and Society in the Age of Jonson* (1937), uses his hero as a club with which to beat Jonson's less celebrated contemporary; but if in the chapter, 'Middleton and the New Social Classes', Knights is unfair (he claims that all which remains with us after a second or third reading of *A Chaste Maid in Cheapside* is the plot), he nevertheless has some useful things to say about the social context for the plays. The relation of drama to economic and political developments is also studied, but to a rather different effect, by Brian Gibbons in *Jacobean City Comedy*; he compares Middleton and Jonson without prejudice against the former. Bradbrook's *Growth and Structure of Elizabethan Comedy* offers a brief, lively account of Middleton, not without insights but altogether scrappier than her earlier treatment of the tragedies. Richard Levin dissects half a dozen Middleton plays (including *The Changeling*) in *The Multiple Plot in English Renaissance Drama* (1971). Readers will not always agree with the way Levin organizes and interprets the plot data, and he does not always avoid the dangers of over-ingenuity and high abstraction; but his analyses are admirable for their sustained intelligence. One especially welcomes the sections on *A Fair Quarrel*, where Levin takes the novel position that the play achieves structural integration and tonal synthesis, and on *A Trick to Catch the Old One*, where he strives valiantly to account for the presence of the puzzling Dampit scenes. A similar purpose underlies Ruby Chatterji's 'Unity and Disparity in *Michaelmas Term*' (1968); she argues that structural unity is reinforced by 'a more fundamental thematic unity', and finds the play better integrated than does Levin. Alan C. Dessen, 'Middleton's *The Phoenix* and the Allegorical Tradition' (1966), explores the 'pseudo-allegorical mode' of this early comedy, and shows how Middleton manages to maintain a realistic surface while simultaneously 'achieving the scope and general significance characteristic of the morality tradition'.

Of Middleton's City Comedies, *A Chaste Maid in Cheapside* has properly stimulated the most interest. This play provides, with *Bartholomew Fair*, the climax for Levin's investigation. In '*A Chaste Maid in Cheapside* and Middleton's City Comedy' (1959), Schoenbaum sees the comedy as the dramatist's greatest triumph of 'fantastic realism', and he notes Middleton's special concern 'with the effects of the competitive struggle on family relationships—on ties of blood or marriage'. This line of interpretation is pursued by Chatterji, who, in 'Theme, Imagery, and Unity in *A Chaste Maid in Cheapside*' (1965), finds the family 'the nexus of the play's various complications, the basis of its thematic as well as structural unity'. Chatterji is particularly illuminating on the imagery of the play. Robert I. Williams, in 'Machiavelli's *Mandragola*, Touchwood Senior, and the Comedy of Middleton's *A Chaste Maid in Cheapside*' (1970), compares *Mandragola* with *A Chaste Maid* to get at the paradoxical nature of a 'comedy of anguish' that 'equivocates between romance and cynicism'. If criticism since Eliot has brought about a new and higher valuation of *Women Beware Women*, it has also instated *A Chaste Maid in Cheapside* as Middleton's comic master-piece.

In conclusion, one may cite two articles, R. C. Bald's 'The Chronology of Thomas Middleton's Plays' (1937) and David George's 'Thomas Middleton's Sources: A Survey' (1971), of which the interest is not critical at all, but rather, if one may use the term, pre-critical. Subsequent investigation has necessitated the revision of some of Bald's dates, and future scholars will no doubt point out sources that George missed. But both essays furnish essential points of reference for anyone interested in Middleton's work as a whole.

Philip Massinger

TEXTS

Massinger early engaged editorial attention. The first critical editor of Shakespeare, Nicholas Rowe, apparently contemplated issuing a complete Massinger, but nothing came of the scheme. Several other abortive attempts at an edition in the eighteenth century preceded Thomas Coxeter's *Dramatic Works of Philip Massinger*, issued in four volumes in 1759, and reissued by T. Davies in 1761. J. Monck Mason's edition, two decades later, included Davies's 'Short Essay on the Life and Writings of Massinger'. These collections were superseded by William Gifford's *The Plays of Philip Massinger* (1805). For the second edition in 1813, Gifford revised some of his notes, and incorporated readings from a lately recovered copy of the first edition of *The Duke of Milan*, with corrections in the author's hand. Otherwise, however, except for the most minor changes, he let his text stand, boasting of the 'unwearied pains with which it was at first established, not only from a collation of all the editions, but of numerous copies of the same edition'. Gifford exaggerated his achievement (in the text of *The Parliament of Love* he made over

130 blunders, according to the Malone Society editor's count), and by modern standards he took liberties with his texts which are unconscionable. Still the 1813 edition was for its day remarkable, and Gifford's text—in modern spelling and punctuation but without line numbering—became the basis of all the later nineteenth-century editions. A one-volume version, published posthumously in 1840, went through several reprintings, as did the combined *Massinger and Ford* of the same year, with an introduction by Hartley Coleridge. Lt.-Col. F. Cunningham based his 1871 edition on Gifford's text, but added *Believe as you List*, a manuscript tragedy which holds much interest, for it is in Massinger's autograph, and has theatrical revisions in another hand, as well as alterations by the Master of the Revels. 'Concealed in a vast mass of rubbish', the play had turned up in 1844, and was five years later edited for the Percy Society by T. Crofton Croker, who had trouble deciphering the script, and pieced out deficiencies in the text with the natural sprouts of his own wit. Meanwhile, in 1830–1, W. Harness had brought out three volumes of Massinger's plays, with the texts 'adapted for family reading, and the use of young persons, by the omission of objectionable matter'. The interest of this edition is primarily sociological.

Although more than a century and a half has passed, Gifford's remains the last essay at a complete edition. A. K. McIlwraith undertook a new edition for the Clarendon Press, but, although he was well equipped for the task, he did not live to finish it. His papers were passed down to Philip Edwards, who in collaboration with Colin Gibson has carried on with the work; so one day the Clarendon *Massinger* should be a reality. It is much needed.

Of smaller collections, the amplest is the selection of ten pieces edited by Arthur Symons for the Mermaid Series (2 vols., 1887–9). The texts for the first volume derive from Gifford, but, for the second, S. W. Orson collated British Museum copies of the plays; Symons reprints *Believe as you List* from Croker. R. A. Sherman edited a volume of four plays for the Masterpieces of English Drama series in 1912. Donald S. Lawless's *The Poems of Philip Massinger*, a 1968 Ball State Monograph, brings together the eight poems that the dramatist is known to have written.

A number of plays have had separate editions. Seven were prepared as dissertation exercises for the Ph.D., with T. M. Parrott of Princeton or Samuel C. Chew of Bryn Mawr in most cases the supervisor. This series, if it may be called that, comprises *The Duke of Milan*, ed. T. W. Baldwin (1918); *The Fatal Dowry*, ed. Charles Lacy Lockert, Jr. (1918); *The Maid of Honour*, ed. Eva A. W. Bryne

(1927); *The Roman Actor,* ed. William Lee Sandidge, Jr. (1929); *The Bondman,* ed. Benjamin Townley Spencer (1932); *The Great Duke of Florence,* ed. Johanne M. Stochholm (1933); and *The City Madam,* ed. Rudolf Kirk (1934). These editions feature elaborate introductions, old-spelling texts that generally reproduce the accidentals of the originals, and commentary. Some of the interpretative views expressed in the introductions, e.g. Stochholm on the political relevance of *The Great Duke of Florence,* may be taken *cum grano salis.* The Malone Society has published authoritative transcripts, with full textual introductions, of *Believe as you List* and *The Parliament of Love,* the former prepared by Charles J. Sisson (1927), the latter by Kathleen Lea (1928 [1929]). A collotype facsimile of *Believe as you List* is to be had in Farmer's Tudor Facsimile Texts series (1907). Frequently anthologized, *A New Way to Pay Old Debts* was edited by Brander Matthews for *Representative English Comedies* (vol. 3, 1914); also by, among others, A. H. Cruickshank (1926), Muriel St. Clare Byrne (1949), and T. W. Craik (New Mermaids, 1964). Most readers will find the last-mentioned the most convenient. Cyrus Hoy has ably edited *The City Madam* for his own Regents Renaissance Drama series (1964), and *The Fatal Dowry* is available in an old-spelling text edited by T. A. Dunn for Fountainwell (1969).

CRITICAL STUDIES AND COMMENTARY

To conclude this chapter with Massinger is to end on a note of decrescendo. He has had in general a bad press; better, like Marston, to outrage good taste by literary excesses than to lull readers into lethargy, and inspire the faint praise that damns. Robert Hamilton Ball reminds us, in *The Amazing Career of Sir Giles Overreach* (1939), that one Massinger piece, *A New Way to Pay Old Debts,* held the boards until well into the Victorian age—'a stock play, one of the regular starring vehicles for important actors, a popular success in London and the provinces'. Still, criticism has for some time tended to regard Massinger as the inheritor of fulfilled renown; an apostle of enervation.

The earliest critique, John Ferriar's 'Essay on the Dramatic Writings of Massinger' (1786), sufficiently impressed Gifford to be reprinted in the latter's edition. Ferriar praises Massinger's plot-management, his 'exact discrimination and consistency of character', and his melodious and varied versification. While ranking Massinger immediately beneath Shakespeare, this early critic also discerns a fault subsequent commentary would make much of: Massinger's 'want of passion'. To Lamb, in his *Specimens,* Massinger is deficient in 'poetical enthusiasm', and compares disadvantageously with his collaborator Dekker, endowed with 'poetry enough for anything'. Coleridge uses Massinger not as a whipping boy for Dekker but, more expectedly, 'our sweet Shakspeare' in his miscellaneous remarks, which are as suggestive as they are fragmentary. For Coleridge the plays, always entertaining, have a novelistic appeal; he devotes most space to the blank verse, which, if prosy, is 'the very model of dramatic versification'. The touch-stone however for Massinger criticism comes later, with Leslie Stephen's urbane essay, 'Massinger', included in *Hours in a Library* (1874-9). Stephen presents Massinger as a sentimentalist and rhetorician, prone to indulgence in 'elaborate didactic utterances upon moral topics'. But the morality is morbid, a blossom flourishing in 'exhausted soil'. Massinger's defect is, 'in one word, a want of vital force'. This influential essay, which repeats Ferriar's stricture but makes it central rather than peripheral to the act of critical judgement, left its mark on Symons, Swinburne, and latterly, Eliot, all of whom cite Stephen. Symons finds delight in *The Great Duke of Florence*, admires Massinger's story-telling skills and dramatic construction, but concludes: 'He has no real mastery over the passions, and his eloquence does not appeal to the heart.' Even Swinburne must treat Stephen with deference, and end with tepid commendation of 'a most admirable and conscientious writer, who was also a most rational and thoughtful patriot'. This essay struck Eliot as 'Swinburne's criticism at its best'; his own 'Philip Massinger' (1920) completes the demolition of an already battered edifice. Mainly Eliot compares Massinger's borrowings, in his view base echoes, with their Shakespearian originals. Eliot determined that 'Massinger's feeling for language had outstripped his feeling for things; that his eye and his vocabulary were not in co-operation'. Suffering from cerebral anaemia, Massinger initiates the dissociation of sensibility.

A severe judgement; but Massinger has not entirely wanted defenders in this century, although one is naïve, and the other presents his case in a foreign tongue. In his *Philip Massinger* (1920), avowedly an attempt to rehabilitate the reputation of a writer of the second rank, Canon Cruickshank can say, without embarrassment, 'in the main, I must confess, I plead for Massinger because I love him.' The plea consists of simple impressionism: '*The Maid of Honour* is well planned, and the characters well contrasted', 'No student of our comic drama can ignore the brilliant vigour of *The City Madam*', etc. Altogether more sophisticated and substantial is Maurice Chelli's *Le Drame de Massinger*. A Sorbonne thesis completed on the eve of the Great War, it was not published until 1923, five years after the author's death. It is a very superior example of the genre to which it belongs. Chelli devotes chapters to the life and posthumous reputation, to Massinger and the school of Fletcher, to characterization, the treatment of the passions, and the dramatist's sentiments with respect to love, politics, and religion. A chapter on 'L'Art de l'intrigue chez Massinger' gives detailed summaries of the fifteen plays of his unaided authorship. Chelli writes with intelligence and perception, but inevitably in the shadow of a scholarship which time has passed by. We can no longer share his confidence that the metrical authorship tests of Fleay and the New Shaksperians offer a method of assured utility, and in other ways too our understanding of the period, not to mention our sensibility, has altered.

It cannot be claimed, however, that the only more recent general book on the subject, T. A. Dunn's *Philip Massinger: The Man and the Playwright* (1957), provides the needed reassessment. Dunn begins with a long and useful biographical section; chapters follow on plotting, stagecraft, characterization, criticism of life, and style—an arrangement rather like Chelli's, and one which never permits the critic to come to grips with the aesthetic object in all its aspects. Dunn is oddly unenthusiastic about the author to whom he has devoted so much time and effort. 'I have not . . . attempted to claim for Massinger a position or an importance that does not accord with his worth', he announces ominously in his preface. 'He is not, it must be admitted, a great, or even always a very good dramatist.' The depreciatory tone persists in the book that follows. Massinger has 'a stock method of handling his plots', the characters come only intermittently to life, the inelastic style is that of a 'man temperamentally humourless, lacking in the warm fire of the sensuous imagination and sicklied o'er with the pale cast of convention and abstraction'. Dunn limits his discussion to the fifteen plays which Massinger wrote independently, and, while one can sympathize with his unwillingness to lose himself in the dark forest of attributional speculation, still no comprehensive revaluation of this author can dismiss the substantial body of collaborative writing. (In this respect Cyrus Hoy has made a major contribution in his monograph, 'The Shares of Fletcher and his Collaborators in the Beaumont and Fletcher Canon', the first two instalments of which deal with Massinger; Hoy distinguishes Massinger's share by the presence or absence of certain linguistic forms, e.g. pronominal *ye*, the verb form *hath*—more reliable guides than the metrical criteria favoured by earlier investigators.) Dunn has thoroughly familiarized himself with previous criticism and scholarship, and his book is well documented; but it will not drive any uncommitted student back to the plays. Lawless's *Philip Massinger and his Associates* (1967) is not, as its title might lead one to expect, a critical study at all, but a brief monograph, abridged from a doctoral dissertation, which adds to biographical knowledge and to our understanding of the playwright in relation to his patrons and other connections.

In addition to the foregoing, a number of Massinger studies have appeared in books or journals. Benjamin Townley Spencer's 'Philip Massinger' (1933), a revised graduate paper by a student of the history of ideas, explores at length and in pedestrian fashion Massinger's moral ideas, religious and philosophical concepts, social theories, and the idea of the state. Spencer does not disdain platitude, nor does he recognize the dangers of separating utterances made in a play from their dramatic context. The point made by Peter F. Mullany in 'Religion in Massinger's *The Maid of Honour*' (1969)— that in this play 'Religion . . . is Massinger's dramatic means to a brilliant display of heightened and conflicting emotions' but 'has no other real significance'—is not one to recommend itself to Spencer. A more complex and acceptable working assumption is Philip Edwards's, in 'Massinger the Censor' (1962), that the playwright made 'a very determined effort . . . to present convincing theatrical action which should at the same time be the figured language of morality'. This essay discusses a number of plays, and makes an excellent, if all too brief, general introduction to Massinger. On the comedies Eliot provides a point of departure and return for L. C. Knights (*Drama and Society in the Age of Jonson*). Knights acknowledges the derivative in Massinger—the borrowings, not only from Shakespeare but from Jonson as well—but, on the basis of *A New Way to Pay Old Debts* and *The City Madam*, he takes issue with Eliot's charge that Massinger was incapable of 'vivifying' the Elizabethan morality. The same two comedies occupy Allen Gross in 'Social Change and Philip Massinger' (1967). Gross sees Massinger's attitude towards the upward-mobile trading class as not being static in these plays. The same author, in 'Contemporary Politics in Massinger' (1966), challenges the 'received opinion' that Massinger's plays abound in specific references to contemporary persons and events; but, in such works as *Believe as you List* and *The Bondman*, the dramatist does evince an interest in military intervention and domestic taxation, vital issues of the day. This paper is of value for its methodological strictures. Peter Davison, in 'The Theme and Structure of *The Roman Actor*' (1963), and A. P. Hogan, in 'Imagery of Acting in *The Roman Actor*'

(1971), argue, albeit on different grounds, for the unity and integrity of a tragedy that Massinger regarded as 'the most perfit birth of my Minerva'. In '*The Virgin Martyr* and the *Tragedia Sacra*' (1964), Louise George Clubb examines the 'striking' resemblances between this dramatization of the Dorothea legend and the *tragédie sacré* about virgin martyrs which flourished in the wake of the Counter-Reformation. Philip Edwards compares two 'pretender' plays, *Believe as you List* and Ford's *Perkin Warbeck*, relating them to 'the period of perturbed and perplexed relationships between monarch and people about the year 1630' ('The Royal Pretenders in Massinger and Ford', 1974).

These studies testify to some reawakening of interest in Massinger, but on the whole he remains a neglected figure. Neglect may, of course, sometimes be benign, and it is true that Massinger had his share of detractors even in his own time. In this writer's opinion, however, criticism has not sufficiently addressed itself to what is interesting and distinctive in the art of this prolific Stuart dramatist. Perhaps the Clarendon edition, when it appears, will inspire—and contribute to—a needed revaluation.

REFERENCES

John Marston (1575?–1634)

BIBLIOGRAPHIES

C. A. Pennel and W. P. Williams, *Elizabethan Bibliographies Supplements IV: George Chapman and John Marston* (London, 1968).
S. Tannenbaum, *John Marston: A Concise Bibliography* (New York, 1940).

TEXTS

The Workes of Mr. John Marston (London, 1633; two issues).
ed. A. H. Bullen, *The Works of John Marston*, 3 vols. (London, 1887; repr. 1970).
ed. A. Davenport, *The Poems of John Marston* (Liverpool, 1961).
ed. J. O. Halliwell, *The Works of John Marston*, 3 vols. (London, 1856).
ed. H. H. Wood, *The Plays of John Marston*, 3 vols. (Edinburgh, 1934–9).

Antonio and Mellida

ed. W. W. Greg (Malone Society Reprints, London, 1921).
ed. G. K. Hunter (Regents Renaissance Drama, Lincoln, Nebr., 1965).

Antonio's Revenge

ed. W. W. Greg (Malone Society Reprints, London, 1921).
ed. G. K. Hunter (Regents Renaissance Drama, Lincoln, Nebr., 1965).

The Dutch Courtesan

ed. P. Davison (Fountainwell Drama Texts, Edinburgh, 1968).
cd. M. L. Wine (Regents Renaissance Drama, Lincoln, Nebr., 1965).

The Malcontent

ed. B. Harris (The New Mermaids, London, 1967).
ed. G. B. Harrison (London, 1933).
ed. M. L. Wine (Regents Renaissance Drama, Lincoln, Nebr., 1964).

CRITICAL STUDIES AND COMMENTARY

M. Allen, *The Satire of John Marston* (Columbus, Ohio, 1920).
A. J. Axelrad, *Un Malcontent élisabéthain: John Marston (1576–1634)* (Paris, 1955).
P. J. Ayres, 'Marston's *Antonio's Revenge*: The Morality of the Revenging Hero', *SEL* 12 (1972).
E. Berland, 'The Function of Irony in Marston's *Antonio and Mellida*', *SP* 66 (1969).
M. C. Bradbrook, *The Growth and Structure of Elizabethan Comedy* (London, 1955).
A. Caputi, *John Marston, Satirist* (Ithaca, N.Y., 1961).
G. Cross, 'Marston, Montaigne and Morality: *The Dutch Courtesan* Reconsidered', *ELH* 27 (1960).
——, 'The Retrograde Genius of John Marston', *Review of English Literature* 2 (1961).
——, 'Some Notes on the Vocabulary of John Marston', *N & Q* 199 (1954); 200 (1955); 201 (1956); 202 (1957); 203 (1958); 204 (1959); 205 (1960); 206 (1961); 208 (1963).
T. S. Eliot, 'John Marston' (1934), in *Selected Essays* (enlarged edn., London, 1951).
P. Finkelpearl, '*Histriomastix* as an Inns of Court Play: A Hypothesis', *HLQ* 29 (1964).
——, *John Marston of the Middle Temple* (Cambridge, Mass., 1969).
B. Gibbons, *Jacobean City Comedy* (London, 1968).
A. Harbage, *Shakespeare and the Rival Traditions* (New York, 1952).
W. Hazlitt, *Lectures on the Dramatic Literature of the Age of Elizabeth* (London, 1820); in *Complete Works*, ed. P. P. Howe, 21 vols. (London, 1930–4), vol. 6 (1931).
G. K. Hunter, 'English Folly and Italian Vice: The Moral Landscape of John Marston', *Jacobean Theatre* (Stratford-upon-Avon Studies 1, ed. J. R. Brown and B. Harris, London, 1960).
E. Jensen, 'Theme and Imagery in *The Malcontent*', *SEL* 10 (1970).
J. Kaplan, 'John Marston's *Fawn*: A Saturnalian Satire', *SEL* 9 (1969).

A. Kernan, *The Cankered Muse* (New Haven, Conn., 1959).
——, 'John Marston's Play *Histriomastix*', *MLQ* 19 (1958).
A. H. King, *The Language of Satirized Characters in 'Poëtaster'* (Lund, 1941).
C. Lamb, *Specimens of English Dramatic Poets* (London, 1808).
R. Ornstein, *The Moral Vision of Jacobean Tragedy* (Madison, Wis., 1960).
J. H. Penniman, *The War of the Theatres* (Philadelphia, Pa., 1897).
S. Schoenbaum, 'The Precarious Balance of John Marston', *PMLA* 67 (1952).
R. A. Small, *The Stage Quarrel between Ben Jonson and the So-called Poetasters* (Breslau, 1899).
T. Spencer, 'John Marston', *Criterion* 13 (1934).
A. C. Swinburne, *The Age of Shakespeare* (London, 1908).
T. Warton, *A History of English Poetry*, 4 vols. (London, 1824).
P. M. Zall, 'John Marston, Satirist', *ELH* 20 (1953).

Thomas Middleton (1580–1627)

BIBLIOGRAPHIES

D. G. Donovan, *Elizabethan Bibliographies Supplements 1: Thomas Middleton and John Webster* (London, 1967).
S. A. Tannenbaum, *Thomas Middleton: A Concise Bibliography* (New York, 1940).

TEXTS

ed. A. H. Bullen, *The Works of Thomas Middleton*, 8 vols. (London, 1885–6).
ed. A. Dyce, *The Works of Thomas Middleton (With Some Account of the Author)*, 5 vols. (London, 1840).
ed. H. Ellis, *Thomas Middleton*, 2 vols. (The Mermaid Series, London, 1887–90).
ed. M. W. Sampson, *Thomas Middleton* (Masterpieces of the English Drama, New York, 1915).

The Changeling

ed. N. W. Bawcutt (The Revels Plays, London, 1958).
ed. M. W. Black (Philadelphia, Pa., 1966).
ed. P. Thomson (The New Mermaids, London, 1964).
ed. G. W. Williams (Regents Renaissance Drama, Lincoln, Nebr., 1966).

A Chaste Maid in Cheapside

ed. C. Barber (Fountainwell Drama Texts, Edinburgh, 1969).
ed. A. Brissenden (The New Mermaids, London, 1968).
ed. R. B. Parker (The Revels Plays, London, 1969).

A Game at Chess

ed. R. C. Bald (Cambridge, 1929).
ed. J. W. Harper (The New Mermaids, London, 1966).

The Ghost of Lucrece

ed. J. Q. Adams (New York, 1937).

Hengist, King of Kent; or The Mayor of Queenborough

ed. R. C. Bald (New York, 1938).

Honourable Entertainments

ed. R. C. Bald (Malone Society Reprints, Oxford, 1953).

The Inner Temple Masque, or Masque of Heroes

ed. R. C. Bald, in *A Book of Masques in Honour of Allardyce Nicoll* (Cambridge, 1967).

A Mad World, My Masters

ed. S. Henning (Regents Renaissance Drama, Lincoln, Nebr., 1965).

Michaelmas Term

ed. R. Levin (Regents Renaissance Drama, Lincoln, Nebr., 1966).

The Roaring Girl

ed. F. Bowers, in *The Works of Thomas Dekker*, 4 vols. (Cambridge, 1953–61), vol. 3 (1958).

The Spanish Gypsy

ed. C. M. Gayley, in *Representative English Comedies*, vol. 3 (New York, 1914).
ed. E. C. Morris (Belles-Lettres Series, Boston, Mass., 1908).

A Trick to Catch the Old One

ed. C. Barber (Fountainwell Drama Texts, Edinburgh, 1968).

The Triumphs of Honour and Virtue

ed. J. L. Pearson (London, 1845).

The Witch

ed. L. Drees and H. De Vocht (Materials for the Study of the Old English Drama, Louvain, 1945).
ed. W. W. Greg and F. P. Wilson (Malone Society Reprints, Oxford, 1948).
ed. I. Reed (London, 1778).

Women Beware Women

ed. C. Barber (Fountainwell Drama Texts, Edinburgh, 1969).
ed. R. Gill (The New Mermaids, London, 1968).

CRITICAL STUDIES AND COMMENTARY

Anon., 'Middleton's Plays', *Retrospective Review* 8 (1823).
R. C. Bald, 'The Chronology of Thomas Middleton's Plays', *MLR* 32 (1937).

R. H. Barker, *Thomas Middleton* (New York, 1958).

M. C. Bradbrook, *The Growth and Structure of Elizabethan Comedy* (London, 1955).

——, *Themes and Conventions of Elizabethan Tragedy* (Cambridge, 1935).

R. Chatterji, 'Theme, Imagery, and Unity in *A Chaste Maid in Cheapside*', *Ren. Dr.* 8 (1965).

——, 'Unity and Disparity in *Michaelmas Term*', *SEL* 8 (1968).

A. C. Dessen, 'Middleton's *The Phoenix* and the Allegorical Tradition', *SEL* 6 (1966).

W. D. Dunkel, *The Dramatic Technique of Thomas Middleton in his Comedies of London Life* (Chicago, Ill., 1925).

T. S. Eliot, 'Thomas Middleton' (1927), in *Elizabethan Essays* (London, 1934).

W. Empson, *Some Versions of Pastoral* (London, 1935).

D. M. Farr, *Thomas Middleton and the Drama of Realism* (Edinburgh, 1973).

H. Gardner, 'Milton's "Satan" and the Theme of Damnation in Elizabethan Tragedy', *ES*, N.S. 1 (1948).

D. George, 'Thomas Middleton's Sources: A Survey', *N & Q* 216 (1971).

B. Gibbons, *Jacobean City Comedy* (London, 1968).

G. R. Hibbard, 'The Tragedies of Thomas Middleton and the Decadence of the Drama', *University of Nottingham Renaissance and Modern Studies* 1 (1957).

W. Hazlitt, *Lectures on the Dramatic Literature of the Age of Elizabeth* (London, 1820); in *Complete Works*, ed. P. P. Howe, 21 vols. (London, 1930–4), vol. 6 (1931).

D. Holmes, *The Art of Thomas Middleton* (Oxford, 1970).

K. J. Holzknecht, 'The Dramatic Structure of *The Changeling*', *Renaissance Papers*, ed. A. H. Gilbert (Columbia, S.C., 1954).

L. Hunt, *Imagination and Fancy; or Selections from the English Poets* (London, 1844).

R. Jordan, 'Myth and Psychology in *The Changeling*', *Ren. Dr.*, N.S. 3 (1970).

A. C. Kirsch, *Jacobean Dramatic Perspectives* (Charlottesville, Va., 1972).

L. C. Knights, *Drama and Society in the Age of Jonson* (London, 1937).

C. Lamb, *Specimens of English Dramatic Poets* (London, 1808).

R. Levin, *The Multiple Plot in English Renaissance Drama* (Chicago, Ill., 1971).

R. Ornstein, *The Moral Vision of Jacobean Tragedy* (Madison, Wis., 1960).

R. B. Parker, 'Middleton's Experiments with Comedy and Judgement', *Jacobean Theatre* (Stratford-upon-Avon Studies 1, ed. J. R. Brown and B. Harris, London, 1960).

I. Ribner, *Jacobean Tragedy: The Quest for Moral Order* (London, 1962).

C. Ricks, 'The Moral and Poetic Structure of *The Changeling*', *Essays in Criticism* 10 (1960).

——, Word-play in *Women Beware Women*', *RES* 12 (1961).

——, 'The Tragedies of Webster, Tourneur and Middleton: Symbols, Imagery and Conventions', in *English Drama to 1710*, ed. C. Ricks (*Sphere History of Literature in the English Language*, vol. 3, London, 1971).

S. Schoenbaum, *Internal Evidence and Elizabethan Dramatic Authorship: An Essay in Literary History and Method* (Evanston, Ill., 1966).

——, *Middleton's Tragedies: A Critical Study* (New York, 1955).

——, 'A Chaste Maid in Cheapside and Middleton's City Comedy', in *Studies in the English Renaissance Drama in Memory of Karl Julius Holzknecht*, ed. J. W. Bennett and others (New York, 1959).

——, 'Peut-on parler d'une "décadence" du théâtre au temps des premiers Stuarts?', *Dramaturgie et société*, ed. J. Jacquot (Paris, 1968).

A. C. Swinburne, 'Thomas Middleton', *Nineteenth Century* 19 (1886).

A. Symons, 'Middleton and Rowley', in *The Cambridge History of English Literature*, vol. 6, pt. 2 (Cambridge, 1907).

T. B. Tomlinson, *A Study of Elizabethan and Jacobean Tragedy* (Cambridge, 1964).

P. Wiggins, *An Inquiry into the Authorship of the Middleton–Rowley Plays* (Boston, Mass., 1897).

R. I. Williams, 'Machiavelli's *Mandragola*, Touchwood Senior, and the Comedy of Middleton's *A Chaste Maid in Cheapside*', *SEL* 10 (1970).

Philip Massinger (1583–1640)

BIBLIOGRAPHIES

C. A. Pennel and W. P. Williams, *Elizabethan Bibliographies Supplements VIII: Philip Massinger* (London, 1968).

S. A. Tannenbaum, *Philip Massinger: A Concise Bibliography* (London, 1938).

TEXTS

ed. T. Coxeter, *The Dramatic Works of Philip Massinger*, 4 vols. (London, 1759, reissued 1761).

ed. F. Cunningham, *The Plays of Philip Massinger*, 4 vols. (London, 1871).

ed. W. Gifford, *The Plays of Philip Massinger*, 4 vols. (Edinburgh, 1805; 2nd edn., 1813).

ed. W. Harness, *The Plays of Philip Massinger adapted for Family Reading*, 3 vols. (London, 1830–1).

ed. D. Lawless, *The Poems of Philip Massinger* (Ball State Monographs No. 13, Muncie, Ind., 1968).

ed. J. M. Mason, *The Dramatic Works of Philip Massinger*, 4 vols. (London, 1779).

ed. R. A. Sherman, *Philip Massinger* (Masterpieces of the English Drama, New York, 1912).

ed. A. Symons, *Philip Massinger*, 2 vols. (The Mermaid Series, London, 1887–9).

Believe as you List

ed. J. S. Farmer (Tudor Facsimile Texts, London, 1907).

ed. C. J. Sisson (Malone Society Reprints, Oxford, 1927).

The Bondman

ed. B. T. Spencer (Princeton, N.J., 1932).

The City Madam

ed. C. Hoy (Regents Renaissance Drama, Lincoln, Nebr., 1964).
ed. R. Kirk (Princeton, N.J., 1934).

The Duke of Milan

ed. T. W. Baldwin (Lancaster, Pa., 1918).

The Fatal Dowry

ed. T. A. Dunn (Fountainwell Drama Texts, Edinburgh, 1969).
ed. C. L. Lockert (Lancaster, Pa., 1918).

The Great Duke of Florence

ed. J. M. Stochholm (Baltimore, Md., 1933).

The Maid of Honour

ed. E. A. W. Bryne (London, 1927).

A New Way to Pay Old Debts

ed. T. W. Craik (The New Mermaids, London, 1964).
ed. A. H. Cruickshank (Oxford, 1926).
ed. B. Matthews in *Representative English Comedies*, vol. 3 (New York, 1914).
ed. M. St. Clare Byrne (New York, 1949).

The Parliament of Love

ed. K. M. Lea (Malone Society Reprints, Oxford, 1928).

The Roman Actor

ed. W. L. Sandidge (Princeton, N.J., 1929).

CRITICAL STUDIES AND COMMENTARY

R. H. Ball, *The Amazing Career of Sir Giles Overreach* (Princeton, N.J., 1939).
M. Chelli, *Le Drame de Massinger* (Paris, 1923).
L. G. Clubb, '*The Virgin Martyr* and the *Tragedia Sacra*', *Ren. Dr.* 7 (1964).
S. T. Coleridge, *Coleridge on the Seventeenth Century*, ed. R. F. Brinkley (Durham, N.C., 1955).
A. H. Cruickshank, *Philip Massinger* (Oxford, 1920).
P. Davison, 'The Theme and Structure of *The Roman Actor*', *AUMLA* 19 (1963).
T. A. Dunn, *Philip Massinger: The Man and the Playwright* (Edinburgh, 1957).
P. Edwards, 'Massinger the Censor', in *Essays on Shakespeare and Elizabethan Drama in Honor of Hardin Craig*, ed. R. Hosley (Columbia, Mo., 1962; London, 1963).

——, 'The Royal Pretenders in Massinger and Ford', *Essays and Studies 1974*, N.S.27 (London, 1974).

T. S. Eliot, 'Philip Massinger' (1920), in *Elizabethan Essays* (London, 1934),

J. Ferriar, 'Essay on the Dramatic Writings of Philip Massinger', in *The Plays of Philip Massinger*, ed. W. Gifford (London, 1805; 2nd edn., 1813).

A. Gross, 'Contemporary Politics in Massinger', *SEL* 6 (1966).

——, 'Social Change and Philip Massinger', *SEL* 7 (1967).

A. P. Hogan, 'Imagery of Acting in *The Roman Actor*', *MLR* 66 (1971).

C. Hoy, 'The Shares of Fletcher and his Collaborators in the Beaumont and Fletcher Canon', *Studies in Bibliography* 8 (1956); 9 (1957).

L. C. Knights, *Drama and Society in the Age of Jonson* (London, 1937).

C. Lamb, *Specimens of English Dramatic Poets* (London, 1808).

D. S. Lawless, *Philip Massinger and his Associates* (Ball State Monograph No. 10, Muncie, Ind., 1967).

P. F. Mullany, 'Religion in Massinger's *The Maid of Honour*', *Ren. Dr.* N.S. 2 (1969).

B. T. Spencer, 'Philip Massinger', in *Seventeenth Century Studies*, ed. R. Shafer (Princeton, N.J., 1933).

L. Stephen, 'Massinger', in *Hours in a Library* (London, 1874–9).

7. BEAUMONT and FLETCHER, HEYWOOD, and DEKKER

MICHAEL TAYLOR
Francis Beaumont and John Fletcher

TEXTS

THE standard edition is still *The Works of Beaumont and Fletcher* (1905–12) in ten volumes edited by A. Glover and A. R. Waller, 'whose fidelity to copy [the 1679 Folio] involves the preservation of obvious error, including much mislineation' (Clifford Leech). A coeval Variorum edition, easier to cite from, and more reliably edited by A. H. Bullen and others, extends only to four volumes, and includes some twenty of the fifty-four plays associated with Beaumont and Fletcher. These editions are being superseded by *The Dramatic Works in the Beaumont and Fletcher Canon* under the general editorship of Fredson Bowers. There are some useful collections, notably the Everyman, the popular two-volume Mermaid, and a selection by F. E. Schelling with notes, glossary, and line-numbering. Few plays have appeared as single editions, although *The Knight of the Burning Pestle* is a popular choice. Michael Hattaway's New Mermaid edition (1969) is easily the most helpful, comparable to Andrew Gurr's highly recommended *Philaster* (1969) in the Revels Plays. R. K. Turner has edited *A King and No King* and H. B. Norland *The Maid's Tragedy* in the Regents Renaissance Drama Series. The Malone Society has reprinted *Bonduca* and *The Humorous Lieutenant* (under the Folio title of *Demetrius and Enanthe*), while J. D. Jump has carefully edited *Rollo Duke of Normandy*.

CRITICAL STUDIES AND COMMENTARY

The most authoritative discussion of the intricate problem of collaboration is to be found in a series of articles by Cyrus Hoy in *Studies in Bibliography* called 'The Shares of Fletcher and his Collaborators in the Beaumont and Fletcher Canon'. Of the fifty-four plays, Fletcher is the sole or partial author of fifty-one, Beaumont the sole or partial author of fourteen. The most prominent of Fletcher's many collaborators is Massinger, with a hand in nineteen plays. Beaumont, of course, looms larger than Fletcher's other colleagues because his name is associated with recognized masterpieces —*The Knight of the Burning Pestle* (solely his), *The Maid's Tragedy*,

A King and No King, Philaster, and the rather underestimated comedy *The Scornful Lady*. Yet Beaumont is an elusive figure. The very success of the collaboration makes disentanglement difficult. Despite the attention that the problem has received (for example, in the writings of E. H. C. Oliphant and in Baldwin Maxwell's book *Studies in Beaumont, Fletcher and Massinger*), as recently as 1969 Andrew Gurr in his introduction to *Philaster* can talk of the 'impenetrability' of Beaumont and Fletcher, inviting us, albeit tongue-in-cheek, to question Beaumont's existence.

We learn from works such as A. C. Sprague's *Beaumont and Fletcher on the Restoration Stage*, D. J. Rulfs's 'Beaumont and Fletcher on the London Stage, 1776–1833', J. H. Wilson's *The Influence of Beaumont and Fletcher on Restoration Drama*, and L. B. Wallis's *Fletcher, Beaumont and Company, Entertainers to the Jacobean Gentry* that the stock of Beaumont and Fletcher was high until the eighteenth century. 'In the opinion of the Stuart world of the mid-seventeenth century', writes Wallis, ' "Beaumont and Fletcher" were the twin stars, the Castor and Pollux, in the shining galaxy of English playwrights.' The decline in their popularity in the eighteenth century has never really been reversed, despite a short-lived upsurge of interest in them during the Romantic period, and despite a persistent admiration for the four great plays. Beaumont and Fletcher have suffered (and still suffer) from a form of critical puritanism. They can be forgiven for lacking Shakespeare's genius, but not, it seems, for apparently disavowing the moral earnestness of a Dekker or a Heywood. Their decadence as writers has been linked repeatedly to the immorality of James's court and to the role they played in providing entertainment (the word itself is patronizing) for the shallowly sophisticated patrons of the private theatres. The most trenchant criticism along these lines is J. F. Danby's. In his 'Jacobean Absolutists: The Placing of Beaumont and Fletcher' he describes Beaumont and Fletcher as 'inferior Sidneys of the second generation', believing that they exemplify the 'degeneration of a tradition, impelled by . . . bread-and-butter needs'. His *Poets on Fortune's Hill* contrasts a symbiotic Elizabethan society with a decadent Jacobean; a kingly Sidney on the hill's pinnacle with Beaumont and Fletcher, like the dirty rascals in the rhyme, languishing below. Yet it is noticeable that when Danby deals with individual plays (*Philaster* in the article, *The Maid's Tragedy* in the book) he is very respectful of their merits.

Even those critics who find much that is worthwhile in Beaumont and Fletcher feel obliged to point out their shortcomings, especially their 'moral inertia' in O. L. Hatcher's phrase in her *John Fletcher :*

A Study in Dramatic Method (1905). They lack 'deep spirituality'; they are 'melodramatic' according to C. M. Gayley in *Francis Beaumont, Dramatist* (1914). Even Arthur Mizener's seminal essay, 'The High Design of *A King and No King*' (1940), stresses the play's lack of moral seriousness, while Philip Edwards in an important and largely sympathetic article on Fletcher's tragicomedy, 'The Danger Not the Death: The Art of John Fletcher', writes: 'They do little to explain the human condition; their comment on contemporary society is trifling; their psychology and politics are often (not always) jejune; identification with the characters is a superhuman effort.'

In the face of so much judicious withdrawal, it is, in some ways, heartening to turn to the exuberant partisanship of John Masefield in an article in the *Atlantic Monthly* (1957), who quotes approvingly Shelley's remark that 'Incest is a highly poetical circumstance', even though his enthusiasm leads to excesses such as his conviction that *Beggars' Bush* is 'one of the best plays ever made'. Yet there *is* much artistry to praise in Beaumont and Fletcher, and it is at least arguable that the most valuable modern criticism attempts its assessment of them with due deference to their imaginative power, and with a sympathetic understanding of the literary and dramatic conventions they employ and of the social circumstances in which they had to work. A good introductory essay from these points of view, though perhaps somewhat crudely schematic, is Marco Mincoff's 'The Social Background of Beaumont and Fletcher'. A later article by him, 'Fletcher's Early Tragedies', usefully investigates their conventions, emphasizing the baroque nature of their characterization where 'Burning rage gives place to melting sentiment, each represented in its chemical purity.'

Some of the most helpful criticism of Beaumont and Fletcher, therefore, expects us to consider the plays on their own terms. Andrew Gurr, for example, asks us to set aside our 'chronic over-familiarity with subtle characterization', and explains that Beaumont and Fletcher were particularly interested in exploring 'the Sidneian scheme of moral paradigms or patterns of situations'. This note is frequently struck. While conceding to the neo-classicists the plays' lack of a strong or convincing narrative line, Arthur Mizener argues that they are constructed 'in terms of what might be called emotional or psychological form'. His argument is extended (though by no means eclipsed) in an essay by R. K. Turner. Clifford Leech in his sensible book, *The John Fletcher Plays*, also believes that the plays 'attempt to record the case-history not of a man but of a situation', and he is critical too of Coleridge's famous accusation against

Beaumont and Fletcher that they were courtly sycophants, deeming the 'element of open debate' about kingship in their plays to be extraordinary. In this he echoes M. G. M. Adkins who, in an article of 1946, convincingly demonstrates the degree of scepticism in *Philaster* about kingship; her argument is taken up and expanded in Peter Davison's impressive essay 'The Serious Concerns of *Philaster*'. This relatively new serious concern for Beaumont and Fletcher, particularly for a greater precision in defining the conventions of their art, owes a debt to the work of E. M. W. Waith, especially to his valuable book *The Pattern of Tragicomedy in Beaumont and Fletcher*.

Philip Edwards's 'The Danger Not the Death' persuasively recommends Fletcher's tragicomedies, describing their shaping elements as 'mystification, debate and persuasion, prurience, improbable plots with elaborate complications, strong scenes'. His essay goes on to explore the plays under these categories, and is a striking example of what can be achieved when Fletcher's plays are granted the right to exist in their own world. Similarly, Michael Neill's essay in *Renaissance Drama* (1970) demonstrates that a close-reading analysis can reveal subtleties and complexities of construction hitherto considered un-Fletcherian. His article, Klaus Steiger's in *Essays and Studies* (1967), and Suzanne Gossett's in *Modern Philology* (1972) (especially in her concern for the 'aesthetic logic' of the masques in the plays) illustrate fruitful possibilities for the direction that criticism might now take, though it is ironic that Steiger's analysis should reinforce the traditional position that Fletcher had 'neither need nor impulse to go deeper and search for an inner value'.

Finally, a word concerning some miscellaneous items. John Doebler has an interesting piece which argues that *The Knight of the Burning Pestle*, while embodying aristocratic values, failed initially because its satire against the citizens was too gentle. Although this explanation runs counter to the usual one, it seems to me to be true. The problem of the influence of Beaumont and Fletcher on Shakespeare and Shakespeare on Beaumont and Fletcher is explored, among other considerations, by Richard Proudfoot in 'Shakespeare and the New Dramatists of the King's Men, 1608–1613' (mutually influencing), F. H. Ristine's *English Tragi-comedy*, D. M. McKeithan's *The Debt to Shakespeare in the Beaumont-and-Fletcher Plays*, and A. H. Thorndike's *The Influence of Beaumont and Fletcher on Shakespeare*. Useful introductions are Peter Ure's article in the 1964 edition of the *Encyclopaedia Britannica*, Ian Fletcher's *Beaumont and Fletcher*, and W. W. Appleton's *Beaumont and Fletcher: A Critical Study*.

Thomas Heywood

TEXTS

The standard edition (whose 'defects are many and serious', in Arthur Brown's words) is *The Dramatic Works of Thomas Heywood* (1874) in six volumes edited by R. H. Shepherd. The Mermaid Series has a selection of the plays edited by A. W. Verity, but only *The Rape of Lucrece*, edited by Allan Holaday in the Illinois Studies in Language and Literature Series, and *A Woman Killed with Kindness* in the Revels Plays, edited by R. W. Van Fossen, have been accorded a rigorous editing on modern principles. The two parts of *The Fair Maid of the West* have been edited by R. K. Turner in the Regents Renaissance Drama Series. *The Captives*, *The Fair Maid of the Exchange*, and *If You Know Not Me, You Know Nobody* have appeared as Malone Society Reprints.

CRITICAL STUDIES AND COMMENTARY

The Prefatory Epistle to *The English Traveller* tells us that Thomas Heywood had 'either an entire hand or at least a main finger' in some 220 plays, which averages five a year over his working life as a dramatist. Of these only twenty-four are extant (and only sixteen of these bear his name on the title-page); seven are on classical themes, the rest are concerned largely with the dramatization of 'domestic' issues, laced with exotic episodes of adventure in far-flung places. Criticism has tended to concentrate on the seventeen plays dealing with domestic themes, seeing in them Heywood's essential contribution to seventeenth-century English drama. The very titles of some full-length studies reveal the main tendency: Mowbray Velte's *The Bourgeois Elements in the Dramas of Thomas Heywood* (1924), Otelia Cromwell's *Thomas Heywood: A Study of the Elizabethan Drama of Everyday Life* (1928), Michel Grivelet's *Thomas Heywood et le drame domestique élisabéthain* (1957). Despite their awareness of its centrality to any study of Heywood, however, few critics can give their full assent to this obsession with the bourgeoisie, perhaps in the belief that the drama of everyday life only produces everyday drama. Certainly, few can match Swinburne's enthusiasm in his depiction of Heywood in *The Age of Shakespeare* (1908) as a 'writer who at his ethical best might be defined as something of a plebeian Sidney', and fewer still can give credence to the raptures of Otelia Cromwell over his 'wholesome types of Elizabethan men and women in a richly varied atmosphere of Elizabethan life'. Wholesomeness tends rather to invite a certain scepticism, as is the case with Dekker. H. H. Adams, for example, censures the didactic quality of Heywood's tragedies, concluding that 'Domestic tragedy was thus the dramatic equivalent of the homiletic tract and the broadside ballad.'

Indeed, Heywood's interest in bourgeois life has always been viewed somewhat patronizingly, though not often from quite so reductively determinist a position as Francis Kirkman's in 1660: 'many of his plays being composed loosely in taverns, occasions them to be so mean.' It is T. S. Eliot's famous essay which is most acerbic, arguing that Heywood has 'no vision', 'no reality of moral synthesis', and, worst of all, 'no imaginative humour'. At best he is 'a facile and sometimes felicitous purveyor of goods to the popular taste'. As one might expect, the most rewarding commentary steers a course between Miss Cromwell's rapture and Eliot's opprobrium. The standard biography by A. M. Clark, *Thomas Heywood: Playwright and Miscellanist* (1931), presents the facts straightforwardly and, accord ing to Arthur Brown, is 'still the most useful and reliable' book on him. F. S. Boas's *Thomas Heywood* also has the merit of a quiet lucidity while making points that require further thought. He notes, for example, how *Edward IV* domesticates, as it were, the Revenge tradi tion, when the queen forgives Jane Shore for becoming the king's mistress, and how this action seems to presage the subdued moral climate of *A Woman Killed with Kindness*. J. Q. Adams praises Heywood's *Ages* plays as indicating a 'philanthropic attempt to popularize Greek culture among the middle class in London'; Arthur Brown, in 'Thomas Heywood's Dramatic Art', commends his striking openings, his speed and timing, believing that he 'cries out to be played', and in his essay in *Renaissance Papers* argues that more attention should be paid to Heywood's use of imagery. Allan Holaday invites us to approve of Heywood's democratic leanings; Norman Rabkin thinks that Heywood handles delusion brilliantly in *The English Traveller*; Freda Townsend praises his artistry in the use of the double plot, and L. B. Wright sees much to commend in Heywood's missionary cultivation of the bourgeoisie.

Many of the above items illustrate a tendency, becoming more and more pronounced in modern criticism (as we have seen with Beaumont and Fletcher), to acknowledge a complexity at once more craftsmanly and more moral in the work of Elizabethan and Jaco bean dramatists. It is not a tendency to be despised. While we may not be able to agree completely with Michel Grivelet, in his 'The Simplicity of Thomas Heywood', that Heywood exposes the 'endless ironies of life', it seems undeniable that he is a good deal less facile than has hitherto been allowed. And explorations into his most popular play, *A Woman Killed with Kindness*, support such an opinion. P. M. Spacks, for example, talks of the 'areas of darkness' in the play which do not allow us merely to view the action through the smug pietisms of Frankford's 'kindness', while in similar fashion David Cook directs our attention to the very real wickedness of Frankford's 'inflexible morality'. And John Canuteson in his brilliant article, 'The Theme of Forgiveness in the Plot and Subplot of *A Woman Killed with Kindness*', reveals the inadequacy of most previous commentary in showing us how Heywood clearly *intends* us to see Frankford as a beast, and Sir Charles as a fool. Such criticism invests Heywood with a new sophistication, and it can be found elsewhere in his work.

Thomas Dekker

TEXTS

Unlike the situation with Beaumont and Fletcher and with Heywood, Dekker's plays and dramatic entertainments have been gathered together and carefully edited in this century, by Fredson Bowers. His edition is in four volumes, comprising some twenty-six works including three plays—*Lust's Dominion, The Noble Spanish Soldier, The Welsh Ambassador*—from the list of those merely attributed to Dekker. Most of the plays are collaborative ventures; only four— *Old Fortunatus, The Whore of Babylon, If This Be Not a Good Play the Devil Is in It*, and *Match Me in London*—are certainly Dekker's alone. (*The Shoemaker's Holiday* and the second part of *The Honest Whore* are likely candidates.) Students should note that Bowers's is a textual edition; the editor's effort has been exclusively taken up with the establishment of a text. No other aids to comprehension obtrude. Five plays—*The Shoemaker's Holiday, The Honest Whore* (both parts), *Old Fortunatus, The Witch of Edmonton*—comprise the Mermaid selection (1887) edited by Ernest Rhys, with an introduction and notes. Only *The Shoemaker's Holiday* has appeared as a single edition. J. R. Sutherland's is sensibly annotated. J. B. Steane's is textually unreliable. There is an old-spelling edition, by Paul C. Davies, in the Fountainwell Series.

CRITICAL STUDIES AND COMMENTARY

Despite Lamb's belief that Thomas Dekker had 'poetry enough for anything', and despite the ardency of the admiration for him in such full-length studies as M. L. Hunt's *Thomas Dekker: A Study* (1911) which praises Dekker's 'sane, sweet and democratic mind', M. T. Jones-Davies's exhaustive two-volume study *Un Peintre de la vie londonienne: Thomas Dekker*, and Aldo Maugeri's *Studi su Thomas Dekker*, Dekker has not generally been considered to be as rewarding for study as Beaumont and Fletcher or even Heywood. Modern criticism, in particular, is uncomfortable with the literature of good cheer. 'The simple humour of high spirits is not in fashion', as J. B. Steane wistfully remarks in his introduction to *The Shoemaker's Holiday*, perceiving in Lady Sneerwell's witticism, 'there's no possibility of being witty without a little ill-nature', a description of our own jaded expectations. The customary view of Dekker is admirably summed up by Normand Berlin as 'the gentle, tolerant, lovable, "moral sloven" who had his hand in too many plays, who occasionally sang a sweet song, who could at times present lively characters'. (Berlin makes out a strong case, however, for the need to qualify this view.) Thus Arthur Brown in *Jacobean Theatre* echoes Swinburne in talking of Dekker's 'Loyalty and patriotism . . . added to . . . love, forgiveness and tolerance', while Peter Ure, in *Essays and Studies* (1966), thinks that Dekker treats city life in a 'kindly and wholesome manner' until he comes under the malign influence of Middleton, an odd opinion of Dekker and an extraordinary one of Middleton.

Often, in this view, Dekker is not only remorselessly cheerful, but also unsophisticated and old-fashioned. He seems unaware of the darker side of Jacobean life, that anatomized and censured by satirists like Jonson and Marston. Patricia Thomson, for example, in her article contrasting Massinger's *A New Way to Pay Old Debts* with *The Shoemaker's Holiday*, thinks Dekker's play closer to *A Midsummer Night's Dream* than to *A New Way*, its ethos feudal rather than capitalist, representing the acquisitive individual as tamed in the solidarity of a guild morality. Symptomatic of such anachronistic optimism, according to Russell Potter, is the way in which the presence of the devil in *If This Be Not a Good Play* is made comic merely, or the way, according to Michael Manheim, in which in *The Shoemaker's Holiday* inner qualities triumph, where 'Good will and honest industry link the true cobbler and the true courtier.'

There are other opinions. As early as 1925 Gamaliel Bradford described Dekker in what must have been distinctly unfamiliar terms: 'Dekker is, perhaps, the most complicated genius among the lesser Elizabethan dramatists. With a faculty for keen and biting satire approaching that of Marston he unites a subtle and simple pathos, less sweet and gentle, but more intense, than that of Heywood.' The unfamiliar is becoming less so. L. L. Brodwin, for example, thinks that the main plot of *The Witch of Edmonton* contains the most sophisticated treatment of domestic tragedy in Elizabethan drama. James Conover in *Thomas Dekker: An Analysis of Dramatic Structure* (1969) praises Dekker's craftsmanship highly, although believing him to have dissipated his talents. Alfred Harbage, in a fine essay, 'The Mystery of *Perkin Warbeck*', also thinks Dekker an able craftsman, finding, for this reason, L. C. Knights's dismissal of him in *Drama and Society in the Age of Jonson* one of the 'most incomprehensible judgements of our time'. And in articles reconsidering *The Shoemaker's Holiday*, allegedly Dekker's most 'merry piece', modern criticism has discovered significant tensions, ambiguities, and subtleties. F. M. Burelbach has noticed (correctly I believe) how the play demonstrates a shrewd awareness of the commercial value of fraternal love, while J. H. Kaplan thinks that the play's 'central episodes seem to bristle with moral ambiguities' and that Eyre's exuberant, asyndetic rhetoric points to a 'cockney utopia' based on mercantile opportunism. Finally, H. E. Toliver deftly brings together traditional and modern views, describing the play's theme as the 'struggle between the exigencies imposed upon one's free will by a life of commodity and compromise, and the desire to escape these necessities, to be an entirely free and romantic agent perpetually on "holiday".'

REFERENCES

Francis Beaumont (1584–1616) and John Fletcher (1579–1625)

TEXTS

ed. F. T. Bowers, *The Dramatic Works in the Beaumont and Fletcher Canon* (Cambridge, 1966–).

ed. A. H. Bullen and others, *The Works of Francis Beaumont and John Fletcher*, 4 vols. (London, 1904–12).

ed. A. Glover and A. R. Waller, *The Works of Beaumont and Fletcher*, 10 vols. (Cambridge, 1905–12).

ed. E. Rhys, *Beaumont and Fletcher's Plays* (Everyman's Library, London, 1911).

ed. F. E. Schelling, *Beaumont and Fletcher* (New York, 1912).

ed. J. Strachey, *Beaumont and Fletcher*, 2 vols. (The Mermaid Series, London, 1893).

Bonduca

ed. W. W. Greg and F. P. Wilson (Malone Society Reprints, Oxford, 1951).

Demetrius and Enanthe

ed. M. Cook and F. P. Wilson (Malone Society Reprints, Oxford, 1950).

A King and No King

ed. R. K. Turner, Jr. (Regents Renaissance Drama Series, Lincoln, Nebr., 1963).

The Knight of the Burning Pestle

ed. M. Hattaway (The New Mermaids, London, 1969).

The Maid's Tragedy

ed. H. B. Norland (Regents Renaissance Drama Series, Lincoln, Nebr., 1968).

Philaster

ed. A. Gurr (The Revels Plays, London, 1969).

Rollo Duke of Normandy or *The Bloody Brother*

ed. J. D. Jump (Liverpool, 1948).

CRITICAL STUDIES AND COMMENTARY

M. G. M. Adkins, 'The Citizens in *Philaster*: Their Function and Significance', *SP* 43 (1946).

W. W. Appleton, *Beaumont and Fletcher: A Critical Study* (Fair Lawn, N.J., 1956).

J. F. Danby, 'Jacobean Absolutists: the Placing of Beaumont and Fletcher', *Cambridge Journal* 3 (1949–50); repr. in his *Poets on Fortune's Hill* and in *Elizabethan Drama: Modern Essays in Criticism*, ed. R. J. Kaufmann (Oxford, 1961).

——, *Poets on Fortune's Hill* (London, 1952; repr. as *Elizabethan and Jacobean Poets*, London, 1964).

P. Davison, 'The Serious Concerns of *Philaster*', *ELH* 30 (1963).

J. Doebler, 'Beaumont's *The Knight of the Burning Pestle* and the Prodigal Son Plays', *SEL* 5 (1965).

P. Edwards, 'The Danger Not the Death: The Art of John Fletcher', in *Jacobean Theatre* (Stratford-upon-Avon Studies 1, ed. J. R. Brown and B. Harris, London, 1961).

I. Fletcher, *Beaumont and Fletcher* (Writers and Their Works, London, 1967).

C. M. Gayley, *Francis Beaumont, Dramatist* (London, 1914).

S. Gossett, 'Masque Influence on the Dramaturgy of Beaumont and Fletcher', *MP* 69 (1972).

O. L. Hatcher, *John Fletcher: A Study in Dramatic Method* (Chicago, Ill., 1905).

C. Hoy, 'The Shares of Fletcher and his Collaborators in the Beaumont and Fletcher Canon', *Studies in Bibliography* 8 (1956), 9 (1957), 11 (1958), 12 (1959), 13 (1960), 14 (1961), 15 (1962).

C. Leech, *The John Fletcher Plays* (London, 1962).

D. M. McKeithan, *The Debt to Shakespeare in the Beaumont-and-Fletcher Plays* (London, 1938).

J. Masefield, 'Beaumont and Fletcher', *Atlantic Monthly* 199 (1957).

B. Maxwell, *Studies in Beaumont, Fletcher and Massinger* (New York, 1939).

M. Mincoff, 'Fletcher's Early Tragedies', *Ren. Dr.* 7 (1964).

——, 'The Social Background of Beaumont and Fletcher', *English Miscellany* 1 (1950).

A. Mizener, 'The High Design of *A King and No King*', *MP* 38 (1940).

M. Neill, ' "The Simetry, Which Gives a Poem Grace": Masque, Imagery, and the Fancy of *The Maid's Tragedy*', *Ren. Dr.* n.s. 3 (1970).

E. H. C. Oliphant, *The Plays of Beaumont and Fletcher* (London, 1927).

R. Proudfoot, 'Shakespeare and the New Dramatists of the King's Men, 1608–1613', in *Later Shakespeare* (Stratford-upon-Avon Studies 8, ed. J. R. Brown and B. Harris, London, 1966).

F. H. Ristine, *English Tragi-comedy* (New York, 1910; repr. 1963).

D. J. Rulfs, 'Beaumont and Fletcher on the London Stage, 1776–1833', *PMLA* 63 (1948).

A. C. Sprague, *Beaumont and Fletcher on the Restoration Stage* (Cambridge, Mass., 1926; repr. New York, 1965).

K. Steiger, ' "May a Man be Caught with Faces?": The Convention of "Heart" and "Face" in Fletcher and Rowley's *The Maid in the Mill*', *Essays and Studies* 20 (1967).

A. H. Thorndike, *The Influence of Beaumont and Fletcher on Shakespeare* (Worcester, Mass., 1901).

R. K. Turner, Jr., 'The Morality of *A King and No King*', in *Renaissance Papers 1958, 1959, 1960*, ed. G. W. Williams (Southeastern Renaissance Conference, 1961).

P. Ure, 'Beaumont and Fletcher', *Encyclopaedia Britannica* (London, 1964, vol. 3).

E. M. W. Waith, *The Pattern of Tragicomedy in Beaumont and Fletcher* (Yale Studies in English 120, New Haven, Conn., 1952).

L. B. Wallis, *Fletcher, Beaumont and Company, Entertainers to the Jacobean Gentry* (New York, 1947).

J. H. Wilson, *The Influence of Beaumont and Fletcher on Restoration Drama* (Columbus, Ohio, 1928).

Thomas Heywood (1575?–1641)

TEXTS

ed. R. H. Shepherd, *The Dramatic Works of Thomas Heywood*, 6 vols. (London, 1874).

ed. A. W. Verity, *Thomas Heywood* (The Mermaid Series, London, 1888).

The Captives

ed. A. Brown and R. E. Alton (Malone Society Reprints, Oxford, 1953).

The Fair Maid of the Exchange
ed. A. Brown and P. H. Davison (Malone Society Reprints, Oxford, 1962).

The Fair Maid of the West, Parts I and II
ed. R. K. Turner, Jr. (Regents Renaissance Drama Series, Lincoln, Nebr., 1967).

If You Know Not Me, You Know Nobody
ed. M. Doran (Malone Society Reprints, London, 1935).

The Rape of Lucrece
ed. A. Holaday (Illinois Studies in Language and Literature, Urbana, Ill., 1950).

A Woman Killed with Kindness
ed. R. W. Van Fossen (The Revels Plays, London, 1961).

CRITICAL STUDIES AND COMMENTARY

H. H. Adams, *English Domestic or Homiletic Tragedy* (New York, 1943).
J. Q. Adams, 'Shakespeare, Heywood, and the Classics', *MLN* 34 (1919).
F. S. Boas, *Thomas Heywood* (London, 1950).
A. Brown, 'An Edition of the Plays of Thomas Heywood: A Preliminary Survey of Problems', in *Renaissance Papers*, ed. A. H. Gilbert (Ann Arbor, Mich., 1954).
A. Brown, 'Thomas Heywood's Dramatic Art', in *Essays on Shakespeare and the Elizabethan Drama in Honor of Hardin Craig*, ed. R. Hosley (Columbia, Mo., 1962; London, 1963).
J. Canuteson, 'The Theme of Forgiveness in the Plot and Subplot of *A Woman Killed with Kindness*', *Ren. Dr.* N.S. 2 (1969).
A. M. Clark, *Thomas Heywood: Playwright and Miscellanist* (New York, 1931).
D. Cook, '*A Woman Killed with Kindness*: An Unshakespearian Tragedy', *ES* 45 (1964).
O. Cromwell, *Thomas Heywood: A Study of the Elizabethan Drama of Everyday Life* (Yale Studies in English 78, New Haven, Conn., 1928).
T. S. Eliot, 'Thomas Heywood', in *Elizabethan Dramatists* (London, 1963).
M. Grivelet, 'The Simplicity of Thomas Heywood', *Shakespeare Survey 14* (1961).
——, *Thomas Heywood et le drame domestique élisabéthain* (Paris, 1957).
A. Holaday, 'Thomas Heywood and the Puritans', *JEGP* 49 (1950).
N. Rabkin, 'Dramatic Deception in Heywood's *The English Traveller*', *SEL* 1 (1961).
P. M. Spacks, 'Honor and Perception in *A Woman Killed with Kindness*', *MLQ* 20 (1959).
A. C. Swinburne, 'Thomas Heywood', in his *The Age of Shakespeare* (London, 1908).
F. L. Townsend, 'The Artistry of Thomas Heywood's Double Plots', *PQ* 25 (1946).

M. Velte, *The Bourgeois Elements in the Dramas of Thomas Heywood* (Mysore City, India, 1924).

L. B. Wright, 'Thomas Heywood and the Popularizing of History', *MLN* 43 (1928).

Thomas Dekker (1570?–1632)

TEXTS

ed. F. T. Bowers, *The Dramatic Works of Thomas Dekker*, 4 vols. (Cambridge, 1953–61).

ed. E. Rhys, *Thomas Dekker* (The Mermaid Series, London, 1887).

The Shoemaker's Holiday

ed. P. C. Davies (Fountainwell Drama Texts, Edinburgh, 1968).
ed. J. B. Steane (Cambridge, 1965).
ed. J. R. Sutherland (Oxford, 1928).

CRITICAL STUDIES AND COMMENTARY

N. Berlin, 'Thomas Dekker: A Partial Reappraisal', *SEL* 6 (1966).

G. Bradford, 'The Women of Dekker', *Sewanee Review* 33 (1925).

L. L. Brodwin, 'The Domestic Tragedy of Frank Thorney in *The Witch of Edmonton*', *SEL* 7 (1967).

A. Brown, 'Citizen Comedy and Domestic Drama', in *Jacobean Theatre* (Stratford-upon-Avon Studies 1, ed. J. R. Brown and B. Harris, London, 1960).

F. M. Burelbach, Jr., 'War and Peace in *The Shoemaker's Holiday*', *Tennessee Studies in Literature* 13 (1968).

J. Conover, *Thomas Dekker: An Analysis of Dramatic Structure* (The Hague, 1969).

A. Harbage, 'The Mystery of *Perkin Warbeck*', in *Studies in the English Renaissance Drama*, ed. J. W. Bennett and others (New York, 1959).

M. L. Hunt, *Thomas Dekker: A Study* (New York, 1911).

M. T. Jones-Davies, *Un Peintre de la vie londonienne: Thomas Dekker*, 2 vols. (Paris, 1958).

J. H. Kaplan, 'Virtue's Holiday: Thomas Dekker and Simon Eyre', *Ren. Dr.* N.S. 2 (1969).

L. C. Knights, *Drama and Society in the Age of Jonson* (London, 1937).

M. Manheim, 'The Construction of *The Shoemaker's Holiday*', *SEL* 10 (1970).

A. Maugeri, *Studi su Thomas Dekker* (Messina, 1958).

R. Potter, 'Three Jacobean Devil Plays', *SP* 28 (1931).

P. Thomson, 'The Old Way and the New Way in Dekker and Massinger', *MLR* 51 (1956).

H. E. Toliver, '*The Shoemaker's Holiday*: Theme and Image', *Boston University Studies in English* 5 (1961).

P. Ure, 'Patient Madman and Honest Whore: The Middleton-Dekker Oxymoron', *Essays and Studies* 19 (1966).

8. WEBSTER, TOURNEUR, and FORD

INGA-STINA EWBANK

GENERAL AND BACKGROUND STUDIES

STUDENTS of John Webster, Cyril Tourneur, and John Ford, searching for guides to the best understanding and enjoyment of these playwrights, are liable to find themselves in the position of Webster's Flamineo who, when he looks up to heaven, confounds knowledge with knowledge. All three playwrights—despite their very different artistic temperaments and talents—shared an appetite for absolutes, extremes, and paradoxes. And, perhaps not coincidentally, the outstanding characteristic of the scholarly and critical literature about them is its tendency towards extreme statements and antithetical, or even paradoxical, positions. On the same library shelf, Ford the modernist is next to Ford the traditional moralist; Tourneur both is and is not the author of *The Revenger's Tragedy*, which is either the most cynical or the most thoroughly medieval play of the Jacobean era; and Webster is on the one hand a decadent melodramatist, on the other a deviser of experimental dramatic structures which body forth a new tragic, or absurd, vision. More radically still, their very *raison d'être*, on a shelf devoted to serious English dramatic literature, is now questioned, now affirmed. The appearance, in 1969, of a collection of Webster criticism as the first of the Penguin Critical Anthologies would have seemed to confirm, for Webster at least, an approved status; but a reviewer of that volume was soon to demonstrate at considerable length that 'the dramatist is not worth the critical attention that is being lavished on him' (Wilbur Sanders in *Essays in Criticism*, 1972). And at much the same time Christopher Ricks, the General Editor of the Penguin Critical Anthologies, in an important essay in volume 3 of the *Sphere History of Literature in the English Language*, not only questioned many of the unthinking assumptions behind much criticism of Jacobean and Caroline drama, but also challenged the whole reputation of these playwrights as 'responsible' artists. The dichotomy has not changed much since, in 1919, T. S. Eliot published his poem on Webster as the supreme metaphysical poet 'Who found no substitute for sense, / To seize and clutch and penetrate; / Expert beyond experience', at about the same time as William Archer fulminated against *The Duchess of Malfi* as 'coarse and sanguinary melodrama'. Only the battle-ground has, typically, shifted to the academic arena. An inspection of the valuable bibliographies of Webster, Ford, and Tourneur, compiled by S. A. Tannenbaum and later supplemented by C. A. Pennel and others, will show a flourishing thesis industry as well as a formidable array of published books and articles.

The initial certainty that the student can take away from such a thick mist of antithetical opinions is that, with so many writers protesting so much, and moreover with some of the best scholarly and critical minds of the last couple of generations exercising themselves on these playwrights, they must be important. Soon he will discover that a major reason for their importance is the way in which writing about them tends to involve a reconsideration of some of our basic assumptions about art: the relationship of poetry to drama, of verbal to visual art, of realism to artifice, of tragedy to comedy, of the individual talent to tradition, and of the dramatist to his audience—to mention but a few. Accordingly, some of the most illuminating comments on them will be found in works of a general nature: in *The Language of Tragedy* by Moody Prior, in Wylie Sypher's *Four Stages of Renaissance Style*, and in Alfred Harbage's still provocative study of *Shakespeare and the Rival Traditions*. Next the student will discover that they are important because of their proximity to Shakespeare. At worst—as in David Frost, *The School of Shakespeare*—he will find that Shakespeare is a stick to beat them with; at best—as in Robert Ornstein, *The Moral Vision of Jacobean Tragedy*—he will find the kind of cross-illumination which comes from seeing Shakespeare along with dramatists who shared his theatre and his world. And, finally, he will discover that an interest in that world—and, at least since the time of the original Mermaid editions, a widely held sense of its modernity—has made Webster, Tourneur, and Ford peculiarly important.

The most incisive introduction to that world, and one which is in effect the academic prose version of Eliot's lines on Webster's sensibility, is F. P. Wilson's short book, *Elizabethan and Jacobean*. Theodore Spencer's study of *Shakespeare and the Nature of Man*, together with his *Death and Elizabethan Tragedy*, will illuminate central beliefs and conventions of the playwrights' world; and the way these were translated and manifested in the actual contemporary scene is best illustrated by G. P. V. Akrigg in his *Jacobean Pageant*. As all three playwrights tend to set the action of their plays outside England, chiefly in Italy, G. K. Hunter's essay on 'English Folly and Italian Vice' is an essential pointer to the kind of moral—rather than physical or historical—geography they found in the Italian court settings. On the other hand, J. W. Lever's book, *The Tragedy of State*, stimulatingly, if one-sidedly, insists on the acute political and social relevance of these plays and, therefore, on their peculiar *rapport* with their own audiences as well as with modern audiences who also inhabit 'a world controlled by huge aggregations of power'.

It is such intimations of importance which lie behind the continued critical questioning of the achievements of Webster, Tourneur, and Ford. The seminal mind here is undoubtedly T. S. Eliot, through his essays on Tourneur and on Ford and his brief but brilliant analysis of Webster in 'Four Elizabethan Dramatists'. His rationalized verdicts on the playwrights have started many false hares, and indeed they are often in contradiction to his quotations from the plays. It is in them— as in the cadences which haunt Eliot's own verse—that he alerts us to the ability of each of these playwrights to catch memorable moments of human experience and render them in memorable language. Eliot's problem with these writers as *playwrights*, not only as poets, was that he could never really forgive them their 'impure art'; and it was left to more academic criticism to illuminate the dramatic structures they created, the traditional elements they had to work with, and the conventions through which they communicated with their audiences. M. C. Bradbrook's *Themes and Conventions of Elizabethan Tragedy* (with separate chapters on Webster and Tourneur and with Ford discussed as part of 'The Decadence') remains the basic work in this vast area: its insights into the art of these playwrights, though sometimes apparently impressionistic, tend brilliantly to anticipate much of what has later been seen, and said at tedious length, in many books and articles. Above all, the book sends one to the plays themselves— a signal quality, as Jacobean dramatic criticism all too often degenerates into the art of berating other critics for using the wrong criteria. T. B. Tomlinson's *A Study of Elizabethan and Jacobean Tragedy* exemplifies this unhappy trend; and even Christopher Ricks's chapter in the *Sphere History* conveys more exasperation with other critics than enjoyment of the plays. In contrast, the other general study from that dawn, in the 1930s, when it must have been bliss to be a student of Jacobean drama, conveys all the excitement of discovery. U. M. Ellis-Fermor's *Jacobean Drama* may not always be a safe guide to an objective appraisal of these playwrights; but it helps one to see their uniqueness as experimental artists, each finding a form germane to his own purpose and mirroring his own thoughts. The value of this becomes apparent through another contrast: with the many generic studies which were an almost inevitable result of the reaction from the absolute, 'Ibsenite', standards of Archer's *The Old Drama and the New*, and of the interest in traditional 'themes and conventions'.

The study of generic forms has obviously made a very great contribution to our understanding of Webster, Tourneur, and Ford. The danger, in studies of kinds or modes of drama, is that conventions may be allowed to become, as it were, self-authenticating and the definition of genres an end in itself. For all the useful background information they impart, neither W. Thorp, in *The Triumph of Realism in Elizabethan Drama, 1558–1612*, nor H. H. Adams, in *English Domestic or Homiletic Tragedy, 1575–1642*, nor even F. T. Bowers, in *Elizabethan Revenge Tragedy, 1587–1642*—the last so clearly relevant to three authors who all employ the revenge motif—can be altogether acquitted of this tendency. Their critical value is therefore limited; and the same is true for the evolutionary gallops through the playwrights which are forced upon authors of historical surveys. Even one of the best of these, *A Short View of Elizabethan Drama* by T. M. Parrott and R. H. Ball, defines Tourneur as one who 'stripped the Senecan drama of its supernatural trappings' and 'raised domestic tragedy to a loftier ethical pitch than it had attained before'. But J. M. R. Margeson, in *The Origins of English Tragedy*, manages to put Webster and Tourneur into an evolutionary context without entirely making their plays into examples of types. The most valuable genre studies are those which help us to see how kinds and modes reflect certain basic ways of looking at experience: Webster and Tourneur are thus illuminated in John Peter's *Complaint and Satire* and Alvin Kernan's *The Cankered Muse*, and all three playwrights in R. B. Heilman's *Tragedy and Melodrama*. The invaluable guide to the relation between theory and practice, tradition and individual talent, in these dramatists is Madeleine Doran's book *Endeavors of Art: A Study of Form in Elizabethan Drama*. When Miss Doran speaks of Tourneur, Webster, and Ford as illustrating 'the uncertainties of dramatic form that are consequent on the deeper uncertainties of the ethical bases of tragedy', she gives us the terms in which the playwrights have been most profitably discussed. How serious is their morality, how serious their art, and what is the relation between the two? Two major attempts to answer these questions are Irving Ribner's *Jacobean Tragedy: The Quest for Moral Order* and Robert Ornstein's *The Moral Vision of Jacobean Tragedy*. Ribner's book can mislead by being too unquestioning: it tends to assume the (once) received picture of the ordered world of Shake-

speare and Hooker being called in doubt by New Philosophy, and to
level the plays down to varieties of orthodox piety. Ornstein's book,
on the other hand, stimulates further questioning because of its
open-mindedness and its subtle insights into the art of individual
plays. The last page of its opening chapter, where the author refuses
to generalize about Jacobean tragedy and instead refers us to 'a small
handful of great dramatists who weighed the conventional form of
tragedy with the splendour of their personal intuition', ought to be
required reading for anyone studying Webster, Tourneur, and
Ford.

In the end, it would seem that the best guides to the splendour of
which Ornstein speaks are those who have the kind of knowledge of
and sensitivity to the text that is nourished on a very close reading,
and who combine this with a knowledge not only of contemporary
drama and its traditions but also of contemporary life and its conventions—its social habits and ways of thought. Not surprisingly,
those who come closest to this ideal are the modern editors of individual plays—notably John Russell Brown in his Revels editions of
Webster, R. A. Foakes and Irving Ribner as Revels editors of
Tourneur, and Peter Ure in editing Ford's *Perkin Warbeck*, also for
the Revels Plays. Good modern editions may have done more than
anything to spread understanding of these playwrights.

TEXTS

A number of anthologies of Tudor and Stuart drama include two,
and occasionally three, plays by Webster, Tourneur, and Ford. The
plays chosen tend to be much the same. F. E. Schelling's *Typical
Elizabethan Plays*, a companion piece to his massive study of *Eliza-
bethan Playwrights*, initially included *The Duchess of Malfi* and *Perkin
Warbeck*; but later editions apparently consider Ford's historical play
too untypical and substitute for it *The Broken Heart*. This tragedy by
Ford can be found also in C. F. Tucker Brooke and N. B. Paradise's
English Drama, 1580–1642, in Hazelton Spencer's *Elizabethan Plays*,
and in the anthology of *Elizabethan and Stuart Plays* edited by
Baskervill, Heltzel, and Nethercot. All these also print either *The
White Devil* or *The Duchess of Malfi*, and the last named adds *Perkin
Warbeck*. All have modernized texts and some explanatory notes.
Though often reprinted, they all stem from the days before modern
textual scholarship. In contrast, *The Anchor Anthology of Jacobean
Drama*, edited by R. C. Harrier (1963), is a scholarly text which
prints variants and has much fuller notes. Though it includes fewer
plays in all than the anthologies just mentioned, it has *The Revenger's*

Tragedy as well as *The White Devil* and the ubiquitous *Broken Heart.*
Portability is the main virtue of the two unannotated World's
Classics volumes relevant in this context: *Six Plays by Contemporaries
of Shakespeare,* edited by C. B. Wheeler and containing both of
Webster's tragedies, and *Five Stuart Tragedies,* edited by A. K.
McIlwraith, which has *The Duchess of Malfi* and *'Tis Pity She's A
Whore.* It was only in the 1960s that Tourneur started to appear in
collections of plays. A. H. Gomme's *Jacobean Tragedies* makes available a modernized and sparsely annotated text of both the Tourneur
plays; and for the student who is prepared to manage without too
many notes, there is good value for money in the Penguin volume of
Three Jacobean Tragedies, edited by G. Salgādo and including a
modernized text of *The Revenger's Tragedy* and *The White Devil.*

Modern scholarship has concentrated on editions of single plays
by these playwrights rather than on providing collected works.
Accordingly, the standard collected edition of Webster remains that
by F. L. Lucas, first published in 1927 and notable for its compre-
hensiveness (though for the *Ho!* plays and *Sir Thomas Wyatt,* which
Webster wrote together with Dekker, it needs to be supplemented
with volumes 1 and 2 of Fredson Bowers's edition of Dekker), its old-
spelling text, and its voluminous and often picturesque notes. Nor is
there a modern, or modernized, successor to Allardyce Nicoll's
edition of *The Works of Cyril Tourneur* (1929). The standard collected
edition of Ford remains *The Dramatic Works* originally edited by
Gifford in 1827, revised by Dyce in 1869, and again revised by
Bullen in 1895—a monument to nineteenth-century ways with texts.
The non-specialist may still find the original Mermaid series (in so
far as the volumes are available) the pleasantest medium in which to
read (within one cover) the two Webster and the two Tourneur
tragedies, edited by J. A. Symonds (1888), and a good selection of
Ford plays, edited by Havelock Ellis (1888), though the texts are
unreliable. The Penguin English Library has made available a
modernized text of all three of Webster's unaided plays, with an
introduction and notes by D. C. Gunby, and in the same format
Three Plays by Ford, edited by Keith Sturgess.

But for the student who wishes for texts edited according to
modern principles, and for more extensive annotation, the choice
must be with one of the several series of one-volume texts, all of
which include the obvious plays by the three playwrights, as detailed in the list of References at the end of this chapter. The value
of the 'normalized' old-spelling texts in the Fountainwell Drama
Texts series is doubtful; whereas both the Regents Renaissance

Drama Series and the New Mermaids provide (generally) soundly edited modernized texts and an apparatus of notes as well as short critical introductions. The explanatory notes in the Regents volumes might be fuller; in the New Mermaids they vary considerably in extent and quality from volume to volume. The series of texts which will best equip the student to understand each play is, without doubt, The Revels Plays. Whether his interest is bibliographical, biographical, historical, linguistic, or theatrical—or, as one would hope, a combination of all these—the Revels text, notes, and introduction will be a sound base for his approach to the play and its author.

CRITICAL STUDIES OF INDIVIDUAL AUTHORS

John Webster

To T. S. Eliot, 'the case of John Webster, and in particular *The Duchess of Malfi*', would have provided—had he written his book on Four Elizabethan Dramatists—'an interesting example of a very great literary and dramatic genius directed toward chaos'. Though this remained one of the great unwritten books, his tantalizing sentence could stand as the motto of practically all the books and articles which have been written on Webster, variously stressing the 'genius' and the 'chaos', and occasionally seeing the genius *in* the chaos.

Students may find a guide, if a somewhat pedestrian one, through the Webster controversy in D. D. Moore's thorough but uncritical (and sometimes inaccurate) disquisition on *John Webster and his Critics* (1966). There is much more excitement in the editors' introductions to the various, chronologically arranged, sections of Webster commentary in G. K. and S. K. Hunter's Penguin anthology; and the pieces they have chosen to reprint form a most valuable conspectus of Webster criticism from his own day to ours. Naturally, Norman Rabkin's partly overlapping collection of *Twentieth-Century Interpretations of 'The Duchess of Malfi'* appears thin by comparison.

It is perhaps deceptively easy to divide Webster critics into two camps. On the one hand there are the *Scrutiny* essayists, notably Ian Jack and W. A. Edwards, and their latter-day followers, notably T. B. Tomlinson in *A Study of Elizabethan and Jacobean Tragedy* and C. O. MacDonald in *The Rhetoric of Tragedy*, who see Webster as morally confused and artistically incoherent, a failed and decadent Shakespeare. On the other hand, there are those who take him seriously—without enthusing like Lamb, or Swinburne, or Rupert

Brooke, but also without falling back on arguments that he wrote 'as they liked it', as F. L. Lucas tends to do—and attempt to explain his art in its own terms. The best representatives of this camp, apart from Ribner and Ornstein, would be Travis Bogard, exploring Webster's counterpointing of modes in *The Tragic Satire of John Webster*; J. R. Mulryne, writing on Webster's theatrical art and particularly his language, in an essay in *Jacobean Theatre*; and H. T. Price on 'The Function of Imagery in Webster'. The most extreme, and least convincing, followers of this camp would be those who try to turn Webster into a didactic Christian optimist: D. C. Gunby, in '*The Devil's Law-Case*: An Interpretation', and E. B. Benjamin, in 'Patterns of Morality in *The White Devil*.'

But such an easy polarization would leave out not only the purely objective scholarly writings on Webster—like John Russell Brown's articles on 'The Printing of John Webster's Plays'—but also some important books in which scholarship is allowed impartially to illuminate the art of this difficult, bookish, and deliberate writer: Gunnar Boklund's two studies of the sources of Webster's tragedies; R. W. Dent's disconcerting examination of *John Webster's Borrowing*; Ingeborg Glier's dissertation on Webster's concept of structure; and Gabriele Baldini on *John Webster e il linguaggio della tragedia*. It would also leave out the sane and balanced general introduction to Webster in Clifford Leech's *John Webster*, as well as the same author's somewhat modified statement on *The Duchess of Malfi* in the Arnold 'Studies in English Literature' series.

Perhaps, then, a more helpful way through Webster criticism is to distinguish those who have tried to 'cover' all of Webster from those who have seized on single, outstanding, features of his art. P. B. Murray, in *A Study of John Webster*, is the greatest coverer since E. E. Stoll wrote on *John Webster: The Periods of his Work as Determined by his Relations to the Drama of his Day* (1905); both may be lacking in critical finesse, but they remind us—as does G. E. Bentley in his convenient summary of what is known of Webster's life and theatrical career—that there is more to Webster than the Devil and the Duchess. The plays in which Webster had only a share have tended to be discussed in terms of the authorship problem as such, though I.-S. Ekeblad (Ewbank), in an essay on 'Webster's Constructional Rhythm', attempts to use *A Cure for A Cuckold* to trace certain consistently Websterian stylistic and formal habits. As against those who try to cover all, there are those who from a small entry-point make a large assault on Webster's art. M. C. Bradbrook, writing on 'Fate and Chance in *The Duchess of Malfi*', manages to illuminate both his theatre and his doctrine; James Smith, in a *Scrutiny* essay on 'The Tragedy of Blood' which does not toe the Webster line of that periodical, points up central qualities of Websterian dramatic structure and dialogue; and I.-S. Ekeblad (Ewbank), through an analysis of masque elements in the Duchess of Malfi's death-scene, tackles the problem of the relation between convention and realism in 'The "Impure Art" of John Webster'. The several reprints of this essay, together with J. L. Calderwood's on '*The Duchess of Malfi*: Styles of Ceremony', would seem to suggest that modern readers are fascinated by an experimental, rather than chaotic, and ritualistic, rather than decadent, Webster.

The two kinds of approaches just outlined point, when seen together, to the dream of all Webster critics: to arrive, through specific examples, at a general principle whereby his art can be understood. Several of the essays in the Mermaid Critical Commentaries volume on *John Webster*, edited by Brian Morris, try to do so. Despite its claims, Ralph Berry's book, *The Art of John Webster*, fails to do so— mainly because it confounds one general principle with another, a Baroque Webster with an Absurd Webster. The moral is clear: if we try too hard to find a single answer to the case of John Webster, we are likely to find that 'chaos is come again.'

Cyril Tourneur

Two obsessions have bedevilled the study of the art of Cyril Tourneur. One is a speculative concern with the mind behind the plays, rather than with the plays themselves—perpetuated by T. S. Eliot's essay on Tourneur, by U. M. Ellis-Fermor's chapter on him in *Jacobean Drama*, and even by scholarly articles like Harold Jenkins's attempt, in 'Cyril Tourneur', to trace the road from *The Transformed Metamorphoses* through *The Revenger's Tragedy* to *The Atheist's Tragedy* by exploring 'the nature of the mind in which such conceptions could have arisen'. The other is the problem of the authorship of the anonymously published *Revenger's Tragedy*. Anyone studying 'Tourneur' has sooner or later to decide whether or not to accept this play as his; and much of the critical—as well as bio- graphical and bibliographical—discussion of Tourneur has taken place in the penumbra of the authorship controversy, acquiring thereby a peculiar ardour of tone and tendency towards special pleading. The smallness of Tourneur's corpus means that he has not really provided book-material, except to the indefatigable Peter B. Murray. His book, *A Study of Cyril Tourneur*, illustrates the central paradox of Tourneur criticism: while claiming to be the first 'full-

scale interpretation' of the works of Tourneur, it yet devotes nearly
half of its total number of pages to arguing that Thomas Middleton
wrote *The Revenger's Tragedy*.

By far the best—most balanced but also, as a bonus, most entertaining—account of the authorship controversy, from its inception
in the late nineteenth century to its state of deadlock (which does not
mean that it is dead) in the mid-1960s, is in S. Schoenbaum's book
Internal Evidence and Elizabethan Dramatic Authorship. Like several
other critics, Schoenbaum started out as a firm champion of one
side—in his case that of Middleton, so that there is a chapter on
The Revenger's Tragedy in his earlier book *Middleton's Tragedies*—but
has come to accept that the evidence is inconclusive. What is remarkable is the strength of the evidence on both sides. There is a
formidable bibliographical argument for Middleton in G. R. Price's
article, 'The Authorship and the Bibliography of *The Revenger's
Tragedy*'; but R. A. Foakes argues equally strongly for Tourneur in
his Revels edition of the play. The Revels text provided Foakes with
the opportunity to sort out the tangle—which he himself drew attention to in an important essay 'On the Authorship of *The Revenger's
Tragedy*'—of mislineation in the 1607–8 quarto and in many later
editions: a particularly disconcerting feature since stylistic details
such as weak line-endings have been used as major ammunition in
the authorship battle. There is convincing argument for Middleton
on the grounds of stylistic idiosyncrasies, especially by P. B. Murray;
but there are also a number of convincing demonstrations of stylistic
and thematic connections between *The Revenger's Tragedy* and *The
Atheist's Tragedy*: notably, apart from Peter, Ornstein, and Ribner
(in both *Jacobean Tragedy* and his Revels edition of *The Atheist's
Tragedy*), H. H. Adams in 'Cyril Tourneur on Revenge', I.-S.
Ekeblad (Ewbank) in 'On the Authorship of *The Revenger's Tragedy*',
and Clifford Leech in '*The Atheist's Tragedy* as a Dramatic Comment
on Chapman's *Bussy* Plays'. There is evidence for Tourneur, on the
basis of a Spurgeon-type analysis of 'The Imagery of *The Revenger's
Tragedy* and *The Atheist's Tragedy*', by U. M. Ellis-Fermor; but
Marco K. Mincoff, using the same method of analysis, came down
on the side of Middleton, in his long essay on 'The Authorship of
The Revenger's Tragedy'. Attempts at rescuing something of methodological value from this kind of disconcerting clash are made by
I.-S. Ekeblad (Ewbank) in 'An Approach to Tourneur's Imagery',
where the imagery of the two plays is seen in its relation to dramatic
function; and by Allardyce Nicoll, who in '*The Revenger's Tragedy* and
the Virtue of Anonymity' pleads for the study of the play *an sich*.

The only studies of Tourneur which have been able to steer relatively clear of the authorship problem are those dealing with sources. N. W. Bawcutt, in 'The Revenger's Tragedy and the Medici Family'; G. K. Hunter, in 'A Source for The Revenger's Tragedy'; and Pierre Legouis, in 'Réflexions sur la recherche des sources à propos de la Tragédie du Vengeur', have all illuminated Tourneur's background reading. L. G. Salingar, in 'The Revenger's Tragedy: Some Possible Sources', manages not only to trace further borrowings but to relate their nature and use to the whole conception of drama behind The Revenger's Tragedy.

It is also Salingar, through his influential Scrutiny essay, 'The Revenger's Tragedy and the Morality Tradition', and his chapter on 'Tourneur and the Tragedy of Revenge' in the Pelican Guide to English Literature, who more than anyone else has helped to formulate the standard critical reading of Tourneur (assuming him to be the author of both tragedies). This is an interpretation which stresses the moral fervour of Tourneur's plays (often at the expense of Webster's), relating The Revenger's Tragedy to a medieval tradition of satire and complaint, seeing the irony-laden Morality of The Revenger's Tragedy as the greater artistic achievement and The Atheist's Tragedy as a kind of after-vibration in the shape of a thesis play. While this is no doubt a sound outline, it is dangerously close to hardening into orthodoxy and producing a self-perpetuating Tourneur industry, with articles—like P. Lisca's 'The Revenger's Tragedy: A Study in Irony', or A. L. and M. K. Kistner's 'Morality and Inevitability in The Revenger's Tragedy'—written for the poor benefit of finding more ironies and more Morality inheritance, rather than to provoke new insights or refined discriminations. One would like to conclude with Clifford Leech's timely reminders, in his review of Murray's book, that not all Moralities have the same moral tone, and that it is critical obtuseness to forget that Tourneur's plays are about people, not moral principles.

John Ford

Ford produced a larger and more varied corpus of plays than either Webster or Tourneur, so it is perhaps natural that he should have been the subject of a larger number of book-length studies than either of the other two. But the reason for this lies also in his way of writing plays: his concentration on characters and their psychological make-up, rather than on explicitly moral issues; and, therefore, the absence of obvious ideological significance in his work. T. S. Eliot was clearly haunted by Ford's verse, 'that slow solemn rhythm which is Ford's distinct contribution to the blank verse of the period'; at the same time he felt constrained to protest about the lack of 'an action or struggle for harmony in the soul of the poet' and the resultant 'poetry of the surface'. This ambivalence of feeling about Ford has tended, in critics less able than Eliot to be in two minds at once, to produce extremely partisan interpretations. The student new to Ford is well advised to begin with the more objective accounts before facing the polarization of opinions which characterizes much Ford criticism.

The first full-length study of the life and works of Ford was M. Joan Sargeaunt's book, *John Ford* (1935). In many ways undated, her untendentious account needs, when it comes to Ford's somewhat enigmatic theatrical career, to be supplemented with the pages on Ford in volume 3 of G. E. Bentley's *The Jacobean and Caroline Stage*. Robert Davril's book, *Le Drame de John Ford*, is the fullest, most learned, and least biased treatment that the dramatist has received. Less ambitious, but more immediately helpful to the student who wants to acquire a sense of Ford's dramatic context, is Clifford Leech's compact book, *John Ford and the Drama of his Time*, which also has a valuable *catalogue raisonné* of all Ford's writings, dramatic and non-dramatic. H. J. Oliver, in *The Problem of John Ford*, has careful analyses of all the main plays; he is also particularly illuminating in the obscure area of Ford's dramatic collaboration, trying to make a meaningful pattern of the collaborative works and to decide what Ford may have learnt from, respectively, Dekker, Rowley, and Middleton. This area has raised some interesting general issues, particularly in two controversial essays by Alfred Harbage. 'The Mystery of *Perkin Warbeck*' is a not wholly convincing attempt to explain the difference of this late history from other Ford plays in terms of yet another collaboration between Ford and Dekker; and 'Elizabethan–Restoration Palimpsest' argues that *The Great Favourite, or The Duke of Lerma*, acted and published as the work of Sir Robert Howard in 1668, was in fact a rewriting of a Ford manuscript play. No one should miss the fascinating account, in C. J. Sisson's *Lost Plays of Shakespeare's Age*, of the fortunes of the topical play, *A Late Murther of the Sonn upon the Mother*, or *Keep the Widow Waking*, which Ford, with embarrassing consequences, wrote together with Webster, Dekker, and Rowley.

It is when we move to the more exclusively interpretative criticism that the division of opinions on Ford becomes obvious: a division rooted in the early nineteenth century when Lamb saw Ford as a great poet celebrating, despite the often shocking nature of his subjects, the greatness in the soul of man; whereas Hazlitt found in him nothing but sensationalism and 'an artificial elaborateness'. For a short cut to these arguments, Davril has a chapter on 'Ford devant la critique'; John Wilcox sketches them out in an essay 'On Reading Ford' (whereas W. Bacon's 'The Literary Reputation of John Ford' is a misleadingly titled piece of axe-grinding); and the Introduction to Mark Stavig's book on *John Ford and the Traditional Moral Order* summarizes and categorizes criticism up to the early 1960s.

The division of opinions is into two overlapping and intertwining lines: Ford the decadent versus Ford the moralist; and Ford the modernist versus Ford the traditionalist. The *locus classicus* for the decadence is S. P. Sherman's prefatory essay to the first volume of the type-facsimile text of Ford: 'Ford's Contribution to the Decadence of the Drama'; the seminal reference to modernism is in Havelock Ellis's brief introduction to the Mermaid edition of Ford's plays. Havelock Ellis compared Ford's psychological insight to that of Flaubert and Stendhal and so introduced a tradition of comparative name-dropping which seems to have dominated Ford criticism ever since. Thus, in G. F. Sensabaugh's tendentious book, *The Tragic Muse of John Ford*, in which decadence and modernism meet in 'scientific determinism', we learn that 'what Freud seems to have done for Eugene O'Neill, Burton accomplished for John Ford'. And R. J. Kaufmann's essay, 'Ford's Tragic Perspective', while ultimately stimulating, at first disconcerts the reader by trying to define Ford's tone and purpose through an array of names including Emily Brontë, E. M. Forster, Hawthorne, Scott Fitzgerald, Anouilh, Giraudoux, Sartre, Camus, Henry James, Conrad, Euripides, Aristophanes, D. H. Lawrence, Edgar Allan Poe, and Plato.

The central point of the counter-argument to the determinist–modernist school is Ford's share in a historical context. In fairness to Sensabaugh one must point out that he has, as Sherman also has, a helpful account of Ford's connection with the Platonic love-cult at the court of Queen Henrietta. Two extensive studies of Ford's dependence on Burton's *Anatomy of Melancholy*—Lawrence Babb's general survey, *The Elizabethan Malady*, and S. Blaine Ewing's more specific examination of *Burtonian Melancholy in the Plays of John Ford*—are interesting in terms of sheer information but not very helpful as critical guides. Perhaps the most forceful statement of Ford being, morally and artistically, 'very much of his time' comes from a historian: Veronica Wedgwood in an essay in *Penguin New Writing*. But she is only the harbinger of a whole group of critics anxious to see Ford in relation to his time and tradition: Oliver's book and

Leech's both belong here, and so do two important essays by Peter Ure, 'Marriage and the Domestic Drama in Heywood and Ford' and 'Cult and Initiates in Ford's *Love's Sacrifice*', and also an essay by G. H. Blayney on 'Convention, Plot, and Structure in *The Broken Heart*'. Cyrus Hoy, in '"Ignorance in Knowledge"', puts the hero of *'Tis Pity She's A Whore* in the same moral tradition as Marlowe's Doctor Faustus; and Irving Ribner, predictably, sees Ford as an Elizabethan *manqué*—a Caroline sceptic who yet longed for the certitude of his forbears, bred on Hooker and the Great Chain of Being. Mark Stavig, in *John Ford and the Traditional Moral Order*, completes the rejection of the modernist view by giving Ford that Elizabethan certitude and thus turning the tragedies into, ultimately, *exempla horrenda*. At this stage we have a much less complex and dramatically exciting Ford than a sensitive first-hand response to the plays might suggest; and it is a solace to come to the balanced and discriminating appraisal by Ornstein, who points out that Ford is neither more nor less modern than John Donne.

It is a solace, too, to turn from the large and general issues of most of the works mentioned to the attention to specific details of subject-matter and style in some modern editions of Ford plays. Peter Ure's very full introduction to the Revels edition of *Perkin Warbeck* brings one as close to the essential Ford as one could hope to get. It is a model for how to read the otherness of Ford. Ure refuses—as does Jonas Barish in a stimulating article on '*Perkin Warbeck* as Anti-History'—to read historical sources, doctrines, and traditions back into the play, as has been done by Mildred Clara Struble and P. K. Anderson in their respective editions of the play, as well as by Irving Ribner in his discussion of it in *The English History Play in the Age of Shakespeare*. But he also refuses to take a narrowly modernist view. In his concluding comments on the play, he recognizes Ford's ability to sustain a complex set of truths and counter-truths and, in the most exciting moments and lines of the drama, to blend 'some of them together, softly cradled in an antithesis'.

It is the ability, or inability, of critics to respond to apparently contradictory impulses and to hold their responses together 'softly cradled in an antithesis' which ultimately decides their value as guides to the understanding of not only Ford but also Webster and Tourneur.

REFERENCES

GENERAL AND BACKGROUND STUDIES

H. H. Adams, *English Domestic or Homiletic Tragedy, 1575–1642* (New York, 1943; repr. 1965).

G. P. V. Akrigg, *Jacobean Pageant* (London, 1962).

W. Archer, *The Old Drama and the New: An Essay in Re-Valuation* (London, 1923).

F. T. Bowers, *Elizabethan Revenge Tragedy, 1587–1642* (Princeton, N.J., 1940; repr. 1966).

M. C. Bradbrook, *Themes and Conventions of Elizabethan Tragedy* (Cambridge, 1935).

M. Doran, *Endeavors of Art: A Study of Form in Elizabethan Drama* (Madison, Wis., 1954).

U. M. Ellis-Fermor, *The Jacobean Drama: An Interpretation* (London, 1936; 4th edn., 1958).

D. L. Frost, *The School of Shakespeare* (Cambridge, 1968).

A. Harbage, *Shakespeare and the Rival Traditions* (New York, 1952).

R. B. Heilman, *Tragedy and Melodrama: Versions of Experience* (Seattle, Wash., and London, 1968).

G. K. Hunter, 'English Folly and Italian Vice: John Webster', in *Jacobean Theatre* (Stratford-upon-Avon Studies 1, ed. J. R. Brown and B. Harris, London, 1960).

A. Kernan, *The Cankered Muse: Satire of the English Renaissance* (New Haven, Conn., 1959).

J. W. Lever, *The Tragedy of State* (London, 1971).

J. M. R. Margeson, *The Origins of English Tragedy* (Oxford, 1967).

R. Ornstein, *The Moral Vision of Jacobean Tragedy* (Madison, Wis., 1960).

T. M. Parrott and R. H. Ball, *A Short View of Elizabethan Drama* (New York, 1943).

ed. C. A. Pennel, *Elizabethan Bibliographies Supplements*, 1 (Webster), 2 (Tourneur) (London, 1967), 8 (Ford) (London, 1968).

J. Peter, *Complaint and Satire in Early English Literature* (Oxford, 1956).

M. Prior, *The Language of Tragedy* (New York, 1947).

I. Ribner, *Jacobean Tragedy: The Quest for Moral Order* (London, 1962).

C. Ricks, 'The Tragedies of Webster, Tourneur and Middleton: Symbols, Imagery and Conventions', in *English Drama to 1710*, ed. C. Ricks (*Sphere History of Literature in the English Language*, vol. 3, London, 1971).

T. Spencer, *Death and Elizabethan Tragedy* (Cambridge, Mass., 1936).

——, *Shakespeare and the Nature of Man* (New York, 1942).

W. Sypher, *Four Stages of Renaissance Style: Transformations in Art and Literature, 1400–1700* (New York, 1956).

S. A. Tannenbaum, *Elizabethan Bibliographies*, 19 (Webster), 20 (Ford) (New York, 1941), 33 (Tourneur) (New York, 1946).

W. Thorp, *The Triumph of Realism in Elizabethan Drama, 1558–1612* (Princeton Studies in English 3, Princeton, N.J., 1928).

T. B. Tomlinson, *A Study of Elizabethan and Jacobean Tragedy* (Cambridge, 1964).

F. P. Wilson, *Elizabethan and Jacobean* (London, 1945).

John Webster (1580?–1625?)

TEXTS

ed. D. C. Gunby, *John Webster. Three Plays* (Harmondsworth, 1972).

ed. F. L. Lucas, *The Complete Works of John Webster*, 4 vols. (London, 1927; repr. 1966).

The Devil's Law-Case

ed. F. A. Shirley (Regents Renaissance Drama Series, Lincoln, Nebr., 1972).

The Duchess of Malfi

ed. C. R. Baskervill, V. B. Heltzel, and A. N. Nethercot, in *Elizabethan and Stuart Plays* (New York, 1934).

ed. E. M. Brennan (The New Mermaids, London, 1964).

ed. C. F. T. Brooke and N. B. Paradise, in *English Drama, 1580–1642* (Boston, Mass., 1933).

ed. J. R. Brown (The Revels Plays, London, 1964).

ed. Clive Hart (The Fountainwell Drama Texts, Edinburgh, 1972).

ed. A. K. McIlwraith, in *Five Stuart Tragedies* (The World's Classics, London, 1953).

ed. F. E. Schelling, in *Typical Elizabethan Plays by Contemporaries and Immediate Successors of Shakespeare* (New York, 1926; rev. edn., 1931).

ed. J. A. Symonds, in *Webster and Tourneur* (The Mermaids, London, 1888; repr. 1954).

ed. C. B. Wheeler, in *Six Plays by Contemporaries of Shakespeare* (The World's Classics, London, 1915).

The White Devil

ed. E. M. Brennan (The New Mermaids, London, 1966).

ed. J. R. Brown (The Revels Plays, London, 1960).

ed. R. C. Harrier, in *The Anchor Anthology of Jacobean Drama*, 2 vols. (Garden City, N.Y., 1963).

ed. J. R. Mulryne (Regents Renaissance Drama Series, Lincoln, Nebr., 1970).

ed. G. Salgādo, in *Three Jacobean Tragedies* (Harmondsworth, 1965).

ed. H. Spencer, in *Elizabethan Plays* (Boston, Mass., 1933).

ed. J. A. Symonds, in *Webster and Tourneur* (The Mermaids, London, 1888; repr. 1954).

ed. C. B. Wheeler, in *Six Plays by Contemporaries of Shakespeare* (The World's Classics, London, 1915).

CRITICAL STUDIES AND COMMENTARY

G. Baldini, *John Webster e il linguaggio della tragedia* (Rome, 1953).

E. B. Benjamin, 'Patterns of Morality in *The White Devil*', *ES* 46 (1965).

G. E. Bentley, *The Jacobean and Caroline Stage*, 7 vols. (Oxford, 1941–68), vol. 5 (1958).

R. Berry, *The Art of John Webster* (Oxford, 1972).

T. Bogard, *The Tragic Satire of John Webster* (Berkeley and Los Angeles, Calif., 1955).

G. Boklund, '*The Duchess of Malfi*: *Sources, Themes, Characters* (Cambridge, Mass., 1962).

——, *The Sources of 'The White Devil'* (Uppsala, 1957).

M. C. Bradbrook, 'Fate and Chance in *The Duchess of Malfi*', *MLR* 42 (1947).

R. Brooke, *John Webster and the Elizabethan Drama* (London, 1916).

J. R. Brown, 'The Printing of John Webster's Plays' (3 parts), *Studies in Bibliography* 6 (1954), 8 (1956), 15 (1962).

J. L. Calderwood, '*The Duchess of Malfi*: Styles of Ceremony', *Essays in Criticism* 12 (1962).

R. W. Dent, *John Webster's Borrowing* (Berkeley and Los Angeles, Calif., 1960).

W. A. Edwards, 'Revaluations: John Webster', *Scrutiny* 2 (1933).

I.-S. Ekeblad (Ewbank), 'Webster's Constructional Rhythm', *ELH* 24 (1957).

——, 'The "Impure Art" of John Webster', *RES*, N.S. 9 (1958).

T. S. Eliot, 'Four Elizabethan Dramatists. A Preface to an Unwritten Book', in his *Selected Essays* (London, 1932) and *Elizabethan Essays* (London, 1934).

I. Glier, *Struktur und Gestaltungsprinzipien in den Dramen John Websters* (Munich, 1957).

D. C. Gunby, '*The Devil's Law-Case*: An Interpretation', *MLR* 63 (1968).

ed. G. K. and S. K. Hunter, *John Webster* (Penguin Critical Anthologies, Harmondsworth, 1969).

I. Jack, 'The Case of John Webster', *Scrutiny* 16 (1949).

C. Lamb, *Specimens of the English Dramatic Poets* (London, 1808).

C. Leech, *John Webster. A Critical Study* (London, 1951).

——, *Webster: 'The Duchess of Malfi'* (Studies in English Literature 8, London, 1963).

C. O. MacDonald, *The Rhetoric of Tragedy: Form in Stuart Drama* (Amherst, Mass., 1966).

D. D. Moore, *John Webster and his Critics, 1617–1964* (Baton Rouge, La., 1966).

ed. B. Morris, *John Webster* (Mermaid Critical Commentaries, London, 1970).

J. R. Mulryne, '*The White Devil* and *The Duchess of Malfi*', in *Jacobean Theatre* (Stratford-upon-Avon Studies, 1, ed. J. R. Brown and B. Harris, London, 1960).

P. B. Murray, *A Study of John Webster* (The Hague and Paris, 1969).

H. T. Price, 'The Function of Imagery in Webster', *PMLA* 70 (1955).

ed. N. Rabkin, *Twentieth-Century Interpretations of 'The Duchess of Malfi'* (Englewood Cliffs, N.J., 1968).

J. Smith, 'The Tragedy of Blood', *Scrutiny* 8 (1939).

E. E. Stoll, *John Webster: The Periods of his Work as Determined by his Relations to the Drama of his Day* (Boston, Mass., 1905; repr. New York, 1967).

A. C. Swinburne, 'John Webster', *Nineteenth Century* 19 (1886).

Cyril Tourneur (1575?–1626)

TEXTS

ed. A. Nicoll, *The Works of Cyril Tourneur* (London, 1929; rev. edn., New York, 1963).

The Atheist's Tragedy

ed. A. H. Gomme, in *Jacobean Tragedies* (London, 1969).

ed. I. Ribner (The Revels Plays, London, 1964).

ed. J. A. Symonds, in *Webster and Tourneur* (The Mermaids, London, 1888; repr. 1954).

The Revenger's Tragedy

ed. R. A. Foakes (The Revels Plays, London, 1966).

ed. B. Gibbons (The New Mermaids, London, 1967).

ed. A. H. Gomme, in *Jacobean Tragedies* (London, 1969).

ed. R. C. Harrier, in *The Anchor Anthology of Jacobean Drama*, 2 vols. (Garden City, N.Y., 1963).

ed. L. J. Ross (Regents Renaissance Drama Series, Lincoln, Nebr., 1967).

ed. G. Salgādo, in *Three Jacobean Tragedies* (Harmondsworth, 1965).

ed. A. J. Symonds, in *Webster and Tourneur* (The Mermaids, London, 1888; repr. 1954).

CRITICAL STUDIES AND COMMENTARY

H. H. Adams, 'Cyril Tourneur on Revenge', *JEGP* 48 (1949).

N. W. Bawcutt, '*The Revenger's Tragedy* and the Medici Family', *N & Q* 202 (1957).

I.-S. Ekeblad (Ewbank), 'An Approach to Tourneur's Imagery', *MLR* 54 (1959).

——, 'On the Authorship of *The Revenger's Tragedy*', *ES* 41 (1960).

T. S. Eliot, 'Cyril Tourneur', in his *Selected Essays* (London, 1932) and *Elizabethan Essays* (London, 1934).

U. M. Ellis-Fermor, 'The Imagery of *The Revenger's Tragedy* and *The Atheist's Tragedy*', *MLR* 30 (1935).

R. A. Foakes, 'On the Authorship of *The Revenger's Tragedy*', *MLR* 48 (1953).

G. K. Hunter, 'A Source for *The Revenger's Tragedy*', *RES*, n.s. 10 (1959).

H. Jenkins, 'Cyril Tourneur', *RES* 17 (1941).

A. L. and M. K. Kistner, 'Morality and Inevitability in *The Revenger's Tragedy*', *JEGP* 71 (1972).

C. Leech, '*The Atheist's Tragedy* as a Dramatic Comment on Chapman's Bussy Plays', *JEGP* 52 (1953).

——, review of P. B. Murray, *A Study of Cyril Tourneur*, in *JEGP* 64 (1965).

P. Legouis, 'Réflexions sur la recherche des sources à propos de la *Tragédie du Vengeur*', *Études Anglaises* 12 (1959).

P. Lisca, '*The Revenger's Tragedy*: A Study in Irony', *PQ* 38 (1959).

M. K. Mincoff, 'The Authorship of *The Revenger's Tragedy*', *Studia Historico-Philologica Serdicensia* 2 (1940).

P. B. Murray, *A Study of Cyril Tourneur* (Philadelphia, Pa., 1964).

A. Nicoll, '*The Revenger's Tragedy* and the Virtue of Anonymity', in *Essays on Shakespeare and Elizabethan Drama*, ed. R. Hosley (Columbia, Mo., 1962; London, 1963).

G. R. Price, 'The Authorship and the Bibliography of *The Revenger's Tragedy*', *The Library*, 5th Ser. 15 (1960).

L. G. Salingar, '*The Revenger's Tragedy* and the Morality Tradition', *Scrutiny* 6 (1938).

——, '*The Revenger's Tragedy*: Some Possible Sources', *MLR* 60 (1965).

——, 'Tourneur and the Tragedy of Revenge', in *The Age of Shakespeare*, ed. Boris Ford (*Pelican Guide to English Literature*, 2, Harmondsworth, 1955).

S. Schoenbaum, *Internal Evidence and Elizabethan Dramatic Authorship* (London, 1966).

——, *Middleton's Tragedies: A Critical Study* (New York, 1955).

John Ford (1586–1640?)

TEXTS

ed. W. Bang and H. de Vocht, *John Ford's Dramatic Works*, 2 vols.(*Materialien zur Kunde des älteren englischen Dramas*, 23 and N.S. 1, Louvain, 1908 and 1927).

cd. William Gifford and A. Dyce, *The Dramatic Works of John Ford*, 3 vols. (London, 1869; rev. edn. by A. H. Bullen, London, 1895).

The Broken Heart

ed. D. K. Anderson (Regents Renaissance Drama Series, Lincoln, Nebr., 1966).

ed. C. R. Baskervill, V. B. Heltzel, and A. N. Nethercot, in *Elizabethan and Stuart Plays* (New York, 1934).

ed. C. F. T. Brooke and N. B. Paradise, in *English Drama, 1580–1642* (Boston, Mass., 1933).

ed. H. Ellis, in *John Ford* (The Mermaids, London, 1888).

ed. R. C. Harrier, in *The Anchor Anthology of Jacobean Drama*, 2 vols. (Garden City, N.Y., 1963).

ed. B. Morris (The New Mermaids, London, 1965).

ed. F. Schelling, in *Typical Elizabethan Plays* (rev. edn., New York, 1931).
ed. H. Spencer, in *Elizabethan Plays* (Boston, Mass., 1933).
ed. K. Sturgess, in *John Ford. Three Plays* (Harmondsworth, 1970).

The Lover's Melancholy
ed. H. Ellis, in *John Ford* (The Mermaids, London, 1888).

Love's Sacrifice
ed. H. Ellis, in *John Ford* (The Mermaids, London, 1888).

Perkin Warbeck
ed. D. K. Anderson (Regents Renaissance Drama Series, Lincoln, Nebr., 1966).
ed. W. A. Armstrong, in *Elizabethan History Plays* (London, 1965).
ed. C. R. Baskervill, V. B. Heltzel, and A. N. Nethercot, in *Elizabethan and Stuart Plays* (New York, 1934).
ed. H. Ellis, in *John Ford* (The Mermaids, London, 1888).
ed. F. Schelling, in *Typical Elizabethan Plays* (New York, 1926; not in later edns.).
ed. M. C. Struble, *A Critical Edition of Ford's 'Perkin Warbeck'* (University of Washington Publications in Language and Literature 3, Seattle, Wash., 1926).
ed. K. Sturgess, in *John Ford. Three Plays* (Harmondsworth, 1970).
ed. P. Ure (The Revels Plays, London, 1968).

'Tis Pity She's a Whore
ed. N. W. Bawcutt (Regents Renaissance Drama Series, Lincoln, Nebr., 1966).
ed. H. Ellis, in *John Ford* (The Mermaids, London, 1888).
ed. A. K. McIlwraith, in *Five Stuart Tragedies* (The World's Classics, London, 1953).
ed. B. Morris (The New Mermaids, London, 1968).
ed. K. Sturgess, in *John Ford. Three Plays* (Harmondsworth, 1970).

CRITICAL STUDIES AND COMMENTARY

L. Babb, *The Elizabethan Malady: A Study of Melancholia* (East Lansing, Mich., 1951).
W. A. Bacon, 'The Literary Reputation of John Ford', *HLQ* 11 (1947–8).
J. A. Barish, '*Perkin Warbeck* as Anti-History', *Essays in Criticism* 20 (1970).
G. E. Bentley, *The Jacobean and Caroline Stage*, 7 vols. (Oxford, 1941–68), vol. 3 (1956).
G. H. Blayney, 'Convention, Plot, and Structure in *The Broken Heart*', *MP* 56 (1958).
R. Davril, *Le Drame de John Ford* (Paris, 1954).
T. S. Eliot, 'John Ford', in his *Selected Essays* (London, 1932) and *Elizabethan Essays* (London, 1934).

S. B. Ewing, *Burtonian Melancholy in the Plays of John Ford* (Princeton Studies in English 19, Princeton, N.J., 1940).

A. Harbage, 'Elizabethan–Restoration Palimpsest', *MLR* 35 (1940); repr. in his *Shakespeare Without Words' and other Essays* (Cambridge, Mass., 1972).

——, 'The Mystery of *Perkin Warbeck*', in *Studies in the English Renaissance Drama*, ed. J. W. Bennett, O. Cargill, and V. Hall, Jr. (New York, 1959).

W. Hazlitt, 'Lectures chiefly on the Dramatic Literature of the Age of Elizabeth', *Complete Works*, ed. P. P. Howe, 21 vols. (London, 1930–4), vol. 6 (1931).

C. Hoy, ' "Ignorance in Knowledge": Marlowe's Faustus and Ford's Giovanni', *MP* 57 (1960).

R. J. Kaufmann, 'Ford's Tragic Perspective', *Texas Studies in Literature and Language* 1 (1960).

C. Lamb, *Specimens of the English Dramatic Poets* (London, 1808).

C. Leech, *John Ford and the Drama of his Time* (London, 1957).

H. J. Oliver, *The Problem of John Ford* (Melbourne, 1955).

I. Ribner, *The English History Play in the Age of Shakespeare* (Princeton, N.J., 1957).

M. J. Sargeaunt, *John Ford* (Oxford, 1935).

G. F. Sensabaugh, *The Tragic Muse of John Ford* (Stanford, Calif., 1944).

S. P. Sherman, 'Ford's Contribution to the Decadence of the Drama', in *Materialien zur Kunde des älteren englischen Dramas*, ed. W. Bang, 23 (1908).

C. J. Sisson, *Lost Plays of Shakespeare's Age* (Cambridge, 1936).

M. Stavig, *John Ford and the Traditional Moral Order* (Madison, Wis., 1968).

P. Ure, 'Cult and Initiates in Ford's *Love's Sacrifice*', *MLQ* 11 (1951).

——, 'Marriage and the Domestic Drama in Heywood and Ford', *ES* 32 (1951).

C. V. Wedgwood, 'John Ford', in *Penguin New Writing* 38 (1949).

J. Wilcox, 'On Reading John Ford', *Shakespeare Association Bulletin* 21 (1946).

9. THE COURT MASQUE

K. M. LEA

> Spring all the Graces of the age,
> And all the Loves of time;
> Bring all the pleasures of the stage,
> And relishes of rhyme;
> Adde all the softnesses of Courts,
> The lookes, the laughters and the sports,
> And mingle all their sweets, and salts,
> That none may say the Triumph halts.
> (*Neptune's Triumph*)

ROSSETTI once called the sonnet 'a moment's monument'; the phrase might be appropriated by the masque as it celebrates a betrothal, a marriage, an arrival, a coming-of-age, or the more commonly shared days of high festivity.

A. H. Gilbert goes so far as to claim that 'without appreciation of the masque, the epitome of its age, no one can hope to feel at ease with the artists from Machiavelli to Milton.' He was referring to the dissemination of learned symbolism. And yet, as another critic remarks, 'we have lost the language of the masque.' The purpose of this chapter is to suggest some of the methods and recommend some of the means by which this language may be recovered. It is a language as much visual, or indeed physical, as verbal; it involves an activity as well as a show, and the threads of its web are drawn almost equally from music, dance, spectacle, poetry, and mime. It was probably the most elaborate form of aristocratic entertainment ever devised.

To calculate the achievement of the makers of masque is to appraise what is involved in selecting, proportioning, combining, tempering, and trimming its several elements into a unity for one night's display. Whatever notion or theme it was that effected a harmony might be thought of as the soul animating the intricate mass of sensuous appeal. Suitability to a particular occasion and novelty from one season to another are subsidiary tests of quality. A fine masque is not to be described as a single bloom but rather as a composed bunch. Attempts at closer definition must allow for the slant of the definer. For the courtier a masque was an opportunity for dancing, flirtation, the fun of dressing up, and the advantageous display of accomplishments; and nearly as much may be said for the court lady. To a smaller segment of the courtly circle the occasion invited diplomatic intrigue; the ambassadorial jockeying for invitation, and then for places of honour, became notorious. At the peak, for the Royal persons under the state canopy the acceptability was pointed by the discreetly complimentary conveyance of bland moralizing and sometimes by gifts. Much may be gathered from Finett and, more racily and briefly, from the letters to and from Chamberlain.

For the spectators, masque meant amazement at scene, lights, music, movement, and for the more knowing, some interest in the mechanisms by which the sumptuous illusions were produced. For the engineers and craftsmen it meant chances to refine upon traditional techniques of pageantry either by native ingenuity or slyly imported devices from Italy and France; there were similar chances for musicians, dance-masters, and scene-painters, and for some professional actors and clowns, each after his own kind and quality.

From the contriver, poet or dramatist or both, masque demanded a controlling conceit followed by the ingenuity and learning to draw out from mythology or topical and personal allusion a scenario draped with rhetoric, both serious and comic, and jewelled with lyrics. Since it was the poet's prerogative to record more of his part in the work than that of his fellow artists he was tempted to regard his function as having primacy; first in time it may have been, but not necessarily first in importance.

Since the initial question—what is the nature of masque?—does not admit of a neat and adequate answer, the modern inquirer must take into account the views from these different angles in constructing his survey. Further, he must allow for minimum and maximum effects. Some very simple entertainments comprising a procession with torches, some form of disguise, leading to a game of dice or a presentation or a dance could be referred to as masquing: while at the other extreme stood the complex of scenic effect and change, vertical as well as horizontal and in depth; of choral and instrumental music as well as solo singing; of planned and rehearsed dancing in character preceding the sequence of formal court measures; of the extension of a simple speech of introduction into grave address, witty dialogue, and the balancing of serious themes against grotesque parodying turns constituting the anti-masque. All this still went under the name of masque once that term had ousted the older 'disguising'.

For this reason it is hard to recommend a single example, or even a few specimens, as a reliable first showing in the hope of doing justice both to the recorded actuality and the imagined potentiality of the form. In this uncourtly age other methods must be used to enable our thoughts to piece out the imperfections of what of the 'rack' remains. We may make a way in by following up some subordinate questions: where does masque come from? who made it? who enjoyed it? who paid for it? is there anything to it beyond the evening's pleasure? is there any lasting intellectual satisfaction behind its heavy sensuousness?

The authoritative historical studies are, in order of appearance, those by Soergel, Brotanek, Reyher, and Welsford.

The men commissioned to devise masques whose names are recorded are Jonson, Daniel, Chapman, Campion, Beaumont, Carew, Shirley, Davenant, Townshend, Marston, Middleton, Montague, Nabbes, Cokayne, and William Browne.

Those for whose delectation it was cultivated constituted a sophisticated, critical clientèle having on the side (quite literally) as many of the London or local common people as could squeeze into what space remained in the hall—often the Whitehall Banqueting House, discussed by Palme—hot with torch- and candle-light and human crush.

The expenses were met variously from the royal purse via the Office of the Revels as for masques of the Christmas season; or by the occasional enterprise of members of the Inns of Court; or by affluent or aspiring nobles entertaining the greater ones in the city or, more often, in their own homes when visited in Royal Progress; or by the courtly masquers themselves as they furnished the dress and jewels required for their allotted parts. The figures which have been extracted from the Revels accounts by Feuillerat and here and there from gossip in letters (as by Steele and Sullivan) are hard to interpret accurately now but even without allowing for the appropriate multiplication, looked at 'raw', though they may not surprise, they still shock. 'In spite of this penury we speak of a maske', wrote Chamberlain in 1614. It is no wonder that Puritan conscience, economic as well as moral, killed off masque as such and left the stump of a desire for such pleasure to shoot up later in other forms such as opera and ballet or carnival. As for the last question posed, the answer can best be elicited by following up some of the special studies made by recent scholars, notably Gordon, Gilbert, Allen, Talbert, and Wheeler, who have taken pains to interpret the score in accordance with the learning to be found in Renaissance compendia and books of reference.

The symbolism is often intricate and sometimes esoteric, but if it escapes or baffles a modern intellectual that is surely because of his different upbringing. It would be impertinent to suppose that the points were not taken by any of the original participants. Much still yields to patient investigation and shows great nicety and some subtlety underlying the dazzle which catches immediate attention.

To learn about masque by the long way round would be to acquaint oneself with the range of Tudor and Stuart entertainment, thanks to the publications of scholars such as Withington, Wickham, Anglo, Bergeron, Fairholt, Yates, Strong, and some volumes of the Malone Society Collections. Ultimately it is not irrelevant to know about their processions, tableaux, and arches; their May Day and Mis-rule celebrations; the furniture and procedure for the reception of foreign visitors, and for national and domestic events; the practice of show-jousting and the formal presentation of gifts and loyal addresses. Although such pieces of pageantry are not properly masques it is well to be reminded of their cults at least in order to be saved from supposing that masque-making had nothing to draw on; certainly there was the endeavour to surpass, but there was equally a substantial base from which to manœuvre. The two bumper crops of masquing and its associated growths ripened under Henry VIII and James I. But this is not to say that the Elizabethan and Caroline years were barren; indeed, it may be that the chance of having a Hall to chronicle at one end and a Jonson to describe at the other a little biases our view.

For the modern reader, the shortest cut would be to the masquing incorporated into six Shakespearian plays and referred to in four others serving as samples of the Tudor and Jacobean practices: notably one should look at *Henry VIII* and *The Tempest*. To these add the few packed pages 'Of Masques and Triumphs' that Bacon added to the third edition of his *Essays* in 1625; laconic, succinct, informal, shrewd, these constitute the best digest ever provided, and Bacon had made masque speeches for fellow lawyers in his early days and in his affluence stood the whole cost (some £2,000, it is said) of a masque for King James in 1613, not to mention what he learned by sitting through the productions of other men, perforce.

The longest way, that of total survey, which has been mentioned, could in turn be shortened by the use of one or two of the excellent brief accounts by Bayne, Evans, Simpson, or Chambers.

Yet another mode of introduction could be to choose a dozen or so of the masques that reached print and read the libretti of those collected by Evans or admirably edited in honour of Allardyce Nicoll.

The method to be recommended in this chapter takes a middle course and sketches-in a rather more analytical approach intended to enable masque to be imagined as an experience, complex, exciting, overwhelming, and ephemeral. It is focused upon Ben Jonson whose masque-making—quality apart—is best documented not only by the author himself but by the superb editing of Herford and Simpson followed up by the attention of Orgel and specialized studies by Dolora Cunningham and W. Todd Furniss and Parrott, and only paralleled by the care given by Lefkowitz to three post-Jonsonian masques by Shirley and Davenant.

Before taking the Jonsonian masques apart a couple of other exercises may prove worth the trouble. First, it is not amiss to read the texts of two or three whole and unhurriedly, as much for what the printed words convey as for what they admit they cannot do justice to; and secondly, to consider briefly what it was that Jonson had to work on both of native practice and imported resources.

The invaluable sources of information for Tudor masquing are Hall and Nichols. These may be supplemented by modern studies (such as Wickham's) which take the practices further back into the fifteenth century and indicate Lydgate's place in the tradition. Hall's accounts are graphic and plentiful. According to a famous entry the grafting of an Italian custom upon English habits of mumming and disguising took place in 1512.

On the daie of the Epiphanie at night, the Kyng with a xi other were disguised, after the maner of Italie, called a maske, a thyng not seen afore in Englande, thei were appareled in garmentes long and brode, wrought all with gold, with visers and cappes of gold, and after the banket doen, these Maskers came in, with sixe gentlemen disguised in silke bearyng staff torches, and desired the ladies to daunce, some were content, and some that knewe the fashion of it refused, because it was not a thyng commonly seen. And after thei had daunced and commoned together, as the fashion of the maskes is, they toke their leave.

What, it has often been debated, was precisely the novelty? Judging by descriptions on later occasions it seems it lay in the social move, in the 'commoning' and subsequent invitation to dance from the masked strangers to the resident ladies. Taking it on the chronicler's authority that this *was* an innovation, we may turn over Hall's pages to find illustration of allied entertainments of tilting,

pageants, disguising, and May-Daying to feel how strong the briar
stock of revelling already was to support the new shoots of recognized
masquing. We catch sight of these from a mundane angle of the
Revels Records as edited by Feuillerat. Similar documents analysed
by E. K. Chambers show that Elizabeth countenanced the con-
tinuance of her father's indulgence through the Christmas season,
though presumably with less zest and personal involvement. More
lively impressions of what went on during her reign can be gathered
from the three volumes of *Progresses* collected by John Nichols. Once
again, the accounts are not exclusively of masques; but much can be
learned by inference from noticing the variety of provincial endeavours to please. The sole unifying principle of this great compilation must be the Queen's memory: so much (and more) had
Elizabeth seen, heard, and sat through, and enjoyed or suffered,
including the vicissitudes of English weather. The proceedings at
Oxford in 1566 and the more famous Kenilworth series in 1575 are
well worth looking at again, and perhaps the efforts made at Norwich
in 1578 are even more engaging thanks to the naïve narration and
gracious response; a more perfect comment on the last act of *A
Midsummer Night's Dream* could not be found. The most important
account, as far as masque proper is concerned, is that of the Gray's
Inn revels, printed as *Gesta Grayorum*. Setting aside the 'Night of
Errors' quip and all the wrappings of mock rules and procedures,
speeches, and reports, we come upon the minor masque of Russians
and the major development of *Proteus and the Adamantine Rock* which
has been hailed by Miss Welsford as the masque's coming of age.
Two more accounts are rewarding for the intrinsic interest of
amateur ingenuity and country goodwill and for incidental relevance
to the general cult of royal entertainment: these are for Harefield
and Elvetham, and can be read in Nichols's *Progresses* and in Bond's
edition of Lyly.

The initial association with Italy seems to have remained recognized but relatively unexploited during the sixteenth century; but,
as Miss Welsford has shown, the parallel developments in Florence
and Paris offered a store of ideas for a well-travelled Jacobean like
Inigo Jones. Jones's life and work were summarized by Summerson
and have been expertly illustrated in the quatercentenary exhibition
at the Banqueting House, Whitehall, in 1973 and recorded in its
admirable catalogue prepared by Harris, Orgel, and Strong. Fuller
accounts of Italian and French entertainments have been given by
Solerti, and in the articles collected by Jacquot in *Les Fêtes de la
Renaissance*.

Jonson was the chief but not the sole provider for the Stuarts. Daniel made two contributions, but the first, the *Masque of the Twelve Goddesses*, seems old-fashioned even for 1604. Chapman and Campion could have been formidable rivals, but no one kept it up as Jonson did, and since novelty was so important the sheer number must count. Between 1605 and 1631 Jonson thought up and worked out some two dozen masques, recast two of them, and organized half a dozen entertainments and tilts. The ritual as Jonson devised it consisted of an introduction by speech, or invocation with dialogue, or procession, or anti-masque leading to the disclosure of courtly masquers by one or more stages; the provision of songs to cover resting between dances, and the gracing of the retiring by some slight excuse and music. Even this simple formula was flexible, and both order and proportion might vary so long as the descent of the noble masquers for the dances leading to the revels was placed as a climax and their exit decorated by speech and song. The whole confection is complicated enough to merit breaking up into its three main constituents, each involving subdivision.

Music and dance are so closely allied that it is convenient to consider them together. Some idea of both may be recovered from the stage directions and retrospective description in the printed masques where occasionally the choreographer or musician is named. There are indications of the instruments used: fiddles, lutes, harps, drums, fifes, bagpipes, cymbals. Arrangements for continuous playing and imitative sounds for choral and lyric are noted both for their intrinsic charm and to amuse while dancers rested. Lanier singing recitative as a novelty is associated with *Lovers Made Men* (1617), though the accuracy of this dating has been questioned. Masque music and musicians have been studied by Cutts, Dent, Gombosi, Lawrence, Meagher, Pattison, Sabol, Stevens, Woodfill, Willetts, and contributors to Jacquot's *Les Fêtes de la Renaissance*.

The dancing was of two kinds: patterned and so to be rehearsed, or social and conventional. There is a fine description of the second kind in a letter quoted by Herford and Simpson (Jonson, *Works*, vol. 10, p. 522). The texts of *Beautie*, *Hymenaei*, and *Queen's* refer to the graphic patterns drawn, a number of them spelling out royal names. Personal prowess catches an occasional mention, while the notion that true dancing 'maketh the beholders wise' is commended in song in *Pleasure Reconciled to Virtue*. In the anti-masques there were capricious movements, contortions, and posturing. Such hints can be supplemented and interpreted by contemporary theorists and further explained by the modern study by Meagher.

The attraction for the eyes might also be subdivided into the stage architecture, ornaments, and structures; the painting, often of landscape, used for curtain, back-cloth, and sliding wings; and the mechanisms for scenic change, for descent, ascent, and suspension, and the lighting.

The main resources to be kept in mind lie in the stores of pageantry used on various occasions and at different levels of simplicity and pomp. Glynne Wickham illustrates and discusses the chief stock constructions, the castle, cave, arch, bower, ship, chariot, and mountain, arguing that these constitute the base on which improvements such as the shell, palace, island, globe, split rock could be fashioned. The simultaneous setting of the medieval style gave way to a centralized set with scenic disclosures, changes, and transformations. How these shifts were effected, the machinery adapted; or how the techniques of sliding and revolving structures were introduced, the tricks to simulate the movement of water, to produce moonlight and storm and much else are best demonstrated, first, by L. B. Campbell and later by Allardyce Nicoll.

The decorated frames for the curtain, often adorned with complimentary emblems and hieroglyphics, called on learning as well as the painter's skill. The effects can be glimpsed at from the sketches and some of the descriptions interpolated in Jonson's printed texts, and the splendid sketches left by Inigo Jones and published from the Chatsworth collection by Bell and Simpson and later by Orgel and Strong.

Sumptuous and fantastic scenes called for equivalent extravagance in dress. The designer was evidently consulted at the highest level. 'The Cullors are in hir may choyse but my oppinion is that severall fresh greenes mixt with gould and siller will bee most propper' reads a note endorsing Inigo Jones's sketch for the royal dress for *Chloridia* (Jonson, *Works*, vol. 10, p. 685). Nymphs, knights, queens, witches, fairies, satyrs, Olympians, elements, abstractions, fantastics, gypsies, pilgrims, tumblers, pickled sailors, Rosicrucian eccentrics—to select from Jonson's demands upon Jones—all had to be got up.

In addition to the set of noble masquers, some dozen of each sex have their uniform laid down; Inigo must have directed the tailors and tirewomen how to fit out the professional actors who took those parts that required more mimetic or musical accomplishment; in addition, all the torch-bearers and pages had to be clad and equipped. It was a huge, various, and demanding task to be planned for.

In 1613, when Jonson was in France, Chapman gilded his gold

in the *Masque of the Middle Temple and Lincoln's Inn*, ordering an immense procession through the Strand of fifty gentlemen with mock music of baboons. Campion's contrivances in his *Lords' Masque* of the same year were equally elaborate but in better taste. What could be done when sartorial and mechanical expertise was at full stretch and the lust for spectacle at its height, ripe to burst, can best be realized by turning to Carew's *Coelum Britannicum* (1634) and Davenant's *Salmacida Spolia* (1640): glorious technicolour would not be out of place were one to attempt the equivalent now.

What may be thought of as the content of a masque is palpably twofold: the serious and the mocking. The reason for considering both under one heading is that ideally, and occasionally in fact, there is a connection between solemn and profane providing the tension upon which the unity and distinction of a given masque depend. Meanwhile each is important and complicated enough to require separate treatment, provided they are not severed in a final appraisal.

What intellectual appeal was proper or possible in masque depended upon the controlling theme or conceit and the opportunities its conduct afforded for speeches in the ample and euphonious rhetoric which might also be moral and mildly philosophical. It is the main purpose of another of Meagher's studies to extract and expound the didactic strain that Jonson was at pains to introduce and 'to make the spectators understanders'. He judged it suitable to remind royal personages of what was expected of them—clemency and good order—or to let his good sense play upon some fashionable cult such as that of heroic love in *Love's Triumph through Callipolis*. It was left for Davenant to put a political edge upon the old flattering commonplaces.

The masque-maker sought not a plot-line but a pivot, as Jonson has it of the conceit for *Chloridia*: 'upon this hinge the whole invention turned.' The appropriateness of some masques is obvious as they depend upon some special occasion such as a marriage or a home-coming (as in *Albion's Triumph*, made over into the *Fortunate Isles* when Prince Charles who went to woo in Spain returned with a French bride). Once the *donnée*, or leading idea, was the Queen's and Jonson was ordered to play with the idea of blackamoor masquers. More often it was left to his ingenuity to pick up some myth, legend, custom, or current topic and play with it to advantage. It is one thing to have an idea and another to get it to root, branch, and flower. Happy the day when a conceit was sighted with 'capabilities', both sensuous and intellectual, and giving the poet a chance to air his learning. Jonson was not averse to pointing his meaning (as in *The Masque of Queens*) but for a fuller explication the modern reader turns to the special studies made by Gordon, Allen, Gilbert, Talbert, and Wheeler.

Wit, *vis comica*, was tapped to supplement, though not, at least in Jonson's usage, to supersede the learning: hence the development of contrast on every side and level; in décors, dance, or purport in the anti-masque. The prefix remains ambiguous though this may have been more of a happy accident than deliberate punning. Thus the spelling 'ante' suggests the placing, the comic usually led up to the glorious appearances, and by foiling them picked up the meaning of 'anti' and later of 'antic'. Jonson's satire makes Vangoose protest, 'O Sir, all de better, vor an Antick-maske, de more absurd it be, and vrom de purpose, it be ever all de better. If it goe from de Nature of de ting, it is de more Art.'

As in the search for dominant notions for entertaining Jonson had never disdained working up what had already been tried out— witness his use of Christmas gambols, teasing riddles, tilting, and pastoral—so he took advantage of the taste for burlesque which had often provided relief in Tudor practice. The layout of Progress amusements almost invariably included rustic or grotesque episodes, not always related closely to the other items. Jonson and other Jacobeans saw their chance too, and moved through neat adaptations to blatant exploitation of the semi-dramatic and satiric possibilities.

While Jonson was in full command, anti-masques must have greatly enhanced the total artistic effectiveness. This part of the show was scaled and related to the main masque with skill, as when the warring humours and affections led on to the significance of marital harmony, or the turmoil of witches, dancing hip to hip, suddenly vanished before the virtuous queens. The satyrs and sileni were foils to Oberon and his fairy chivalry, but hardly ugly; and they were not banished, only subdued. Later Jonson began to try out topical matter with more realism, allowing always for comic heightening: alchemists, frantic lovers, news-mongers, Venus burlesqued as a deaf tirewoman, disputing poets, and cooks. It is peculiarly hard to assess the effect of anti-masques at this distance; clowning, like poetry, does not translate well into prose, though the virtues of Jonson's comic prose as such have been admirably pointed by Barish. Towards the end of his career there are signs of the anti-masque calling the tune, as in *Augurs* and *Time Vindicated*. Whether this was Jonson's intent or the result of the pressure of Inigo Jones may be debated. The series of comic turns in *Chloridia* suggests that the control was weakening as the partnership cracked. When Carew, Shirley, and Davenant are on their own the hold seems to lapse completely. It is a question whether this great bubble might not have burst by its own inflation without the prick of war.

It has seemed wise to stress how relatively small a responsibility dramatist and poet had for the popularity and success of masquing since it is largely by way of the printed word that the knowledge of the art is preserved for us at all, and the claims of rhetoric and lyric are disproportionately available and so, slyly, biased; and yet, when the corrective stress has been allowed for, it is undeniable that it is to literature that we must turn once more for a further supply of oblique and secondary evidence. Masque proper seeded itself into the adjacent fields of poetry and drama. Spenser took his chances to indulge in ideal description in the Masque of Cupid (*The Faerie Queene*, III. 12) and elsewhere in processional effects approximating to some of the Tudor practices. Chapman tucks a nuptial masque into the Tale of Teras in his continuation of *Hero and Leander*. Davies's *Orchestra* makes many telling allusions, as might be expected. Marvell has reminiscential phrases in 'On Appleton House' and 'The Unfortunate Lover'. Milton comes into the open with *Comus* so that it is equally important to recognize that though masque should not be illustrated by *Comus*, *Comus* cannot be properly understood without reference to the masque. Partially in *Arcades*, in the manuscripts of early drafts for *Paradise Lost*, latent in the ode 'On the Morning of Christ's Nativity', in the framework of *L'Allegro* and *Il Penseroso*; in the style of the Pandemonium passage in Hell, and in the magical banquet in the wilderness, there are signs of what masquing meant to Milton's imagination.

Playwrights saw the potentialities of masques inset and used them frequently and for a variety of dramatic as well as spectacular effects. Full, partial, simple, elaborate, straight, rehearsed, old-fashioned, and new masques in plays of the period have been listed by Reyher and admirably commented upon in Mrs. Ewbank's article, 'These Pretty Devices', and by Allardyce Nicoll in relation to Shakespeare.

The purpose of analysis and specialized study is not to break this butterfly of a form upon the critic's wheel but rather to encourage the reanimation and rearticulation of remains which lie dispersed, dried, broken, and, until this century, disregarded. How much has been done in the last fifty years can be gathered from Mrs. Ewbank's other article 'The Eloquence of Masques' reviewing masque criticism. The justification is in bringing into imaginative grasp what was once so notable a form of civilized pleasure. Anything well made will bear analysis and it is up to those who take apart to see that things come together again. To realize how far this is possible one might turn to chapter three of Stanley Wells's *Literature and Drama*, or to C. V. Wedgwood's reconstruction of 'The Last Masque' in *Truth and Opinion*: what she has done for Davenant's *Salmacida Spolia* is within scope for many another night.

Splendour and pathos dominate the impression left by masque, and essentially when in conjunction. The form is the very image of an awareness of time by its momentary arrest; it is both caught and transcended in the unforgettable speech dismissing a masque which has itself been part of a play—illusion within illusion—as it is 'melted into air, into thin air'.

REFERENCES

GENERAL SURVEYS

R. Brotanek, *Die englischen Maskenspiele* (Vienna and Leipzig, 1902),
P. Reyher, *Les Masques anglais* (Paris, 1909; repr. New York, 1964).
A. Soergel, *Die englischen Maskenspiele* (Halle, 1882).
E. Welsford, *The Court Masque* (Cambridge, 1927).

SHORTER ACCOUNTS

F. Bacon, 'Of Masques and Triumphs', in *Essays* (1625; World's Classics, London, 1937).
R. Bayne, 'Masque and Pastoral', in *Cambridge History of English Literature*, vol. 6 (Cambridge, 1910).
E. K. Chambers, *The Elizabethan Stage*, 4 vols. (Oxford 1923), vol. 1, chs. 5 and 6.
H. A. Evans, Introduction to *English Masques* (London, 1897).
ed. C. H. Herford and P. and E. Simpson, *Ben Jonson: Life and Works*, 11 vols. (Oxford, 1925–52), vol. 2.
P. Simpson, 'The Masque', in *Shakespeare's England*, ed. C. T. Onions, etc., 2 vols. (Oxford, 1917), vol. 2.
M. Sullivan, *The Court Masque of James I* (New York, 1913).

LISTS AND DOCUMENTS

W. W. Greg, *A List of Masques, Pageants, etc. Supplementary to a List of English Plays* (London, 1902).
M. S. Steele, *Plays and Masques at Court during the Reigns of Elizabeth, James and Charles, 1558–1642* (New Haven, Conn., and London, 1926).

146   K. M. LEA

TEXTS

Allardyce Nicoll, in honour of, A Book of Masques, ed. T. J. B. Spencer and
S. Wells (Cambridge, 1967).
Anon., *Gesta Grayorum*, in Malone Society Reprints (Oxford, 1914), and
ed. D. Bland (Liverpool, 1968).
——, *Masque of Flowers* (1614): see Evans and Nicoll.
F. Beaumont, *The Masque of the Inner Temple and Gray's Inn* (1613): see Evans
and Nicoll.
W. Browne, *The Masque of the Inner Temple* (1615): see Evans and Nicoll.
T. Campion, *The Lords' Masque* (1613): see Evans and Nicoll.
T. Carew, *Coelum Britannicum* (1634); in *Collected Poems*, ed. R. Dunlap
(Oxford, 1949).
G. Chapman, *The Masque of the Middle Temple and Lincoln's Inn* (1613), in
The Comedies of George Chapman, ed. T. M. Parrott (London, 1913).
A. Cokayne, *A Masque presented at Bretbie* (1640), in *Dramatic Works*, ed.
J. Maidment and W. H. Logan (Edinburgh, 1874).
S. Daniel, *Works*, ed. A. B. Grosart, 5 vols. (London, 1885-6), vol. 3.
——, *The Vision of the Twelve Goddesses* (1604): see Evans and Nicoll.
W. Davenant, *Salmacida Spolia* (1640): see Evans and Nicoll.
ed. H. A. Evans, *English Masques* (London, 1897).
B. Jonson, *Life and Works*, ed. C. H. Herford and P. and E. Simpson, 11 vols.
(Oxford, 1925-52), vol. 2 (Introductions), vol. 7 (Texts), and vol. 10
(Commentary).
ed. M. Lefkowitz, *Trois masques à la cour de Charles Ier d'Angleterre* (*The
Triumph of Peace; The Triumphs of the Prince d'Amour; Britannia Triumphans*)
(Paris, Éditions du Centre National de la Recherche Scientifique, 1970).
J. Lyly, *The Complete Works of John Lyly*, ed. R. W. Bond, 3 vols. (London,
1902).
T. Middleton, *The Inner Temple Masque* (1619): see Nicoll.
W. Montague, *The Shepherd's Paradise* (1633) (London, 1639).
T. Nabbes, *The Spring's Glory* (1638): see Nicoll.
ed. S. Orgel, *Ben Jonson: The Complete Masques* (New Haven, Conn., 1969).
J. Shirley, *The Triumph of Peace* (1634): see Evans and Nicoll.
A. Townshend, *Albion's Triumph* and *Tempe Restored*, in his *Poems and Masks*,
ed. E. K. Chambers (Oxford, 1912).

BACKGROUND, COMMENT, AND CRITICISM

S. Anglo, 'The London Pageants for the Reception of Katharine of Aragon
in November 1501', *Journal of the Warburg and Courtauld Institutes* 26 (1963).
——, *The Evolution of the Early Tudor Disguising, Pageant and Masque* (Evans-
ton, Ill., 1968).
J. A. Barish, *Ben Jonson and the Language of Prose Comedy* (Cambridge, Mass.,
1960).
D. Bergeron, *English Civic Pageantry, 1558-1642* (London, 1971).
J. Chamberlain, *Letters*, ed. N. E. McClure, 2 vols. (Philadelphia, Pa., 1939).
E. K. Chambers, *The Medieval Stage*, 2 vols. (Oxford, 1903).

D. Cunningham, 'The Jonsonian Masque as a Literary Form', *ELH* 22 (1955).

E. J. Dent, *Foundations of English Opera* (Cambridge, 1928).

I.-S. Ewbank, ' "The Eloquence of Masques". A Retrospective View of Masque Criticism', *Ren. Dr.*, N.S. 1 (1968/9).

F. W. Fairholt, *Lord Mayors' Pageants* (London, 1843).

A. Feuillerat, *Documents relating to the Office of the Revels in the Time of Queen Elizabeth*, in *Materialien zur Kunde des älteren englischen Dramas*, Bd. 21 (Louvain, Leipzig, London, 1908; repr. Vaduz, Liechtenstein, 1963).

——, *Documents Relating to the Revels at Court in the Time of King Edward VI and Queen Mary* (the Loseley MSS.), in *Materialien*, Bd. 44 (Louvain, 1914; repr. Vaduz, Liechtenstein, 1963).

J. Finett, *Finetti Philoxenis* (London, 1656).

W. T. Furniss, 'Ben Jonson's Masques', in *Three Studies in the Renaissance* (New Haven, Conn., 1958).

E. Hall, *The Union of the Two Noble and Illustre Families of Lancastre and Yorke* (1548, repr. London, 1809; facsimile, Scolar Press, Menston, Yorks., 1970).

ed. J. Jacquot, *Les Fêtes de la Renaissance* (Centre National de la Recherche Scientifique, Paris, 1956).

Malone Society *Collections*, vol. 1.2 (Oxford, 1908).

——, vol. 1.3 (Oxford, 1909).

——, vol. 3 (Oxford, 1954).

J. Meagher, *Method and Meaning in Jonson's Masques* (South Bend, Ind., 1966).

J. Nichols, *The Progresses and Public Processions of Queen Elizabeth*, 3 vols. (London, 1788–1807; 2nd edn., 1823).

——, *The Progresses, Processions, and Magnificent Festivities of King James the First*, 4 vols. (London, 1828).

S. Orgel, *The Jonsonian Masque* (Cambridge, Mass., 1965).

T. M. Parrott, 'Comedy in the Court Masque, a Study of Ben Jonson's Contribution', *PQ* 20 (1941).

A. Solerti, *Le origini del melodramma* (Torino, 1903).

R. Strong, 'Inigo Jones and the Revival of Chivalry', *Apollo* (August 1967).

C. V. Wedgwood, 'The Last Masque', in *Truth and Opinion* (London, 1960).

S. Wells, *Literature and Drama, with Special Reference to Shakespeare and his Contemporaries* (London, 1970).

G. Wickham, *Early English Stages, 1300–1660*, vol. 1 (London, 1959); vol. 2, Part One (London, 1963), Part Two (London, 1972).

R. Withington, *English Pageantry* (Cambridge, Mass., 1918–20).

F. Yates, 'Elizabethan Chivalry: the Romance of the Accession Day Tilts', *Journal of the Warburg and Courtauld Institutes* 20 (1957).

SCENE

G. E. Bentley, *The Jacobean and Caroline Stage*, 7 vols. (Oxford, 1941–68), vol. 6.

L. B. Campbell, *Scenes and Machines on the English Stage* (Cambridge, 1933).

ed. J. Harris, S. Orgel, and R. Strong, *The King's Arcadia: Inigo Jones and the Stuart Court, Catalogue of the Quatercentenary Exhibition . . . 1973* (London, 1973).

I. Jones, *Designs by Inigo Jones for Masques and Plays at Court*, ed. P. Simpson and C. F. Bell (Oxford, 1924).

M. T. Jones-Davies, *Inigo Jones, Ben Jonson et le masque* (Paris, 1967).

A. Nicoll, *Stuart Masques and the Renaissance Stage* (London, 1937).

S. Orgel, ' "To make Boards Speak": Inigo Jones's Stage and the Jonsonian Masque', *Ren. Dr.*, n.s. 1 (1968).

S. Orgel and R. Strong, *Inigo Jones, The Theatre of the Stuart Court* (London, 1973).

P. Palme, *Triumph of Peace. A Study of the Whitehall Banqueting House* (London, 1957).

J. Summerson, *Inigo Jones* (Harmondsworth, 1966).

MUSIC AND DANCE

J. P. Cutts, 'Jacobean Masque and Stage Music', *Music and Letters* 35 (1957).

E. J. Dent, *Foundations of English Opera* (Cambridge, 1928).

O. Gombosi, 'Some Musical Aspects of the English Court Masque', *Journal of the American Musicological Society* I (Autumn 1948).

ed. J. Jacquot, *Les Fêtes de la Renaissance* (Centre National de la Recherche Scientifique, Paris, 1956).

W. J. Lawrence, 'Notes on a Collection of Masque Music', *Music and Letters* 3 (1922).

J. C. Meagher, 'The Dance and the Masques of Ben Jonson', *Journal of the Warburg and Courtauld Institutes* 25 (1962).

B. Pattison, *Music and Poetry of the English Renaissance* (London, 1948).

A. J. Sabol, *Songs and Dances for the Stuart Masque* (Providence, R.I., 1959).

——, *A Score for 'Lovers Made Men'* (Providence, R.I, 1963).

——, 'New Documents on Shirley's Masque', *Music and Letters* 47 (1966).

J. Stevens, *Music and Poetry in the Early Tudor Court* (London, 1961).

P. J. Willetts, 'Sir Nicholas Le Strange's Collection of Masque Music', *British Museum Quarterly* 29 (1965).

W. L. Woodfill, *Musicians in English Society from Elizabeth to Charles* (Princeton, N.J., 1953).

POETRY AND DRAMA

D. C. Allen, 'Ben Jonson and the Hieroglyphics', *PQ* 18 (1939).

A. H. Gilbert, *The Symbolic Personages in the Masques of Ben Jonson* (Durham, N.C., 1948).

——, 'The Function of the Masques in *Cynthia's Revels*', *PQ* 22 (1943).

D. J. Gordon, 'Ben Jonson's *Haddington Masque*: the Story and the Fable', *MLR* 47 (1947).

——, 'The Imagery of Ben Jonson's *The Masque of Blacknesse* and *The Masque of Beautie*', *Journal of the Warburg and Courtauld Institutes* 6 (1943).

——, *'Hymenaei*: Ben Jonson's Masque of Union', *Journal of the Warburg and Courtauld Institutes* 8 (1945).

——, 'Poet and Architect: the Intellectual Setting of the Quarrel between Ben Jonson and Inigo Jones', *Journal of the Warburg and Courtauld Institutes* 12 (1949).

——, 'Le "Masque mémorable" de Chapman', see Jacquot, *Les Fêtes de la Renaissance.*

D. T. Starnes and E. W. Talbert, *Classical Myth and Legend in Renaissance Dictionaries* (Chapel Hill, N.C., 1955).

E. W. Talbert, 'New Light on Ben Jonson's Workmanship', *SP* 40 (1943).

——, 'The Interpretation of Jonson's Courtly Spectacles', *PMLA* 61 (1946).

C. F. Wheeler, *Classical Mythology in the Plays, Masques and Poems of Ben Jonson* (Princeton, N.J., 1938).

MASQUES IN PLAYS

I.-S. Ewbank, 'These Pretty Devices', in *A Book of Masques in Honour of Allardyce Nicoll* (Cambridge, 1967).

A. Nicoll, 'Shakespeare and the Court Masque', *Shakespeare Jahrbuch* 94 (1958).

10. DAVENANT, DRYDEN, LEE, and OTWAY

H. NEVILLE DAVIES

WILLIAM Davenant's interrupted career as a dramatist belongs to two periods, each of about a dozen years or so, one before he reached his mid-thirties, and the other after he was fifty. During the time that he was, as we may suppose, in his prime, theatres in England were closed. That a man who was above all a practical man of the theatre should have been frustrated in this way was a wry twist of fate, and it is similarly ironic that Davenant now holds a secure place in the library having become virtually unknown on the stage. When, we may wonder, was one of his plays last given in a commercial theatre, and when will one be performed there again? Yet two large biographical studies were published in the 1930s, a critical study of his comedy was published thirty years later, and no book on the drama of his period, or periods, can overlook Davenant's immense importance. *The Wits* (acted 1633/4; published 1636 and, in a revised form, 1673), Davenant's best play, enjoyed by Charles I and a favourite with Pepys and Restoration audiences, is easily available to modern readers (in its unrevised form) in a World's Classics anthology, and could well succeed with a university audience; but it is doubtful whether any of the other plays has much chance, now, of a performance. As it happens, Davenant's most considerable work and, as far as its title goes, his most famous, is a long, heroic, unfinished epic-romance, *Gondibert* (pronounced 'Gundibart'; 1651) written during those theatrically barren middle years, and constructed on the model of a five-act play. Dryden thought it 'rather a play in narration . . . than a heroic poem' and it seems that the energy of a dramatist *manqué* found release in its composition. But it is not just the form of *Gondibert* that recalls the drama. So revealingly does it illuminate the taste of Restoration audiences and the concerns of the heroic play that no serious student of Davenant's work for the stage, or of the drama that he influenced, can afford to neglect it. For a similar reason, its Preface (published in advance of the poem, Paris 1650), the first long preface of its type in English and a model for Dryden, is, with Hobbes's rejoinder, an important document. J. E. Spingarn's collection of *Critical Essays of the Seven-*

teenth Century, volume 2, *1650–1685*, presents both preface and reply. The modern neglect of *Gondibert* itself, once excusable because the only easily available text of its almost 7,000 lines was dauntingly hard on the eye, can now be rectified. A handsomely printed critical edition by D. F. Gladish was published in 1971. A complementary volume of *The Shorter Poems* (1972), edited by A. M. Gibbs, will also interest the reader of the plays because it includes, and excellently annotates, eighty-one songs from the plays and masques.

The standard collection of Davenant's plays is the five-volume set edited by J. Maidment and W. H. Logan in 1872–4, two hundred years after the important folio collection that appeared four years after Davenant's death. It goes without saying that this edition is now out of date and needs to be supplemented by a number of other volumes. The most important of these is Christopher Spencer's edition of a manuscript acquired by Yale University in 1953, *Davenant's 'Macbeth' from the Yale Manuscript: An Edition, with a Discussion of the Relation of Davenant's Text to Shakespeare's*. Another Shakespeare adaptation, *The Law Against Lovers* (acted 1662), an ingenious attempt to combine the main plot of *Measure for Measure* with the Beatrice and Benedick story from *Much Ado About Nothing*, has been reproduced in facsimile from the folio *Works* of 1673 and provided with a useful, short introduction by A. M. Gibbs. The most celebrated of Davenant's adaptations, however, is undoubtedly *The Tempest* (acted 1667; published 1670) altered in collaboration with Dryden who probably did most of the work. It is famous for the addition of Hippolito to the dramatis personae, an addition for which Dryden gave the credit to his senior colleague:

Sir *William D'avenant* as he was a man of quick and piercing imagination, soon found that somewhat might be added to the Design of *Shakespear*, of which neither *Fletcher* nor *Suckling* [who had imitated *The Tempest*] had ever thought: and therefore to put the last hand to it, he design'd the Counterpart to *Shakespear's* Plot, namely that of a Man who had never seen a Woman; that by this means those two Characters of Innocence and Love might the more illustrate and commend each other. This excellent contrivance he was pleas'd to communicate to me, and to desire my assistance in it. I confess that from the very first moment it so pleas'd me, that I never writ any thing with more delight.

Additions necessitated compensating deletions, and it has been calculated that only about 31 per cent of Shakespeare's play was carried over into the adaptation. The best edition of this Davenant–Dryden production is in volume 10 of the California edition of Dryden's *Works* (see under Dryden). If other editions are used, special care must be taken not to confuse this particular adaptation with the more popular 'operatic *Tempest*' (acted and published 1674), a revision by Thomas Shadwell (1642–92), and possibly some others, that was regularly mistaken for it in the nineteenth century. It is the revised version that Noyes has described as 'the most popular play of the Restoration period'. Undoubtedly *some* of the credit should go to Davenant. Shakespeare and Fletcher's *The Two Noble Kinsmen* was also adapted by Davenant as *The Rivals* (acted 1664): the printed quarto of 1668 has been reproduced in facsimile with an introductory note by Kenneth Muir. Facsimiles of a number of Davenant's other plays have been announced as forthcoming by the Scolar Press. The extent to which Davenant's alterations influenced productions of Shakespeare, even when his adaptations had themselves been superseded or relegated, may be seen by examining the Cornmarket Press facsimiles of adaptations and acting versions (the first series without introductions, London, 1969, the second series with introductions, London, 1970–73). In his 1853 *Macbeth*, Charles Kean not only retained supernatural operatic *divertissements* inherited ultimately from Davenant, but even attempted to justify them. In *The Tempest*, Davenant's 'excellent contrivance', Hippolito, remained on the stage until 1838. George R. Guffey's collection of four texts, *After 'The Tempest'*, includes the Davenant–Dryden text (1670), the 'operatic' revision (1674), Thomas Duffett's burlesque, *The Mock-Tempest* (1673), and David Garrick's libretto for J. C. Smith's music, *The Tempest, An Opera* (1756), not to be confused with Garrick's acting version of Shakespeare's original play.

That Davenant's work should have retained its foothold in the theatre longest in the context of productions of Shakespeare, productions that many audiences must have regarded simply as legitimate presentations of Shakespeare's plays with never a thought of Davenant, seems almost symbolically appropriate when we recall that Davenant regarded himself as Shakespeare's child. There seems to be no good reason to disbelieve the pleasant tale that Davenant's Christian name was derived from that of his godfather, that his godfather was a customer at the Davenants' inn at Oxford who travelled between London and Stratford, and even that this customer was Shakespeare. But to suppose that William was the natural son of Shakespeare and Mrs. Davenant is to give credence to an altogether more elaborate story and one unsupported by any evidence other than Davenant's possibly inherited theatrical talent. We are wise to be cautious about falling victim to a tall story. The Gallic affectation of an apostrophe in the spelling of his name (D'Avenant) certainly demonstrates an attempt to rise above a humble origin. His knight-hood, however, at the Siege of Gloucester in 1643 was no affectation. Davenant served the crown well, and quite apart from theatrical and literary achievement, his career affords biographers with much exciting material: high office, imprisonment, and three marriages. Of the two major biographical studies, by Harbage and Nethercot, the former focuses more sharply on his work as a dramatist. The critical study of the comedies is by H. S. Collins.

In the history of the English stage, Davenant has unique importance as the only significant dramatist to span the Stuart, Caroline, Commonwealth, and Restoration periods. His ability to adjust to changing circumstances shows the greatest resourcefulness. He was a remarkably successful innovator, but he also transmitted theatrical expertise and tradition to Restoration dramatists and managers after the long and damaging break of the Interregnum. John Dryden's account of this debt to a man 'whose memory I love and honour', in the essay 'Of Heroick Plays' prefixed to *The Conquest of Granada* and published the year before the Davenant folio appeared, is memorable. In a converted tennis court at Lincoln's Inn Fields, Davenant managed the Duke of York's company, one of the two companies of actors in early Restoration London, putting on a programme of old and new plays. His makeshift theatre with its proscenium arch, use of complex scenery and machinery, and regular employment of actresses, was a new departure for public entertainment in England. Its replacement, the purpose-built Dorset Gardens theatre designed for Davenant by Wren, did not open until 1671, when it was run by Davenant's widow and his leading actor, Thomas Betterton; but it was, in effect, a monument to Davenant's energy, vision, and practicality. The new style of Restoration theatre is described in Leslie Hotson's *The Commonwealth and Restoration Stage* and Montague Summers's *The Restoration Theatre*. J. H. Wilson has given the fullest account of Restoration actresses in *All the King's Ladies*.

Another innovation credited to Davenant is the introduction of opera into England. To circumvent Commonwealth legislation against the performance of plays, Davenant publicly presented *The First Dayes Entertainment at Rutland House by Declamations and Musick: after the manner of the Ancients* in 1656, more or less a costumed debate with music. This was followed later the same year by *The Siege of Rhodes* (published 1656, and in an expanded form together with a second part, 1663), often regarded as the first English opera, and by Dryden as the first heroic play. The music has not survived, though

John Webb's designs for the scenery have. One of them is reproduced in Ann-Mari Hedbäck's authoritative edition. *The Cruelty of the Spaniards in Peru* and *Sir Francis Drake* presented at The Cockpit, one of the old pre-Commonwealth theatres, in 1658 and 1659, similarly avoided censorship. But Davenant's interest in musical drama was not merely in an ingenious subterfuge to mount quasi-dramatic performances. He had had similar plans in 1639, and had written masques for the Caroline court (see Chapter 9), collaborating with Inigo Jones, and becoming, to all intents and purposes, Ben Jonson's successor as Poet Laureate. E. J. Dent's *Foundations of English Opera* (1928) gives the fullest broad account, but it is a pioneer work by a distinguished scholar now rather out of date and unfortunately not yet superseded. Eugene Haun's *But Hark! More Harmony* (1971) is a useful specialized study of the libretti of Restoration opera. Texts of *The Cruelty of the Spaniards in Peru* and *Sir Francis Drake* are to be found only in Acts III and IV of Davenant's *The Play-house to be Lett*, a medley of plays acted in 1663 that includes in Act V yet another of Davenant's innovations, a burlesque of the Antony and Cleopatra story, the first burlesque on the Restoration stage. For a history of the form, see V. C. Clinton-Baddeley's *The Burlesque Tradition in the English Theatre after 1660*.

Thomas Duffett is specially remembered for three lively burlesques, one of which, *Psyche Debauch'd* (acted 1675, published 1678; after Shadwell's *Psyche*, acted earlier in 1675) makes fun of operatic conventions, while another, a burlesque of Settle's *The Empress of Morocco* (acted 1673, published 1674), includes ridicule of *Macbeth*, a play which Davenant had turned into a musical spectacular with flying witches. Duffett's most amusing piece is *The Mock-Tempest* (acted 1674, published 1675), which transposes the action of the 'operatic' *Tempest* of 1674 from its Shakespearian setting on an enchanted island to Bridewell, and transforms Prospero, Peachum-like, into a jailer. All three burlesques have been edited by R. E. Dilorenzo. The best-known of Restoration burlesques is *The Rehearsal* (performed by the King's company in 1661, published 1672 etc., 'with amendments and large additions' 1675) first drafted in the early 1660s by George Villiers, the second Duke of Buckingham (1628–87) assisted by others, Thomas Sprat, Samuel Butler, and Martin Clifford possibly among them. By representing the rehearsal of an absurd mock-heroic play the authors satirized, by parody and caricature, the heroic play as it was established by Davenant and exploited by Dryden. Mr. Bayes, the supposed dramaturge of the mock play, was originally intended as a satirical portrait of Davenant, but became instead a portrait of Dryden. The change has symbolic force. John Dryden, already mentioned as Davenant's collaborator and eulogist, was in many ways Davenant's successor. But with Dryden we move to an unquestionably major figure in English literature, and the most considerable literary man of the Restoration period. Of the many modern editions of *The Rehearsal*, that by Montague Summers is particularly useful, and that in Simon Trussler's anthology, *Burlesque Plays of the Eighteenth Century*, conveniently available.

Dryden wrote twenty-three plays counting his adaptation of Shakespeare's *Troilus and Cressida* and the operatic pieces. In five more he collaborated in turn with his brother-in-law, Sir Robert Howard (1626–98), with William Cavendish, Duke of Newcastle (1593–1676), with Davenant, and with Nathaniel Lee; and he may have contributed to the anonymous *The Mistaken Husband* (acted 1674, published 1675). At the very end of his life he wrote a song and a masque, as well as the prologue and epilogue, for an adaptation of Fletcher's *The Pilgrim*. The corpus thus makes a substantial and varied collection, and prospective readers are often uncertain where to begin.

The best introduction to Dryden's plays is, without doubt, provided by the two elegant and scholarly volumes in the attractive Curtain Playwrights series, one volume of comedies and tragicomedies (*Secret Love*, *Sir Martin Mar-All*, *An Evening's Love*, and *Marriage à-la-Mode*) all from the short period 1667–73, and one of tragedies and heroic plays (*The Indian Emperor*, *Aureng-Zebe*, *All for Love*, and *Don Sebastian*) spanning the whole of Dryden's career. Unfortunately, these volumes are too expensive to be bought by most students, though in selection and in presentation they are distinctly preferable to the likely alternative, George Saintsbury's two much-used Mermaid volumes (vol. 1, *The Conquest of Granada*, parts 1 and 2, *Marriage à-la-Mode*, and *Aureng-Zebe*; vol. 2, *All for Love*, *The Spanish Friar*, *Albion and Albanius*, and *Don Sebastian*). The Curtain Playwrights volumes provide a critical, old-spelling text, prepared by Fredson Bowers, that is authoritative and easy to read, substantive variants being presented without undue fuss. *The Indian Emperor* has special textual interest, and Bowers bases his text on the Trinity College manuscript of 1665 rather than on the first quarto (1667) which the 'California' edition selects as copy text. The rights and wrongs of this issue defy simple explanation or a totally acceptable solution, and the readers for whom Bowers has prepared his text are unlikely to appreciate the attempted justification with which it is buttressed. But the textual apparatus is not, after all, compulsory reading. The other textual decision of note is the sensible omission of dedicatory epistles, but not prefaces, except 'A Defense of An Essay of Dramatic Poesie' which Dryden published in the second quarto of *The Indian Emperor*.

The reader who wishes to have the plays complete is faced with a problem. The finely printed six volumes of plays and *Of Dramatick Poesie* edited by Montague Summers would provide what is wanted were they not unreliable and flawed by eccentricity. They must simply be discounted. Well-preserved copies, their green spines not faded by sunlight, their marbled boards not rubbed by normal use, their pages unopened, are valuable possessions which readers are often discouraged from handling. The only other complete, post-eighteenth century edition is that included in what was for a long time the standard edition of Dryden's works, originally edited by Sir Walter Scott in 1808, and then revised by George Saintsbury (1882–92). Needless to say, this is without benefit of modern scholarship, and a reader of *The Tempest*, for instance, using this edition would, as we have seen, be unwittingly reading Shadwell's adaptation of the Davenant–Dryden *Tempest* instead of the Davenant–Dryden version itself. It is not just the annotation, then, that is out of date. Work on a full modern edition is in progress at the University of California, and this I have already referred to in passing as the 'California' edition. It is to be a complete edition of Dryden's works, and nine volumes (8–16) have been set aside for plays. So far, the first nine plays (vols. 8–10) have been published, and also *Of Dramatick Poesie: An Essay*, which appears in volume 17 (*Prose 1668–1691*). The text is a reliable one, prepared by computer, and supplied with an elaborate textual apparatus; and there are extensive commentaries and notes. The project as a whole is a major work of collaborative scholarship, but progress has been slow.

For texts and annotation for which Scott–Saintsbury is inadequate, which Bowers and Beaurline have not selected, and which the 'California' edition has not yet reached, the reader must shop around. A complete, chronological list of the plays may make this easier. (Titles are followed by date of first performance. Dates of first publication and facsimiles are in brackets.)

The Wild Gallant 1663 (1669). Comedy.
The Rival Ladies 1664 (1664; facsimile announced by The Scolar Press). Tragicomedy.

The Indian Queen (with Sir Robert Howard) 1664 (1665). Heroic tragedy.
Operatic version *c.* 1695 with music by Henry and Daniel Purcell.

The Indian Emperor 1665 (1667; facsimile, Menston, 1971). Heroic tragedy
written as a sequel to the previous play. [2a]

Secret Love 1667 (1668). Tragicomedy. [2b]

Sir Martin Mar-All (with the Duke of Newcastle) 1667 (1668). Comedy. [2b]

The Tempest; or, the Enchanted Island (with Davenant) 1667 (1670; facsimile,
London, 1969); revised by Thomas Shadwell and others (?)—the
'operatic *Tempest*'—1674 (1674; facsimile 1969), and in this form revived
c. 1695 with music formerly attributed to Henry Purcell. Adapted from
Shakespeare.

An Evening's Love 1668 (1671). Comedy. Often known by its subtitle, *The
Mock Astrologer.* [2b]

Tyrannic Love 1669 (1670; expanded dedication 1672). Heroic tragedy.

[*Present limit of the 'California' edition*]

The Conquest of Granada, part 1 1670 ⎱ ('1671' for ?1672). Heroic tragedy.
                        part 2 1671 ⎰ [3a]

Marriage à-la-Mode 1672 (1673). Comedy. [1c, 2b, 3a]

The Assignation 1672 (1673). Comedy.

Amboyna 1673 (1673). Heroic tragedy.

The Mistaken Husband (anon. One scene by Dryden?) 1674 (1675). Comedy.
Adapted from a lost play by Alexander Brome?

The State of Innocence. Unacted. Written *c.* 1674 (1677; facsimile announced
by The Scolar Press). 'An opera. Written in heroique verse' without
music. (Edward Ecclestone's *Noah's Flood* (1679) is a sequel.)

Aureng-Zebe 1675 (1676). Heroic tragedy. [1b, 2a, 3a]

All for Love 1677 (1678; facsimiles, San Francisco, 1929, and Menston,
1969). Blank verse tragedy. [1a. 2a. 3b]

The Kind Keeper 1678 (1680). Comedy.

Oedipus (with Lee) 1678 (1679). Blank verse tragedy.

Troilus and Cressida; or, Truth Found Too Late 1679 (1679; facsimile, London,
1969). Adapted from Shakespeare.

The Spanish Friar 1680 (1681). Comedy. [3b]

The Duke of Guise (with Lee) 1682 (1683). Blank verse tragedy.

Albion and Albanius 1685 (1685). Allegorical opera: music by Louis Grabu
(London, 1687). [3b]

Don Sebastian 1689 (1690). Blank verse tragedy. [2a. 3b]

Amphitryon 1690 (1690). Comedy.

King Arthur 1691 (1691). Dramatic opera: music by Henry Purcell.

Cleomenes (? with Thomas Southerne, 1660–1746) 1692 (1692). Blank verse
tragedy.

Love Triumphant 1694 (1694). Tragicomedy.

The Pilgrim (Vanbrugh's adaptation of Fletcher's comedy to which Dryden
contributed 'Song of a Scholar and his Mistress' and 'The Secular
Masque') 1700 (1700).

[1a *Five Restoration Tragedies*, edited by B. Dobrée (World's Classics, London, 1928); 1b *Five Heroic Plays*, edited by B. Dobrée (World's Classics, London, 1960); 1c *Restoration Comedies*, edited by D. Davison (World's Classics, London, 1970). 2a John Dryden, *Four Tragedies*, edited by L. A. Beaurline and Fredson Bowers (Chicago, Ill., and London, 1967); 2b John Dryden, *Four Comedies*, edited by L. A. Beaurline and Fredson Bowers (Chicago, Ill., and London, 1967). 3a–3b *Selected Plays of John Dryden*, edited by G. Saintsbury, 2 vols. (Mermaid edition, London, 1904).]

Dryden's contributions to *The Pilgrim* are included in the Oxford English Texts edition of his poems by James Kinsley, and may be read *in situ* in *The Complete Works of Sir John Vanbrugh*, edited by B. Dobrée, vol. 2. The two plays written in collaboration with Lee are to be found in Lee's *Works* edited by Stroup and Cooke (see below). The disadvantage of using Scott–Saintsbury rather than this edition is well illustrated by Anne Davidson Ferry when she quotes Lee's commendatory poem prefixed to Dryden's *The State of Innocence*. (See *Milton and The Miltonic Dryden*, Cambridge, Mass., 1968, pp. 7–8.) Dryden based his work on *Paradise Lost* and Lee commented, according to Mrs. Ferry:

> To the dead bard your fame a little owes
> For Milton did the wealthy mind disclose,
> And rudely cast what you could well dispose . . .
> He was the golden ore, which you refined.

Had she consulted Stroup and Cooke's edition, Mrs. Ferry would have found 'wealthy mine' and 'His was the golden ore', and the passage would have made sense.

Besides being included in various anthologies, *Aureng-Zebe* and *All for Love* have been edited in single, annotated volumes. The fullest edition of *All for Love* is Arthur Sale's (1957). Annotation is extensive, taking up over half the volume, and including quotations indicating Dryden's indebtedness to Shakespeare and Samuel Daniel. But Sale is not a scholarly editor, and the running commentary on the action, the characters, and the quality of the poetry is tiresome. Another curious edition is that by Benjamin W. Griffith (1961), designed to give the reader the impression of the play in performance. It could have been much better done, and omits Dryden's Preface, presumably because prefaces suggest a printed book rather than stage action. The latest edition is by David M. Vieth, in the Regents Restoration Drama Series. It has a sound text and a sensible introduction, but rather sparse annotation. *Aureng-Zebe* (the trisyllabic name is that of a seventeenth-century Mogul

emperor of India) is available in the same series, edited by Frederick
M. Link. Again there are some notes and a helpful introduction.

In spite of there being no properly adequate edition, *All for Love*,
Dryden's version of the popular Antony and Cleopatra story, is far
and away his best-known, most studied play, and probably the most
famous English tragedy written between the time of *Samson Agonistes*
and *Murder in the Cathedral*. Unlike Milton's play and Eliot's, it was
written for the commercial London theatre, though in the present
century it has been only rarely performed. Until the nineteenth
century, *All for Love* was frequently given, its popularity possibly
being the major factor in keeping Shakespeare's *Antony and Cleopatra*
off the stage: the first *recorded* performance of Shakespeare's play is of
Garrick's 1758 abridgement. Even Henry Brooke's unacted, radical
adaptation of Shakespeare's tragedy (written between 1740 and
1778) makes use of *All for Love*. Nowadays, comparison of the
Dryden and Shakespeare plays is a standard academic exercise, one
of John Bailey's contributions to the *Times Literary Supplement*
(1 January 1904; reprinted in his *Poets and Poetry* (1911), and slightly
abridged in *Twentieth Century Interpretations of 'All for Love'*, edited by
Bruce King) being an accomplished example. A different type of
comparison is that attempted by F. R. Leavis in *Scrutiny* 5 (reprinted
in abridged form in B. King's anthology) who rather unfairly uses
Dryden's Cydnus speech as a foil to demonstrate the qualities of
Shakespeare's Cydnus speech, unfairly because Leavis seeks only to
notice what is lacking in Dryden, and makes no attempt to see either
speech within its dramatic context. Hazlitt, on the other hand, was
well aware of the dramatic context of Shakespeare's lines, as he
revealingly shows in *The Characters of Shakespear's Plays* (1817), but
his grasp of this probably came from seeing what happened when the
speech was displaced in the 1813 production of *Antony and Cleopatra* at
Covent Garden which combined, not for the last time on the stage,
Shakespeare's play and Dryden's. (The text of the 1813 production
as it was when the production opened has been reprinted in facsimile (1970).) In general, Hazlitt found Shakespeare's style and
Dryden's incompatible, a point worth pursuing since Dryden's play
was avowedly written in imitation of Shakespeare's style, though
what he meant by 'imitation' is a difficult matter: see H. D.
Weinbrot, *The Formal Strain*, where the subject is helpfully discussed,
though without explicit reference to *All for Love*. The title of Dryden's
play alludes, though I have never seen it acknowledged, to the first
scene of *The Two Gentlemen of Verona*, and there are throughout frequent borrowings from Shakespeare's plays, by no means only the

Roman ones. It helps to recognize them, for through their allusive quality Dryden expands the meaning of what he writes. The non-Shakespearian sources also repay looking into, particularly the earlier Antony and Cleopatra plays, if Dryden's dramatic design is to be understood. Vieth's introduction to his Regents Restoration Drama edition provides a guide to work on the sources, and Mario Praz's *The Neurotic in Literature* draws attention to Dryden's use of traditional elements in the presentation of Antony's melancholy.

The criticism of *All for Love* has special interest because there is a good deal of vigorous disagreement about how successful the play is; whether, for instance, it is a coherent poetic drama or a play decorated with poetry, whether there is a discrepancy between moral intention and achievement, whether its confrontations are merely mechanical or compelling and lucid. Vieth's edition raises these issues, and some of the essays to which he refers are represented in King's anthology. Bruce King himself in the introduction to his anthology writes about *All for Love* more enthusiastically than he had in his earlier *Dryden's Major Plays*, where he reacts against the way in which *All for Love* has been admired at the expense of denigrating or ignoring some of the best of Dryden's other plays. But King's earlier point should not be forgotten. The other plays *have* been neglected, and *Dryden's Major Plays* is a good introduction to them. Among other recent books, Arthur C. Kirsch's *Dryden's Heroic Drama* on plays up to and including *Aureng-Zebe*, and Frank H. Moore's *The Nobler Pleasure*, on the comedies, are particularly valuable.

Perhaps the major difficulty for a modern reader of Dryden's plays is to judge accurately the tone of the heroic plays. Some critics, notably Bruce King and his teacher D. W. Jefferson, see in them a considerable element of mockery, taking them to be plays that prompt our sophisticated laughter. Other critics see Dryden's heroic plays as wholly serious in purpose. With the heroic drama as with any literary form, or other cultural phenomenon, that has very strongly marked characteristics, and that rises suddenly to fashionable prominence to enjoy a brief but intense popularity, it is difficult, perhaps impossible, to tell where the boundaries lie between stylish exploitation, parody, and ridicule. The attitudes of the audience may be diverse, depending on the level of sophistication, and even on the date. The time factor can be vital, with a few months making all the difference between one response and another. In such a situation the intention of the writer may well not be simple. Reflection on a cultural fad which one has experienced at first hand, like the James Bond craze for instance, soon exposes the nature of the difficulty.

If the drama has all too frequently been neglected, the prologues and epilogues—around a hundred of them—with which Dryden equipped his own and other people's plays are enjoyed by all who take pleasure in Dryden's occasional verse. Dryden is the unrivalled master of the form, and these verses are his most effective writing for the theatre. Though not usually 'dramatic' in themselves, they show his concern for dramatic poesy, and the nine Oxford prologues and epilogues in particular show their author's genuine respect for an intelligent critical response to plays:

> *London* likes grossly, but this nicer Pit
> Examines, Fathoms all the depths of Wit:
> The ready Finger lays on every Blot,
> Knows what shou'd justly please, and what shou'd not.

Readers of the non-dramatic poetry who remember only the lines of self-recrimination from the ode on Anne Killigrew,

> O wretched We! why were we hurry'd down
> This lubrique and adult'rate age,
> (Nay added fat Pollutions of our own)
> T'increase the steaming Ordures of the Stage?

and those prologues and epilogues that berate the fashionable London audience for silliness and poor taste, are apt to undervalue Dryden's commitment to the stage.

There is a handsome critical edition of the prologues and epilogues by W. B. Gardner, and Mark Van Doren has written enthusiastically about them in his study of *The Poetry of John Dryden* (1920, reissued as *John Dryden: a Study of his Poetry*, 1946), comparing Dryden's verses with those of other sixteenth-, seventeenth-, and eighteenth-century dramatists. For further guidance on Dryden's poetry, see James Kinsley's chapter in *English Poetry* edited by A. E. Dyson, a companion to the present volume.

Dryden's repute as a critic and prose-writer also exceeds his repute as a dramatist, but the two activities are closely linked because much of the critical writing takes the form of prefaces to plays. All too often it is assumed that the printing of a play merely provided Dryden with a convenient vehicle in which a largely unrelated critical essay could achieve publication. In fact, the context matters in many cases, and Eugene Waith has even argued for a significant relationship between heroic dedicatory epistles and heroic plays ('The Voice of Mr Bayes').

Some of the more important critical prefaces to plays have

independent titles and can therefore be referred to either by their own title or by the title of the accompanying play. A list of these pieces may help to avoid confusion:

'A Defence of *An Essay of Dramatic Poesy*' prefaces early copies of the second quarto of *The Indian Emperor* (1668).

'Of Heroic Plays: An Essay' prefaces *The Conquest of Granada* ('1671').

'Defence of the Epilogue: or an Essay on the Dramatic Poetry of the Last Age' is from the same volume, but was dropped from the fourth edition (1687) and not reprinted until Congreve's edition (1717).

'The Author's Apology for Heroic Poetry and Poetic Licence' prefaces *The State of Innocence* (1677).

'The Grounds of Criticism in Tragedy' is the second and principal part of the preface to *Troilus and Cressida* (1679).

Two more critical documents relating to drama, but which do not preface plays, still remain. First, some manuscript notes (now destroyed) written towards the end of 1677 on the end-papers of Thomas Rymer's *The Tragedies of the Last Age* which had just been published. They show Dryden's initial reaction to a book that greatly impressed him, and were first published in the 1711 edition of Beaumont and Fletcher, and then in Johnson's Life of Dryden (1779). Known by the editorial title 'Heads of an Answer to Rymer' they have been much and variously interpreted by modern scholars. See, for instance, R. D. Hume's *Dryden's Criticism*. The second item is Dryden's only independently published work of criticism, and the only one that he troubled to revise. *Of Dramatick Poesie: An Essay* ('1668' for ?1667, facsimile, Menston, 1969; revised 1684, reprinted 1693) has always been popular. The three editions during Dryden's lifetime, extensive scholarly investigation since the eighteenth century, and frequent new editions all attest to that. L. C. Gatto's 'An Annotated Bibliography of Critical Thought Concerning Dryden's *Essay of Dramatic Poesy*' shows the interest that the *Essay* has provoked, though since Donald Davie's unappreciative 'Dramatic Poetry: Dryden's Conversation Piece' (1952), there has been a tendency to grumble that the *Essay* has been extravagantly praised. Besides the 'California' edition, based on the '1668' text, which provides a good account of scholarly investigation into the *Essay*, there is an edition by James T. Boulton, based on the 1684 text, that also includes Sir Robert Howard's Preface to *The Great Favourite*, which attacks the *Essay*, and Dryden's 'Defence of an Essay' which replies to the attack. In D. D. Arundell's *Dryden and Howard, 1664–68* (1929) all the publications in the Dryden–Howard controversy are conveniently collected. Although many aspects of the *Essay* have been

subjected to detailed study, the strategy of its quasi-dramatic form
has received far too little attention.

Readers of Dryden's prose will find George Watson's '*Of Dramatic
Poesy*' *and Other Critical Essays* a convenient though incomplete collection. Some items relevant to students of the drama must be found
elsewhere, for instance, the interesting dedicatory letter accompanying *King Arthur* which is printed in the big Scott–Saintsbury edition.
But even Scott-Saintsbury is not absolutely complete. The frequently
quoted dedicatory letter signed by Henry Purcell, but written on his
behalf by Dryden, that prefaces the published score of *The
Prophetess; or, The History of Diocletian* (performed and published
1690), a dramatic opera with music by Purcell and a text adapted
by Betterton from Fletcher and Massinger, can be most conveniently
read in Roswell G. Ham's 'Dryden and *The Music of The Prophetesse*
1691'. A complete, uniform edition would indeed make things simpler
for readers of Dryden.

Nathaniel Lee, Dryden's younger collaborator in *Oedipus* and *The
Duke of Guise*, is remembered almost entirely as a dramatist, though
he also published verses which include the eulogy on Dryden's *The
State of Innocence* quoted some pages back; Dryden duly returned the
compliment by praising one of Lee's plays, *The Rival Queens*. The
standard complete edition is *The Works of Nathaniel Lee* edited in two
volumes by Thomas B. Stroup and Arthur L. Cooke. It incorporates
a short biography, editorial notes and introductions, Lee's few occasional poems, and the thirteen plays (including the two written with
Dryden). If, as Tom Brown asserts, Lee composed a twenty-five-act
play in Bedlam it has not survived. Single-volume editions of the two
best-known of Lee's plays are included in the Regents Restoration
Drama Series, *The Rival Queens* (first performed and published 1677;
facsimile, Menston, 1971) edited by P. F. Vernon, and *Lucius Junius
Brutus* (acted 1680, published 1681) edited by John Loftis. *Sophonisba*
(acted 1675, published 1676) is conveniently included in Bonamy
Dobrée's anthology, *Five Heroic Plays*. Other editions, as well as books
and articles about Lee, are listed in A. L. McLeod's 'A Nathaniel
Lee Bibliography, 1670–1960'.

Both Dryden's and Lee's plays were provided with music by their
great contemporary, Henry Purcell (1659–95). Much of this is
available in *The Works of Henry Purcell*, a multi-volume publication
of The Purcell Society, and it should not be neglected. There are
six relevant volumes:

Volume 9, edited by Frederick J. Bridge and John Pointer (London,

1900) revised by Margaret Laurie (London, 1961), provides the
musical score for the dramatic opera *Dioclesian* together with the
'Purcell' dedicatory letter written by Dryden.

Volume 16, *Dramatic Music—Part I*, edited by Alan Gray (London,
1906), includes the music for *Amphitryon*, *Aureng-Zebe*, and *Cleomenes*.

Volume 19, edited by E. J. Dent (London, 1912), supplies Daniel and
Henry Purcell's music for the operatic revival (*c.* 1695) of *The Indian
Queen*, and the new music, formerly attributed to Henry Purcell, for
the revival of the 'operatic' *Tempest* (also *c.* 1695).

Volume 20, *Dramatic Music—Part II*, edited by Alan Gray (London,
1916), includes the music for the 1691 revival of *The Indian Emperor*,
and music for the original productions of *Love Triumphant* and *The
Massacre at Paris*.

Volume 21, *Dramatic Music—Part III*, edited by Alan Gray (London,
1917), includes music for *Oedipus*, *Sophonisba*, *The Spanish Friar*,
Theodosius, and *Tyrannic Love*.

Volume 26, *King Arthur*, is edited by Dennis Arundell (London,
1928), and revised by Margaret Laurie (London, 1971). Dr. Laurie
has also edited a vocal score, *The Music in 'King Arthur'* (London,
1972).

Robert Etheridge Moore's *Henry Purcell and the Restoration Theatre*
analyses both libretti and music, and is of great interest to the
student of Restoration drama. The standard works on Purcell are
by F. B. Zimmerman: *Henry Purcell, 1659–1695: His Life and Times*,
and *An Analytical Catalogue of his Music*; a critical study is expected.
The popularity of Purcell's music has given unexpected currency to
some of Dryden's words, for example, in *The Shipwreck* (1780), yet
another derivative of the Davenant–Dryden *Tempest*, this time for
puppets, and in the 1842 Covent Garden *Comus* (see A. Thaler,
'Milton in the Theatre', *Studies in Philology* 17, 1920), where, in both
cases, *King Arthur* provided words and music.

Thomas Otway is, like Lee, known primarily as a tragic dramatist,
like Lee died young and in miserable circumstances, and, like Lee,
was a failed actor. It is natural to compare the two men, and the
standard biography of each of them is an interesting attempt to
present a joint study, Roswell G. Ham's *Otway and Lee. Biography
from a Baroque Age*. Otway's *Works*, which comprise ten plays, some
effective poetry including a prologue to Lee's *Constantine the Great* that
may be by Otway, and an agonized series of six love letters, have
been edited in two volumes by J. C. Ghosh. The letters are addressed
to Elizabeth Barry, Rochester's mistress and the greatest actress of

the Restoration period. Ghosh's edition includes an introduction, a short biography, and notes. Roden Noel's selection of plays in the Mermaid series reprints the four best-known plays: *Don Carlos* (performed and printed 1676), *The Orphan* (performed and published 1680), *The Soldier's Fortune* (performed 1680, published 1681) a comedy, and *Venice Preserv'd* (performed and published 1682). *Caius Marius* (performed 1679, published 1680), a free adaptation of *Romeo and Juliet* transposed to a setting reminiscent of *Coriolanus*, has been reprinted in facsimile, and so has Otway's best play, *Venice Preserv'd*. The fullest edition of *Venice Preserv'd* is that of Malcolm Kelsall in the Regents Restoration Drama Series. Kelsall's introduction provides a guide to studies of this powerful and intense play, sensibly rejecting the over-schematized political–allegorical interpretations that have been proposed, and A. M. Taylor's *Next to Shakespeare* describes the distinguished record on the stage of this play and of *The Orphan*, another popular success. One of Robert Birley's 1960–61 Clark Lectures, on forgotten masterpieces (in *Sunk Without Trace*, 1962) was devoted to Lee's most popular play, *The Rival Queens*. Such a lecture could not possibly be delivered on Otway's most popular play, for *Venice Preserv'd* is a far from forgotten masterpiece. Among a number of recent studies of it, Derek W. Hughes's 'A New Look at *Venice Preserv'd*' (1971) is worth singling out as an enthusiastic appraisal of the play's coherent density.

No full-scale critical work on either Lee or Otway is available, but various studies of Restoration drama include sections devoted to them. Best known is Bonamy Dobrée's classic, pioneering study, *Restoration Tragedy 1660–1720* (Oxford 1929, repr. 1950). It is still the natural starting-point. The next book to cover the same field did not appear for almost forty years, but when it did, Eric Rothstein's intelligent and astute *Restoration Tragedy: Form and the Process of Change* (1967) proved to be, in its very different way, another distinguished contribution. It includes a valuable study of Lee's *Sophonisba*. Meanwhile, a more limited book, C. V. Deane's *Dramatic Theory and the Rhymed Heroic Play* (1931), provided a sound survey of appropriate Restoration plays up to the time when dramatists grew weary of their 'long-lov'd Mistris, Rhyme' in the mid-1670s. As far as general histories of drama are concerned, G. Wilson Knight's idiosyncratic *The Golden Labyrinth. A Study of British Drama* is notable for a glowing response to Nathaniel Lee, and Moody E. Prior's *The Language of Tragedy* includes a fine chapter on 'Tragedy and the Rhymed Heroic Play' (*Dryden. A Collection of Critical Essays* edited by Bernard N. Schilling, prints only about a third of it). Some of the most interesting recent writing on Restoration tragedy and heroic drama has been by Eugene M. Waith. His lively, ranging book on *The Herculean Hero in Marlowe, Chapman, Shakespeare and Dryden*, which offers studies of *The Conquest of Granada, Aureng-Zebe*, and *All for Love*, has been followed by *Ideas of Greatness. Heroic Drama in England* which extends his investigation into the Herculean hero to Davenant, Lee, and Otway, and sets the heroic drama in a larger context than has hitherto been allowed. He distinguishes a major road where previously only a cul-de-sac had been signposted.

Among short accounts, Professor Waith's 'Dryden and the Tradition of Serious Drama' in Earl Miner's collection in the Writers and Their Background series, and Philip Parsons's stimulating essay 'Restoration Tragedy as Total Theatre' in Harold Love's collection, *Restoration Literature. Critical Approaches*, can be strongly recommended. Clifford Leech's 'Restoration Tragedy: A Reconsideration' is another short and spirited introduction.

The indispensable work of reference for details about performances in the Restoration theatres is *The London Stage 1660–1800. Part 1: 1660–1700*, edited by E. L. Avery, A. H. Scouten, and W. Van Lennep. The adaptation of earlier plays is described in G. C. D. Odell's now rather old-fashioned *Shakespeare—from Betterton to Irving* (1920), Hazelton Spencer's censorious *Shakespeare Improved; the Restoration Versions in Quarto and on the Stage* (1927), and Gunnar Sorelius's '*The Giant Race Before the Flood': Pre-Restoration Drama on the Stage and in the Criticism of the Restoration* (Uppsala 1966).

For additional guidance on Dryden, Lee, and Otway, the reader is referred to *The New Cambridge Bibliography of English Literature* edited by George Watson, volume 2, *1660–1800*, and to the comprehensive and annotated annual bibliographies published each November in the journal *Restoration and Eighteenth Century Theatre Research*. A cumulation of these from the time the journal began has been published in book form: Carl J. Stratman, Edmund A. Napieralski, and Jean E. Westbrook, *Restoration and Eighteenth Century Theatre Research Bibliography 1961–1968*. Volume 1 of Watson's *New Cambridge Bibliography* provides guidance on Davenant, which can be supplemented by fuller and more specialized, but less up-to-date, information from G. E. Bentley's *The Jacobean and Caroline Stage*, volume 3.

DAVENANT, DRYDEN, LEE, AND OTWAY 167

REFERENCES

BIBLIOGRAPHIES

G. E. Bentley, *The Jacobean and Caroline Stage*, 7 vols. (Oxford, 1941–68), vol. 3 (1956) for Davenant.

L. C. Gatto, 'An Annotated Bibliography of Critical Thought Concerning Dryden's *Essay of Dramatic Poesy*', *Restoration and Eighteenth Century Theatre Research* 5 (1965).

J. Kinsley, 'Dryden', in *English Poetry. Select Bibliographical Guides*, ed. A. E. Dyson (Oxford, 1971). Includes essential references not duplicated here.

A. L. McLeod, 'A Nathaniel Lee Bibliography, 1670–1960', *Seventeenth and Eighteenth Century Theatre Research* 1 (1961).

C. J. Stratman, E. A. Napieralski, and J. E. Westbrook, *Restoration and Eighteenth Century Theatre Research Bibliography 1961–1968* (Troy, N.Y., 1969).

ed. G. Watson, *The New Cambridge Bibliography of English Literature*, vol. 1, *600–1660* (Cambridge, 1974); vol. 2, *1660–1800* (Cambridge, 1971).

F. B. Zimmerman, *Henry Purcell 1659–1695: An Analytical Catalogue of his Music* (London, 1963).

GENERAL

ed. E. L. Avery, A. H. Scouten, and W. Van Lennep, *The London Stage 1660–1800. Part 1: 1660–1700* (Carbondale, Ill., 1965).

Buckingham, George Villiers, Duke of, and others, *The Rehearsal*
  ed. M. Summers (Stratford-upon-Avon, 1914).
  ed. S. Trussler in *Burlesque Plays of the Eighteenth Century* (London, 1969).

V. C. Clinton-Baddeley, *The Burlesque Tradition in the English Theatre after 1660* (London, 1952; repr. 1973).

ed. D. Davison, *Restoration Comedies* (The World's Classics, London, 1970).

C. V. Deane, *Dramatic Theory and the Rhymed Heroic Play* (London, 1931; repr. New York, 1968).

E. J. Dent, *Foundations of English Opera. A Study of Musical Drama in England during the Seventeenth Century* (Cambridge, 1928; repr. New York, 1965).

B. Dobrée, *Restoration Tragedy 1660–1720* (Oxford, 1929; repr. 1950).

ed. B. Dobrée, *Five Heroic Plays* (The World's Classics, London, 1960).

——, *Five Restoration Tragedies* (The World's Classics, London, 1928).

T. Duffett, *Three Burlesque Plays*, ed. R. E. Dilorenzo (Iowa City, Iowa, 1972).

E. Haun, *But Hark! More Harmony. The Libretti of Restoration Opera in English* (Ypsilanti, Mich., 1971).

L. Hotson, *The Commonwealth and Restoration Stage* (Cambridge, Mass., 1928; repr. New York, 1962).

G. Wilson Knight, *The Golden Labyrinth. A Study of British Drama* (London, 1962).

ed. A. S. Knowland, *Six Caroline Plays* (The World's Classics, London, 1962).

C. Leech, 'Restoration Tragedy: A Reconsideration', *Durham University Journal* 11 (1950); repr. in *Restoration Drama. Modern Essays in Criticism*, ed. J. Loftis (New York, 1966).

R. E. Moore, *Henry Purcell and the Restoration Theatre* (London, 1961).

G. C. D. Odell, *Shakespeare—from Betterton to Irving*, 2 vols. (New York, 1920; repr. 1963).

P. Parsons, 'Restoration Tragedy as Total Theatre', in *Restoration Literature: Critical Approaches*, ed. H. Love (London, 1972).

M. E. Prior, *The Language of Tragedy* (New York, 1947; repr. Bloomington, Ind., and London, 1966).

H. Purcell: *see* pp. 163–4 for relevant volumes in the Purcell Society edition of his works.

E. Rothstein, *Restoration Tragedy: Form and the Process of Change* (Madison, Wis., Milwaukee, Wis., and London, 1967).

G. Sorelius, '*The Giant Race Before the Flood*': *Pre-Restoration Drama on the Stage and in the Criticism of the Restoration*, Studia Anglistica Upsaliensia 4 (Uppsala, 1966).

H. Spencer, *Shakespeare Improved; the Restoration Versions in Quarto and on the Stage* (Cambridge, Mass., 1927).

M. Summers, *The Restoration Theatre* (London, 1934; repr. New York, 1964).

E. M. Waith, *The Herculean Hero in Marlowe, Chapman, Shakespeare and Dryden* (New York and London, 1962).

——, *Ideas of Greatness. Heroic Drama in England* (London, 1971).

J. H. Wilson, *All the King's Ladies. Actresses of the Restoration* (Chicago, Ill., 1968).

F. B. Zimmerman, *Henry Purcell, 1659–1695: His Life and Times* (London, 1967).

William Davenant (1606–68)

TEXTS

The Works of Sr William D'avenant K^t (London, 1673; facsimile, New York, 1968).

ed. J. Maidment and W. H. Logan, *The Dramatic Works of Sir William D'Avenant*, 5 vols. (Edinburgh and London, 1872–4; repr. New York, 1964).

Gondibert

facsimile of 1651 edition (Menston, 1970).

ed. D. F. Gladish (Oxford, 1971).

'The Author's Preface' and 'The Answer of Mr Hobbes to Sr Will. D'Avenant's Preface', ed. J. E. Spingarn in *Critical Essays of the Seventeenth Century*, vol. 2, *1650–1685* (London, 1908; repr. 1957).

The Law Against Lovers

facsimile of 1673 edition, introduced by A. M. Gibbs (Cornmarket Press, London, 1970).

Macbeth

ed. C. Spencer (Yale Studies in English 146, New Haven, Conn., 1961).

The Rivals

facsimile of 1668 edition, introduced by K. Muir (Cornmarket Press, London, 1970).

The Shorter Poems

ed. A. M. Gibbs (Oxford, 1972).

The Siege of Rhodes

ed. A.-M. Hedbäck (Studia Anglistica Upsaliensia 14, Uppsala, 1973).

The Tempest
See under Dryden.

The Wits

ed. A. S. Knowland, in *Six Caroline Plays* (The World's Classics, London, 1962).

CRITICAL STUDIES AND COMMENTARY

H. S. Collins, *The Comedy of Sir William Davenant* (Studies in English Literature 24, The Hague and Paris, 1967).

A. Harbage, *Sir William Davenant, Poet Venturer 1606–1668* (Philadelphia, Pa., 1935).

A. Nethercot, *Sir William D'Avenant, Poet Laureate and Playwright–Manager* (Chicago, Ill., 1938; rev. New York, 1967).

John Dryden (1631–1700)

TEXTS

ed. L. A. Beaurline and F. Bowers, *Four Comedies* (Curtain Playwrights, Chicago, Ill., and London, 1967).

ed. L. A. Beaurline and F. Bowers, *Four Tragedies* (Curtain Playwrights, Chicago, Ill., and London, 1967).

ed. E. N. Hooker, H. T. Swedenberg, and others, *The Works of John Dryden* (Berkeley and Los Angeles, Calif., 1956–).

ed. G. Saintsbury, *Selected Plays*, 2 vols. (Mermaid Edition, London, 1904).

ed. W. Scott, *The Works of John Dryden* (London, 1808), revised by G. Saintsbury (Edinburgh, 1882–92).

ed. M. Summers, *Dramatic Works* (London, 1931–2).

ed. G. Watson, *Of Dramatic Poesy and Other Critical Essays*, 2 vols. (Everyman's Library, London, 1962).

Albion and Albanius
Musical score by L. Grabu (London, 1687).

All for Love
ed. B. W. Griffith (Great Neck, N.Y., 1961).
ed. A. Sale (rev. edn., London, 1957).
ed. D. Vieth (Regents Restoration Drama Series, Lincoln, Nebr., 1972; London, 1973).
facsimiles of 1678 edition (San Francisco, Calif., 1929, and Menston, 1969).

Aureng-Zebe
ed. F. M. Link (Regents Restoration Drama Series, Lincoln, Nebr., and London, 1972).

The Duke of Guise
See under Lee.

Of Dramatick Poesie: An Essay
ed. D. D. Arundell, in *Dryden and Howard 1664–1668* (Cambridge, 1929).
ed. J. T. Boulton (London, 1964).
facsimile of '1668' edition (Menston, 1969).

The Indian Emperor
facsimile of 1667 edition (Menston, 1971).

King Arthur
Purcell's score, ed. D. Arundell (London, 1928), revised by M. Laurie (London, 1971) as volume 26 of the Purcell Society edition of *The Works of Henry Purcell*.
The Music in 'King Arthur', vocal score, ed. M. Laurie (London, 1971).

Oedipus
See under Lee.

The Pilgrim
'Song of a Scholar and his Mistress' and 'The Secular Masque', in *The Complete Works of Sir John Vanbrugh*, ed. B. Dobrée and G. Webb, 4 vols. (London, 1927; repr. New York, 1967), vol. 2; also in *The Poems of John Dryden*, ed. J. Kinsley, 4 vols. (Oxford, 1958), vol. 4.

Prologues and Epilogues
ed. W. B. Gardner (New York, 1951).

The Secular Masque
See under The Pilgrim.

DAVENANT, DRYDEN, LEE, AND OTWAY 171

The Tempest

facsimile of 1670 edition (Cornmarket Press, London, 1969).
facsimile of 1674 revision (Cornmarket Press, London, 1969).
facsimiles of 1670 edition, 1674 revision, Duffett's burlesque (1675), and
Garrick's libretto (1756), ed. G. R. Guffey in *After 'The Tempest'* (Augustan Reprint Society, special publication, Los Angeles, Calif., 1969).
facsimile of puppet version, *The Shipwreck* (1780), ed. R. Speaight (Cornmarket Press, London, 1970).

Troilus and Cressida

facsimile of 1679 edition (Cornmarket Press, London, 1969).

CRITICAL STUDIES AND COMMENTARY

(This list should be supplemented by J. Kinsley's chapter on Dryden in
English Poetry. Select Bibliographical Guides, ed. A. E. Dyson (Oxford, 1971).)
J. Bailey, *Poets and Poetry* (Oxford, 1911).
Henry Brooke, *Antony and Cleopatra* (1778), introduced by H. N. Davies
(Cornmarket Press, London, 1970).
D. Davie, 'Dramatic Poesy: Dryden's Conversation Piece', *Cambridge
Journal* 5 (1952).
ed. H. N. Davies, *Antony and Cleopatra 1813* (Cornmarket Press, London,
1970).
R. G. Ham, 'Dryden and *The Music of The Prophetesse*, 1691', *PMLA* 50
(1935).
R. D. Hume, *Dryden's Criticism* (Ithaca, N.Y., and London, 1970).
D. W. Jefferson, 'Aspects of Dryden's Imagery', *Essays in Criticism* 4 (1954);
repr. with revisions in *Dryden's Mind and Art*, ed. B. King (Edinburgh,
1969).
——, 'The Significance of Dryden's Heroic Plays', *Proceedings of The Leeds
Literary and Philosophical Society* (*Literary and Historical Section*) 5 (1940).
B. King, *Dryden's Major Plays* (Edinburgh and London, 1964).
——, ed., *Twentieth Century Interpretations of 'All for Love'* (Englewood Cliffs,
N.J., 1968).
A. C. Kirsch, *Dryden's Heroic Drama* (Princeton, N.J., 1965).
F. R. Leavis, '*Antony and Cleopatra* and *All for Love*: A Critical Exercise',
Scrutiny 5 (1936; repr. Cambridge, 1963).
F. H. Moore, *The Nobler Pleasure: Dryden's Comedy in Theory and Practice*
(Chapel Hill, N.C., 1963).
M. Praz, *The Neurotic in Literature* (Occasional Paper no. 9 of The Australian Humanities Research Council, Melbourne and Cambridge, 1965).
B. N. Schilling, ed., *Dryden. A Collection of Critical Essays* (Englewood Cliffs,
N.J., 1963).
A. Thaler, 'Milton in the Theatre', *SP* 17 (1920).
M. Van Doren, *The Poetry of John Dryden* (New York, 1920, Cambridge,
1931), reissued as *John Dryden: A Study of his Poetry* (New York, 1946;
Bloomington, Ind., 1960).

E. M. Waith, 'The Voice of Mr Bayes', *SEL* 3 (1963).
——, 'Dryden and the Tradition of Serious Drama', in *Writers and Their Background. John Dryden*, ed. E. Miner (London, 1972).
H. D. Weinbrot, *The Formal Strain. Studies in Augustan Imitation and Satire* (Chicago, Ill., and London, 1969).

Nathaniel Lee (1653?–92)

TEXTS

ed. T. B. Stroup and A. L. Cooke, *The Works of Nathaniel Lee*, 2 vols. (New Brunswick, N.J., 1954–5; repr. Metuchen, N.J., 1968).

Lucius Junius Brutus

ed. J. Loftis (Regents Restoration Drama Series, Lincoln, Nebr., 1967; London, 1968).

The Rival Queens

facsimile of 1677 edition (Menston, 1971).
ed. P. F. Vernon (Regents Restoration Drama Series, Lincoln, Nebr., and London, 1970).

CRITICAL STUDIES AND COMMENTARY

R. Birley, *Sunk Without Trace* (Clark Lectures, 1960–1, London, 1962).
R. G. Ham, *Otway and Lee. Biography from a Baroque Age* (New Haven, Conn., 1931).

Thomas Otway (1652–85)

TEXTS

ed. J. C. Ghosh, *The Works of Thomas Otway*, 2 vols. (Oxford, 1932; repr. 1968).
ed. R. Noel, *Selected Plays* (Mermaid Edition, London, 1888).

Caius Marius

facsimile of 1680 edition (Cornmarket Press, London, 1969).

Venice Preserv'd

facsimile of 1682 edition (Menston, 1972).
ed. M. Kelsall (Regents Restoration Drama Series, Lincoln, Nebr., and London, 1969).

CRITICAL STUDIES AND COMMENTARY

R. G. Ham, *Otway and Lee. Biography from a Baroque Age* (New Haven, Conn., 1931).
D. W. Hughes, 'A New Look at *Venice Preserv'd*', *SEL* 12 (1971).
A. M. Taylor, *Next to Shakespeare. Otway's 'Venice Preserv'd' and 'The Orphan' and their History on the London Stage* (Durham, N.C., 1950).

11. ETHEREGE, SHADWELL, WYCHERLEY, CONGREVE, VANBRUGH, and FARQUHAR

JOHN BARNARD

THE twentieth-century texts of Restoration comedy (discussed in more detail and listed under individual authors) mirror its changing critical fortunes. In the 1920s and 1930s the lavish Nonesuch volumes, aimed at the gentleman's library rather than the general public, reflected the somewhat anomalous attitude to the plays' mingling of sophisticated stylization with a frank treatment of sexuality. In the same years scholars had begun to amass the details of theatrical and literary history, which were to expose the weaknesses and inaccuracies of the main Nonesuch editor, Montague Summers (a clergyman whose rather prurient interest in the period was equalled by a devotion to the occult). Most critics either attacked its moral irresponsibility, or stressed the style and took an apologetic attitude to the content. A decisive change in attitude is probably marked by the successful productions of several major Restoration comedies on the London stage during the 1960s, signalling the return of a vigorous period of English drama to the permanent repertory. Simultaneously, the Regents Restoration Drama Series and the New Mermaid series began to make cheap modernized and annotated texts of single plays easily available. Both series draw on the increased knowledge of theatre history and on growing interest in the plays. The great virtue of the Regents series is its willingness to go beyond the major names to include the work of minor dramatists. However, there are as yet no definitive editions to compare with the California Dryden, and the reader has to rely on editions of individual plays and be willing to fall back upon the Nonesuch texts or the old Mermaids.

GENERAL WORKS

From its beginnings Restoration comedy excited strong disagreement. The claims (made in prologues, epilogues, and prefaces) that the dramatists wrote in the tradition of earlier English comedy or sought to correct society's follies by ridicule, were countered by the traditional Puritan hostility to the stage which culminated in

Jeremy Collier's *A Short View of the Immorality and Profaneness of the English Stage* (1698). Collier attacked the comedies for being in themselves blasphemous, immoral, and obscene, and for encouraging these vices in society. The subsequent controversy, chronicled by Sister Rose Anthony, generated more feeling than critical analysis. Even so, Collier's essential charge that the comedies trivialized human feelings and sexuality and endorsed the rake-heroes, who, having lost their fortunes to the whore and the bottle, are rewarded with the heroine's virginal purity and considerable fortune, was shrewd. In various forms the moral questions have continued to trouble critics. Macaulay's Victorian sensibilities were outraged by the plays' 'earthy, sensual, devilish' moral standards, which he thought a 'disgrace to our language and our national character'. Hostile reaction in this century is markedly less hysterical, but L. C. Knights's powerful and influential indictment in *Scrutiny*, 'Restoration Comedy: The Reality and the Myth' (1937), found the comedies characterized by a superficial cynicism, dominated by a narrow code of sexual ethics, and in the last analysis, 'trivial, gross, and dull'. This attitude has been supported and extended by John Wain, while George Parfitt's critique of the sharp limitations of Congreve's sensibility and art indicates the continuing relevance of the moral issue. Even a perceptive and largely sympathetic critic like Ian Donaldson insists upon the relative narrowness of Wycherley and Congreve when set within the context of English comedy from Jonson to Fielding.

The problems thrown up by Restoration comedy, the relationship between literature and morality, and the nature of the exchange between conventional types or situations and reality, are difficult ones. It is often assumed that the dramatists themselves were unable to supply a coherent answer to Collier, but the essays and prefaces of Dryden and Shadwell, and the pamphlet replies of Congreve, Vanbrugh, and Farquhar do outline a clear, if circumscribed, position. Comedy held up a mirror to the everyday world, and by mocking folly sought to cure it: the comic writer's business was not with incurable vices but with hypocrisy, affectation, and stupidity (Dennis, Congreve, Vanbrugh, Farquhar). Its concern, in the phrase of James Drake, was 'Civil Prudence'. With Dryden, the playwrights saw themselves working in a satiric tradition related to Jonson and the Roman satirists and comic dramatists. Shadwell's prefaces take up the Jonsonian notion of humours, and Congreve's 'Concerning Humour in Comedy' introduced a valuable distinction between humour and affectation. Despite their shortcomings, these formulations are valuable for the light thrown on the dramatists' own opinions and for their comments on specific dramatic effects. In the following century, Voltaire's reaction to the English stage remains interesting, and Horace Walpole's discussion of 'genteel comedy' gives a penetrating, but brief, analysis of the relationship between emotion and passion, and the 'forms' and 'decorums' common to 'polite' society and the comedy of manners.

The stress upon imitation and corrective satire among these early writers placed a false weight upon didacticism and realism. Avoiding this, and at the same time neatly side-stepping Collier's objections, Charles Lamb wrote in 1822 that the comedies create their own world, a 'land . . . of cuckoldry—the Utopia of gallantry', which 'is altogether a speculative scene of things' with 'no reference whatever to the world that is'. Lamb's position is in essence that adopted by Hazlitt, and shares with Macaulay's subsequent attack the assumption that the characters are heartless. Towards the end of the century, George Meredith's perception (in 'On the Idea of Comedy . . . ') that the comedies belong to a line of critical comedy pointed a way out of this dilemma, and John Palmer's *The Comedy of Manners* (1913) is the first attempt to define Restoration comedy as a genre. In the early years of the twentieth century Montague Summers began his editorial work, and several writers extended the base laid by Palmer. Allardyce Nicoll's *Restoration Drama 1660–1700* (1923) gave the first comprehensively documented dramatic history of the period. Bonamy Dobrée's *Restoration Comedy* (1924) emphasized its stylistic achievement, though with little close analysis, and argued that the overriding theme is the rationalization of sexual relationships. In the same year J. W. Krutch examined the literary antecedents and background, and the following year H. T. E. Perry explored *The Comic Spirit in Restoration Drama*. Meanwhile, Kathleen Lynch established the comedies' link with the *précieuse* tradition and with Cavalier drama. It was this gradual reinstatement of the plays that provoked L. C. Knights's attack (1937), and in fact the emphasis upon genre, social and dramatic history, and upon style, had left the critical question begging.

Knights's challenge was left virtually unanswered until the 1950s, when T. H. Fujimura's *The Restoration Comedy of Wit*, followed by Dale Underwood's more tightly argued and substantiated book on Etherege, sought to give a dimension of seriousness to the comedies by stressing their common roots in a tradition of scepticism. With differing emphases both writers analyse the tensions between 'libertinism', Epicureanism, and naturalism in the plays, setting them within the history of ideas in the seventeenth century, and showing the relevance of particular thinkers, notably Hobbes, to their concerns. F. W. Bateson, who had earlier shown the term 'comedy of manners' to be an anachronism, gave an explicit, but regrettably brief, reply to Knights, discussing the way in which the comedy works upon the audience. In his book, *The First Modern Comedies*, Norman N. Holland, building on the ground gained by Fujimura and Underwood, saw the plays as explorations of the 'split-consciousness' of modern man. His close analyses of all the three major dramatists' comedies are perhaps most valuable for their discussion of characteristic image patterns and thematic development. The comedies can also be studied in terms of contemporary dramatic theory (S. Singh), though the limitations of neoclassical critical thought and the strong affiliations between the dramatists and poets have made studies of the comedies as a mode of satire a more illuminating approach. Rose Zimbardo's book on Wycherley is sub-titled 'A Link in the Development of English Satire', and C. O. McDonald's important article examines the seventeenth-century concept of satire as a basis for Restoration comedy. The parallels between the plays and the satiric tradition in poetry are usefully discussed in Roger Sharrock's 'Modes of Satire'.

As much as an over-moralistic approach, the use of the history of ideas and background studies to explain the comedies runs the risk of drawing attention away from the plays as plays. V. O. Birdsall's *Wild Civility* makes this important point firmly within the bounds of a discussion of the rake-hero figure, whose origins are traced back to Morality plays, while Harriett Hawkins's *Likenesses of Truth in Elizabethan and Restoration Drama* attempts an examination of the nature of theatrical illusion in Shakespeare, Etherege, and Congreve (most of the space going to Shakespeare). But though there has been an increasing and proper concern for the stage dynamics of these comedies, and a good deal is now known about the Restoration stage and its actors, the results of the exchange between critics and scholars remain generalized. Hugh Hunt has written a good introductory essay on 'Restoration Acting'. More specifically, Gareth Lloyd Evans has shown the effect of Congreve's actors and stage upon his plays. For further reading in this interesting field, students should consult the relevant sections in the *New Cambridge Bibliography of English Literature* (which gives bibliographies of both primary and secondary material), and the journal, *Theatre Notebook*. On a wider scale, Allardyce Nicoll's account of Restoration drama has long been a basic source for theatrical history. Essential for any detailed work on performances, actors, repertories or changing taste is W. Van Lennep's calendar of the London stage between 1660 and 1700, which has a packed and judicious introduction by E. L. Avery and A. H. Scouten.

An understanding of the social milieu is particularly relevant to the comedy of manners. Many of the general works include commentary on this area as a matter of course (see, for instance, Fujimura and Holland). The constant theme of the conflict between love and 'interest' (financial as well as personal), and between youth and age, is in part a response to the affront offered to the dignity of the individual by the arranged marriages of the day, as well as to the emergence after 1660 of a generation with more liberal ideas about personal relationships than their elders. In an article on Wycherley, which has important implications for other writers, P. F. Vernon examines the connections between the *mariage de convenance* and the ethos of Restoration comedy, while the emergence of the 'new woman' in the years 1600 to 1730 has been followed by Jean Gagen. A great deal of interesting factual information (with virtually no critical discussion) is contained in G. S. Alleman's comparison of stage marriages with the actual marriage laws obtaining at the time.

There is as yet no satisfactory single study of the interplay between the conventional types of Restoration comedy and the changing social and economic structure of English society between 1660 and 1710. Unfortunately John Loftis's excellent *Comedy and Society from Congreve to Fielding* deals only with the latter end of the period, though he makes apparent the widening gap between fictional type and reality after the Glorious Revolution of 1688. The consequent change in mood, and indeed themes, in these years noted in Clifford Leech's articles on the first phase of Restoration comedy and on Congreve and the 1690s, has been underlined by other writers and by subsequent studies of individual writers. A. H. Scouten regards the last decade as a distinct period within Restoration comedy as a whole, and one of the good things about M. E. Novak's book on Congreve is its clear awareness of the altered tone of comedy during these years.

More particular studies include E. Mignon's account of the dramatists' treatment of old men and women in the plays, J. H. Smith's *The Gay Couple in Restoration Comedy*, and studies of the rake-hero by John Traugott and V. O. Birdsall. Contemporary courtesy books throw light on the satire upon gallants and fops (D. R. M. Wilkinson), and C. D. Cecil and David Berkeley have published

valuable studies of the comedies' stylized language and raillery, and
their use of *libertin* and *précieux* elements. Molière's influence, for
which Saintsbury made excessive claims, has been sensibly discussed
by J. Wilcox, and with stimulating critical awareness by Norman
Suckling in a short essay. The influence of Beaumont and Fletcher
is detailed by J. H. Wilson.

Among introductory studies, Kenneth Muir's book is informative. It stresses the difference between the individual dramatists,
insists that the Saturnalian element does not overwhelm the dramatists' awareness of moral issues, and claims that its heroines are
'moral beings and not merely sexual objects'. J. H. Wilson's *Preface*
is useful, though more concerned with background information.
P. A. W. Collins and John Barnard have written chapters on
Restoration comedy in the Pelican and Sphere histories of English
literature. Earl Miner and John Loftis have collected several important essays into handy paperback volumes, and J. R. Brown and
B. Harris's *Restoration Theatre* has ten specially commissioned essays.
For a more detailed historical account of the period, which gives
unusual and welcome attention to lesser figures, James Sutherland's
chapter in his volume of the Oxford History of English Literature
should be consulted.

BIBLIOGRAPHIES

The entries in the *New Cambridge Bibliography of English Literature*,
which has sections on the major and minor writers, foreign influences, dramatic theory, the Collier controversy, and on theatres and
actors, will prove adequate for most students. However, it only lists
works published before about 1969; for subsequent publications, the
annual bibliography printed in *Philological Quarterly*, which gives
brief reviews of important books and articles, should be used. Copies
of specific early editions can be located through Woodward and
McManaway's *Check-List of English Plays 1641–1700* and Fredson
Bowers's supplement. Wing's *Short-Title Catalogue* will help track
down both plays and other works printed in these years. Similar
bibliographies do not exist for comedies published after 1700, and
individual items can only be found by consulting the printed catalogues of major libraries. A bibliography of 'libertine' literature,
ephemeral by its nature, has been brought together by David Foxon,
and Fredson Bowers's lecture gives an introduction to the problems
facing the bibliographer and textual critic working on Restoration
drama.

BACKGROUND

Contemporary Literary and Intellectual Context

The work of other comic dramatists working in the period is the most immediately relevant background. Dryden's comedies and his essays on drama and satire (see Chapter 10) are readily available, but it is difficult to go beyond the central figures without falling back upon the original editions or upon nineteenth-century collections like the twenty-six volumes of Dibdin's *The London Theatre* or *Oxberry's New English Drama*. Aphra Behn's works have been edited by Montague Summers, who also edited Buckingham's *The Rehearsal*, and the Regents series has published single plays by Mrs. Behn, Colley Cibber, and John Crowne. The strong satiric tradition represented by the poetry of Dryden, Rochester, and Oldham is important as an analogous and related genre, while Suckling's poems and plays throw valuable light on the transition from the Cavalier to Restoration periods.

Clarendon's first-hand description of the profound changes wrought by the Civil War in English society, political alignments, and manners, gives a vivid sense of the sources of tension in Restoration society which are reflected in the themes and character types of Restoration comedy. So too Hobbes's *Leviathan* (1651), whose political philosophy assumes the innate selfishness and violence of a mankind governed by appetite, suggests links between themes raised by the comedy of manners and larger movements in seventeenth-century thought. Locke's *Essay concerning Humane Understanding* is the major philosophic expression of the rationalism which characterized the period, and which is reflected by the dramatists. At a more personal level, Pepys's diaries give an unrivalled insight into the everyday life of Restoration London, while the urbanity of Halifax's *Essays* is a representative example of the views of a contemporary man of the world, whose values are in many ways similar to those embodied in Restoration comedy. Some of the major critical writings of the period are reprinted in Spingarn's anthology.

Modern Studies

James Sutherland's comprehensive and lucid account of the period as a whole in the Oxford History of English Literature is the most convenient introduction. On English social history in these years G. M. Trevelyan provides an inclusive survey, and B. S. Allen's guide gives a summary indication of the changes in taste and sensibility, though it does not pretend to take the place of more specialist works on music or the visual and decorative arts. The shifting position of the writer in society and the altering system of patronage is documented by A. Beljame in a book which, though written over seventy years ago, remains essential reading. Some grasp of English history is helpful: G. N. Clark's *The Later Stuarts* gives a general history, and David Ogg's two books treat the reigns of Charles II, James II, and William III in greater detail. Valuable insights into the relationship between history and literature within the period occur in several chapters of Christopher Hill's *Puritanism and Revolution*. J. H. Wilson's book on the court wits is colourful and readable, though Etherege's letters contain vivid accounts of the life of an ageing rake and wit with an authenticity and directness otherwise difficult to capture. The study of the history of ideas is best approached through A. O. Lovejoy's work and Basil Willey's introductory book. The importance of scepticism is explored in L. I. Bredvold's *The Intellectual Milieu of John Dryden* and in Margaret Wiley's *The Subtle Knot*. An interesting portrait of a typical cultured wit is given by Clara Marburg in *Sir William Temple: A Seventeenth Century 'Libertin'*.

Sir George Etherege

TEXTS

The basic text of the plays, which is annotated and has a good biographical introduction, is by H. F. B. Brett-Smith. Frederick Bracher's edition of the letters from new manuscript material supersedes Sybil Rosenfeld's earlier work. The poems are edited by James Thorpe. W. B. Carnochan has published a modern-spelling edition of *The Man of Mode* with useful notes and a short but incisive introduction. *She Would if She Could* is edited by Charlene M. Taylor.

CRITICAL STUDIES AND COMMENTARIES ·

Of Etherege's three plays it was his last, *The Man of Mode*, which established the note of urbane scepticism characteristic of the best Restoration comedy. Most earlier criticism centres on this play, and either advances or rejects the proposition that its sophistication is front for cynicism or worse. Steele thought Dorimant 'a Direct Knave', to which John Dennis replied with an appeal to the twin doctrines of imitation and moral correction—*The Man of Mode* is an accurate portrait of its age concerned with the correction of vice not the depiction of virtue. Later writers set greater store by Etherege's 'ease' and wit, though tending to slide away from the moral questions, or looked to the history of ideas to explain Etherege's concerns (Palmer, Dobrée, Lynch, Fujimura; *see* General Works). The first, and so far only, book devoted to Etherege, Dale Underwood's *Etherege and the Seventeenth Century Comedy of Manners* (1957), offers an illuminating examination of the way in which the plays mould the traditions of pre-Restoration drama into a distinctively Restoration idiom, and the manner in which the rake-hero figure focuses Epicurean, libertine, and naturalistic strains of thought within an open-ended discussion of contemporary manners. For Underwood, Etherege's comedies are a tough, dialectical exploration of the notions of love and honour inherited from Cavalier drama within the context of a realistic depiction of the Restoration world. Scepticism and the 'libertine' rake have been discussed by later writers, notably Norman N. Holland and V. O. Birdsall (*see* General Works), though Jocelyn Powell, in an essay fully aware of Etherege's variety and skill, concludes that 'manners no longer express but contradict reality', and that the 'comedy of experience' forces us to a double view of 'the lightness and elegance of fashion on the surface and the underlying reality of passion it conceals'. The ambiguity of Dorimant's role is a subject common to most critics. J. G. Hayman has written on the tension between Dorimant's nature and the requirements of society, and P. C. Davies has reconsidered *The Man of Mode*'s thematic handling of the 'state of nature' and the 'state of war'. The kind of seriousness evident in some twentieth-century writers is questioned by Harriett Hawkins (*see* General Works), who argues the irrelevance of harsh moral judgements, emphasizing instead *The Man of Mode*'s lightness and charm. Over all, the most interesting discussion is Underwood's which, though demanding, perceives the intellectual energy of the comedies, and provides a challenging analysis of the link between Etherege's plays and the literature of the period.

Thomas Shadwell

The only complete text with pretensions to scholarship is Summers's edition. *Epsom Wells* and *The Volunteers* were edited by D. M. Walmsley, and four other plays may be read in Saintsbury's Mermaid collection. *The Virtuoso* has been more recently edited by M. H. Nicolson and D. Rodes with a good introduction on its satire of scientific projectors. Apart from A. S. Borgman's now dated biographical and critical account (1928), M. Alsidd has written the only book on Shadwell, though discussions of his work appear in some of the general outlines (*see*, for instance, Sutherland, Nicoll, and Muir under General Works). Despite his vigorous directness and an openness to a wider range of society than is common in Restoration comedy, Shadwell has been often overlooked. In part this is due to the effectiveness of Dryden's satiric portrait, but also because as the self-announced heir of Ben Jonson (a claim which his prefaces seek to substantiate) he has been thought to stand outside the comedy of manners. With the growing awareness of the limitations of this concept, Shadwell's individual, if inferior, contribution to comedy of the period is likely to receive due recognition.

William Wycherley

TEXTS

Unfortunately, Montague Summers's Nonesuch edition is the only comprehensive text of Wycherley's output, which includes poems as well as comedies. The text is careless and the annotation uneven, though a good deal of somewhat miscellaneous information is supplied. Gerald Weales's *Complete Plays* is based on the first editions, is well annotated, and has taken the place of W. C. Ward's old Mermaid edition. *The Country Wife* and *The Plain Dealer* have been edited by T. H. Fujimura and Leo Hughes respectively in the Regents series, and J. D. Hunt has edited *The Country Wife*.

CRITICAL STUDIES AND COMMENTARIES

Willard Connely's *Brawny Wycherley* is a popular biography, now somewhat out-of-date and not always accurate. A useful brief introduction to the life and work has been written by P. F. Vernon. The history of his eighteenth-century popularity has been recorded by Emmett L. Avery.

Wycherley's comedy is distinguished by its violence and energy. His contemporaries, if they did not damn him for indecency, saw clearly that he stood apart from the ease and sophistication of Etherege or Congreve, and praised his comedies for lashing the hypocrisies and vices of the age. Modern critics have been less certain of Wycherley's aims, often finding it difficult to accommodate his directness within unduly narrow definitions of the comedy of manners. Most general works discuss Wycherley, though frequently limiting themselves to *The Country Wife* and *The Plain Dealer*. Assessments of the nature of Wycherley's achievement differ widely. At one extreme, a critic like T. W. Craik believes that Wycherley's overriding interest lay in theatrical effect—'his satire is not intended to be more than a source of amusement for his fashionable audience.' Where Palmer and Dobrée had placed the source of his violence in a Puritanical hatred

of the bestiality of man (*see* General Works), Anne Righter sees
a 'covert sympathy with excess', giving force to the darkness of the
satire. Rose Zimbardo, like J. Auffret, believes him to be a satirist as
distinct from a comic writer, working in the Juvenalian tradition.
Indeed, in her eagerness to place the comedies within a formal genre
of satire as defined by Renaissance and Restoration theory and
example, Zimbardo denies that the plays are 'comedies at all'. For
Fujimura they are 'comedies of wit', for Holland they turn on pitting
a 'right way' against a 'wrong way', while V. O. Birdsall argues that
Wycherley is basically an idealist who fuses elements of comedy and
satire, directing them at our sense of guilt and hypocrisy (*see* General
Works).

The two final plays have attracted a number of interesting essays.
David Vieth makes a useful analysis of the interplay of characters
and plots in *The Country Wife*, Ronald Berman regards the Machia-
vellian Horner as an analogue for the satirist himself, while L. J.
Morrissey argues that a preoccupation with moral problems has
obscured the baroque stylization which patterns the comedy on the
model of a formal dance. *The Plain Dealer*, where the realistic and
idealistic sides of Wycherley are most obviously juxtaposed, is the
most problematic of the plays. The main difficulty is to know whether
Manly, the plain-dealing hero, is himself satirized as a misfit and
surly hypocrite, or whether, as Dryden assumed, he acts as Wycherley's satiric *persona*. Fujimura, Holland (*see* General Works), Zimbardo, and A. H. Chorney all deny the identification—plain-dealing
is a folly to be castigated. K. M. Rogers cuts through the difficulty
by suggesting that the play is inconsistent, working on two different
levels which are dramatically incompatible, while A. M. Friedson
has restated the classic case, that Manly is used to satirize a corrupt
society. It is, however, rewarding to see the conflict between idealistic and satiric modes in *The Plain Dealer* as crucial to the play's
effect, an ambiguity which denies the audience any easy resting-
point (Ian Donaldson, and, from a different viewpoint, V. O.
Birdsall; *see* General Works).

William Congreve

TEXTS

Ewald's old Mermaid text is still useful, and Summers's Nonesuch
edition, for all its shortcomings, remains the most complete. Congreve's 1710 text, which makes minor changes, is available in
Dobrée's two World's Classics volumes, and is the basis of F. W.

Bateson's edition of the comedies. The Curtain Playwrights edition by H. J. Davis has an introduction, notes, and an (incomplete) list of variants. *Incognita*, Congreve's novel, has been edited by H. F. B. Brett-Smith, and is reprinted by Dobrée, Summers, and in A. N. Jeffares's edition of *The Way of the World*. *Love for Love* can be read in editions by Emmett L. Avery, Malcolm Kelsall, and A. N. Jeffares (old spelling). *The Way of the World* has been published in annotated editions by K. M. Lynch (modernized), A. N. Jeffares (old spelling), Brian Gibbons (modernized), and John Barnard (old spelling). John C. Hodges has edited Congreve's letters and documents, giving sound texts and annotation in place of Summers's casual treatment in his Nonesuch text.

CRITICAL STUDIES AND COMMENTARIES

The basic biography is by Hodges (1941), who draws on new source material which illuminates Congreve's working career and makes important discoveries about his private life. It replaces Gosse's outdated study, and the untrustworthy, carelessly written account by D. Crane Taylor. An interesting collection of essays on several of Congreve's friends has been written by Kathleen Lynch, though its interest is biographical rather than critical. The list of books owned by Congreve, which was discovered and edited by Hodges, is an invaluable starting-point for the study of the dramatist's mind and art, while the bibliography by A. M. Lyles and J. Dobson of early editions of Congreve's works and associated items in the Hodges Collection at Knoxville gives a basis for the further study of the history of the printed texts of Congreve's works.

Congreve has received more critical attention than any other Restoration comic writer. Dryden quickly discerned that he ranked with Etherege and Wycherley, and Voltaire admired the perfection and finish of his art. The eighteenth-century reputation of the comedies and of *The Mourning Bride*, his tragedy, has been recorded by Emmett L. Avery.

Nineteenth-century criticism centres on Congreve's style and elegance, largely to the exclusion of the plays' analysis of manners and society. Lamb's influential essay (1822; *see* General Works for this and other writings mentioned in this paragraph), which regarded theirs as a fantasy world, set the tone for much subsequent criticism, even though Hazlitt considered the comedies a brilliant and realistic portrayal of an artificial society. Palmer's establishment of the 'comedy of manners' as a genre (1913) encouraged a view of Congreve as the apex of the comedy written from 1660 to 1700. A tendency to divorce style and formal organization from subject-matter is most marked in H. T. E. Perry, though it is also evident in Dobrée's humane and sympathetic account. With other writers, Congreve has benefited from the studies of the *précieuse* tradition by Lynch, Cecil, and Berkeley, from Fujimura's discussion of the comedy of wit (though his treatment ought to be compared with R. A. Foakes's essay on 'Wit and Convention in Congreve's Comedies' in *William Congreve*, ed. Brian Morris), and from Norman Holland's exploration of the theme of appearance and reality in his comedies.

The common assumption that Congreve brought Restoration comedy to perfection has often obscured the fact that he was writing during the transitional period following 1688. Clifford Leech, John Loftis (*see* General Works), and M. E. Novak have all stressed how far Congreve's achievement is distinguished by its response to the new sensibility apparent in the drama written during these years, and by a growing concern with the nature of the marital relationship. Some critics have gone so far as to regard Congreve's comedies as moving towards 'sentimental comedy', though Ernest Bernbaum long ago drew a firm distinction between Congreve's anti-sentimentalism and the emergent 'drama of sensibility'. An attempt to show Time as the recurrent theme of Congreve's art is made in W. H. Van Voris's *The Cultivated Stance*, where it is related to the dramatist's social and personal values, conceived of as those of the Whig aristocracy. Alone among critics, Aubrey Williams has pursued a Christian reading, discerning the workings of Providential Grace in the disguise of Poetic Justice, but the position is more ingenious than convincing, and most writers stress the secularity of Congreve's vision. The tacit assumption among some writers that the moral questions raised by Knights and Wain are irrelevant is challenged by several of the essays in Brian Morris's collection of essays (see particularly the very interesting and constructive piece by William Myers) and by Ian Donaldson's cogent expression of unease before *The Way of the World* (*see* General Works).

Congreve's debt to Jonson in *The Old Batchelour* has been discussed by Brian Gibbons, a relationship dealt with in part by P. and M. Mueschke's *A New View of Congreve's 'The Way of the World'*, which also gives a convincing and illuminating analysis of the play's structure, frequently found to be mystifying or non-existent by earlier writers. Mirabell's role as Congreve's 'ideal gentleman' is explored by Jean Gagen, though it is an interpretation which should be compared with Donaldson's. Sensible introductions to Congreve's work will be found in Kenneth Muir's essay and Bonamy Dobrée's booklet, but the best introduction to Congreve as a whole is M. E. Novak's *William Congreve* (1971), which strikes a difficult balance between an awareness of the comedies' seriousness and the element of 'play' common to all comedy.

The use of song and music in Congreve's drama is discussed in two brief articles by Stoddard Lincoln, and I. Simon has considered the theory of fiction demonstrated in his novel, *Incognita*. *The Mourning Bride*, whose considerable eighteenth-century popularity is most reliably discussed by Avery, has received little critical attention, but Novak devotes an interesting chapter to the tragedy, and Aubrey Williams has given it a Christian interpretation.

Sir John Vanbrugh

TEXTS

Vanbrugh's dramatic output contains more translations and adaptations than original comedies. The only complete modern edition is that published by Bonamy Dobrée and Geoffrey Webb in 1927. More dependable than most Nonesuch texts, it is essential for anyone wishing to study Vanbrugh as a whole, though the more recent editions of *The Provoked Wife* and *The Relapse* by C. A. Zimansky, James L. Smith, and Bernard Harris are more easily available, and together provide better annotation and discussion of textual matters, along with helpful introductions. Peter Dixon's edition of *The Provoked Husband*, Cibber's altered and completed version of Vanbrugh's final comedy, *A Journey to London*, gives a valuable account of the play's genesis and interest. A selection of the plays can be found in A. E. H. Swaen's old Mermaid edition.

CRITICAL STUDIES AND COMMENTARIES

Like Farquhar, Vanbrugh has often been regarded as a poor relation of the major exponents of Restoration comedy. Yet his first play, *The Relapse*, satirizes the shift towards sentimentality in Cibber's *Love's Last Shift* and at the same time broadens the base of the traditional comedy of courtship to include married relationships, which are treated with a frankness and unsentimental factuality not found in earlier writers. Vanbrugh's achievement of a new formulation of the conventions and ethos of Restoration comedy needs to be seen within the context of the final decade of the century, and compared with the plays of Congreve, Southerne, Cibber, and Farquhar rather than those of Wycherley or Etherege. Despite its over-argumentative style, a sympathetic reading of Vanbrugh's own defence of his two original plays against Jeremy Collier's assault describes the basis of his realistic mode, and among earlier critics Hazlitt (*see* General Works) communicates an intelligent and lively perception of Vanbrugh's comic vitality. The best single modern defence of Vanbrugh against the charge of amorality is still the article published by P. Mueschke and J. Fleischer in 1934, though C. A. Zimansky's and Bernard Harris's introductions are valuable and informative. Harris has also written a concise assessment of Vanbrugh's career. Laurence Whistler's two biographical works throw light on Vanbrugh's extraordinarily energetic life as playwright, theatrical entrepreneur, and architect, though the main emphasis falls upon the latter. No satisfactory account of Vanbrugh's translations and adaptations has yet been published.

George Farquhar

TEXTS

The handsome *Complete Works* (1930), edited by Charles Stonehill, is the only attempt at a full-dress text, though its annotation is sometimes misleading. William Archer's selection for the Mermaid series has a useful preface, and L. A. Strauss's selection (1915) is preceded by an essay which is still interesting. *The Beaux' Stratagem* has been edited by V. C. Hopper and G. B. Lahey, and by A. N. Jeffares, the latter being an old-spelling text, with commentary and an informative introduction. *The Recruiting Officer* is available in M. Shugrue's dependable edition in the Regents series, in A. N. Jeffares's old-spelling text, and has also been edited, with photographs of the National Theatre production, by Kenneth Tynan.

CRITICAL STUDIES AND COMMENTARIES

A recognition of Farquhar's achievement has been hindered by the tendency to regard him as a late practitioner of Restoration comedy. Pope's comment on his 'pert, low Dialogue' assumes Farquhar to have attempted, and failed, to equal the stylized elegance of Congreve, and is typical of many later critics' response, who offset an awareness of Farquhar's increased verisimilitude and broader social canvas with the conviction that he was caught in a transitional phase in which the comedy of manners was in the process of decay. In varying degrees the analyses given by Palmer, Perry, Nicoll, and Dobrée (*see* General Works) all suffer from this simplistic approach. With the realization that Congreve's comedies cannot be described

as 'Restoration' in the same sense as Etherege's, came a new willingness to admit Farquhar's originality. Eric Rothstein in his article on
The Twin-Rivals (1964) and his subsequent book presents him as an
accomplished and intelligent dramatist in his final plays, testing the
implicitly aristocratic assumptions and conventions of Restoration
comedy against the realities of bourgeois existence, and concerned
not simply with the reform of the individual hero but with the
patterns of relationship within a broader and more naturalistic
description of society. Farquhar's expansion of the Restoration
formula is matched by a new directness in handling human problems—*The Beaux' Stratagem* meets the problem of divorce head-on.
His technique of examining conventional comic values by setting
them against reality is investigated by Ronald Berman's essay on the
play, which concentrates on the obsession with money, at first
claimed as a permanent good, only to be exploded and replaced by
passion.

A popular biography has been written by Willard Connely; it is
informative but not always trustworthy. The best introduction to
Farquhar is Rothstein's book (1967), and A. J. Farmer's pamphlet
is helpful (1966). W. Sharp has written on the problems of staging
Restoration comedy using Farquhar as the centre of his discussion.

REFERENCES

GENERAL WORKS

(References to studies of individual writers mentioned in this section are
given under the writers, below.)

G. S. Alleman, *Matrimonial Law and the Materials of Restoration Comedy*
(Philadelphia, Pa., 1942).

Sister R. Anthony, *The Jeremy Collier Stage Controversy 1698–1726* (Marburg,
1937).

J. Barnard, 'Drama from the Restoration till 1710', in *English Drama to 1710*,
vol. 3 of the *Sphere History of Literature in the English Language*, ed. C. Ricks
(London, 1971).

F. W. Bateson, 'Contributions to a Dictionary of Critical Terms: I. Comedy
of Manners', *Essays in Criticism* 1 (1951); repr. J. Loftis (ed.) (1966).

——, 'Second Thoughts: II. L. C. Knights and Restoration Comedy',
Essays in Criticism 7 (1957).

D. S. Berkeley, '*Préciosité* and the Restoration Comedy of Manners', *HLQ*
18 (1954–5).

V. O. Birdsall, *Wild Civility: The English Comic Spirit on the Restoration Stage*
(Bloomington, Ind., 1970).

ed. J. R. Brown and B. Harris, *Restoration Theatre* (Stratford-upon-Avon Studies 6, London, 1965).

C. D. Cecil, 'Libertine and *Précieux* Elements in Restoration Comedy', *Essays in Criticism* 9 (1959).

——, 'Raillery in Restoration Comedy', *HLQ* 29 (1965–6).

——, 'Une Espèce de l'éloquence abrégée: The Idealized Speech of Restoration Comedy', *Études Anglaises* 19 (1966).

J. Collier, *A Short View of the Immorality and Profaneness of the English Stage* (London, 1698).

P. A. W. Collins, 'Restoration Comedy', in *From Dryden to Johnson*, vol. 4 of *The Pelican Guide to English Literature*, ed. B. Ford (Harmondsworth, 1957; rev. 1965).

B. Dobrée, *Restoration Comedy: 1660–1720* (Oxford, 1924).

I. Donaldson, *The World Upside-Down: Comedy from Jonson to Fielding* (Oxford, 1970).

J. Drake: *see* E. E. Williams *below*.

J. Dryden, *Of Dramatic Poesy: An Essay*, Preface to *An Evening's Love*, and *A Discourse concerning the Original and Progress of Satire*: in *'Of Dramatic Poesy' and other Critical Essays*, ed. G. Watson, 2 vols. (Everyman's Library, London, 1962).

T. H. Fujimura, *The Restoration Comedy of Wit* (Princeton, N.J., 1952; repr. London, 1968).

J. E. Gagen, *The New Woman: Her Emergence in English Drama 1600–1730* (New York, 1954).

B. Harris, 'The Dialect of those Fanatic Times', in *Restoration Theatre* (Stratford-upon-Avon Studies 6, ed. J. R. Brown and B. Harris, London, 1965).

H. Hawkins, *Likenesses of Truth in Elizabethan and Restoration Drama* (Oxford, 1972).

W. Hazlitt, *Lectures on the English Comic Writers* (London, 1819); repr. in *Complete Works*, ed. P. P. Howe, 21 vols. (London, 1930–4), vol. 6 (1931).

N. N. Holland, *The First Modern Comedies: The Significance of Etherege, Wycherley, and Congreve* (Cambridge, Mass., 1959).

H. Hunt, 'Restoration Acting', in *Restoration Theatre* (Stratford-upon-Avon Studies 6, ed. J. R. Brown and B. Harris, London, 1965).

G. W. Knight, *The Golden Labyrinth: A Study of English Drama* (London, 1962).

L. C. Knights, 'Restoration Comedy: The Reality and the Myth', *Scrutiny* 6 (1937); repr. in his *Explorations* (London, 1946).

J. W. Krutch, *Comedy and Conscience after the Restoration* (New York, 1924; rev. edn., 1949).

C. Lamb, 'On the Artificial Comedy of the Last Century', in *Essays of Elia* (London, 1823; World's Classics, London, 1901).

C. Leech, 'Restoration Comedy: The Earlier Phase', *Essays in Criticism* 1 (1951).

J. Loftis, *Comedy and Society from Congreve to Fielding* (Stanford, Calif., 1959).

J. Loftis, ed., *Restoration Drama: Modern Essays in Criticism* (New York, 1966).

K. M. Lynch, *The Social Mode of Restoration Comedy* (New York, 1926).

T. B. Macaulay, Lord, 'The Dramatic Works of Wycherley, Congreve, Vanbrugh, and Farquhar', *Edinburgh Review* 72 (1840–1); repr. as 'The Comic Dramatists of the Restoration' in *Critical and Historical Essays* (London, 1843).

C. O. McDonald, 'Restoration Comedy as Drama of Satire: An Investigation into Seventeenth-Century Aesthetics', *SP* 61 (1964).

G. Meredith, 'On the Idea of Comedy and of the Uses of the Comic Spirit', *New Quarterly Magazine* 8 (1877); repr. in *Works*, 27 vols. (London, 1909–11).

E. Mignon, *Crabbed Age and Youth: The Old Men and Women in the Restoration Comedy of Manners* (Durham, N.C., 1947).

ed. E. Miner, *Restoration Dramatists* (Twentieth Century Views, Englewood Cliffs, N.J., 1966).

K. Muir, *The Comedy of Manners* (London, 1970).

A. Nicoll, *Restoration Drama 1660–1700*: vol. 1, *History of the English Drama 1660–1900* (Cambridge, 1923; 4th edn. rev., 1952).

J. L. Palmer, *The Comedy of Manners* (London, 1913).

G. Parfitt, 'The Case against Congreve', in *William Congreve* (Mermaid Critical Commentaries, ed. B. Morris, London, 1972).

H. T. E. Perry, *The Comic Spirit in Restoration Drama* (New Haven, Conn., 1925).

B. R. Schneider, *The Ethos of Restoration Comedy* (Urbana, Ill., 1971).

A. H. Scouten, 'Notes towards a History of Restoration Comedy', *PQ* 45 (1966).

R. Sharrock, 'Modes of Satire', in *Restoration Theatre* (Stratford-upon-Avon Studies 6, ed. J. R. Brown and B. Harris, London, 1965).

S. Singh, *The Theory of Drama in the Restoration Period* (Calcutta, 1963).

J. H. Smith, *The Gay Couple in Restoration Comedy* (Cambridge, Mass., 1948).

N. Suckling, 'Molière and English Restoration Comedy', in *Restoration Theatre* (Stratford-upon-Avon Studies 6, ed. J. R. Brown and B. Harris, London, 1965).

J. R. Sutherland, *English Literature of the Late Seventeenth Century* (Oxford History of English Literature, vol. 6, Oxford, 1969).

J. Traugott, 'The Rake's Progress from Court to Comedy', *SEL* 6 (1966).

ed. W. Van Lennep, introduction by E. L. Avery and A. H. Scouten, *The London Stage 1660–1800: Part I (1660–1700)* (Carbondale, Ill., 1965).

P. F. Vernon, 'Marriage of Convenience and the Moral Code of Restoration Comedy', *Essays in Criticism* 12 (1962).

F. M. A. de Voltaire, 'Sur la comédie', in *Lettres Philosophiques* (Paris, 1733); English translation published as *Letters Concerning the English Nation* (London, 1733).

J. Wain, 'Restoration Comedy and its Modern Critics', *Essays in Criticism* 6 (1956); repr. in his *Preliminary Essays* (London, 1957).

H. Walpole, 'Thoughts on Comedy', in *The Works of Horatio Walpole, Earl of Orford*, 4 vols. (London, 1798); repr. in *Essays in Criticism* 15 (1965).

J. Wilcox, *The Relation of Molière to Restoration Comedy* (New York, 1938).

D. R. M. Wilkinson, *The Comedy of Habit: An Essay on the Use of Courtesy Literature in a Study of Restoration Comic Drama* (Leiden, 1964).

E. E. Williams, 'Dr. James Drake and the Restoration Theory of Comedy', *RES* 15 (1939).

J. H. Wilson, *The Influence of Beaumont and Fletcher on Restoration Drama* (Columbus, Ohio, 1928).

——, *A Preface to Restoration Drama* (Cambridge, Mass., 1965).

BIBLIOGRAPHIES

F. Bowers, *Bibliography and Restoration Drama* (Los Angeles, Calif., 1966).

D. Foxon, 'Libertine Literature in England 1660–1745', *Book Collector* 12 (1963); repr. and rev., New Hyde Park, N.Y., 1965).

Philological Quarterly 5 (1926–), 'English Literature 1660–1800: A Current Bibliography', ed. R. S. Crane, *et al.*; continued annually. First twenty-five lists for 1926–50 repr., 2 vols. (Princeton, N.J., 1950–2), the following ten lists for 1951–60 repr., 2 vols. (Princeton, N.J., 1962).

D. G. Wing, *Short-Title Catalogue of Books Printed in England, Scotland, Ireland, Wales, and British America, and of English Books Printed in Other Countries 1641–1700*, 3 vols. (New York, 1945–51); for corrections and supplements, see *New Cambridge Bibliography of English Literature*.

G. L. Woodward and J. G. McManaway, *A Check List of English Plays 1641–1700* (Chicago, Ill., 1945); supplement by F. Bowers (Charlottesville, Va., 1949).

BACKGROUND

Contemporary Literary and Intellectual Context

A. Behn, *The Works of Aphra Behn*, ed. M. Summers, 6 vols. (London, 1915).

——, *The Rover*, ed. F. Link (Regents Restoration Drama Series, Lincoln, Nebr., and London, 1967).

Buckingham, G. Villiers, Duke of, *The Rehearsal*, ed. M. Summers (Stratford-upon-Avon, 1914); ed. G. G. Fall, in *Three Restoration Comedies* (New York, Toronto, and London, 1964).

C. Cibber, *The Careless Husband*, ed. W. W. Appleton (Regents Restoration Drama Series, Lincoln, Nebr., 1966).

Clarendon, E. Hyde, Earl of, *The History of the Rebellion and Civil Wars in England*, ed. W. D. Macray, 6 vols. (Oxford, 1888).

J. Crowne, *The City Politiques*, ed. J. H. Wilson (Regents Restoration Drama Series, Lincoln, Nebr., 1967).

——, *Sir Courtly Nice*, ed. C. Hughes (The Hague, 1966).

T. J. Dibdin, ed., *The London Theatre*, 26 vols. (London, 1815–18).

J. Dryden: see Chapter 10.

Halifax, G. Saville, Marquis of, *Halifax: Complete Works*, ed. J. P. Kenyon (Harmondsworth, 1969).

T. Hobbes, *Leviathan*, ed. M. Oakeshott (Oxford, 1946).

J. Locke, *An Essay concerning Humane Understanding*, ed. A. C. Fraser, 2 vols. (Oxford, 1894; repr. New York, 1959); new edition, ed. P. H. Nidditch (Oxford, 1974).

Sir John Oldham, *Poetical Works* [a selection], ed. R. Bell (London, 1854; repr. 1960). There is as yet no satisfactory edition.

ed. W. Oxberry, *Oxberry's New English Drama*, 20 vols. (London, 1818–25).

S. Pepys, *The Diary of Samuel Pepys*, ed. R. Latham and W. Matthews, 11 vols. (London, 1970–).

Rochester, J. Wilmot, Earl of, *Poems*, ed. V. de S. Pinto (Muses' Library, London, 1953, 1964); ed. D. M. Vieth (New Haven, Conn., 1968).

J. E. Spingarn, ed., *Critical Essays of the Seventeenth Century*, 3 vols. (Oxford, 1908–9).

Sir John Suckling, *The Works of Sir John Suckling*, ed. L. A. Beaurline and T. Clayton, 2 vols. (Oxford, 1971).

Modern Studies

B. S. Allen, *Tides in English Taste, 1619–1800: A Background for the Study of Literature*, 2 vols. (Cambridge, Mass., 1937).

A. Beljame, *Le Public et les hommes de lettres en Angleterre au dix-huitième siècle* (Paris, 1897); English translation, as *Men of Letters and the English Public, 1660–1744*, by E. O. Lorimer (London, 1948).

L. I. Bredvold, *The Intellectual Milieu of John Dryden* (Ann Arbor, Mich., 1934).

G. N. Clark, *The Later Stuarts, 1660–1714* (Oxford, 1934; 2nd edn., 1956).

C. Hill, *Puritanism and Revolution* (London, 1958).

A. O. Lovejoy, *The Great Chain of Being: A Study in the History of an Idea* (Cambridge, Mass., 1936).

——, *Essays in the History of Ideas* (Baltimore, Md., 1948).

C. Marburg, *Sir William Temple: A Seventeenth Century 'Libertin'* (New Haven, Conn., 1932).

D. Ogg, *England in the Reign of Charles II*, 2 vols. (Oxford, 1934; 2nd edn., 1956).

——, *England in the Reigns of James II and William III* (Oxford, 1955).

J. Sutherland, *English Literature in the Late Seventeenth Century* (Oxford History of English Literature, vol. 6, Oxford, 1969).

G. M. Trevelyan, *Illustrated English Social History*, vol. 2 (London, 1949).

M. L. Wiley, *The Subtle Knot: Creative Scepticism in Seventeenth-Century England* (Cambridge, Mass., 1952).

B. Willey, *The Seventeenth-Century Background: Studies in the Thought of the Age in relation to Poetry and Religion* (London, 1934).

J. H. Wilson, *The Court Wits of the Restoration* (Princeton, N.J., 1948; repr. London, 1967).

Sir George Etherege (1635?–91)

TEXTS

ed. F. Bracher, *Letters of Sir George Etherege* (Berkeley and Los Angeles, Calif., and London, 1974).

ed. H. F. B. Brett-Smith, *The Works of Sir George Etherege*, 2 vols. (Oxford, 1927; repr. 1971).

ed. J. Thorpe, *The Poems of Sir George Etherege* (Princeton, N.J., 1963).

She Would if She Could

ed. C. M. Taylor (Regents Restoration Drama Series, Lincoln, Nebr., 1972; London, 1973).

The Man of Mode, or, Sir Fopling Flutter

ed. W. B. Carnochan (Regents Restoration Drama Series, Lincoln, Nebr., 1966; London, 1967).

CRITICAL STUDIES AND COMMENTARY

P. C. Davies, 'The State of Nature and the State of War: A Reconsideration of *The Man of Mode*', *University of Toronto Quarterly* 39 (1969).

J. Dennis, *A Defense of Sir Fopling Flutter* (London, 1722; repr. in *The Critical Works of John Dennis*, ed. E. N. Hooker, 2 vols. (Baltimore, 1939–43)).

J. G. Hayman, 'Dorimant and the Comedy of a Man of Mode', *MLQ* 30 (1969).

J. Powell, 'Etherege and the Form of a Comedy', in *Restoration Theatre* (Stratford-upon-Avon Studies 6, ed. J. R. Brown and B. Harris, London, 1965); repr. in *Restoration Dramatists*, ed. E. Miner; *see* General Works, above.

D. Underwood, *Etherege and the Seventeenth-Century Comedy of Manners* (New Haven, Conn., 1957).

Thomas Shadwell (1642?–92)

TEXTS

ed. G. Saintsbury, *Thomas Shadwell* (Mermaid Series, London, 1903). Includes *The Sullen Lovers*, *A True Widow*, *The Squire of Alsatia*, and *Bury Fair*.

ed. M. Summers, *The Complete Works of Thomas Shadwell*, 5 vols. (London, 1927).

ed. D. M. Walmsley, *'Epsom Wells' and 'The Volunteers'* (Boston, Mass., 1930).

The Virtuoso

ed. M. H. Nicolson and D. S. Rodes (Regents Restoration Drama Series, Lincoln, Nebr., and London, 1966).

CRITICAL STUDIES

M. W. Alsidd, *Thomas Shadwell* (New York, 1967).
A. S. Borgman, *Thomas Shadwell: His Life and Comedies* (New York, 1928).

William Wycherley (1640?–1716)

TEXTS

ed. M. Summers, *The Complete Works of William Wycherley*, 4 vols. (Nonesuch Press, London, 1924).
ed. W. C. Ward, *William Wycherley* (Mermaid Series, London, 1888).
ed. G. Weales, *The Complete Plays of William Wycherley* (New York, 1967).

The Country Wife

ed. T. H. Fujimura (Regents Restoration Drama Series, Lincoln, Nebr. and London, 1965).
ed. J. D. Hunt (New Mermaids, London, 1973).

The Plain Dealer

ed. L. Hughes (Regents Restoration Drama Series, Lincoln, Nebr., 1967; London, 1968).

CRITICAL STUDIES AND COMMENTARY

J. Auffret, 'Wycherley et ses maîtres les moralistes', *Études Anglaises* 15 (1962).
E. L. Avery, '*The Country Wife* in the Eighteenth Century', *Washington State University Research Studies* 10 (1942).
——, '*The Plain Dealer* in the Eighteenth Century', ibid. 11 (1943).
R. Berman, 'The Ethic of *The Country Wife*', *Texas Studies in Literature and Language* 9 (1967).
A. H. Chorney, 'Wycherley's Manly Reinterpreted', in *Essays Critical and Historical Dedicated to Lily B. Campbell* (Berkeley, Calif., 1950).
W. Connely, *Brawny Wycherley* (New York, 1930).
T. W. Craik, 'Some Aspects of Satire in Wycherley's Plays', *ES* 41 (1960).
I. Donaldson, 'Tables Turned: *The Plain Dealer*', *Essays in Criticism* 17 (1967); repr. in his *The World Upside-Down* (Oxford, 1970).
A. M. Friedson, 'Wycherley and Molière: Satirical Point of View in *The Plain Dealer*', *MP* 64 (1967).
L. J. Morrissey, 'Wycherley's Country Dance', *SEL* 8 (1968).
A. Righter, 'William Wycherley', in *Restoration Theatre* (Stratford-upon-Avon Studies 6, ed. J. R. Brown and B. Harris, London, 1965); repr. in *Restoration Dramatists*, ed. E. Miner; *see* General Works, above.
K. M. Rogers, 'Fatal Inconsistency: Wycherley and *The Plain Dealer*', *ELH* 28 (1961).
P. F. Vernon, *William Wycherley* (Writers and Their Work, London, 1965).
D. M. Vieth, 'Wycherley's *The Country Wife*: An Anatomy of Masculinity', *Papers on Language and Literature* 2 (1966).

ETHEREGE, SHADWELL, WYCHERLEY 195

R. Zimbardo, *Wycherley's Drama: A Link in the Development of English Satire* (New Haven, Conn., 1965).

William Congreve (1670–1729)

TEXTS

ed. F. W. Bateson, *The Works of William Congreve* (London, 1930).
ed. H. J. Davis, *The Complete Plays of William Congreve* (Curtain Playwrights, Chicago, Ill., 1967).
ed. B. Dobrée, *Comedies by William Congreve* (World's Classics, London, 1925).
ed. B. Dobrée, *The Mourning Bride, Poems, and Miscellanies by William Congreve* (World's Classics, 1928).
ed. A. C. Ewald, *William Congreve* (Mermaid Series, London, 1887; repr. New York, 1956).
ed. J. C. Hodges, *William Congreve: Letters and Documents* (New York and London, 1964).
ed. M. Summers, *The Complete Works of William Congreve*, 4 vols. (Nonesuch Press, London, 1923; repr. New York, 1964).

Incognita, or Love and Duty Reconcil'd: A Novel

ed. H. F. B. Brett-Smith (Oxford, 1922); also printed in *The Mourning Bride . . .*, ed. Dobrée, Summers's edn., and *The Way of the World*, ed. Jeffares.

Love for Love

ed. E. L. Avery (Regents Restoration Drama Series, Lincoln, Nebr., 1966; London, 1967).
ed. A. N. Jeffares (London, 1967).
ed. M. Kelsall (New Mermaids, London, 1969).

The Way of the World

ed. A. N. Jeffares (London, 1966); includes *Incognita*.
ed. K. Lynch (Regents Restoration Drama Series, Lincoln, Nebr., and London, 1965).
ed. J. Barnard (Fountainwell Drama Texts, Edinburgh, 1972).
ed. B. Gibbons (New Mermaids, London, 1971).

CRITICAL STUDIES AND COMMENTARY

E. L. Avery, *Congreve's Plays on the Eighteenth-Century Stage* (New York, 1951).
W. Congreve, *Amendments of Mr. Collier's False and Imperfect Citations . . .* (London, 1698; repr. Summers, ed., and *The Mourning Bride*, ed. Dobrée).
——, 'Concerning Humour in Comedy', in *Letters upon Several Occasions . . .* (London, 1696; repr. Summers, ed., *Comedies*, ed. Dobrée, and J. C. Hodges, ed.).
B. Dobrée, 'William Congreve', in *A Variety of Ways* (Oxford, 1932).
——, *William Congreve* (Writers and Their Work, London, 1963).

I. Donaldson, ' "Dear Liberty": *The Way of the World*', in his *The World Upside-Down* (Oxford, 1970).

J. Dryden, 'To my Dear Friend Mr. Congreve', poem prefixed to *The Double Dealer* (London, 1694).

G. L. Evans, 'Congreve's Sense of Theatre', in *William Congreve* (Mermaid Critical Commentaries, ed. B. Morris, London, 1972).

R. A. Foakes, 'Wit and Convention in Congreve's Comedies', in *William Congreve* (Mermaid Critical Commentaries, ed. B. Morris, London, 1972).

J. Gagen, 'Congreve's Mirabell and the Ideal of the Gentleman', *PMLA* 79 (1964).

B. Gibbons, 'Congreve's *The Old Batchelour* and Jonsonian Comedies', in *William Congreve* (Mermaid Critical Commentaries, ed. B. Morris, London, 1972).

E. Gosse, *Life of William Congreve* (Great Writers Series, London, 1888; rev. for English Men of Letters Series, London, 1924).

H. Hawkins, 'Offending against Decorums', in *Likenesses of Truth* (*see* General Works).

ed. J. C. Hodges, *The Library of William Congreve* (New York, 1955).

——, ed., *William Congreve the Man: A Biography from New Sources* (New York, 1941).

C. Leech, 'Congreve and the Century's End', *PQ* 41 (1962).

S. Lincoln, 'The First Setting of Congreve's *Semele*', *Music and Letters* (London) 44 (1963).

——, 'Eccles and Congreve: Music and Drama on the Restoration Stage', *Theatre Notebook* 18 (1963).

A. M. Lyles and J. Dobson, *The John C. Hodges Collection of William Congreve . . . A Bibliographical Catalogue* (Knoxville, Tenn., 1970).

K. M. Lynch, *A Congreve Gallery* (Cambridge, Mass., 1951).

ed. B. Morris, *William Congreve* (Mermaid Critical Commentaries, London, 1972).

P. and M. Mueschke, *A New View of Congreve's 'Way of the World'* (Ann Arbor, Mich., 1958).

K. Muir, 'The Comedies of William Congreve', in *Restoration Theatre* (Stratford-upon-Avon Studies 6, ed. J. R. Brown and B. Harris, London, 1965).

W. Myers, 'Plot and Meaning in Congreve's Comedies', in *William Congreve* (Mermaid Critical Commentaries, ed. B. Morris, London, 1972).

M. E. Novak, *William Congreve* (New York, 1971).

——, 'Love, Scandal, and the Moral Milieu of Congreve's Comedies', in *Congreve Reconsider'd: Papers Read at a Clark Library Seminar December 5, 1970* (Los Angeles, Calif., 1971).

I. Simon, 'Early Theories of Prose Fiction: Congreve and Fielding', in *Imagined Worlds: Essays in Honour of John Butt*, ed. M. Mack and I. Gregor (London, 1968).

D. C. Taylor, *William Congreve* (Oxford, 1931; repr. New York, 1963).

W. H. Van Voris, *The Cultivated Stance: The Designs of Congreve's Plays* (Dublin, 1965).

F. M. A. de Voltaire: *see* General Works.

A. Williams, 'Congreve's *Incognita*, the Contrivances of Providence', in *Imagined Worlds: Essays in Honour of John Butt*, ed. M. Mack and I. Gregor (London, 1968).

——, 'The "Just Decrees of Heav'n" and Congreve's *Mourning Bride*', in *Congreve Reconsider'd: Papers Read at a Clark Library Seminar December 5, 1970* (Los Angeles, Calif., 1971).

——, 'Poetical Justice, the Contrivances of Providence, and the Works of William Congreve', *ELH* 35 (1968).

Sir John Vanbrugh (1664–1726)

TEXTS

ed. B. Dobrée and G. Webb, *The Complete Works of Sir John Vanbrugh*, 4 vols. (Nonesuch Press, London, 1927–8).

ed. A. E. H. Swaen, *Sir John Vanbrugh* (Mermaid Series, London, 1896).

The Relapse

ed. B. Harris (New Mermaids, London, 1972).

ed. C. A. Zimansky (Regents Restoration Drama Series, Lincoln, Nebr., 1969; London, 1970).

The Provoked Wife

ed. B. Harris (New Mermaids, London, 1972).

ed. C. A. Zimansky (Regents Restoration Drama Series, Lincoln, Nebr., 1970).

The Provoked Husband (completed and altered by Cibber)

ed. P. Dixon (Regents Restoration Drama Series, Lincoln, Nebr., 1973).

CRITICAL STUDIES AND COMMENTARY

B. Harris, *Sir John Vanbrugh* (Writers and Their Work, London, 1967).

P. Mueschke and J. Fleisher, 'A Re-evaluation of Vanbrugh', *PMLA* 49 (1934).

Sir John Vanbrugh, *A Short Vindication of 'The Relapse' and 'The Provok'd Wife', from Immorality and Prophaneness* (1698); repr. in Dobrée and Webb (eds.).

L. Whistler, *Sir John Vanbrugh, Architect and Dramatist, 1664–1726* (London, 1938).

——, *The Imagination of Vanbrugh and his Fellow Artists* (London, 1954).

198   JOHN BARNARD

George Farquhar (1678–1707)

TEXTS

ed. W. Archer, *George Farquhar* (Mermaid Series, London, 1906).

ed. L. A. Strauss, *A Discourse upon Comedy, The Recruiting Officer, and The Beaux' Stratagem* (Boston, Mass., 1914).

ed. C. Stonehill, *The Complete Works of George Farquhar*, 2 vols. (Nonesuch Press, London, 1930).

The Recruiting Officer

ed. A. N. Jeffares (Fountainwell Drama Texts, Edinburgh, 1973).

ed. M. Shugrue (Regents Restoration Drama Series, Lincoln, Nebr., 1965; London, 1966).

ed. K. Tynan (London, 1965).

The Beaux' Stratagem

ed. V. C. Hopper and G. B. Lahey (New York, 1963).

ed. A. N. Jeffares (Fountainwell Drama Texts, Edinburgh, 1972).

CRITICAL STUDIES AND COMMENTARY

R. Berman, 'The Comedy of Reason', *Texas Studies in Literature and Language* 7 (1965).

W. Connely, *Young George Farquhar: The Restoration Drama at Twilight* (London, 1949).

A. J. Farmer, *George Farquhar* (Writers and Their Work, London, 1966).

E. Rothstein, 'Farquhar's *Twin-Rivals* and the Reform of Comedy', *PMLA* 79 (1964).

——, *George Farquhar* (New York, 1967).

W. Sharp, 'Restoration Comedy: An Approach to Modern Production', *Drama Survey* 7 (1968).

12. GAY, GOLDSMITH, SHERIDAN and Other Eighteenth-century Dramatists

CECIL PRICE

UNTIL the 1920s it was commonly accepted that the period between 1708 and 1800 had produced only two dramatists of note: Goldsmith and Sheridan. Their comedies, *She Stoops to Conquer*, *The Rivals*, and *The School for Scandal*, were known to everyone and, apart from the more popular of Shakespeare's works, were the only plays more than fifty years old that were constantly performed.

The revolt against accepted ideas after the Great War and the consequent search for novelty led to a new interest in the drama of the Restoration and its associated period, the eighteenth century. In 1927 Allardyce Nicoll remarked that it was quite wrong to believe that Goldsmith and Sheridan shone alone in their period and suggested that any careful examination of other plays of the time would lead to a revision of the popular view. The compilers of *The London Stage* have since brought forward evidence to confirm his judgement as far as popularity in the eighteenth century is concerned. Yet if there were similar volumes cataloguing the repertories of theatres in the nineteenth and twentieth centuries, they would almost certainly indicate that occasional performances of plays like Garrick and Colman's *The Clandestine Marriage* or of Fielding's *Rape upon Rape* (as *Lock up Your Daughters*) do little to disturb the general pattern: Goldsmith's and Sheridan's comedies (and sometimes *The Beggar's Opera*) go on being presented in the English-speaking world when plays by other writers of the age are left to amuse readers only.

The test provided in the playhouse is an important one, since it proves that these dramatists have something to say that is of perennial interest and, in spite of changes in the theatre, the means to accomplish their purposes. Consequently I shall give detailed attention to their work, but shall deal rather summarily with other leading playwrights.

John Gay

TEXTS

No modern collection shows the range of the *Poetical, Dramatic and Miscellaneous Works* (1795), but eight of the theatrical pieces and Johnson's critical essay are to be found in the Abbey Classics edition (1923). The omission of *Three Weeks after Marriage* has been made doubly good in versions edited by J. H. Smith and by R. Morton and W. M. Peterson. Naturally the work that has received greatest attention is Gay's most finished achievement, *The Beggar's Opera*. A. E. Case listed the texts in Nettleton's and his *British Dramatists from Dryden to Sheridan* (p. 937), and noted that the first (octavo) edition of 1728 contained some significant errors or omissions. He therefore used the 'third' (quarto) edition of 1729 as copy-text. This (1729) has since been reproduced in facsimile and with commentaries by L. Kronenberger and M. Goberman. Edgar V. Roberts preferred to print the text of the first edition.

CRITICAL STUDIES AND COMMENTARY

S. M. Armens gives a sound estimate of Gay's achievements in his *John Gay, Social Critic*. F. W. Bateson examines each of the entertainments in turn, and makes some downright but very sensible comments on them. George Sherburn deals with 'The Fortunes and Misfortunes of *Three Hours after Marriage*' in a most informative article. Bertrand H. Bronson's knowledge of the literature and music of the period enables him to present two penetrating critiques. In one of them he suggests that *Acis and Galatea* is one of the greatest works in the English pastoral tradition, and shows that Gay provided Handel with an almost perfect libretto. In the other, he makes a number of valuable points about the songs in *The Beggar's Opera*, stressing that in some of them innocuous words were accompanied by well-known tunes that the audience would immediately associate with the amorous or bawdy. Similarly, Wilfred Mellers makes some subtle points about the comic element in *Acis and Galatea*, and the curious effect created in *The Beggar's Opera* when the corrupt sing in the language of innocence. Gay was a supreme ironist, a point well made in the sixth chapter of William Empson's *Some Versions of Pastoral*, when 'the comic primness' of the Peachums is strikingly contrasted with Macheath's heroic stance. For facts about the sources, composition, and performances of *The Beggar's Opera*, we must turn to Schultz's monograph; and to appreciate the genre, to E. M. Gagey's *Ballad Opera*. A. E. H. Swaen's article on the airs and tunes is also valuable.

On the Life, Lewis Melville's *Life and Letters of John Gay* is still readable, but has been supplanted by W. H. Irving's spirited biography, and by the scholarly edition of eighty-two of Gay's letters brought out by C. F. Burgess.

Oliver Goldsmith

TEXTS

The best texts of *The Good-Natur'd Man* and *She Stoops to Conquer* are to be found in Arthur Friedman's edition of *The Collected Works*. He has also brought out *She Stoops to Conquer* separately and with an introduction. For Goldsmith's poor little afterpiece *The Grumbler*, students must seek a copy of Alice I. Perry Wood's edition.

CRITICAL STUDIES AND COMMENTARY

Goldsmith's 'An Essay on the Theatre; or, A Comparison between Laughing and Sentimental Comedy' made many people think he was hostile to sentimentalism. *She Stoops to Conquer* confirms the impression, but *The Good-Natur'd Man* is not so distinct in its attitude. Ricardo Quintana has concluded that the play was intended to be thoroughly satirical at the expense of sentimental comedy, but that its ironical effects were not obvious enough in the theatre. W. F. Gallaway, Jr., has contributed the suggestion that the title indicated that Goldsmith was ready to ridicule generosity when it was really extravagance, and universal benevolence when marked by gullibility. Arthur Friedman, too, saw Goldsmith attacking 'not the sentimental virtues but the faults that resemble them'. Some French influences on the play are discussed in Byron Gassman's article.

The biographies by Prior and Forster are still useful. Ralph M. Wardle's *Oliver Goldsmith* is a valuable reassessment. Comparatively few of Goldsmith's letters are extant, but those that were available were collected by Katharine C. Balderston and published in 1928. She was also responsible for the perceptive work, *The History and Sources of Percy's Memoir of Goldsmith*.

Richard Brinsley Sheridan

TEXTS

W. Fraser Rae's *Sheridan's Plays Now Printed as He Wrote Them* and R. C. Rhodes's 'critical and comprehensive collection' of Sheridan's plays and poems were important because they showed a turning-away from what was long regarded as the standard edition, the

Works published by Murray in 1821. In particular, Rhodes emphasized the lack of authority in Murray's text of *The School for Scandal*,
and suggested that the best readings were to be found in Thomas
Moore's collations of a manuscript given by Sheridan to Mrs. Crewe
with an authoritative text printed in Dublin in 1799. G. H. Nettleton
improved on this method when he found the Crewe manuscript itself
in Georgetown University Library, and transcribed it for publication in *British Dramatists from Dryden to Sheridan*. When I examined
the material, it seemed to me that Moore's collations indicated that
other Crewe manuscripts might be in existence, and, in fact, one of
them has since come to light. Consequently I have brought together
(in *The Dramatic Works of R. B. Sheridan*) seven manuscripts of the
play that contain corrections by Sheridan, in the hope that his
intentions are best realized when the manuscripts concur. I have
also edited single-volume texts of *The School for Scandal* and *The
Rivals*.

Textually, *The Rivals* presents fewer problems. R. L. Purdy printed
the version sent to the Lord Chamberlain for licensing, and made
clear that it substantially represented the text given at the first performance on 17 January 1775. However, the audience was not
pleased, and Sheridan revised the comedy considerably before the
second performance on 28 January. It has been argued that the first
edition, published a few days later, gives us the play as Sheridan
intended it to be read, but another school of thought believes the
third edition possesses greater authority: Sheridan presented a copy
of it to David Garrick. Editors differ therefore in their practices:
G. H. Nettleton prints the third edition as copy-text and gives the
variants in footnotes. I use the first edition as copy-text, but have
inserted substantives from the third edition.

The best version of *St. Patrick's Day* is to be found in the manuscript submitted to the Lord Chamberlain for licensing, even though
it may omit alterations possibly made before or after the first
performance. Rhodes, however, prefers to use later texts: the
Dublin piracies of 1788–9, the London edition by Cumberland,
and Fraser Rae's transcription of an early manuscript. All reveal
corruptions.

The Duenna was sold to Covent Garden by Sheridan and an
authoritative edition did not appear till 1794. For a fuller discussion
of the problems in this and other Sheridan texts, see my edition of
the *Dramatic Works*. In making my choices, I have been guided by
Sheridan's attitude towards the first edition of *The Critic*, the one
text that seems to have satisfied him.

CRITICAL STUDIES AND COMMENTARY

The only full-length critical study is by Jean Dulck, and is in French. For the most part it is a record of received opinion, but it is valuable in its assessment of possible French influences. A number of shorter pieces have also appeared. I have written introductions to my single-volume editions of *The Rivals* and *The School for Scandal*. Cleanth Brooks and R. B. Heilman deal with the latter in *Understanding Drama*, printing a text and discussing Sheridan's approach as well as the structure and mechanics of the play. All this is thoughtful, but I do not like the practice of setting a number of questions at the end of every act. The student who needs them will also require answers to be given in the style of the old-fashioned arithmetic.

A more hostile attitude to Sheridan is shown by Marvin Mudrick, who finds the plays too literary, too divorced from real life. The staginess of the situations is stressed, and Sheridan is convicted of degrading the tradition of the comedy of manners as found in Congreve. These arguments have not been rebutted, probably because most people are aware that Sheridan took Vanbrugh as much as Congreve for his model, and that his plays have enjoyed even greater success in the theatre than those of his masters.

The three articles that remain to be mentioned all deal with the stage life of *The School for Scandal*. J. R. de J. Jackson examines some of the earliest sketches for the play and shows how Sheridan gave his dialogue greater effectiveness. Christian Deelman proves that the play was almost ideally cast at its first performance, and I have brought forward evidence concerning the topical allusions the play contains and the particular circumstances in which it was completed.

The best biography is still Thomas Moore's *Memoirs of the Life of the Right Honourable Richard Brinsley Sheridan*. Moore had access to papers that are not now available, and though he was rather timid in his handling of them, he did justice to Sheridan's claims as playwright and versifier. W. Fraser Rae also drew on much unpublished material for his *Sheridan*, but was a little too favourably disposed towards his subject. Walter Sichel's biography covers the subject thoroughly, but lacks structure and is sometimes unreliable in its dates. R. C. Rhodes's *Harlequin Sheridan* examines with scholarly care a number of problems in Sheridan's life and work. My edition of Sheridan's letters reveals that Sheridan wrote characteristic letters to his second wife and his women friends, but was too often overcome by pressure of business to give full attention to his less interesting correspondents.

Other Playwrights and their Plays

Readers who can be satisfied with some of the best plays of the age will find an excellent selection in Nettleton and Case's anthology, *British Dramatists from Dryden to Sheridan*: it prints nine Restoration, and fifteen eighteenth-century works. Sentimental comedy is well represented in Cibber's *The Careless Husband* (1704), Steele's *The Conscious Lovers* (1722), and Cumberland's *The West Indian* (1771); satirical burlesque, in Fielding's *The Tragedy of Tragedies* (1731); farce, in Garrick's *The Lying Valet* (1741); and comedy, in Colman the elder's *The Jealous Wife* (1761), as well as in pieces by Goldsmith and Sheridan. Verse tragedy may be appreciated in Addison's *Cato* (1713) and Home's *Douglas* (1756); prose tragedy, in Lillo's *The London Merchant* (1731). MacMillan and Jones's *Plays of the Restoration and Eighteenth Century* contains a similar selection, but includes Kelly's *False Delicacy* (1768) and Kotzebue's *The Stranger* (translated by B. Thompson, 1798). It lacks, however, the very useful set of bibliographical notes on the plays that gives *British Dramatists from Dryden to Sheridan* such distinction.

A good anthology, called *Burlesque Plays of the Eighteenth Century*, has been edited by Simon Trussler and contains ten amusing examples. The only outstanding omission is the one that is still performed: Sheridan's *The Critic*. Fortunately it is included in all editions of his plays as well as in *British Dramatists from Dryden to Sheridan*.

For other light entertainment of the age, students will turn to Mrs. Inchbald's representative collection. More easily available are *Ten English Farces* (ed. Hughes and Scouten) and *Eighteenth Century Drama: Afterpieces* (ed. Bevis). One complements the other, and Mr. Bevis's stimulating introduction makes the point that these shorter plays showed 'more creative activity' than the mainpieces, and carried on the old tradition of laughter in the theatre at a time when sentimentalism was a dangerous influence.

Sentimentalism itself is probably the most controversial issue of the period, and is the subject of a thoughtful survey by Arthur Sherbo. He finds sentimentalism in the theatre well before the eighteenth century, but rightly notes that it is unobjectionable if the general emphasis of the play lies elsewhere. Very few comedies of note have been wholly sentimental in outlook, and even Kelly's *False Delicacy* satirized one aspect of it while praising another. The meaning of 'delicacy' has been carefully scrutinized by C. J. Rawson, and P. E. Parnell has written a subtle essay on the moral ambiguities

of some sentimental comedies. We may also deduce from the
material available that while tearful plays of the kind were congenial
to French audiences, their greatest appeal in England was to the
reading public.

Few writers of sentimental comedy have been given much
scholarly attention. The grand exception is Steele: Shirley Strum
Kenny has presented excellent texts of his plays, and John Loftis
and Calhoun Winter have dealt with his achievements and influence
with considerable success. Rae Blanchard's edition of his correspondence is of high quality. For Cibber, texts are available of *The
Careless Husband* (prepared by W. W. Appleton) and of *The Rival
Queans* (undertaken by W. M. Peterson), as well as an enthusiastic
account of his life and times by F. Dorothy Senior. His fascinating
autobiography, *An Apology for the Life of Mr. Colley Cibber, Comedian*
(1740) has been edited by R. W. Lowe (1889) and by D. R. S. Fone
(1968); it is also included in Everyman's Library. Close consideration of Richard Cumberland's efforts is to be found in S. T.
Williams's monograph.

Nor is the position very much better for some of the other dramatists of the period. Nicholas Rowe's tragedies, *Tamerlane*, *The Fair
Penitent*, and *Jane Shore*, have been well edited by J. R. Sutherland;
and George Lillo's *The London Merchant* and *Fatal Curiosity*, by W. H.
MacBurney. No full, distinctive biographical or critical study of
either dramatist has appeared. Thomas Holcroft's plays have not
been re-edited or collected; but Elbridge Colby brought out a fine
edition of his memoirs and V. R. Stallbaumer published an article
with the significant title of 'Holcroft: a Satirist in the Stream of
Sentimentalism'.

Fielding, Garrick, and Colman the elder have been rather better
treated, the first two for reasons not entirely connected with their
achievements as dramatists. Bernard Shaw said, provokingly rather
than provocatively, that Fielding was the greatest practising English
dramatist after Shakespeare, but that opinion has not been resound-
ingly echoed. The plays are often read as precursors to the novels,
and for reliable texts of the dramatic works we still have to depend
on Henley's five volumes. When we look for single plays, we can
easily become confused because some of them appeared under more
than one title. *The Tragedy of Tragedies*, for example, was originally
Tom Thumb, but in its later and more developed state it has been
excellently edited by J. T. Hillhouse. *The Grub Street Opera* was
earlier *The Welsh Opera*, but the enlarged text has been thoroughly
examined by E. V. Roberts: 'Appendix B' prints words and music

of the songs. In many ways this follows the precedent set by C. B. Woods in his authoritative version of *The Author's Farce*. Two other plays worth study, *The Historical Register* and *Eurydice Hiss'd*, have been very adequately presented by W. W. Appleton. Comment on several of these plays when they were first acted or published in the eighteenth century will be found in *Henry Fielding: The Critical Heritage*, and an assessment of Fielding as a dramatist has been well undertaken by Ronald Paulson. The most comprehensive discussion of Fielding's life and work is still to be found in W. L. Cross's monograph.

The three volumes of *The Dramatic Works of David Garrick* (1798) have been reprinted, and as a supplement to them, Elizabeth P. Stein has given us texts of *Harlequin's Invasion*, *The Jubilee*, and *The Meeting of the Company*, from the original manuscripts in the Huntington and Boston Public Libraries. She commented upon them and on the plays in general in her *David Garrick, Dramatist*, an essential work on the subject. The biographies by Margaret Barton and Carola Oman give good pictures of the man, but he can be best seen in the theatre in Kalman A. Burnim's *David Garrick, Director*, and in F. L. Bergman's thoughtful article on the impact of the player on the creation of dramatic literature. James Boaden brought out a rather slovenly edition of Garrick's private correspondence in 1831–2, but for a very efficient modern text of the great actor's own letters, the reader must see Little and Kahrl's edition.

George Colman's dramatic works, published in four volumes in 1777, have not been reprinted recently, but good texts of *The Clandestine Marriage* (written with Garrick) and of *The Jealous Wife* are in Nettleton and Case's *British Dramatists from Dryden to Sheridan*. Eugene R. Page's monograph presents a well-documented and thorough account of Colman's life and work. For his letters (not yet fully collected), see *Posthumous Letters* and R. B. Peake, *Memoirs of the Colman Family*.

Two actor-dramatists may also be mentioned. Excellent accounts of Foote's life and works have been written by M. M. Belden and by Simon Trefman. A good study of Macklin has been presented by W. W. Appleton, and *Four Comedies* has been edited by J. O. Bartley.

BIBLIOGRAPHIES

Readers will inevitably be referred to the relevant portions of *The New Cambridge Bibliography*, to Stratman's bibliography of tragedy, and to Arnott and Robinson's revision of, and supplement to, Lowe's *Bibliographical Account*. They are of first-rate importance to the advanced student but may well bewilder the beginner with sheer weight of titles. For annual lists, recourse should be had to the *Philological Quarterly*, in which trifles are noted, works of substance are quickly summarized, and major contributions to knowledge are properly reviewed. This system is much to be preferred to the mere lists in *The Annual Bibliography* or the erratic notes in *The Year's Work in English Studies*.

For handlists of plays of the period, the reader must see Allardyce Nicoll's histories and his catalogue. *The Rothschild Library* gives useful collations for a number of plays, and Iolo A. Williams's book is helpful in the same way for work by Goldsmith and Sheridan.

REFERENCES

GENERAL WORKS

J. F. Arnott and J. W. Robinson, *English Theatrical Literature, 1559–1900, A Bibliography incorporating R. W. Lowe's 'A Bibliographical Account of English Theatrical Literature' published in 1888* (London, 1970).

ed. E. L. Avery, *The London Stage 1660–1800*, Part 2, 2 vols. (Carbondale, Ill., 1960); Part 3, ed. A. H. Scouten, 2 vols. (1961); Part 4, ed. G. W. Stone, Jr., 3 vols. (1962); Part 5, ed. C. B. Hogan, 3 vols. (1968).

F. W. Bateson, *English Comic Drama, 1700–1750* (Oxford, 1929).

ed. R. W. Bevis, *Eighteenth Century Drama: Afterpieces* (London, 1970).

ed. L. Hughes and A. H. Scouten, *Ten English Farces* (Austin, Tex., 1948).

ed. E. Inchbald, *A Collection of Farces and other Afterpieces*, 7 vols. (London, 1809).

ed. D. MacMillan and H. M. Jones, *Plays of the Restoration and Eighteenth Century as They were acted at the Theatres-Royal by Their Majesties' Servants* (London, 1931).

ed. G. H. Nettleton and A. E. Case, *British Dramatists from Dryden to Sheridan* (Boston, Mass., and London, 1939; rev. by G. W. Stone, Jr., New York, 1969).

A. Nicoll, *A History of Early Eighteenth-Century Drama, 1700–1750* (Cambridge, 1925; 3rd (rev.) edn., 1952).

——, *A History of Late Eighteenth-Century Drama, 1750–1800* (Cambridge, 1927; 3rd (rev.) edn., 1952).

P. E. Parnell, 'The Sentimental Mask', *PMLA* 78 (1963).

C. J. Rawson, 'Some Remarks on Eighteenth-Century "Delicacy" ', *JEGP* 61 (1962).

The Rothschild Library, 2 vols. (Cambridge, 1954).

A. Sherbo, *English Sentimental Drama* (East Lansing, Mich., 1957).

ed. C. J. Stratman, *Bibliography of English Printed Tragedy, 1565–1900* (Carbondale, Ill., and London, 1966).
ed. S. Trussler, *Burlesque Plays of the Eighteenth Century* (London, 1969).
ed. G. Watson, *The New Cambridge Bibliography of English Literature*, vol. 2 (Cambridge, 1971).
I. A. Williams, *Seven XVIIth-Century Bibliographies* (inc. Goldsmith and Sheridan; London, 1924).

Colley Cibber (1671–1757)

TEXTS

An Apology for the Life of Mr. Colley Cibber, Comedian (London, 1740; ed. R. W. Lowe, 2 vols., London, 1889; Everyman's Library, London, 1914; ed. B. R. S. Fone, Ann Arbor, Mich., 1968).
ed. W. W. Appleton, *The Careless Husband* (Regents Restoration Drama Series, Lincoln, Nebr., 1966).
ed. W. M. Peterson, *The Rival Queans* (Painesville, Ohio, 1965).

CRITICAL STUDIES AND COMMENTARY

F. D. Senior, *The Life and Times of Colley Cibber* (London, 1928).

George Colman the Elder (1732–94)

TEXTS

The Dramatick Works of George Colman, 4 vols. (London, 1777).

CRITICAL STUDIES AND COMMENTARY

ed. G. Colman the younger, *Posthumous Letters* (London, 1820).
E. R. Page, *George Colman the Elder* (New York, 1935).
R. B. Peake, *Memoirs of the Colman Family*, 2 vols. (London, 1841).

Richard Cumberland (1732–1811)

CRITICAL STUDIES AND COMMENTARY

S. T. Williams, *Richard Cumberland: His Life and Dramatic Works* (New Haven, Conn., 1917).

Henry Fielding (1707–54)

TEXTS

ed. W. E. Henley, *The Complete Works of Henry Fielding, Esq.*, 16 vols. (London, 1903; repr. New York and London, 1967). The plays are in vols. 8–12.
ed. W. W. Appleton, '*The Historical Register for the Year 1736*' and '*Eurydice Hiss'd*' (Regents Restoration Drama Series, Lincoln, Nebr., 1966).
ed. J. T. Hillhouse, *The Tragedy of Tragedies* (New Haven, Conn., and London, 1918).

ed. E. V. Roberts, *The Grub Street Opera* (Regents Restoration Drama Series, Lincoln, Nebr., 1969).

ed. C. B. Woods, *The Author's Farce* (Regents Restoration Drama Series, Lincoln, Nebr., 1966).

CRITICAL STUDIES AND COMMENTARY

W. L. Cross, *The History of Henry Fielding*, 3 vols. (New Haven, Conn., 1918).

R. Paulson, *Satire and the Novel in Eighteenth Century England* (New Haven, Conn., and London, 1967).

ed. R. Paulson and T. Lockwood, *Henry Fielding: The Critical Heritage* (London and New York, 1969).

Samuel Foote (1720–77)

CRITICAL STUDIES AND COMMENTARY

M. M. Belden, *The Dramatic Work of Samuel Foote* (New Haven, Conn., 1929; repr. 1969).

S. Trefman, *Sam. Foote, Comedian (1720–1777)* (New York, 1971).

David Garrick (1717–79)

TEXTS

The Dramatic Works of David Garrick, 3 vols. (London, 1798; repr. Farnborough, 1969).

ed. E. P. Stein, *Three Plays by David Garrick* (New York, 1926; repr. 1967).

CRITICAL STUDIES AND COMMENTARY

M. Barton, *Garrick* (London, 1948).

F. L. Bergman, 'David Garrick and *The Clandestine Marriage*', *PMLA* 67 (1952).

[ed. J. Boaden], *The Private Correspondence of David Garrick*, 2 vols. (London, 1831–2).

K. A. Burnim, *David Garrick, Director* (Pittsburgh, Ohio, 1961).

ed. D. M. Little and G. M. Kahrl, *The Letters of David Garrick*, 3 vols. (Cambridge, Mass., 1963).

C. Oman, *David Garrick* (London, 1958).

E. P. Stein, *David Garrick, Dramatist* (New York, 1938).

John Gay (1685–1732)

TEXTS

Poetical, Dramatic, and Miscellaneous Works, 6 vols. (London, 1795).

The Plays of John Gay, 2 vols. (Abbey Classics, London [1923]).

The Beggar's Opera

facsimile of the 'third' edition of 1729, with commentaries by L. Kronenberger and M. Goberman (Larchmont, N.Y., 1961).

ed. E. V. Roberts (Regents Restoration Drama Series, Lincoln, Nebr., 1969).

Three Weeks after Marriage

ed. R. Morton and W. M. Peterson (Painesville, Ohio, 1961).
ed. J. H. Smith (Augustan Reprint Society, London, 1961).

CRITICAL STUDIES AND COMMENTARY

S. M. Armens, *John Gay, Social Critic* (New York, 1954; repr. 1966).
B. H. Bronson, 'The Beggar's Opera', *Studies in the Literature of the Augustan Age . . . in Honor of A. E. Case* (ed. R. C. Boys, Ann Arbor, Mich., 1952).
——, 'The True Proportion of Gay's *Acis and Galatea*', *PMLA* 80 (1965).
ed. C. F. Burgess, *The Letters of John Gay* (Oxford, 1966).
W. Empson, *Some Versions of Pastoral* (London, 1935).
E. M. Gagey, *Ballad Opera* (New York, 1937; repr. 1965).
W. H. Irving, *John Gay, Favorite of the Wits* (Durham, N.C., 1940).
W. Mellers, *Harmonious Meeting* (London, 1965).
L. Melville, *Life and Letters of John Gay* (London, 1921).
W. E. Schultz, *Gay's Beggar's Opera* (New Haven, Conn., and London, 1923; repr. New York, 1967).
G. Sherburn, 'The Fortunes and Misfortunes of *Three Hours after Marriage*', *MP* 24 (1926–27).
A. E. Swaen, 'The Airs and Tunes of Gay's *Beggar's Opera*', *Anglia* 43 (1919).

Oliver Goldsmith (1730?–74)

TEXTS

ed. A. Friedman, *Collected Works of Oliver Goldsmith*, 5 vols. (Oxford, 1966).
——, *Goldsmith's 'She Stoops to Conquer'* (London, 1968).
ed. A. I. P. Wood, *'The Grumbler'*, *An Adaptation by Oliver Goldsmith* (Cambridge, Mass., 1931).

CRITICAL STUDIES AND COMMENTARY

ed. K. C. Balderston, *The History and Sources of Percy's Memoir of Goldsmith* (Cambridge, 1926).
——, *The Collected Letters of Oliver Goldsmith* (Cambridge, 1928).
J. Forster, *The Life and Adventures of Oliver Goldsmith*, 2 vols. (2nd edn., London, 1854).
A. Friedman, 'Aspects of Sentimentalism in Eighteenth Century Literature', in *The Augustan Milieu: Essays Presented to Louis Landa* (Oxford, 1970).
W. F. Gallaway, Jr., 'The Sentimentalism of Goldsmith', *PMLA* 48 (1933).
B. Gassman, 'French Sources of Goldsmith's *The Good Natur'd Man*', *PQ* 39 (1960).
J. Prior, *The Life of Oliver Goldsmith*, 2 vols. (London, 1837).
R. Quintana, 'Goldsmith, Ironist to the Georgians', in *Eighteenth Century Studies in Honor of Donald Hyde* (New York, 1970).
R. M. Wardle, *Oliver Goldsmith* (Lawrence, Kans., and London, 1957).

Thomas Holcroft (1745–1809)

CRITICAL STUDIES AND COMMENTARY

ed. E. Colby, *The Life of Thomas Holcroft, Written by Himself and continued to the Time of his Death From his Diary Notes and other Papers by William Hazlitt*, 2 vols. (London, 1925).

V. R. Stallbaumer, 'Holcroft: a Satirist in the Stream of Sentimentalism', *ELH* 3 (1936).

George Lillo (1693–1739)

TEXTS

ed. W. H. MacBurney, *The London Merchant* (Regents Restoration Drama Series, Lincoln, Nebr., 1965).

——, *Fatal Curiosity* (Regents Restoration Drama Series, Lincoln, Nebr., 1966).

Charles Macklin (1697?–1797)

TEXTS

ed. J. O. Bartley, *Four Comedies by Charles Macklin* (London, 1968). (*Love à la Mode, The School for Husbands, The True-Born Irishman, The Man of the World*).

CRITICAL STUDIES AND COMMENTARY

W. W. Appleton, *Charles Macklin, An Actor's Life* (Cambridge, Mass., 1961).

Nicholas Rowe (1674–1718)

TEXTS

ed. J. R. Sutherland, *Three Plays (Tamerlane, The Fair Penitent, Jane Shore) by Nicholas Rowe* (London, 1929).

R. B. Sheridan (1751–1816)

TEXTS

[Murray, pub.] *The Works of the late Right Honourable Richard Brinsley Sheridan*, 2 vols. (London, 1821).

ed. C. Price, *Sheridan's 'The Rivals'* (London, 1968).

——, *Sheridan's 'The School for Scandal'* (London, 1971).

——, *The Dramatic Works of R. B. Sheridan*, 2 vols. (Oxford, 1973).

ed. R. L. Purdy, *The Rivals, A Comedy, As it was first Acted* (Oxford, 1935).

ed. W. F. Rae, *Sheridan's Plays Now Printed as He Wrote Them* (London, 1902).

ed. R. C. Rhodes, *The Plays and Poems of R. B. Sheridan*, 3 vols. (Oxford, 1928; repr. New York, 1962).

CRITICAL STUDIES AND COMMENTARY

ed. C. Brooks and R. B. Heilman, *Understanding Drama* (New York, 1948).

C. Deelman, 'The Original Cast of *The School for Scandal*', *RES*, N.S. 13 (1962).

J. Dulck, *Les Comédies de Sheridan. Étude littéraire* (Paris, 1962).

J. R. de J. Jackson, 'The Importance of Witty Dialogue in *The School for Scandal*', *MLN* 76 (1961).

T. Moore, *Memoirs of the Life of the Right Honourable Richard Brinsley Sheridan*, 2 vols. (5th edn., London, 1825).

M. Mudrick, 'Restoration Comedy and After', in *English Stage Comedy* (ed. W. K. Wimsatt, New York, 1935).

C. Price, 'The Completion of *The School for Scandal*', *TLS*, 28 December 1967, p. 1265.

ed. C. Price, *The Letters of R. B. Sheridan*, 3 vols. (Oxford, 1966).

W. F. Rae, *Sheridan*, 2 vols. (London, 1896).

R. C. Rhodes, *Harlequin Sheridan: The Man and the Legend* (Oxford, 1933).

W. Sichel, *Sheridan*, 2 vols. (London, 1909).

Richard Steele (1672–1729)

TEXTS

ed. S. S. Kenny, *The Plays of Richard Steele* (Oxford, 1971).

CRITICAL STUDIES AND COMMENTARY

ed. R. Blanchard, *The Correspondence of Richard Steele* (London, 1941).

J. Loftis, *Steele at Drury Lane* (Berkeley and Los Angeles, Calif., 1952).

C. Winter, *Captain Steele: the Early Career of Richard Steele* (Baltimore, Md., and London, 1964).

——, *Sir Richard Steele, M.P. The Later Career* (Baltimore, Md., and London, 1970).

13. NINETEENTH-CENTURY DRAMA

MICHAEL R. BOOTH

TEXTS

THE number of nineteenth-century plays available in modern editions is slowly increasing, but one can hardly say that the choice is plentiful. No editor has accorded a nineteenth-century play the full textual treatment that Elizabethan and Jacobean plays, for instance, have received; indeed, such complete treatment is probably as yet neither necessary nor desirable for plays of this period.

The only major collection in print is *English Plays of the Nineteenth Century*, edited by Michael Booth. This contains in four volumes twenty-four plays illustrative of different genres of dramatic writing: tragedy, melodrama, 'drama', comedy, and farce. (A fifth and final volume of pantomime, extravaganza, and burlesque will also be published.) Each volume also contains a general introduction of some length, individual play prefaces, illustrations, and appendices concerned with acting, production, and critical reception. Nine plays from this collection, with a new introduction, appear in a paperback, '*The Magistrate*' *and Other Nineteenth-Century Plays*. An admirable collection in a single volume is *Nineteenth-Century Plays*, edited by George Rowell: ten melodramas and comedies from 1829 to 1890, an introduction, and a useful brief glossary of terms found in the stage directions of acting editions. The same editor's *Late Victorian Plays*, also an Oxford Paperback, extends past the Edwardian period, but does include two noted plays of the 1890s, Pinero's *The Second Mrs. Tanqueray* and Jones's *The Liars*. The latter play, together with Pinero's *The Notorious Mrs. Ebbsmith*, comprises the text of *The New Drama*, edited and introduced by Carl Selle. *British Plays of the Nineteenth Century*, edited by J. O. Bailey, is a textbook with unpleasantly crowded double columns and sometimes superficial historical and critical comment, but it contains seventeen plays, most of them unavailable in other modern editions. Michael Booth's volume *Hiss the Villain* reprints six English and American melodramas famous in their own time; the introduction defines and discusses the melodramatic form. The largest available collection might produce as much eyestrain as the perusal of the old acting editions, but it has the advantage of immediate accessibility.

This is the Readex *English and American Drama of the Nineteenth Century*, a reproduction on microcard of thousands of printed and some manuscript texts.

Individual nineteenth-century dramatists have not been as well served. A two-volume edition of James Albery's plays, including *Two Roses* and *Pink Dominos*, appeared in 1939, edited by Wyndham Albery. David Krause has edited (or at least selected, for little textual work appears to have been done—a common failing in many of these editions) *The Shaughraun, Arrah-na-Pogue*, and *The Colleen Bawn* in *The Dolmen Boucicault*, with a helpful glossary of Irish expressions. The introduction takes a teleological view of Boucicault in that he is viewed as a precursor of the glories of Synge and O'Casey; this is a fruitful approach, but unfortunately a basic familiarity with nineteenth-century theatre and an awareness of Boucicault's relationship with the drama of his own time do not accompany it. Seven other plays by Boucicault, including *Forbidden Fruit, Louis XI, The Flying Scud*, and *Robert Emmett*, edited by Allardyce Nicoll and F. T. Cloak, can be found in *America's Lost Plays*. Forty-one plays by W. S. Gilbert, including all the Gilbert and Sullivan operas, are in the four volumes of *Original Plays by W. S. Gilbert*, several times reprinted and still the most comprehensive selection of Gilbert published. Five early Gilbert opera burlesques were collected by Isaac Goldberg in *New and Original Extravaganzas*, and six of the burlesques and satires written for the German Reeds' Gallery of Illustration are edited by Jane Stedman in *Gilbert Before Sullivan*. This edition, with its lengthy introduction, is a substantial and illuminating piece of scholarship; the plays are admirably related to their theatrical and dramatic context. The most informative edition of the operas, by Reginald Allen, is *The First Night Gilbert and Sullivan*; the texts are those of the première performances, together with facsimiles of the first-night programmes, reproductions of contemporary drawings, and an introduction and descriptive particulars by the editor. Among the numerous editions and reprints of Oscar Wilde, it is perhaps necessary to indicate only the revised *Complete Works of Oscar Wilde* with the four-act version of *The Importance of Being Earnest*. There is as yet no scholarly edition of Wilde's plays. The 1908 *Bibliography of Oscar Wilde*, by Stuart Mason, is still the standard bibliography of Wilde's writings. The plays of Pinero and Jones began appearing singly in commercial editions after 1891, but the only larger editions of their plays are those by Clayton Hamilton fifty years ago: *The Social Plays of A. W. Pinero* and *Representative Plays of Henry Arthur Jones*, the former a collection of eight plays, the latter of seventeen; only half of them were first performed in the nineteenth century.

THEATRICAL BACKGROUND

An awareness of theatrical conditions is not only helpful but absolutely essential for an understanding and appreciation of nineteenth-century drama. So much criticism of this period is misconceived and faulty because its authors have little knowledge of the theatrical context; they attempt to isolate the drama from the theatre, and are inclined to dismiss the latter contemptuously and to look only for literary values in the former; not finding them, they dismiss the drama as well. Such criticism—and it is still being written— displays a complete misunderstanding of the essentially theatrical nature and intentions of almost all nineteenth-century drama, and is of no assistance to the student who wishes to know it better. Nineteenth-century drama and theatre are of course quite inseparable, and must always be considered together.

Appropriate reference works are Diana Howard's *London Theatres and Music Halls 1850–1950*, a bibliography of information pertaining to the historical, architectural, managerial, and journalistic records of the theatres of the time, and the reports of two parliamentary committees: the Select Committee on Dramatic Literature of 1832 and the Select Committee on Theatrical Licences and Regulations of 1866. These reports contain a mass of information on innumerable aspects of drama and theatre as well as an interesting and representative variety of public attitudes to them. Any edition of *Who's Who in the Theatre*, such as that for 1972, edited by F. Gaye, lists important revivals and long runs, and provides theatrical obituaries, family trees, and the amounts of money left in theatrical wills.

There are few modern studies of nineteenth-century theatre and theatre practice. A useful general introduction is George Rowell's *The Victorian Theatre* (the period actually covered is 1792–1914); like other theatrical studies, it also discusses the drama. A fuller and more detailed examination is E. B. Watson's *Sheridan to Robertson*, although published fifty years ago still one of the most valuable accounts of traditionalists and reformers in the period, with much perceptive comment on acting, staging, and management. Richard Southern's *The Victorian Theatre* is a pictorial impression of some aspects of staging, scene-painting, theatre architecture, acting, and audiences; the book is haphazardly organized and inadequate even as a survey, but the 140 well-chosen illustrations are excellent. Two much earlier but still important books are H. B. Baker's *History of the London Stage* and Erroll Sherson's *London's Lost Theatres of the Nineteenth Century*. Over half the former is concerned with the nineteenth century, and there is a great deal of information on the character and repertory of the smaller theatres as well as the larger. The latter work, though full of inaccuracies, is still the only extended survey of those nineteenth-century theatres that had vanished by the time Sherson published in 1925. Both books provide valuable information on the neglected theatre outside the West End; too many historians still write of the nineteenth-century drama as if it were entirely a West End product. In this conjunction one should also mention A. E. Wilson's *East End Entertainment*, with its discussion of some thirteen East End theatres, and Clive Barker's 'The Chartists, Theatre Reform, and Research', which calls attention to the vigorous and politically sensitive life of the East End working-class theatre in the 1830s. Somewhat peripheral, but vividly conveying the colour and vitality of nineteenth-century theatre, is A. H. Saxon's *Enter Foot and Horse*, a history of that peculiarly nineteenth-century dramatic form, hippodrama, and of the staging of battles and Shakespeare in the circus ring. The toy theatre—the children's stage for pantomime, melodrama, and most other types of contemporary drama—is described in A. E. Wilson's *Penny Plain, Twopence Coloured* and George Speaight's *The History of the English Toy Theatre*, works of rich theatrical flavour. The latter is the more organized and scholarly study; both are handsomely illustrated.

Several books have concentrated on individual figures rather than general areas. Two of the leading actor-managers of the century have been examined in *The Eminent Tragedian: William Charles Macready* by Alan Downer, and *Samuel Phelps and Sadler's Wells Theatre*, by Shirley Allen. Downer's authoritative work on Macready is more of an acting and managerial study than a biography, and centres on Macready's two periods of management (1837-9 and 1841-3) at Covent Garden and Drury Lane. The book on Phelps— interestingly anti-Macready in its earlier sections—has a similar area of emphasis and especially investigates Phelps's achievements as an actor and producer of Shakespeare. Clifford John Williams and William Appleton have written general accounts of Madame Vestris's life in the theatre: *Madame Vestris* and *Madame Vestris and the London Stage* respectively. The latter is the better organized and more scholarly work. Leo Waitzkin's *The Witch of Wych Street* examines her staging reforms at the Olympic Theatre in the 1830s. A knowledge of the work of Macready, Phelps, and Vestris (together with Charles Kean, upon whom his contemporary J. W. Cole's *The*

Life and Theatrical Times of Charles Kean is still the only substantial work) is most important, for it dispels the still-lingering and completely mistaken notion that changes and reforms in the nineteenth-century theatre did not begin until Robertson and the Bancrofts in the 1860s. Richard Findlater's *Grimaldi* is the only twentieth-century biography of the great pantomime clown, and achieves what often escapes historians of acting: a clear and vivid impression of an individual acting technique. A similarly complete impression of a great and distinctive tragic style is obtainable from *Edmund Kean*, by H. N. Hillebrand, the most detailed and reliable of several books on this actor. Laurence Irving's *Henry Irving*, although adulatory, contains much information on Irving's acting and management.

The legal background to playwriting and performance is important for an understanding of the restrictions within which dramatists and managers were required to work. For instance, when one is inclined to attack the alleged triviality of so much nineteenth-century drama, it is as well to remember that successive Lord Chamberlains interpreted their powers under the Licensing Act of 1737 and the Theatres Regulation Act of 1843 to mean that dramatists could be and were forbidden to deal seriously (or even at all) with religious, political, and sexual themes. The practical operation of such restrictions is exemplified in J. F. Stottlar's 'A Victorian Stage Censor: The Theory and Practice of William Bodham Donne'. The relationship of the law to the licensing of theatres and the movement towards freedom from theatrical monopolies culminating in their abolition in 1843 are discussed in a work that is still the authoritative study of the subject, *The Struggle for a Free Stage in London*, by Watson Nicholson. Dewey Ganzel's 'Patent Wrongs and Patent Theatres: Drama and the Law in the Early Nineteenth Century' is a concise summary of the same situation; though incorrect about playwrights' fees it is illuminating on the 1832 Select Committee, the censorship, and copyright.

This section can conclude with a selection of Victorian books of varied uses. Percy Fitzgerald's *The World Behind the Scenes* is the only English book of the century to concern itself significantly with stage technology. The Bancrofts in *Mr. and Mrs. Bancroft On and Off the Stage* offer much information on the plays of Robertson, their own managements at the Prince of Wales's and the Haymarket, and the interesting subject of entering upon an acting career. *Our Recent Actors*, by Westland Marston, is one of the most perceptive accounts of acting and actors; similarly valuable is much of George Henry Lewes's *On Actors and the Art of Acting*. The only significant and general modern study of nineteenth-century acting is Alan Downer's 'Players and Painted Stage: Nineteenth-Century Acting'. It is a subject much neglected by contemporary historians.

THE DRAMATISTS AND THEIR WORK

Biographies of nineteenth-century playwrights are few and far between, and the autobiographical dramatist, like the actor, tended all too readily to anecdote and non-theatrical chit-chat. Two highly informative recollections, however, are *Thirty-Five Years of a Dramatic Author's Life*, by Edward Fitzball, and J. R. Planché's *Recollections and Reflections*. Fitzball was a leading melodramatist and wrote mainly for the minor theatres; Planché, the author of light classical burlesques, virtually the inventor of the extravaganza, and a reformer of theatrical costuming, has much of interest on these matters. *The Memoirs of Charles Dibdin the Younger* is full of valuable material concerning repertory and stage management at Sadler's Wells, Astley's, and the Royal Circus early in the century. Later studies are critical as well as biographical; in most cases they are of some age and represent the only substantial treatment of their subjects. Such are *Sheridan Knowles and the Theatre of his Time*, by L. H. Meeks; Townsend Walsh's *The Career of Dion Boucicault*, and T. E. Pemberton's *The Life and Writings of T. W. Robertson*. All are inadequate as biographies and critical-historical studies, but all contain much useful information; Pemberton's book reprints some of Robertson's excellent theatrical criticism from the *Illustrated Times*. A more thorough study (though light on biography) of a completely representative and eclectic early nineteenth-century dramatist, the author of some of the most popular comedies of the day, is J. F. Bagster-Collins's *George Colman the Younger*. The definitive biography of W. S. Gilbert has yet to be written; still first in the field are Hesketh Pearson's *Gilbert: His Life and Strife* and Isaac Goldberg's *The Story of Gilbert and Sullivan*. Oscar Wilde is also in need of a fresh biography, but one can recommend Pearson's *The Life of Oscar Wilde*. *The Life and Letters of Henry Arthur Jones*, by his daughter, is the only biography of this dramatist, inevitably subjective and uncritical, but valuably informative.

Turning from biography to dramatic criticism, one also notices a paucity of modern material. The most useful collection, *Victorian Dramatic Criticism*, edited by George Rowell, contains 110 reviews ranging in selection from Hunt and Hazlitt to Beerbohm and Desmond MacCarthy, and is divided into sections relating to dramatic genres, theatres, audiences, and theatre criticism itself. A selection of Hunt's reviews in the *Examiner* and *Tatler* is available in the Houtchens edition, *Leigh Hunt's Dramatic Criticism 1808–1831*; an additional selection can be found in the Hunt volume of the Archer–Lowe edition in three parts of *Dramatic Essays*, the other two volumes being occupied by selections from the theatre reviews and essays of Hazlitt, John Forster (*Examiner* reviews 1835–8), and George Henry Lewes (*Leader* reviews 1850–4). A considerable amount of dramatic criticism was reprinted in the nineteenth century; a fair selection of this is available in the Rowell anthology, but a fuller picture of the theatre and drama of the time, as well as the attitudes of particular reviewers, is obtainable from the early collections. In addition to the Archer–Lowe volumes, three can be especially recommended: Morley's *Journal of a London Playgoer* (*Examiner* reviews 1851–66), reprinted with an introduction by Michael Booth; Dutton Cook's *Nights at the Play* (*Pall Mall Gazette* and *World* reviews 1867–81); and Joseph Knight's *Theatrical Notes* (*Athenaeum* reviews 1874–9). Henry James's somewhat denigratory essays on the London theatre (he preferred Parisian theatre) of the late 1870s in *The Scenic Art* are also rewarding.

The 1890s has undoubtedly been the greatest decade of the English dramatic critic. As important a critic as Shaw and probably more influential was William Archer; his five annual volumes of reviews from the *World* provide a comprehensive account of the theatre from 1893 to 1897. Finally, the criticism of Shaw's peerless successor on the *Saturday Review*, Max Beerbohm, has been selected in three volumes: *Around Theatres*, *More Theatres*, and *Last Theatres*; the first two contain reviews written before 1900.

There was also, of course, a wide range of comment on the drama outside the columns of theatre reviews; there is space to mention only two studies here. Percy Fitzgerald's *Principles of Comedy and Dramatic Effect*, published in 1870, takes a despondent view of the stage and of dramatic authors. As well as discussing modern playwriting, staging, and acting, it also contains lengthy chapters on comedy and burlesque—the latter a form, like farce, ignored by most critics and historians. Archer's *English Dramatists of To-Day*, published twelve years later, is more hopeful. Archer politely rejects the 'playwrights of yesterday'—particularly Robertson, Taylor, Boucicault, and Charles Reade—and devotes the rest of the book to a detailed and perceptive examination of the 'dramatists of today', sixteen of them altogether. *English Dramatists of To-Day* is the most thorough review of the state of the contemporary drama written at any time in the nineteenth century.

A Bibliography of British Dramatic Periodicals, edited by Carl Stratman, is a most useful and comprehensive compilation for those wishing to do further research in nineteenth-century dramatic criticism; it includes information on library holdings, dates of publication, number of volumes published, and names of editors when these are known.

Full-length studies of a general nature on the nineteenth-century drama are not common. Since this is the third time this kind of statement has been made in this chapter, it can be gathered that much needs to be done in all areas of research. Apart from Rowell's *The Victorian Theatre*, already mentioned, the two volumes of Allardyce Nicoll's *A History of English Drama* concerned with the nineteenth century constitute a valuable general survey, and the 'Hand-List of Plays' at the end of each volume is an indispensable tool for any research in the field. Joseph Donohue's *Dramatic Character in the English Romantic Age* only partly pertains to the nineteenth century, but his account of how critics, dramatists, and actors arrived at certain conceptions of dramatic character and therefore at certain critical standards, dramatic themes, and acting styles that expressed these standards is masterly; the section on early nineteenth century tragedy and the spectacle-drama *Pizarro* deals fully with material neglected or only superficially treated by other writers. Bertrand Evans's *Gothic Drama from Walpole to Shelley* analyses Gothic themes and techniques in tragedy and melodrama, and discusses the major plays and authors of this kind of drama. It too is a full and perspicacious treatment of a rather neglected and often theatrically sensational area of drama. *Nineteenth Century British Theatre*, edited by Kenneth Richards and Peter Thomson, a collection of papers delivered to a symposium on the subject, contains interesting material on the Victorian theatre and several articles relating to the drama, notably 'The Early Career of George Colman the Younger' (Peter Thomson), 'Early Victorian Farce: Dionysus Domesticated' (Michael Booth), 'George Henry Lewes as Playwright: A Register of Pieces' (John Hopkin), and 'The First Production of *The Importance of Being Earnest*: A Proposal for a Reconstructive Study' (Joseph Donohue).

Dramatic genres have been the subject of several studies, although again not in profusion. Melodrama has attracted the most interest. M. W. Disher's *Blood and Thunder* and *Melodrama* are vigorously if loosely written, and offer descriptive summaries of numerous melodramas and many fine illustrations; the former ranges from about 1790 to 1860, and the latter from about 1860 to 1930. Michael

Booth's *English Melodrama* defines and characterizes melodrama, gives its dramatic and theatrical background, differentiates it according to type (gothic and eastern, military and nautical, domestic, sensation), discusses its decline, and offers a selective bibliography, sixty illustrations, and an appendix on the acting of melodrama which has also appeared as a separate article. The same author's 'The Drunkard's Progress: Nineteenth-Century Temperance Drama' examines this militant and strenuous branch of the parent tree. Frank Rahill's *The World of Melodrama* surveys French and American melodrama as well as English, which comprises about a third of the book. Robin Estill's article, '*The Factory Lad*: Melodrama as Propaganda', points out the radicalism and rebellious political spirit of working-class theatre, taking this play as an example. Lastly, one nineteenth-century work should be mentioned: Jerome K. Jerome's *Stage Land*, delightfully illustrated by Bernard Partridge, humorously and with gentle satire treats the world of late Victorian melodrama as a real place, with curious laws and an odd logic of its own, and its inhabitants—hero, villain, heroine, comic man, villagers, etc.—as real people. The result is not only extremely entertaining but also illuminates the content and character of 1880s melodrama.

Other genres have had less attention. Fred Thomson in 'A Crisis in Early Victorian Drama: John Westland Marston and the Syncretics' discusses the 'unacted drama', the problems facing tragic writers, and the failure of the attempt to express modern life in pseudo-Elizabethan verse forms, with particular reference to George Stephen's *Martinuzzi* and Marston's *The Patrician's Daughter*. The discussion throws light on the sad state of legitimate tragedy in the 1840s, but the author himself is inclined to dismiss Victorian drama as worthless; certainly he looks at it from the legitimist point of view, while at the same time acknowledging the legitimists' failure to write good plays and attract audiences. Martin Meisel's 'Political Extravaganza: A Phase of Nineteenth-Century British Theatre' examines the topical reference and political satire of several burlesque-extravaganzas (as he terms them), as well as the difficulties they caused the Examiner of Plays. The only two books on burlesque are a late Victorian study, *A Book of Burlesque*, by W. D. Adams, and V. C. Clinton-Baddeley's *The Burlesque Tradition in the English Theatre after 1660*. The former goes thoroughly if ploddingly through its subject: classical burlesque, fairy-tale burlesque (Adams includes what we might call extravaganza), and burlesque of history), Shakespeare, contemporary drama, opera, fiction, and song.

The latter contains a brief section on nineteenth-century burlesque, particularly on melodrama, and comments on Planché's extravaganzas. Pantomime has found at least more than one recent historian. A. E. Wilson's *Christmas Pantomime* is devoted mainly to the nineteenth century, and more to the Victorian pantomime of E. L. Blanchard, Augustus Harris, and Dan Leno than to the Regency pantomime of Grimaldi. His *Pantomime Pageant* covers much the same ground, but does contain additional material. Neither book is at all scholarly; by far the most authoritative and scholarly study is *Harlequin in His Element* by David Mayer. The author concentrates on the pantomime of 1806–36; his hero is Grimaldi, and he wishes not only to demonstrate the superiority of Grimaldi-style harlequinade to later pantomime that subordinated the harlequinade to other elements, but also to show the political and social relevance and satirical potential of the Regency pantomime.

Nineteenth-century pantomime and farce are dramatic forms that certainly merit more consideration than they have been given. Individual dramatists have also been long lost to view in the fogs and glooms of critical neglect. Only Planché, Gilbert, and Wilde have been the subject of any sustained examination; two or three other playwrights have received the favour of a single book or an article or two. Several such studies have been mentioned above; of the others, the best is Winston Tolles's *Tom Taylor and the Victorian Drama*. Tolles is careful to establish the theatrical and dramatic context of Taylor's plays, as well as subjecting them to perceptive analysis and classification. *Bulwer and Macready*, Charles Shattuck's edition of the correspondence that passed between Bulwer, Macready, and Forster concerning the production of Bulwer's plays at various theatres between 1837 and 1840, is most informative, not only about Bulwer's development as a playwright, but especially about the role Macready as actor-manager played in suggesting revisions and indeed collaboratively determining the final shape of the plays. *Bulwer and Macready* is the best account we have of the relations between a nineteenth-century dramatist and his actor-manager. Three articles on Planché by Dougald Macmillan—'Planché's Early Classical Burlesques', 'Some Burlesques with a Purpose, 1830–70', 'Planché's Fairy Extravaganzas'—together with Harley Granville-Barker's 'Exit Planché—Enter Gilbert', all but constitute modern criticism of one of the most ingenious and attractive of nineteenth-century playwrights, and all date from the period 1928–32. Granville-Barker's article is an appreciation of the burlesque writers of the fifties and sixties as well as a critique of Planché and the early Gilbert; his affection for this much-maligned variety of Victorian theatre informs his work with sympathy as well as critical understanding. There is also Stanley Wells's 'Shakespeare in Planché's Extravaganzas', an interesting revelation of the extent to which Planché used Shakespeare's plays and wove Shakespearian speeches and allusions into the fabric of his work; of no less interest is Planché's assumption that audiences would immediately recognize his borrowings. All these articles comment more than adequately on Planché's extravaganzas (published in five volumes during his own lifetime) and burlesques but do not refer to his substantial output of melodramas and farces. Charles Reade, author of some forty plays, is the subject of a single article, Sheila Smith's 'Realism in the Drama of Charles Reade', which discusses the spectacular and sensational elements in several of the plays, dismisses Reade as a dramatizer of social problems, and generally patronizes nineteenth-century drama—a not uncommon attitude among modern critics. Tom Robertson receives some mention in any general study of nineteenth-century drama, but that is about all, except for *Thomas William Robertson: His Plays and Stagecraft*, by Maynard Savin, a careful and dogged investigation of Robertson's techniques in writing and staging. Unfortunately, the book is marred by the traditional critical tendency to equate Robertson with the Herald of the Dawn and the pre-Robertsonian period with the Dark Ages of the Drama; and the introductory chapter on the state of the mid-Victorian theatre is a lamentable caricature of acting, staging, and playwriting before the 1860s. Needless to say, not one of the playwrights mentioned has been published in a selected edition in the twentieth century.

W. S. Gilbert, at least, has been granted the honour of both editions and a considerable number of books and articles. Bibliographically, the dramatist Gilbert can hardly be separated from the composer Sullivan, but although the former's satirical powers fully emerged in the collaboration with Sullivan, the following selection concentrates as best as it can upon Gilbert alone. Two useful anthologies are *W. S. Gilbert: A Century of Scholarship and Commentary* and *Gilbert and Sullivan*. The former contains eighteen articles and a selected bibliography; several articles are included for historical interest and read strangely now. Helpful for their introductory remarks on the state of Gilbert bibliography are '*The Gondoliers* and *Princess Ida*', by David Randall, and 'The Printing of *The Grand Duke*: Notes Toward a Gilbert Bibliography', by J. B. Jones. Jane Stedman's 'The Genesis of *Patience*' illustrates the value of textual scholarship when applied to Gilbert—or to any nineteenth-century

dramatist, for that matter. *Gilbert and Sullivan* (nineteen articles) contains more than one contribution betraying a sad lack of knowledge
and understanding of nineteenth-century drama and theatre as a
whole, but there are compensations in Colin Prestige's 'D'Oyly
Carte and the Pirates', Terence Rees's 'W. S. Gilbert and the Pantomime Season of 1866', George McElroy's 'Meilhac and Halévy—
and Gilbert: Comic Converses', and Jane Stedman's 'Gilbert's
Stagecraft: Little Blocks of Wood'. Not especially relevant to
Gilbert, but useful in suggesting possible starting-points for research,
is Michael Booth's article from the same anthology, 'Research
Opportunities in Nineteenth-Century Drama and Theatre.' A listing
of all Gilbert's plays, together with brief critical comment, is
'William Schwenck Gilbert: An Anniversary Survey', by Reginald
Allen; this is expanded in the same author's *W. S. Gilbert: An
Anniversary Survey and Exhibition Check-List*. Two final articles worthy
of mention are E. P. Lawrence's ' "The Happy Land": W. S. Gilbert
as Political Satirist' and Jane Stedman's 'From Dame to Woman:
W. S. Gilbert and Theatrical Transvestism'. The former deals with
the *cause célèbre* of the Lord Chamberlain's brief suppression in 1873
of the burlesque by Gilbert and Gilbert Arthur À Beckett, the latter
with Gilbert's oft-decried treatment of middle-aged women, a study
that carefully places the subject of the older woman in the context
of Victorian dramatic characterization and tradition (especially
burlesque and transvestism), and shows to what extent Gilbert
adapted them for his own purposes.

An awareness of dramatic traditions, the contemporary drama,
and the state of the theatre is almost totally absent from academic
criticism of Oscar Wilde; his plays are treated as literature quite
divorced from the drama and theatre of the 1890s. For example,
Lady Windermere's Fan, *A Woman of No Importance*, and *An Ideal
Husband* are seen as comedies rather than what they were, variants
of the conventional society melodrama of the 1890s. It is therefore
difficult to recommend a selection of recent critical work (biographies and general studies of Wilde of course include comment on
his plays). About the only article that relates Wilde to the drama of
his century is Richard Foster's 'Wilde as Parodist', concerned like
most of the others with *The Importance of Being Earnest*. An exception
to this emphasis is Morse Peckham's 'What Did Lady Windermere
Learn?', which discusses the themes of *Lady Windermere's Fan*, concluding that she learns nothing and is thus opposed to the understanding of Mrs. Erlynne. H. E. Toliver's 'Wilde and the Importance
of "Sincere and Studied Triviality" ' sees 'serious triviality' as the

unifying principle in the comic structure of the plays. Ian Gregor in
'Comedy and Oscar Wilde' views the dramatic creation of the dandy
and the simultaneous creation of a dramatic world projecting the
dandy as Wilde's basic concern. Early writings on him are conveniently assembled in K. Beckson's volume in the 'Critical Heritage' Series.

We can conclude with two of Wilde's contemporaries, Pinero and
Jones. One of the few studies of Pinero is Wilbur Dunkel's *Sir Arthur
Pinero*; it suffers from desultory organization and superficial analysis.
Much superior is Cecil Davies's 'Pinero: The Drama of Reputation',
which demonstrates how central to Pinero's characters and his plays
(and, naturally, his audiences) was the absolute social necessity of
preserving reputation—especially for women—and how this preoccupation motivates the more important dramas. *Henry Arthur Jones
and the Modern Drama*, by R. A. Cordell, possesses the usual introductory and inadequate chapter on the worthlessness of Victorian
drama before the entrance upon the scene of the chosen subject, but
otherwise is a fair attempt at asserting the rightful importance of
Jones as a transitional figure. The best short account of Jones's innovations and significance is Marjorie Northend's 'Henry Arthur Jones
and the Development of the Modern English Drama', although it
mistakenly regards Robertson's comedies as 'the first manifestations
of the social drama', decries the 'artificial absurdities' of melodrama,
and generally belittles pre-Jones drama. Jones's own collection of
eighteen lectures, articles, and prefaces dating from 1883 to 1893,
The Renascence of the English Drama, illuminates his early radicalism as
well as the state of the drama in that decade; it is a valuable book.

REFERENCES

ANTHOLOGIES OF PLAYS

ed. J. O. Bailey, *British Plays of the Nineteenth Century* (New York, 1966).
ed. M. R. Booth, *English Plays of the Nineteenth Century*, 4 vols. (Oxford,
1969–73).
——, *Hiss the Villain* (London, 1964).
——'*The Magistrate*' and Other Nineteenth-Century Plays (London, 1974).
ed. A. Nicoll and G. Freedley, *English and American Drama of the Nineteenth
Century* (New York, 1965–).
ed. G. Rowell, *Late Victorian Plays* (World's Classics, London, 1968; repr.
1972).
——, *Nineteenth-Century Plays* (World's Classics, London, 1953; repr. 1972).
ed. C. M. Selle, *The New Drama* (Miami, Flor., 1963).

THEATRICAL BACKGROUND

S. S. Allen, *Samuel Phelps and the Sadler's Wells Theatre* (Middletown, Conn., 1971).

W. Appleton, *Madame Vestris and the London Stage* (New York, 1974).

H. B. Baker, *History of the London Stage* (London, 1904; repr. New York, 1969).

S. and M. Bancroft, *Mr. and Mrs. Bancroft On and Off the Stage*, 2 vols. (London, 1888).

C. Barker, 'The Chartists, Theatre Reform, and Research', *Theatre Quarterly* 1 (1971).

J. W. Cole, *The Life and Theatrical Times of Charles Kean*, 2 vols. (London, 1859; repr. New York, 1971).

A. S. Downer, *The Eminent Tragedian: William Charles Macready* (Cambridge, Mass., 1966).

——, 'Players and Painted Stage: Nineteenth-Century Acting', *PMLA* 61 (1946).

R. Findlater, *Grimaldi* (London, 1955).

P. Fitzgerald, *The World Behind the Scenes* (London, 1881; repr. New York, 1971).

D. Ganzel, 'Patent Wrongs and Patent Theatres: Drama and the Law in the Early Nineteenth Century', *PMLA* 76 (1961).

ed. F. Gaye, *Who's Who in the Theatre* (15th edn., London, 1972).

H. N. Hillebrand, *Edmund Kean* (New York, 1933; repr. 1966).

D. Howard, *London Theatres and Music Halls 1850–1950* (Woking, 1970).

L. Irving, *Henry Irving* (London, 1951).

G. H. Lewes, *On Actors and the Art of Acting* (London, 1875; repr. Westport, Conn., 1968).

W. Marston, *Our Recent Actors*, 2 vols. (London, 1888; repr. New York, 1971).

W. Nicholson, *The Struggle for a Free Stage in London* (Boston, Mass., 1906; repr. New York, 1966).

Report from the Select Committee on Dramatic Literature (London, 1832; repr. Shannon, 1968).

Report from the Select Committee on Theatrical Licences and Regulations (London, 1866; repr. Shannon, 1970).

G. Rowell, *The Victorian Theatre* (London, 1956; 2nd edn., 1967).

A. H. Saxon, *Enter Foot and Horse* (New Haven, Conn., 1968).

E. Sherson, *London's Lost Theatres of the Nineteenth Century* (London, 1925; repr. New York, 1971).

R. Southern, *The Victorian Theatre* (Newton Abbot, 1970).

G. Speaight, *The History of the English Toy Theatre* (London, 1969); first printed as *Juvenile Drama* (London, 1946).

J. F. Stottlar, 'A Victorian Stage Censor: The Theory and Practice of William Bodham Donne', *Victorian Studies* 13 (1970).

L. Waitzkin, *The Witch of Wych Street* (Cambridge, Mass., 1934).

E. B. Watson, *Sheridan to Robertson* (Cambridge, Mass., 1926; repr. New York, 1963).

C. J. Williams, *Madame Vestris* (London, 1973).
A. E. Wilson, *East End Entertainment* (London, 1954).
——, *Penny Plain, Twopence Coloured* (London, 1932; repr. New York, 1969).

THE DRAMATISTS AND THEIR WORK

W. D. Adams, *A Book of Burlesque* (London, 1891).
W. Archer, *English Dramatists of To-Day* (London, 1882).
——, *The Theatrical 'World' 1893–1897*, 5 vols. (London, 1894–8; repr. New York, 1971).
—— and R. W. Lowe, eds., *Dramatic Essays: William Hazlitt* (repr. as *Hazlitt on Theatre*, Dramabooks, New York, n.d.); *Dramatic Essays: Leigh Hunt; Dramatic Essays: John Forster, George Henry Lewes* (London, 1894–6).
M. Beerbohm, *Around Theatres* (London, 1924; repr. 1953).
——, *More Theatres* (London, 1969).
——, *Last Theatres* (London, 1970).
M. R. Booth, 'The Acting of Melodrama', *University of Toronto Quarterly* 34 (1964).
——, 'The Drunkard's Progress: Nineteenth-Century Temperance Drama', *Dalhousie Review* 44 (1964).
——, *English Melodrama* (London, 1965).
V. C. Clinton-Baddeley, *The Burlesque Tradition in the English Theatre after 1660* (London, 1952; repr. 1973).
D. Cook, *Nights at the Play* (London, 1883; repr. New York, 1971).
M. W. Disher, *Blood and Thunder* (London, 1949).
——, *Melodrama* (London, 1954).
J. Donohue, *Dramatic Character in the English Romantic Age* (Princeton, N.J., 1970).
R. Estill, '*The Factory Lad*: Melodrama as Propaganda', *Theatre Quarterly* 1 (1971).
B. Evans, *Gothic Drama from Walpole to Shelley* (Berkeley and Los Angeles, Calif., 1947).
P. Fitzgerald, *Principles of Comedy and Dramatic Effect* (London, 1870).
H. Granville-Barker, 'Exit Planché—Enter Gilbert, I–II', *London Mercury* 25 (1932); also in *The Eighteen-Sixties*, ed. J. Drinkwater (Cambridge, 1932).
Leigh Hunt's Dramatic Criticism 1808–1831, ed. L. H. and C. W. Houtchens (New York, 1949).
H. James, *The Scenic Art*, ed. A. Wade (London, 1949; repr. New York, 1957).
J. K. Jerome, *Stage-Land: Curious Habits and Customs of its Inhabitants* (London, 1889).
H. A. Jones, *The Renascence of the English Drama* (London, 1895).
J. Knight, *Theatrical Notes* (London, 1893; repr. New York, 1971).
D. Mayer, *Harlequin in His Element* (Cambridge, Mass., 1969).
M. Meisel, 'Political Extravaganza: A Phase of Nineteenth-Century British Theatre', *Theatre Survey* 3 (1962).

H. Morley, *The Journal of a London Playgoer* (London, 1866; repr. Leicester, 1974).
A. Nicoll, *A History of English Drama 1660–1900*, vol. 4 (Cambridge, 1930; 2nd edn. 1955); vol. 5 (Cambridge, 1946; 2nd edn. 1959).
F. Rahill, *The World of Melodrama* (University Park, Pa., 1967).
ed. K. Richards and P. Thomson, *Nineteenth Century British Theatre* (London, 1971).
ed. G. Rowell, *Victorian Dramatic Criticism* (London, 1971).
ed. C. H. Shattuck, *Bulwer and Macready* (Urbana, Ill., 1958).
ed. C. J. Stratman, *A Bibliography of British Dramatic Periodicals* (New York, 1962); rev. as *Britain's Theatrical Periodicals, 1720–1967: A Bibliography* (New York, 1972).
F. C. Thomson, 'A Crisis in Early Victorian Drama: John Westland Marston and the Syncretics', *Victorian Studies* 9 (1966).
A. E. Wilson, *Christmas Pantomime* (London, 1934).
——, *Pantomime Pageant* (London, 1946).

Individual Dramatists
James Albery (1838–89)

ed. W. Albery, *The Dramatic Works of James Albery*, 2 vols. (London, 1939).

Dion Boucicault (1820?–90)

ed. D. Krause, *The Dolmen Boucicault* (Dublin, 1962).
ed. A. Nicoll and F. T. Cloak, *'Forbidden Fruit' and Other Plays*, in *America's Lost Plays*, ed. B. H. Clark, vol. 1 (Princeton, N.J., 1940; Bloomington, Ind., 1963).

T. Walsh, *The Career of Dion Boucicault* (New York, 1915; repr. 1967).

George Colman the Younger (1762–1836)

J. F. Bagster-Collins, *George Colman the Younger* (London, 1946).

Charles Dibdin the Younger (1768–1833)

ed. G. Speaight, *Memoirs of Charles Dibdin the Younger* (London, 1956).

Edward Fitzball (1792–1873)

E. Fitzball, *Thirty-Five Years of a Dramatic Author's Life*, 2 vols. (London, 1859).

Sir William Schwenck Gilbert (1836–1911)

Original Plays by W. S. Gilbert, 4 vols. (London, 1876–1911).
ed. I. Goldberg, *New and Original Extravaganzas* (Cambridge, Mass., 1931).
ed. J. W. Stedman, *Gilbert Before Sullivan* (Chicago, Ill., 1967).

CRITICAL STUDIES AND COMMENTARY

ed. R. Allen, *The First Night Gilbert and Sullivan* (New York, 1963).

'William Schwenck Gilbert: An Anniversary Survey', *Theatre Notebook* 15 (1961).

W. S. Gilbert: An Anniversary Survey and Exhibition Check-List (Charlottesville, Va., 1963).

I. Goldberg, *The Story of Gilbert and Sullivan* (London, 1929; repr. New York, 1970).

ed. J. Helyar, *Gilbert and Sullivan: Papers Presented at the International Conference* (Lawrence, Kans., 1971).

ed. J. B. Jones, *W. S. Gilbert: A Century of Scholarship and Commentary* (New York, 1970).

E. P. Lawrence, ' "The Happy Land": W. S. Gilbert as Political Satirist', *Victorian Studies* 15 (1971).

H. Pearson, *Gilbert: His Life and Strife* (London, 1957).

J. W. Stedman, 'From Dame to Woman: W. S. Gilbert and Theatrical Transvestism', *Victorian Studies* 14 (1970).

Henry Arthur Jones (1851–1929)

TEXTS

ed. C. Hamilton, *Representative Plays*, 4 vols. (London, 1926).

CRITICAL STUDIES AND COMMENTARY

R. A. Cordell, *Henry Arthur Jones and the Modern Drama* (London, 1932; repr. Port Washington, N.Y., 1968).

D. A. Jones, *The Life and Letters of Henry Arthur Jones* (London, 1930; repr. St. Clair Shores, Mich., 1971).

M. Northend, 'Henry Arthur Jones and the Development of the Modern English Drama', *RES* 18 (1943).

Sheridan Knowles (1784–1862)

L. H. Meeks, *Sheridan Knowles and the Theatre of his Time* (Bloomington, Ind., 1933).

Sir Arthur Wing Pinero (1855–1934)

TEXTS

ed. C. Hamilton, *The Social Plays of A. W. Pinero*, 4 vols. (New York, 1917–22).

CRITICAL STUDIES AND COMMENTARY

C. W. Davies, 'Pinero: The Drama of Reputation', *English* 14 (1962).

W. D. Dunkel, *Sir Arthur Wing Pinero* (Chicago, Ill., 1941; repr. Port Washington, N.Y., 1967).

James Robinson Planché (1796–1880)

TEXTS

ed. T. F. Dillon Croker and Stephen Tucker, *The Extravaganzas of J. R. Planché, Esq., 1825–71*, 5 vols. (London, 1879).

J. R. Planché, *Recollections and Reflections* (London, 1872; 2nd edn. 1901; repr. New York, 1968).

CRITICAL STUDIES AND COMMENTARY

H. Granville-Barker, 'Exit Planché—Enter Gilbert, I–II', *London Mercury* 25 (1932); also in *The Eighteen-Sixties*, ed. J. Drinkwater (Cambridge, 1932).

D. Macmillan, 'Planché's Early Classical Burlesques', *SP* 25 (1928).

——, 'Some Burlesques with a Purpose, 1830–70', *PQ* 8 (1929).

——, 'Planché's Fairy Extravaganzas', *SP* 28 (1931).

S. Wells, 'Shakespeare in Planché's Extravaganzas', *Shakespeare Survey 16* (1963).

Charles Reade (1814–84)

S. M. Smith, 'Realism in the Drama of Charles Reade', *English* 12 (1958).

Thomas William Robertson (1829–71)

T. E. Pemberton, *The Life and Writings of T. W. Robertson* (London, 1893).

M. Savin, *Thomas William Robertson: His Plays and Stagecraft* (Providence, R.I., 1950).

Tom Taylor (1817–80)

W. Tolles, *Tom Taylor and the Victorian Drama* (New York, 1940; repr. 1966).

Oscar Wilde (1854–1900)

TEXTS

ed. G. F. Maine, *The Complete Works of Oscar Wilde* (London, 1948; 2nd edn. 1966).

CRITICAL STUDIES AND COMMENTARY

ed. K. Beckson, *Oscar Wilde: The Critical Heritage* (London, 1971).

R. Foster, 'Wilde as Parodist: A Second Look at *The Importance of Being Earnest*', *College English* 18 (1956).

I. Gregor, 'Comedy and Oscar Wilde', *Sewanee Review* 74 (1966).

S. Mason, *Bibliography of Oscar Wilde* (London, 1908, repr. 1967).

H. Pearson, *The Life of Oscar Wilde* (London, 1946; Harmondsworth, 1960).

M. Peckham, 'What Did Lady Windermere Learn?' *College English* 18 (1956).

H. E. Toliver, 'Wilde and the Importance of "Sincere and Studied Triviality" ', *Modern Drama* 5 (1963).

14. SHAW

MARGERY M. MORGAN

J. L. STYAN observes in *The Dark Comedy* (second edition, 1968):
'The Shavian play is still an unexplored field.' This may seem a
surprising statement in view of the quantity of print that has been ex-
pended on George Bernard Shaw (1856–1950) and his long establishment as a 'set author' in the syllabus of schools and colleges. But
the orthodox reading of Shaw that has prevailed in this context
generally continues on the lines laid down by early reviewers of the
plays in performance. The best of them, particularly Max Beerbohm
and Desmond MacCarthy, are still worth reading, not only for a
historical view of the work. The staleness of response set in later.
James Huneker's essay on Shaw, originally included in *Iconoclasts* in
1905, remains a dazzling piece of criticism, a rich mine of hints for
many approaches to his drama. But some of Huneker's conclusions
have been for too long accepted without question; as the commonplaces of later opinion they have lost subtlety as well as freshness and,
most of all, inwardness.

During the years of the development and heyday of the New
Criticism, hardly any thinking about Shaw went on at a high intellectual level; in England it has hardly started yet. One measure of
the dearth is the prominence retained by G. K. Chesterton's modest
and impressionistic study, first published in 1909, though reissued
in 1935 with an additional chapter making cursory review of the
later phases of Shaw's career. The book is essentially an interpretation of his character and cast of mind. It is shot through with a
slightly patronizing affection for its subject. (A modern reader may
reflect that time has dealt more kindly with Shaw's extravagances
on such topics as marriage and the family than it has with Chesterton's sublime common sense.) And there is some justification for
Shaw's own complaint that Chesterton wrote the book without
reading what *he* had written.

It is interesting that most subsequent discussions of Shavian drama
have concentrated on the period of his writing career with which
this early flowering of criticism was most concerned or entirely
concerned. Even in the revival of interest that has proceeded since
the middle 1960s, and that has been closely connected with the
general availability to scholars of the Shaw manuscripts, detailed

commentary on most of the later plays has been very sparse. (*Saint Joan* is the outstanding exception to this statement, and some of the essays on that could be classified as curiosities of literature.) There is not much of significance recorded in T. J. Spencer's survey of writing on the post-*Saint Joan* plays. On the other hand, the early collections of *Plays Pleasant and Unpleasant* have been thoughtfully scrutinized in particular essays by such distinguished scholars as Eric Bentley ('The Making of a Dramatist') and R. J. Kaufmann ('Shaw's Élitist Vision: . . . the Plays of the First Decade'); and Charles Carpenter has devoted a substantial and judicious book to this group; Stephen S. Stanton has been able to compile a *Casebook on 'Candida'* (a Pleasant play), and *Major Barbara* (1905) was chosen as theme for Rose Zimbardo's anthology of 'Twentieth Century Interpretations' (which just missed Barbara Bellow Watson's interesting article on the play); George Rowell, stretching a point, even so, had previously considered Shaw as a Victorian dramatist.

The tendency to found studies of Shaw on the basis of his relation to Ibsen and the Ibsenite 'problem play' (as John Gassner, in 'Shaw on Ibsen and the Drama of Ideas', has done very ably) has been partly responsible for the concentration on earlier, more demonstrably Ibsenite plays and neglect of those formed in a different mould. Dismissive treatment of later plays, from *Getting Married* onward, has been common in general accounts of Shaw's playwriting career (Martin Lamm's standard work on *Modern Drama* is an example). It is a peculiar hazard of such encyclopedic works as Gassner's *Masters of the Drama*, or Allardyce Nicoll's *World Drama*, that they should reflect popular reputation in treating individual plays as more of a piece than they usually are, without making fine critical distinctions; so that the good may be praised as wholly admirable, or a flaw may seem to damn an entire composition. So these authors' appreciation of the virtues of Shaw's dramaturgy, especially lively in the case of Gassner, is withheld from the less well-known plays; a cautious suspension of judgement would seem more appropriate to works that have not undergone the interpretative sifting that others have received in good measure.

Original as it is, and perhaps the most sensitive study of Shaw's imagination that has yet appeared, Alick West's *A Good Man Fallen Among Fabians* also becomes selective in its comment and rather more casual in its survey of the later plays. The Marxist verdict that *Major Barbara* represents Shaw's political capitulation to the enemies of socialism (though West finds signs of grace persisting long after this) is at least as much responsible for the balance of the book as is any influence of critical fashion. Alick West's advantage was that for him there was no contradiction between a concern with politics and a concern with art. His aesthetic appreciation was accompanied by a sympathetic recognition of a deep political commitment in Shaw's character as dramatist, seeking to communicate with his society, against the grain of an impulse to detach himself from it. He read the plays as developing out of the experience represented in Shaw's novels.

It is not chance that one of the few indubitably first-class studies of Shaw as an artist should be Marxist. Similarly, any discussion of the bibliography of Shaw must run into sociological considerations. Initially this follows from the kind of writer he was, his view of the nature and function of art (which may be judged from *The Quintessence of Ibsenism* and *The Perfect Wagnerite*), and the relation of his imaginative work to the rest of his activity, including his experience in local government as a vestryman of St. Pancras, as a leading member of the Fabian Society, author and editor of Fabian tracts and essays, and a maker of modern socialism. As a propounder of creative evolutionism, he claims a place in the post-Darwinian history of ideas; and his practical involvement in the theatre and its economics is another dimension of his art. What would be merely 'background' and of doubtful relevance to another writer is part of the core here. Grasping the how and why of this is part of the critic's task, as Edmund Wilson, and E. Strauss working on a larger scale with less complete success, realized. It will not do to substitute a knowledge of Shaw's opinions or of his public personality for an understanding of his art as a dramatist, though both contributed to the forms as well as to the content of that art. Shaw enthusiasts have paid most attention to the content, and to the character of the author; intellectuals have tended to regard him as a popularizer and vulgarian. Significantly, the scholar most active in Shaw studies from the 1920s to the 1950s was not a specialist in literature but a mathematician: Archibald Henderson, Shaw's 'official' biographer.

It is tempting, indeed, to put the generality of writing on Shaw into the alternative categories of the credulous or the disdainful, taking Hesketh Pearson as an engaging proponent of the first type and Raymond Williams as a representative of the second. Pearson had been an actor in the Edwardian theatre and played in the original Shaw–Granville-Barker production of *Androcles*. When he later chose to present Shaw anecdotally to a mass-readership, he effectively contributed to the myth of a culture hero. He had his subject's full co-operation in this, though Shaw, in styling Pearson his 'Boswell', hinted an awareness of being admired as a phenomenon, a grand exhibit, and understood hardly at all. His purposes were served. For Shaw always wanted to command the attention of the philistine middle class. In doing so he made a great deal of noise and a lot of money. He also rendered himself suspect to old Marxists and New Left, as to those who saw art as necessarily a minority interest in an age corrupted beyond repair by commercial values.

There is something complex to be unravelled here, if the survey of Shaw criticism is to take account not only of changes in time, but of what has happened at different social and cultural levels: a diversity revealed when Colin Wilson, in *The Outsider*, startled the cultural Establishment of 1956 by taking Shaw seriously as a modern intellectual force. It is not a simple matter of Bernard Shaw, self-educated journalist and man of the theatre, continuing to be enjoyed by a popular audience, but in fact lacking the sophistication and mental discipline to be valued by academic critics and creative writers of the first order (Yeats had a dream of Shaw as a clicking and grinning sewing-machine; T. S. Eliot described him as emotionally sub-adolescent). George Orwell's remark, 'In a working class home it is the man who is the master and not, as in a middle class home, the woman or the baby', serves to identify the author of *Candida*, *Man and Superman*, and *Saint Joan* as essentially middle class. What is more, he used his realization of the fact Orwell observed as a central clue in his explorations of English social values and political attitudes. Now the dominant school of literary criticism in Britain has for a generation pursued an anti-bourgeois mystique—and found it in the work of D. H. Lawrence. Shaw certainly did not share any nostalgia for working-class values and mores, the dream of sinking back rather than getting on; he was no grammar school boy.

Raymond Williams's *Drama from Ibsen to Eliot* was a brave book to come out of Cambridge in 1952, for the contributors to *Scrutiny* had shown little interest in drama, except when its dialogue could be read as poetry, and a contempt for theatre that had its roots in puritan tradition, entrenched—along with the usual subtle conservatism—in the critical faculties of other universities, too. The general seriousness of Williams's work and the way in which it extended the horizons of English academic criticism were admirable and helped establish *Drama from Ibsen to Eliot* as a standard reference book. The immediate effect on Shaw studies in Britain was unfortunate, however, as Williams's treatment of Shaw confirmed a prejudice, rather than breaking any new ground, and certainly discouraged others from further exploration. He took his theme from T. S. Eliot's remark referred to above and illustrated it with cursory reference to two Unpleasant plays and *Back to Methuselah* (read unironically) and rather more extended consideration of *Candida* and *Saint Joan*. Examining the texture of passages from these two plays produces some valid observations which need to be checked and supplemented by a consideration of them as dramatic structures; but Williams could not draw on an adequate methodology for this. Instead, his rejection of *Saint Joan* turns curiously on a refusal to believe in psychological hermaphrodites; and the unpretentious farce of *Arms and the Man*, recognized as very funny, is revealingly passed over as if it were artless. Eliot himself, of course, paid some positive tribute to Shaw by imitation, of the Shavian treatment of history, in *Murder in the Cathedral*; and, in his later plays, by embedding myth and ritual in drawing-room comedies or farces written for performance on Broadway or in the West End of London. But time's changes have affected Eliot's own reputation, and the title of the revised edition of Raymond Williams's book, published in 1968, has been altered to *Drama from Ibsen to Brecht*. Whereas the author originally found it difficult to believe that Shaw's 'dynamic as a dramatist can survive its period', in the revised text 'can' has been changed to 'ought to'.

Eric Bentley had already, in 1948, published *The Modern Theatre* (entitled *The Playwright as Thinker* in its American edition), setting Shaw among the modern European masters, including Brecht, and presenting him as an artist in comedy. Although he is English in origin, Bentley's awareness of strictly dramaturgical values and of the relations of drama to performance found a more congenial environment in the United States, where Theatre Studies had a respected place among university faculties long before they were first timidly admitted into the English university system. This must explain why the American commentary on Shaw in the past quarter of a century has been so much more plentiful, various, and interesting than what Britain has produced. It may be invidious to compare J. I. M. Stewart's solidly traditional discussion of Shaw, in *Eight Modern Writers*, with Francis Fergusson's challenging critiques of *Major Barbara* and *Heartbreak House*, in *The Idea of a Theater*, but the difference illustrates how an environment of on-going debate is helpful to the individual critic, and also suggests that the development of an adequate critical theory as background to practice is slower in the absence of a specialized professionalism.

Eric Bentley's monograph on Shaw offers a refinement on the life-and-works approach which is over-represented in the total bibliography of Shaw. The book follows Chesterton's general plan of concentrating on particular aspects of its subject, though it is much more fully documented. Those who have tried to give a general account of Shaw seem commonly to have been overwhelmed by their material. It is not easy to pick out one attempt as much more successful than the rest. On the other hand, to read them all is to be afflicted quite quickly by a sense of redundancy. The constant production of general accounts implies that Shaw has retained the capacity to interest everyman; and his accessibility gives rise to the notion that there is little for the scholar to do here. The sense is often betrayed that Shaw is more, or other, than a man-of-letters, and that his ideas, whether seen in the light of a philosophy or in terms of propaganda, are separable from his art and in some practical way more important than it. A temptation to fit him to a formula which recognizes this is evident in sub-titles from Henderson's *Playboy and Prophet* of 1932 to Leon Hugo's *Playwright and Preacher* of 1971. Apart from Bentley's account, William Irvine's *Universe of G.B.S.* and Colin Wilson's *Bernard Shaw. A Reassessment* are perhaps the most balanced and intelligent general studies, though the latter disappoints by conveying less of the excitement of discovery than one hopes for, in view of the personal meaning Shaw has had for Wilson. Martin Ellehauge has made the most thorough job of linking Shaw's ideas into the fabric of modern European thinking; J. B. Kaye's *Bernard Shaw and the Nineteenth Century Tradition* is more digestible; but both represent a scholarship that has avoided coming to terms with aesthetics.

All later writers on Shaw depend to some extent on Archibald Henderson's volumes, vast rag-bags of information and comment, far too unsystematic and diffuse to be easily used for reference, enlivened by bickerings in which the biographer is involved with a figure of Shaw who seems to be trying to read the manuscript over his shoulder. Whether it is more entertaining or irritating is a question of subjective response. It may be the lack of a consistent critical perspective that provokes doubts about the work's factual authority, unreasonable though such scepticism may be; but we have to take too much on trust in such a record, which is not research. It is a salutary reminder that all biography may properly be regarded as a form of fiction.

The best fiction, in the present instance, is the two-volume composite *Autobiography* expertly compiled by Stanley Weintraub from Shaw's own writings. It has its notable reticences, particularly on his marriage, where it may be supplemented by Janet Dunbar's diplomatic *Mrs. G.B.S.* However, Shaw's view of himself, or the version of himself he wished to be seen, has been challenged in two books published close together in time and covering much of the same ground in his early life: B. C. Rosset's *Shaw of Dublin* and John O'Donovan's slighter *Shaw and the Charlatan Genius.* Though these may be accused of too sensational an interpretation of the part played by his mother's music teacher, George John Vandeleur Lee, in Bernard Shaw's life, they have helped towards replacing the too familiar and over-defined image with intimations of a more private personality, still open to questioning. A new biographical study is expected from Michael Holroyd.

Association with Shaw has been enough to ensure publication of memoirs of his family. Many of his friends have claimed attention on their account, and a reading of Gilbert Murray's *Unfinished Autobiography*, for instance, or the first volume of A. H. Nethercot's two-volume life of Annie Besant (selected here partly in compensation because Nethercot's Shaw book, *Men and Supermen*, commended by many, seems to me indicative of the futility that excessive enthusiasm, equipped with a card index, may run to), certainly helps to put Shaw in perspective with his contemporaries. He touched the life of his time at so many points that relevant background studies would amount to a bibliography of British social and cultural life for the period. Because a lack of interest in politics and political ideas is certainly disabling to any would-be critic of Shaw, Alan McBriar's *Fabian Socialism and English Politics*, together with Beatrice Webb's journals, Margaret Cole's *Story of Fabian Socialism*, and Anne Fremantle's *This Little Band of Prophets* must be mentioned here, alongside the *Fabian Essays* Shaw himself contributed to and edited. The collections of fugitive texts edited by Dan H. Laurence in *How to Become a Musical Critic* and *Platform and Pulpit* and by Warren Sylvester Smith in *The Religious Speeches of G. B. Shaw* are reminders of other Shavian activities that contributed to his equipment as a playwright. Gilbert Murray claims attention partly because he seems to have guided Shaw's interest in the classics and in Greek drama in particular, as well as being closely associated with Shaw and Granville-Barker in their attempt to establish an unofficial national theatre. Shaw's indebtedness to Euripides was long ago discussed in an informed and appreciative paper by Gilbert Norwood, and the effect on his dramaturgy of an apprenticeship to Greek drama is one of the themes taken up in my own *Shavian Playground*.

The literature of Shaw's association with the theatre is already considerable. He is a central figure in Desmond MacCarthy's contemporary *The Court Theatre, 1904–1907*, and almost as central in P. P. Howe's *The Repertory Theatre*. C. B. Purdom's *Harley Granville Barker*, the accounts of Barry Jackson's work by G. W. Bishop and T. C. Kemp, and Lawrence Langner's *G.B.S. and the Lunatic* contain primary material for learning about Shaw's relationships with the managements largely responsible for the first productions of his plays and his own ideas of how those plays should be performed. A great many letters to actors and producers on matters dramatic, theatrical, and general are included in Dan H. Laurence's fine edition of *Collected Letters of G. B. Shaw* (in progress). Out of the number of previously published correspondences with particular individuals, *Ellen Terry and Bernard Shaw*, edited by Christopher St. John, especially justifies separate reading for its unified presentation of a rich friendship carried on almost entirely by letter. The testimony regarding Shaw's methods of work in the theatre, which various actors have given, was drawn on in W. A. Armstrong's article, 'George Bernard Shaw: The Playwright as Producer', and then later in Bernard F. Dukore's excellently researched and presented *Bernard Shaw, Director*. A useful selection of Shaw's writings on the theatre (drawn from outside the volumes of *Our Theatres in the Nineties*, included in the Constable Standard Edition) was edited by E. J. West, and his achievement as a dramatic critic has been discussed by H. Fromm. There have also been a number of books on the filming of Shaw's plays: Donald Costello's *The Serpent's Eye* and Valerie Pascal's biography of the producer-in-chief of Shaw films cover most ground. Mander and Mitchenson produced the standard companion to Shaw's plays in the form of photographic records of them in performance.

But Shaw proves to be more than the sum of his aspects, economist, philosopher, vegetarian, villager, spelling reformer, critic, playwright, and the rest. Like Humpty Dumpty he has been fragmented, and it is almost as hard to put him together again. The unity of his imagination is perhaps better appreciated through what is frankly a glimpse (Kronenberger's and Winsten's anthologies present a variety of such, including comments by experts in fields where Shaw was an active amateur), or by a narrowly defined approach as in Richard Ohmann's linguistically based *Shaw: The Style and the Man*, which might fairly be judged the best short book in the whole bibliography: bringing nothing startlingly new to light, it gives crisp and authoritative definition to what was previously a vague awareness about Shaw as a whole. One reversal of critical opinion, which may be too extreme for accuracy, has been necessary to clear the way for the new discovery of Shaw's unity where it might most properly be expected, in his drama. A. B. Walkley, Shaw's contemporary and theatre critic for *The Times*, argued on an Aristotelian basis that Shaw's plays were entertaining and provocative but 'not plays at all', and his view had great currency; Elder Olson, in *The Theory of Comedy* (1968), typifies the new way of rejecting philistine enthusiasm yet accepting Shaw: 'I do not think much of Shaw as a thinker . . . his ideas are neither original nor profound. Despite his reputation for argument, he is really very poor at it . . . But he *is* a great playwright . . . his contentiousness makes for freshness, and his extravagance for fun.' The anti-Aristotelian Brecht has passed between the two critics, of course, opening minds to the potential varieties of drama and the seriousness there may be in the comic form, even in farcical comedy; and a critical approach to Shaw via Brecht, who knew Shavian drama in the German theatre (which always rated him high) and wrote his own variations of it, can be rewarding. Incidentally, Olson's consideration of 'suspense of form' as characteristic of Shaw answers Raymond Williams's assertion that the plays are adequately accounted for by naming the social problems with which they deal, though it hardly goes far enough in recognizing how Shaw changed tack in methods of play-construction, through his career—a fact that has disconcerted and confused many of his critics.

The new wave of Shaw criticism, which really gets down to studying his art, seems at last to be gathering head. Carpenter's book, mentioned earlier, and Ohmann's belong to it; so does my own, which makes a close study of the majority of the plays, particularly those that have received little attention before, or that have been, in my opinion, misinterpreted or wrongly assessed. But Martin Meisel's *Shaw and the Nineteenth-Century Theater* dominates everything that has been published so far in its scope, scholarship, and the quality of its appreciation of Shaw's genius. (It is least strong in its understanding of the involvement of Shaw's political concerns with the rest.) Meisel has succeeded in establishing beyond doubt the growth of Shaw's art out of the vital modes of popular theatre known to Dublin and to England in the last century. Although he constantly stresses the intellectualizing transformation that this material undergoes in Shaw's hands, his book also manages to serve as a useful introduction to the theatre that, with all its faults, won Shaw's enthusiasm. Opera, spectacle, acting styles, conventions of plot and casting, as well as discussions of melodrama, farce, the well-made play, and romantic

theatre, are covered in this account. At times the reader may wish
for a more rigorous selection and ordering of the material and feel
that the method followed involves some repetition. On the other
hand, the scattered comments on individual plays are commonly
very perceptive. It is the book of one who has read Shaw imaginatively, as well as extensively; and, if it is an overcrowded book, that
must be related to the author's evident desire to convey his whole
and intricate view of a big subject.

Louis Crompton's *Shaw the Dramatist* deals with eleven plays, including *Back to Methuselah* and *Heartbreak House*, and has made use
of Shaw papers only recently available in order to comprehend
more thoroughly the relation between the materials and what Shaw
made out of them. A. M. Gibbs's *Shaw*, in the Writers and Critics
series, is an introduction to Shavian drama which offers original,
alert readings of individual plays, refreshingly uncluttered by
irrelevancies and the dead weight of accepted opinion. The dramatic
texts are the field of John A. Mills's stylistic approach in *Language
and Laughter* (Ohmann looks at Shaw's prose outside the plays),
which contains much useful analysis of dialogue techniques. Fred
Mayne's *The Wit and Satire of Bernard Shaw* is an uneven book, which
contains some sharp critical comments, but does not finally justify
its attempt to contain Shaw's variousness in categories drawn from
older modes of rhetorical study, and it seems to have been hurriedly
finished. There is room for another book on Shaw as a satirist and
for an altogether wider view of his irony. (An earlier article, Walter
N. King's 'The Rhetoric of *Candida*', is not only helpful in the study
of that particular play, it can usefully supplement Mayne's and
Mills's work by its demonstration of a method of composing dialogue
that Shaw used extensively: a verbal patterning of themes, comparable to the iterative imagery in a Shakespeare play.)

The absence from the English scene of an academic periodical
exclusively concerned with modern drama and theatre both reflects
and helps to explain the infrequency with which English critical
studies of Shaw appear in comparison with American. Even the
exceptions tend to vanish under scrutiny: Leon Hugo and Fred
Mayne represent South African scholarship; A. M. Gibbs is
Australian, and *The Shavian Playground* was partly written in Australia. G. Pilecki's study of the evolution of the text of *Geneva* comes
from Canada, as does Norman Rosenblood's edition of critical essays
on Shaw, a fruit of the Shaw Festival and Seminar held at Niagara-
on-the-Lake. It is instructive to compare the American *Shaw
Review*, now a thoroughly academic periodical and indispensable for

its regular listing of Shaviana, as well as its reviews and articles, with the British *Shavian,* which appears less regularly and has retained its amateur flavour, a tribute in this to a popular genius resistant to being cordoned off. Naturally, the articles that appear in periodicals vary greatly in quality and substance and cover a great diversity of topics. It is by a very arbitrary choice that I list a few to represent so many more.

F. P. W. McDowell and D. J. Leary are prominent Shaw scholars, though they have not published in book form on his work. My particular selection of topics, among the articles, is intended to indicate the growth of interest in the later plays, which was fostered by Katherine Haynes Gatch, and in particular to indicate that there is now a considerable critical literature on *Heartbreak House,* to which Robert Brustein, in *The Theater of Revolt,* and A. M. Gibbs have contributed stimulating essays. R. B. Wilkenfeld's article on the play exemplifies a new readiness to experiment with different critical techniques in the study of Shaw: startlingly structuralist in its approach and rather formidable in idiom, for me it succeeded in reaching some fresh and valid understanding of how the play operates. H. Lüdecke's older and more traditional essay is on a more general and an important body of texts, and I am myself indebted to it.

Finally, editions of Shaw's writings have proliferated bewilderingly and serve as a reminder of his frequent rating with Shakespeare and Molière as a 'force' in the theatre. It has been common scholarly practice to refer to the Constable Standard Edition of Shaw's works, which he saw through the press himself. The *Complete Plays* and *Complete Prefaces,* originally issued by Odhams Press, were also authorized by Shaw and carefully printed according to his wishes. It looks at present as though the *Bodley Head Bernard Shaw* may supersede the Constable edition, which runs into many more volumes. Its supervisory editor is Dan H. Laurence, who is editing the *Collected Letters* and has been responsible for several collections of Shaw's writings not included in the Standard Edition. The text of the plays is carefully reproduced from the final version seen through the press by Shaw, and the last volume is to contain some previously unpublished minor dramatic pieces. A rather arbitrary selection of fugitive pieces connected with the plays, often newspaper interviews drafted by Shaw for publicity purposes, is included as supplementary material in each volume.

In the absence of the variorum edition which Shaw's much-revised plays demand, a few editions of single plays may be mentioned as having particular authority and interest for students. They range from the rare Independent Theatre edition of *Widowers' Houses* (1893), which antedates the collection of *Plays Unpleasant*, to the World's Classics edition of *Back to Methuselah*, specially revised and with a Postscript by the author, and to the screen version of *Major Barbara*, first issued in 1945 as a Penguin book. For the text of *Pygmalion* used in the famous first production with Mrs. Patrick Campbell the reader has to go behind the Standard text to the earlier Constable publication of 1918 in the old green casing. Indeed, the Penguin edition of the film script of this play, with illustrations by Felix Topolski, has priority over the text in the Standard Edition. There is relatively little discussion in print on the textual history of Shaw's work. I have listed a note by Harry Geduld, one of Shaw's editors. Charles Shattuck has shown how Shaw improved on his original version of *Widowers' Houses*, and G. Pilecki has made a thorough study of the successive changes in the text of *Geneva*, introduced chiefly in relation to the unfolding of historical events. Loewenstein's pamphlet is a guide to the Rehearsal Copies of Shaw's plays whose value extends beyond the book collector to anyone interested in the stages of composition that lie behind the final published text. Indeed the great libraries now hold ample evidence of the painstaking and almost obsessively patient habit of mind with which Shaw balanced his ability to imagine characters and let them rip. The British Museum's great collection includes shorthand, longhand, and typed versions of plays, from first jottings to promptbooks, scenarios to production notes. The contents of the very important collection at the University of Texas are described in Frederick J. Hunter's *Guide*. But it will be some time yet before a general bibliography of Shaw's writings is available. The huge task has passed from Loewenstein to Laurence, to whose labours all students of Shaw are already greatly indebted. The Broads' *Dictionary*, a valiant piece of work, was never adequate. For research students and others the computerized *Concordance* is an invaluable, and immense, aid.

REFERENCES

TEXTS

The Works of Bernard Shaw, 36 vols. (Constable Standard Edition, London, 1931–50).

ed. Dan H. Laurence, *The Bodley Head Bernard Shaw: Collected Plays with their Prefaces* (London, 1970–). In progress.

The Complete Plays of Bernard Shaw (Constable, London, 1931; Odhams Press, London, 1934; augmented edition, 1950; repr. Hamlyn, London, 1965).

Back to Methuselah, revised edition with a postscript (World's Classics, London, 1945).

Major Barbara: A Screen Version (Harmondsworth, 1945).

Pygmalion (Constable, London, 1916; Harmondsworth, 1941).

Widowers' Houses (Independent Theatre edition, London, 1893).

ed. Dan H. Laurence, *The Collected Letters of Bernard Shaw* (London and New York, vol. 1, 1965; vol. 2, 1972). In progress.

ed. C. St. John, *Ellen Terry and Bernard Shaw: a correspondence* (London, 1931).

The Complete Prefaces of Bernard Shaw (Constable, London, 1934; Odhams Press, 1938; Hamlyn, London, 1965).

ed. Dan H. Laurence, *How to Become a Musical Critic* (London, 1960).

——, *Platform and Pulpit* (New York, 1961).

ed. E. J. West, *Shaw on Theatre* (London, 1958).

ed. W. S. Smith, *The Religious Speeches of G. B. Shaw* (University Park, Pa., 1963).

Autobiography: see S. Weintraub *below*.

Fabian Essays: see below.

CONCORDANCE

ed. E. D. Bevan, *A Concordance to the Plays and Prefaces of Bernard Shaw*, 10 vols. (Detroit, 1972).

BIOGRAPHICAL AND GENERAL STUDIES

E. Bentley, *Bernard Shaw* (Norfolk, Conn., 1947; 2nd edn., London, 1967).

G. K. Chesterton, *George Bernard Shaw* (London, 1909; rev. edn., 1935; repr. 1949).

A. Henderson, *Bernard Shaw, Playboy and Prophet* (London, 1932).

——, *George Bernard Shaw, Man of the Century* (New York, 1956).

——, *Table-Talk of G.B.S. Conversations on Things in General between Bernard Shaw and his Biographer* (London, 1925).

L. Hugo, *Bernard Shaw. Playwright and Preacher* (London, 1971).

W. Irvine, *The Universe of G.B.S.* (New York, 1949).

J. O'Donovan, *Shaw and the Charlatan Genius. A Memoir* (Dublin, 1965).

244   MARGERY M. MORGAN

H. Pearson, *Bernard Shaw. His Life and Personality* (London, 1942).
——, *G.B.S. A Postscript* (London, 1951).
B. C. Rosset, *Shaw of Dublin. The Formative Years* (University Park, Pa., 1964).
S. Weintraub (compiler), *Shaw. An Autobiography 1856–98. Selected from his Writings* (New York, 1969).
——, *Shaw, An Autobiography 1898–1950. The Playwright Years* (London and New York, 1970).
C. Wilson, *Bernard Shaw. A Reassessment* (London, 1969).
ed. S. Winsten, *G.B.S. 90. Aspects of Bernard Shaw's Life and Works* (London, 1940).

BACKGROUND STUDIES

History of Ideas
M. Ellehauge, *The Position of Bernard Shaw in European Drama and Philosophy* (Copenhagen, 1931).
J. B. Kaye, *Bernard Shaw and the Nineteenth Century Tradition* (Norman, Okla., 1958).
C. Wilson, *The Outsider* (London, 1956).
——, *Religion and the Rebel* (Boston, Mass., and London, 1957).

Politics
M. I. Cole, *The Story of Fabian Socialism* (London, 1961).
Fabian Essays in Socialism, ed. G. B. Shaw (London, 1889; with new preface, 1931; with a postscript by the original editor, 1948; 6th edn. with a new introduction by A. Briggs, 1962).
A. Fremantle, *This Little Band of Prophets* (London, 1960).
A. M. McBriar, *Fabian Socialism and English Politics, 1884–1918* (Cambridge, 1962).

The Theatre
G. W. Bishop, *Barry Jackson and the London Theatre* (London, 1933).
P. P. Howe, *The Repertory Theatre. A Record and a Criticism* (London, 1910).
T. C. Kemp, *The Birmingham Repertory Theatre. The Playhouse and the Man* (Birmingham, 1943).
L. Langner, *G.B.S. and the Lunatic* (New York, 1963).
D. MacCarthy, *The Court Theatre, 1904–1907: A Commentary and a Criticism* (London, 1907; reissued, ed. S. Weintraub, Coral Gables, Fla., 1966).
R. Mander and J. Mitchenson, *A Theatrical Companion to Shaw* (London, 1954; 2nd edn. announced).
C. B. Purdom, *Harley Granville Barker* (London, 1955).

The Cinema
D. Costello, *The Serpent's Eye: Shaw and the Cinema* (Notre-Dame, Ind., 1965).
V. Pascal, *The Disciple: Gabriel Pascal, and his Devil: Bernard Shaw* (New York, 1970).

Friends and Associates

J. Dunbar, *Mrs. G.B.S.* (London, 1963).

G. Murray, *An Unfinished Autobiography*, ed. J. Smith and A. Toynbee (London, 1960).

A. H. Nethercot, *The First Five Lives of Annie Besant*, 2 vols. (Chicago, Ill., 1960).

B. Webb, *Diaries, 1912–1924*, ed. M. I. Cole (London, 1952).

——, *Our Partnership*, ed. B. Drake and M. I. Cole (London and New York, 1948).

BIBLIOGRAPHICAL

C. L. and V. M. Broad, *Dictionary to the Plays and Novels of Bernard Shaw, with a bibliography of his works and of the literature concerning him, with a record of the principal Shaw play productions* (London, 1929).

E. Farley and M. Carlson, 'George Bernard Shaw: A Selected Bibliography (1945–1955)', *Modern Drama* 2.ii and iii (September and December, 1959).

H. M. Geduld, 'The Textual Problem in Shaw', *Shaw Review* 5 (1960).

F. J. Hunter (compiler), *A Guide to the Theatre and Drama Collections at the University of Texas* (Austin, Tex., 1967).

F. E. Loewenstein, *The Rehearsal Copies of Bernard Shaw's Plays. A Bibliographical Study* (London, 1950).

T. J. Spencer, 'An Annotated Checklist of Criticism of the Post-*Saint Joan* Plays', *Shaw Review* 2 (1959).

See also I. Adelman and R. Dworkin, *Modern Drama. A Checklist of Critical Literature on 20th Century Plays* (New York, 1967), and H. H. Palmer and A. J. Dyson, *European Drama Criticism* (Hamden, Conn., 1968).

CRITICAL STUDIES AND COMMENTARY

General

M. Beerbohm, *Around Theatres* (London, 1924; repr. 1953).

——, *More Theatres* (London, 1969).

——, *Last Theatres* (London, 1970).

E. Bentley, *The Modern Theatre* (London, 1948; previous pub. as *The Playwright as Thinker*, New York, 1946).

R. Brustein, *The Theater of Revolt* (Boston, Mass., 1964).

F. Fergusson, *The Idea of a Theater* (Princeton, N.J., 1949).

J. Gassner, *Masters of the Drama* (New York, 1940; rev. and enlarged edn., 1954).

J. Huneker, *Iconoclasts* (New York, 1905; repr. Greenwood Press, New York, 1969).

M. Lamm, *Modern Drama*, trans. K. Elliott (Oxford, 1952).

A. Nicoll, *World Drama* (London, 1949).

E. Olson, *The Theory of Comedy* (Bloomington, Ind., and London, 1968).

G. Rowell, *The Victorian Theatre. A Survey* (London, 1956).

J. I. M. Stewart, *Eight Modern Writers* (Oxford History of English Literature, Oxford, 1963).

246   MARGERY M. MORGAN

J. L. Styan, *The Dark Comedy* (Cambridge, 1962; 2nd edn., 1968).
R. Williams, *Drama from Ibsen to Eliot* (London, 1952; rev. edn. with change of title to *Drama from Ibsen to Brecht*, London, 1968).

Specific Studies

W. A. Armstrong, 'George Bernard Shaw: The Playwright as Producer', *Modern Drama* 8 (1966).

E. Bentley, 'The Making of a Dramatist (1892–1903)', Foreword to *Plays by Bernard Shaw* (New American Library, New York, 1963; repr. in *Modern Drama. Essays in Criticism*, ed. T. Bogard and W. I. Oliver (London and New York, 1965) and in R. J. Kaufmann, ed., *G. B. Shaw*, listed below.

C. Carpenter, *Bernard Shaw and the Art of Destroying Ideals* (Madison, Wis., 1969).

L. Crompton, *Shaw the Dramatist* (Lincoln, Nebr., 1969).

B. F. Dukore, *Bernard Shaw, Director* (London and Washington, D.C., 1971).

H. Fromm, *Bernard Shaw and the Theater in the Nineties. A Study of Shaw's Dramatic Criticism* (Lawrence, Kans., 1967).

J. Gassner, 'Shaw on Ibsen and the Drama of Ideas', in *Ideas in the Drama*, ed. J. Gassner (English Institute Essays, New York, 1964).

K. H. Gatch, 'The Last Plays of Bernard Shaw: Dialectic and Despair', in *English Stage Comedy*, ed. W. K. Wimsatt, Jr. (English Institute Essays, New York, 1955).

A. M. Gibbs, *Shaw* (Writers and Critics, Edinburgh, 1969).

R. Hornby, 'The Symbolic Action of *Heartbreak House*', *Drama Survey* 7 (1968).

R. J. Kaufmann, ed., *G. B. Shaw. A Collection of Critical Essays* (Twentieth Century Views, Englewood Cliffs, N.J., 1965).

——, 'Shaw's Elitist Vision. A Serial Criticism of the Plays of the First Decade', *Komos* I (Monash University, Clayton, Vic., Australia, 1968).

W. N. King, 'The Rhetoric of *Candida*', *Modern Drama* 2 (1959).

ed. L. Kronenberger, *George Bernard Shaw, A Critical Survey* (Cleveland, Ohio, 1953).

D. J. Leary, 'The Moral Dialectic in *Caesar and Cleopatra*', *Shaw Review* 5 (1962).

——, 'Shaw's Blakean Vision: A Dialectic Approach to *Heartbreak House*', *Modern Drama* 15 (1972).

H. Lüdecke, 'Some Remarks on Shaw's History Plays', *ES* 36 (1955).

D. MacCarthy, *Shaw* (London, 1951).

F. P. W. McDowell, 'The Eternal against the Expedient: Structure and Theme in Shaw's *The Apple Cart*', *Modern Drama* 2 (1959).

——, 'Heaven, Hell and Turn-of-the-Century London. Reflections on Shaw's "Man and Superman" ', *Drama Survey* 2 (1963).

——, 'Spiritual and Political Reality: *The Simpleton of the Unexpected Isles*', *Modern Drama* 2 (1960).

——, 'Technique, Symbol and Theme in *Heartbreak House*', *PMLA* 68 (1953).

F. Mayne, *The Wit and Satire of Bernard Shaw* (London, 1967).

M. Meisel, *Shaw and the Nineteenth-Century Theater* (Princeton, N.J., 1963).

J. A. Mills, *Language and Laughter: Comic Diction in the Plays of Bernard Shaw* (Tucson, Ariz., 1969).

M. M. Morgan, *The Shavian Playground* (London, 1972).

G. Norwood, *Euripides and Mr. Bernard Shaw* (London, 1913); repr. in *Euripides and Shaw, with Other Essays* (London, 1921).

R. Ohmann, *Shaw: The Style and the Man* (Middletown, Conn., 1962).

G. Pilecki, *Shaw's 'Geneva': A Critical Study of the Evolution of the Text in relation to Shaw's Political Thought and Dramatic Practice* (The Hague, 1965).

ed. N. Rosenblood, *Shaw. Seven Critical Essays* (Toronto, 1971).

C. Shattuck, 'Bernard Shaw's "Bad Quarto" ', *JEGP* 54 (1955).

A. H. Silverman, 'Bernard Shaw's Political Extravaganzas', *Drama Survey* 5 (1966–7).

S. S. Stanton, *A Casebook on 'Candida'* (New York, 1962).

E. Strauss, *Bernard Shaw: Art and Socialism* (London, 1942).

B. B. Watson, 'Sainthood for Millionaires: "Major Barbara" ', *Modern Drama* 11 (1968).

A. West, *A Good Man Fallen Among Fabians* (London, 1950).

R. B. Wilkenfeld, 'Perpetual Motion in *Heartbreak House*', *Texas Studies in Literature and Language* 13 (1971).

E. Wilson, 'Bernard Shaw at Eighty', in *The Triple Thinkers* (New York, 1938; rev. edn., 1948) and in L. Kronenberger, ed., *George Bernard Shaw*, listed above.

ed. R. Zimbardo, *Twentieth-Century Interpretations of 'Major Barbara'. A Collection of Critical Essays* (Englewood Cliffs, N.J., 1970).

PERIODICALS devoted to Shaw and Shaviana are: *The Shavian* (Shaw Society, London), *The Shaw Review* (Shaw Society of America, State College, Pa.), and *The Independent Shavian* (New York Shavians). *The Shaw Review* includes a Continuing Checklist of Shaviana.

15. THE IRISH SCHOOL

ANN SADDLEMYER

ALTHOUGH a great many Irishmen have contributed over the centuries to the English stage, it was not until the establishment in 1899 of the Irish Literary Theatre by W. B. Yeats, Lady Gregory, and Edward Martyn that Ireland recognized the possibility of a new school of drama, written for and of Ireland. When the Abbey Theatre was founded in 1904, that possibility had become a reality. The history of Irish theatre before this period has been told by W. S. Clark in *The Early Irish Stage* and *The Irish Stage in the Country Towns*, by Peter Kavanagh in *The Irish Theatre*, and by La Tourette Stockwell in *Dublin Theatres and Theatre Customs*. In addition, the contribution of such Anglo-Irish dramatists as Oscar Wilde and Bernard Shaw is considered in all studies of English drama; but not so generally recognized is the influence of an Irish–American dramatist, Dion Boucicault. But even Boucicault's Irish plays came perilously close to presenting the stock Irish character of ridicule so bitterly disowned by Yeats and his colleagues; *The Stage Irishman* by G. C. Duggan efficiently traces the history of this characterization.

When the founders of the new Irish dramatic movement published their manifesto in the first issue of *Beltaine* and followed their arguments in *Samhain* and *The Arrow* (all reprinted by Yeats in *Explorations*), they were following, therefore—and fighting—a strong theatrical tradition. The story of that battle to give the public 'what we thought good until it became popular' has been told by Lady Gregory herself in *Our Irish Theatre*, by Yeats in a slightly more creative fashion in *Autobiographies*, and by George Moore with more distinctive colouring still in *Hail and Farewell*. Other highly personal interpretations can be found in W. G. Fay and Catherine Carswell's *The Fays of the Abbey Theatre* and Gerard Fay's *The Abbey Theatre: Cradle of Genius*, while Frank Fay's essays, *Towards a National Theatre*, serve as a valuable background to the theories of the two brothers who provided Yeats and Lady Gregory with their first company of actors. *The Splendid Years* by Maire NicShiubhlaigh, one of that first company, describes the political involvement of many of the early members, and Herbert Howarth's *The Irish Writers, 1880–1940*, ex-

plores the nationalist bias behind most of the contributors to the
'Celtic Renaissance'. A faithful record of contemporary reaction has
been edited by Robert Hogan and Michael O'Neill from Joseph
Holloway's diaries on deposit in the National Library of Ireland.

There have been many histories of the Abbey Theatre itself, by
Ernest Boyd, A. E. Malone, and others, but the most significant
critical study of the movement remains Una Ellis-Fermor's *The Irish
Dramatic Movement*, first published in 1939. Since that time further
documentation has been made available, to be found in Peter
Kavanagh's *The Story of the Abbey Theatre*, Robin Skelton and Ann
Saddlemyer's *The World of W. B. Yeats*, and James Flannery's *Miss
Annie F. Horniman and the Abbey Theatre*; various aspects of the
theatre's development have also been traced in articles in *Theatre
and Nationalism in Twentieth-Century Ireland*, edited by Robert
O'Driscoll and *The Irish Theatre*, edited by Lennox Robinson.
Robinson's own history, *Ireland's Abbey Theatre*, includes a record of
the casts for each first production and reminiscences of many of the
early company; but *The Story of the Abbey Theatre*, edited by Sean
McCann, is distinguished by hearsay and rumour rather than fact.
A later theatre director, Mícheál O'hAodha, brings the Abbey's
history up to 1969 with his monograph, *The Abbey—Then and Now*.
A Bibliography of Modern Irish Drama, compiled by E. H. Mikhail,
provides an extensive but by no means exhaustive list of critical
articles and books on the history of the dramatic movement in
Ireland in the twentieth century, including a valuable checklist of
unpublished theses, but does not include studies of individual
dramatists.

FROM WILLIAM BUTLER YEATS TO SEAN O'CASEY

Two play-lists, Mathew O'Mahony's *Progress Guide to Anglo-Irish
Plays* and Brinsley MacNamara's *Abbey Plays, 1899–1948*, provide
a survey of plays published and performed in Ireland during the
height of the Abbey Theatre's influence. The prime mover was, of
course, William Butler Yeats, and the industry of scholars digging
in the massive quarry of Yeats manuscripts increases with each year,
now supplemented by the journal *Yeats Studies*, edited by Robert
O'Driscoll and Lorna Reynolds. The variorum edition of Yeats's
plays by Russell Alspach includes works not found in the standard
edition of Yeats's *Collected Plays*. In *Druidcraft: The Writing of 'The
Shadowy Waters'* Michael Sidnell, George Mayhew, and David Clark
examine the creation of a single play; this is the first in a series,
'Manuscripts of W. B. Yeats', first suggested by Curtis Bradford's

study, *Yeats at Work*; another early examination of the creative process is Suheil Bushrui's *Yeats's Verse-Plays: The Revisions 1900–1910*. Two indispensable aids to criticism are Eric Domville's two-volume concordance to the plays and Allan Wade's bibliography of Yeats's writings, revised by Russell Alspach. Of special significance to Yeats's dramatic theory and practice are his essays, especially those collected in *Explorations, Essays and Introductions*, and *The Uncollected Prose*. It should be remembered, however, that Yeats frequently revised his prose as well as his poetry and drama, so that on occasion it is wise to examine the earlier editions of his essays. The first attempt to collect Yeats's letters was made by Allan Wade in 1954; work on a comprehensive edition is in progress by Eric Domville and John Kelly, and this has been supplemented by editions of Yeats's correspondence with individual friends by Clifford Bax, Ursula Bridge, and Roger McHugh. Joseph Hone published the first authorized biography of Yeats in 1943; later studies by A. N. Jeffares, Richard Ellmann, Virginia Moore, and F. A. C. Wilson, all of whom had access to the same manuscript material, probe more deeply into the significance of play-making and theatre management to Yeats's life and work and, incidentally, indicate how much more material is available. Cross and Dunlop's *Bibliography of Yeats Criticism 1887–1965* offers the most comprehensive handbook of criticism; of special interest to students of the plays are works by David Clark, Hiro Ishibashi, Frank Kermode, John Rees Moore, Leonard Nathan, Thomas Parkinson, G. B. Saul, George Steiner, Peter Ure, Helen Vendler, and Thomas Whitaker. Yeats's centenary year, 1965, was the occasion for various collections of essays and revaluations: *An Honoured Guest*, edited by Donoghue and Mulryne; *In Excited Reverie*, by Jeffares and Cross; *Centenary Essays*, by Maxwell and Bushrui; *The World of W. B. Yeats*, by Skelton and Saddlemyer; and the December 1964 issue of *Modern Drama*.

The two-volume definitive edition of John Millington Synge's plays finally appeared in 1968; prepared by Ann Saddlemyer from all available manuscripts, it includes a hitherto unpublished early play, *When the Moon Has Set*, a selection of draft scenarios from Synge's notebooks, and examples from his worksheets of his working method. In the same Oxford series, Synge's *Prose*, edited by Alan Price, includes selections on literary theory; letters to his fiancée, the Abbey actress Maire O'Neill, to Lady Gregory, W. B. Yeats, and Stephen MacKenna contribute further to an understanding of his involvement with the Abbey Theatre. For many years Synge was overshadowed by Yeats, whose essays on him, collected in *Essays and*

Introductions, are probably more revelatory of Yeats than of Synge. Maurice Bourgeois's *J. M. Synge and the Irish Theatre*, written shortly after Synge's death, was a serious attempt to assess the dramatist but there are many omissions; Daniel Corkery gives an interesting if biased insight into the ambiguous attitude towards Synge by his countrymen in *Synge and Anglo-Irish Literature*. In the same year, 1931, *Letters to my Daughter* appeared, a volume of reminiscences by Synge's older brother, but it was not until the Greene and Stephens biography was published in 1959 that an objective view of the playwright was achieved. Since that time interest in Synge has increased remarkably, as Paul Levitt's comprehensive *Bibliography of Synge Criticism* indicates; critical studies by Donna Gerstenberger, Denis Johnston, Alan Price, Ann Saddlemyer and Robin Skelton offer a wide variety of approaches to this intriguing dramatist. Thomas R. Whitaker has compiled *Twentieth-Century Interpretations of 'The Playboy of the Western World'* and James Kilroy provides an interesting account of the riots over *The Playboy*'s first production. The 1972 centenary was the occasion for two volumes of essays, *Sunshine and the Moon's Delight*, edited by Suheil Bushrui, and *Centenary Papers*, edited by Maurice Harmon, the second number of *Yeats Studies* celebrated the centenaries of Synge and his good friend Jack B. Yeats.

Despite the extent of her contribution both directly as playwright and indirectly as director and collaborator with Yeats, surprisingly little attention has been paid to the third member of the Abbey Theatre triumvirate, Lady Gregory. This omission has been in part rectified by Colin Smythe's handsome Coole edition of her complete works, which includes four volumes of *The Collected Plays*, edited by Ann Saddlemyer. Other volumes of importance are her edition of *Ideals in Ireland*, *Poets and Dreamers* (which contains translations from the Irish of Douglas Hyde's plays), the two books used by Yeats as source-books, *Cuchulain of Muirthemne* and *Gods and Fighting Men*, and their joint *Vision and Beliefs in the West of Ireland*. *Our Irish Theatre* and *Journals 1916–1930*, selected by Lennox Robinson, are invaluable aids to an understanding of her contribution to the Abbey Theatre; in addition, selections from her letters have been published by A. C. Edwards and Daniel Murphy. But the first serious biographical study did not appear until 1961, when Elizabeth Coxhead published *Lady Gregory: a Literary Portrait*; this has been followed by Ann Saddlemyer's *In Defence of Lady Gregory, Playwright*, and Hazard Adams's *Lady Gregory*. Anne Gregory has written an interesting memoir of her grandmother in *Me and Nu: Childhood at Coole*.

But the plays of Yeats, Synge, and Lady Gregory could not keep a theatre going, and so a 'two-tier' system of productions tended to develop, with plays by many others in the repertory, including works by William Boyle, Padraic Colum, George Fitzmaurice, Lennox Robinson, Seamus O'Kelly, and T. C. Murray. Most prolific was Lennox Robinson, who in forty years contributed twenty-three plays to the Abbey; Michael O'Neill's *Lennox Robinson* is a readable account of Robinson's life and achievement as playwright and theatre director, while Robinson's own memoirs, *I Sometimes Think*, *Curtain Up*, *Pictures in a Theatre*, and his essay *Towards an Appreciation of the Theatre*, offer further background on the Irish School. Increased interest in the works of these early minor figures has resulted in *Lost Plays of the Irish Renaissance*, edited by Robert Hogan and James Kilroy, and the DePaul University Irish Drama Series edited by William J. Feeney, which includes early plays by Edward Martyn, George Moore, AE (George Russell), Seumas MacManus, James Cousins, and Alice Milligan. The January 1973 issue of *The Journal of Irish Literature* is devoted to Padraic Colum, about whom Zack Bowen has written two critical studies. But perhaps the most serious oversight made by the early directors concerned George Fitzmaurice, whose collected plays were finally published in the late 1960s, followed in 1972 by Howard K. Slaughter's monograph, *George Fitzmaurice and his Enchanted Land*. The role of Edward Martyn, one of the founders of the original Irish Literary Theatre in 1899, is a more complex one. He contributed several plays to the movement, then founded his own theatre; his contribution has been assessed by Denis Gwynn in *Edward Martyn and the Irish Revival* and Sister Marie-Thérèse Courtney in *Edward Martyn and the Irish Theatre*, but his most lasting memorial, if admittedly an unfair one, will doubtless remain George Moore's witty presentation in *Hail and Farewell*.

With the arrival of Sean O'Casey's plays the Abbey Theatre once again gained prominence in world theatre. O'Casey contributed five plays before the famous split occurred over the Abbey directors' rejection of *The Silver Tassie*. But by then O'Casey had established himself in England, where he wrote many more plays about Ireland, his *Autobiographies*, and numerous critical essays, later collected in *Windfalls*, *The Flying Wasp*, *The Green Crow*, *Under a Coloured Cap*, *Feathers from the Green Crow*, and *Blasts and Benedictions*. O'Casey's letters to the American critic George Jean Nathan have been edited by Seymour Rudin, and David Krause writes of his work on the Collected Letters in *A Self-Portrait of the Artist as a Man: Sean O'Casey's*

Letters. Krause's *Sean O'Casey: The Man and His Work* is the most penetrating critical-biographical study of the playwright, although works by Saros Cowasjee, Gabriel Fallon, and Eileen O'Casey all provide insight. Robert Hogan's *The Experiments of Sean O'Casey* and Ronald Ayling's *O'Casey* are valuable critical studies; E. H. Mikhail has compiled a *Bibliography of Criticism*, which indicates that serious treatment of O'Casey as a developing artist is continuing.

THE SECOND GENERATION

By the time O'Casey had left Dublin, Irish playwrights were no longer dependent on the Abbey Theatre, although the work of such dramatists as Paul Vincent Carroll, Brinsley MacNamara (John Weldon), and Michael J. Molloy especially continued to keep the theatre popular. Micheál MacLiammóir describes the rise of alternative theatre movements in his monograph *Theatre in Ireland*, and in *All for Hecuba* relates the story of the foundation, with his partner Hilton Edwards, of the Gate Theatre, which attracted playwrights of the stature of Denis Johnston. Later the Gate was shared with the company established by the Earl of Longford who, together with his wife Christine, Countess of Longford, contributed a great many plays and Irish translations. Dissatisfied with the opportunities for poetry on stage, Austin Clarke established first the Dublin Verse-Speaking Society, then the Lyric Theatre, which produced many of his own plays as well as reviving works by Yeats and Fitzmaurice. Among the younger playwrights the works of John B. Keane and Thomas Kilroy deserve mention; in his anthology *Seven Irish Plays* Robert Hogan has published works by Molloy, Keane, Seamus Byrne, Bryan MacMahon, John O'Donovan, and James Douglas, complementing his critical history, *After the Irish Renaissance*. The brief, tumultuous career of Brendan Behan has received a great deal of attention, beginning with a record of his first plays in Dublin by Alan Simpson of the Pike Theatre, then memoirs by Dominic Behan, Seamus deBurca, and Rae Jeffs; Ulick O'Connor's biography appeared in 1970.

The career of Samuel Beckett is a culmination of this move beyond literary nationalism, with two countries and two languages claiming him. However, Beckett has written as many plays—for stage, television, film, and radio—in English as in French; for those originally written in French, even though translated by the author himself, a comparison of the texts in both languages can be rewarding. Beckett has been reluctant, although not uncooperative, about revealing much concerning his life or working methods, although a great deal of his theory can be gleaned from his prose, especially the early essay on Proust; extracts from his correspondence with Alan Schneider on *Endgame* have been published in *The Village Voice*, and in 'Waiting for Beckett' and his introduction to *Film* Schneider has reported on their collaboration. There are also a great many responses from Beckett included in the critical studies of Richard Coe, Ruby Cohn, Colin Duckworth, John Fletcher and John Spurling, Jacques Guicharnaud, Ronald Hayman, Ludovic Janvier, Hugh Kenner, Michael Robinson, Nathan Scott, and the celebratory *Beckett at 60*. *The Testament of Samuel Beckett* by Josephine Jacobsen and William Mueller is a valuable early attempt to see Beckett's work as a unity, while Alec Reid provides a lucid description of the plays written up to 1968 in *All I Can Manage, More Than I Could*; Martin Esslin's edition of critical essays contains several significant articles on Beckett's plays, as do Ruby Cohn's *Casebook on 'Waiting for Godot'* and Bell Gale Chevigny's *Twentieth Century Interpretations of 'Endgame'*. As early as 1959 Ruby Cohn edited a special issue of *Perspective* devoted to Beckett, and followed this in 1966 with another in *Modern Drama*. Raymond Federman and John Fletcher's all-but-comprehensive bibliography, *Samuel Beckett: His Work and His Critics* testifies to the extraordinary fascination of this remarkable writer; and despite repeated predictions to the contrary, Beckett continues to write more plays.

DRAMA IN ULSTER

A parallel movement of smaller proportions in part influenced by the activity in Dublin took place in Northern Ireland during this century, as described by Sam Hanna Bell in *The Theatre in Ulster*. The most prolific dramatists of the early Ulster Literary Theatre were Rutherford Mayne and Gerald Macnamara, but they, like St. John Ervine (who for a time was one of the Abbey Theatre directors), were well known to southern playgoers as well; later Ulster playwrights, George Shiels (George Morshiel) and Joseph Tomelty, were to contribute a great many plays to the Abbey Theatre also. With the works of Sam Thompson in the 1960s a new voice was heard in the north, and since Thompson's death the plays of Brian Friel have provided some of the most significant work to come out of Ireland in recent years.

REFERENCES

GENERAL WORKS

S. H. Bell, *The Theatre in Ulster: A Survey of the Dramatic Movement in Ulster from 1902 until the Present Day* (London and Dublin, 1972).

E. Boyd, *Ireland's Literary Renaissance* (Dublin, 1916; New York, 1922; repr. Dublin, 1968).

W. S. Clark, *The Early Irish Stage* (Oxford, 1955).

——, *The Irish Stage in the Country Towns, 1720–1800* (Oxford, 1965).

G. C. Duggan, *The Stage Irishman: a History of the Irish Play and Stage Characters from the Earliest Times* (New York and Dublin, 1937).

U. M. Ellis-Fermor, *The Irish Dramatic Movement* (London, 1939; 2nd edn. 1954).

F. J. Fay, *Towards a National Theatre: The Dramatic Criticism of Frank Fay*, ed. R. Hogan (Irish Theatre Series, Dublin, 1970).

G. Fay, *The Abbey Theatre: Cradle of Genius* (London and New York, 1958).

W. G. Fay and C. Carswell, *The Fays of the Abbey Theatre: An Autobiographical Record* (New York and London, 1935).

J. W. Flannery, *Miss Annie F. Horniman and the Abbey Theatre* (Irish Theatre Series, Dublin, 1971).

ed. I. A. (Lady) Gregory, *Ideals in Ireland* (London, 1901).

R. G. Hogan, *After the Irish Renaissance: a Critical History of Irish Drama since 'The Plough and the Stars'* (Minneapolis, Minn., 1967).

——, ed., *Seven Irish Plays, 1946–1964* (Minneapolis, Minn., 1967).

ed. R. Hogan and J. Kilroy, *Lost Plays of the Irish Renaissance* (Newark, Del., 1970).

ed. R. Hogan and M. J. O'Neill, *Joseph Holloway's Abbey Theatre: A Selection from His Unpublished Journal 'Impressions of a Dublin Playgoer'* (Carbondale and Edwardsville, Ill., 1967).

——, eds., *Joseph Holloway's Irish Theatre*, 3 vols. (Dixon, Calif., 1968–70).

H. Howarth, *The Irish Writers, 1880–1940: Literature under Parnell's Star* (London, 1958).

P. Kavanagh, *The Irish Theatre, Being a History of the Drama in Ireland from the Earliest Period up to the Present Day* (Tralee, 1946).

——, *The Story of the Abbey Theatre from Its Origins in 1899 to the Present* (New York, 1950).

M. MacLiammóir, *All for Hecuba* (London, 1946; rev. edn., Dublin, 1961).

——, *Theatre in Ireland* (Dublin, 1950; repr. with additions, 1964).

B. MacNamara [John Weldon], *Abbey Plays, 1899–1948: Including the Productions of the Irish Literary Theatre* (Dublin, 1949).

A. E. Malone, *The Irish Drama 1896–1928* (London and New York, 1929; repr. New York, 1965).

E. H. Mikhail, *A Bibliography of Modern Irish Drama 1899–1970* (London, 1972).

G. Moore, *Hail and Farewell*, 3 vols. (London, 1911–14; repr. 1937, 1947).

M. NicShiubhlaigh, *The Splendid Years: Recollections of Maire NicShiubhlaigh as Told to Edward Kenny* (Dublin, 1955).

M. O'hAodha, *The Abbey—Then and Now* (Dublin, 1969).

ed. R. O'Driscoll, *Theatre and Nationalism in Twentieth-Century Ireland* (Toronto, 1971).

M. O'Mahony, *Progress Guide to Anglo–Irish Plays* (Dublin, 1960).

L. Robinson, *Ireland's Abbey Theatre: A History 1899–1951* (London, 1951; Port Washington, N.Y., 1968).

——, ed., *The Irish Theatre: Lectures Delivered During the Abbey Theatre Festival Held in Dublin in August, 1938* (London, 1939).

L. Stockwell, *Dublin Theatres and Theatre Customs (1637–1820)* (New York, 1938; repr. 1968).

Samuel Beckett (1906–)

TEXTS

Act Without Words II: A Mime for Two Players, trans. by the author, in *New Departures*, I (Summer 1959) (New York, 1960).

All That Fall: A Play for Radio (New York and London, 1957).

Breath and Other Shorts [*Breath*; *Come and Go*; *Act Without Words I*; *Act Without Words II*] (London, 1971).

Cascando: a Radio Piece for Music and Voice, trans. by the author, in *Evergreen Review* 7.30 (May–June 1963).

Cascando, and Other Short Dramatic Pieces [*Words and Music, Eh Joe, Play, Come and Go, Film*] (New York and London, 1968).

Cendres, trans. by R. Pinget and the author, in *Lettres Nouvelles* 36 (30 December 1959).

Come and Go: Dramaticule (London, 1967).

Comédie, trans. by the author, in *Lettres Nouvelles* XII (June–July–August 1964).

Comédie et actes divers [*Va et Vient: Dramaticule, Cascando, Paroles et Musique, Dis Joe, Acte sans Paroles II*] (Paris, 1966).

La Dernière Bande, trans. by P. Leyris and the author, in *Lettres Nouvelles* 1 (4 March 1959).

Dis Joe, trans. by the author, in *Arts: l'Hebdomadaire Complet de la Vie Culturelle* 15 (5–11 January 1966).

Eh Joe: A Piece for Television and Other Writings [*Act Without Words II, Film*] (London, 1967; *Eh Joe*, repr. in *Evergreen Review* 13, January 1969).

Embers: a New Play Written Specially for Broadcasting, in *Evergreen Review* III.15 (November–December 1959).

En attendant Godot: pièce en deux actes (Paris, 1952; ed. D. Duckworth, London, 1966).

Endgame: A Play in One Act, Followed by Act Without Words: A Mime for One Player, trans. by the author (New York and London, 1958).

Film, with an essay on Directing Film by Alan Schneider (New York, 1969).

'Fin de Partie' suivi de 'Acte sans paroles' (Paris, 1957).

Happy Days: A Play in Two Acts for Two Characters (New York, 1961; London, 1962).

Krapp's Last Tape, in *Evergreen Review* 2.5 (Summer 1958).

Krapp's Last Tape and Embers (London, 1959).

Not I (New York, 1973).

Oh, les beaux jours, trans. by the author (Paris, 1963).

Play and Two Short Pieces for Radio [*Words and Music, Cascando*] (London, 1964). (*Play* repr. in *Evergreen Review* 8, April 1965).

Tous ceux qui tombent, trans. R. Pinget (Paris, 1957).

Waiting for Godot: A Tragi-Comedy in Two Acts, trans. by the author (New York, 1954; London, 1956; rev. edn. 1965).

Words and Music: A Short Piece for Radio, to a musical score by John Beckett, in *Evergreen Review* 6.27 (November–December 1962); (repr. London, 1964).

Proust (London, 1931; repr. New York and London, 1957; 3rd edn., London, 1965).

'Samuel Beckett: Extracts from his Correspondence with Director Alan Schneider', in *The Village Voice Reader*, ed. D. Wolf and E. Fancher (New York, 1962).

R. Pinget, *The Old Tune*, trans. S. Beckett (Paris, 1960; New York, 1961; London, 1962, 1963, and 1966).

CRITICAL STUDIES AND COMMENTARY

Beckett at 60: A Festschrift (London, 1967).

B. G. Chevigny, comp., *Twentieth Century Interpretations of 'Endgame'* (Englewood Cliffs, N.J., 1969).

R. Coe, *Samuel Beckett* (Writers and Critics Series, Edinburgh and New York, 1964).

ed. R. Cohn, *Casebook on 'Waiting for Godot'* (New York, 1967).

R. Cohn, *Samuel Beckett: The Comic Gamut* (New Brunswick, N.J., 1962).

C. Duckworth, *Angels of Darkness: Dramatic Effect in Samuel Beckett with Special Reference to Eugène Ionesco* (London, 1972).

ed. M. Esslin, *Samuel Beckett: A Collection of Critical Essays* (Twentieth Century Views, Englewood Cliffs, N.J., 1965).

R. Federman and J. Fletcher, *Samuel Beckett: His Works and His Critics: An Essay in Bibliography* (Berkeley, Calif., and London, 1970).

J. Fletcher and J. Spurling, *Beckett: a Study of his Plays* (London, 1972).

J. Guicharnaud and J. Beckelman, *Modern French Theater from Giraudoux to Beckett* (New Haven, Conn., 1961).

R. Hayman, *Samuel Beckett* (English Contemporary Playwrights Series, London, 1968).

J. Jacobsen and W. Mueller, *The Testament of Samuel Beckett* (New York, 1964).

L. Janvier, *Pour Samuel-Beckett* (Paris, 1966).

H. Kenner, *Samuel Beckett: A Critical Study* (New York and London, 1961; 2nd edn., Berkeley, Calif., 1968).

Modern Drama 9 (December 1966).

Perspective 11 (Autumn 1959).

A. Reid, *All I Can Manage, More Than I Could: An Approach to the Plays of Samuel Beckett* (Dublin and Chester Springs, Pa., 1968).

M. Robinson, *The Long Sonata of the Dead: a Study of Samuel Beckett* (London, 1969).

A. Schneider, 'Waiting for Beckett', *Chelsea Review* 2 (Autumn 1958).

N. A. Scott, *Samuel Beckett* (Studies in Modern Literature and Thought, London, Toronto, and New York, 1965).

A. Simpson, *Beckett and Behan, and a Theatre in Dublin* (London, 1962; New York, 1966).

Brendan Behan (1923–64)

TEXTS

Richard's Cork Leg, ed. A. Simpson (London, 1973).

The Big House: A Radio Play, in *Irish Writing* 37 (Autumn 1957), repr. in *Brendan Behan's Island: An Irish Sketch-Book* (London, 1962).

The Hostage (London, 1958; rev. edn. 1965).

The Quare Fellow: A Comedy-Drama (London and New York, 1956).

The Quare Fellow and The Hostage: Two Plays (New York, 1964).

Two Short Plays: 'Moving Out' and 'A Garden Party', ed. R. Hogan (Short Play Series, Dixon, Calif., 1967).

CRITICAL STUDIES AND COMMENTARY

B. Behan, D. Hickey, G. Smith, *My Life with Brendan* (London, 1973).

D. Behan, *My Brother Brendan* (London, 1965; New York, 1966).

S. deBurca, *Brendan Behan, A Memoir* (Proscenium Chapbooks, Newark, Del., 1971).

R. Jeffs, *Brendan Behan, Man and Showman* (London, 1966).

U. O'Connor, *Brendan Behan* (London, 1970).

A. Simpson, *Beckett and Behan, and a Theatre in Dublin* (London, 1962; New York, 1966).

Isabella Augusta, Lady Gregory (1852–1932)

TEXTS

ed. A. Saddlemyer, *The Collected Plays*, 4 vols. (Coole edition, Gerrards Cross and New York, 1970).

Selected Plays, chosen and introduced by E. Coxhead, with a Foreword by S. O'Casey (New York, 1962).

Cuchulain of Muirthemne: The Story of the Men of the Red Branch of Ulster (London, 1902; New York, 1903; 5th edn. Gerrards Cross and New York, 1970).

Gods and Fighting Men: The Story of the Tuatha de Danaan and of the Fianna of Ireland (London, 1904; 2nd edn. Gerrards Cross and New York, 1970).

Our Irish Theatre: A Chapter of Autobiography (London, 1913; Gerrards Cross, 1973).

Poets and Dreamers: Studies and Translations from the Irish (Dublin, 1903; repr. Port Washington, N.Y., 1967; Gerrards Cross, 1974).

Visions and Beliefs in the West of Ireland: With Two Essays and Notes by W. B. Yeats (London and New York, 1920; repr. Gerrards Cross and New York, 1970).

ed. L. Robinson, *Journals 1916–1930* (London, 1946; New York, 1947).

'The Lady Gregory Letters to Sean O'Casey', ed. A. C. Edwards, *Modern Drama* 8.1 (May 1965).

'Letters from Lady Gregory: A Record of Her Friendship with T. J. Kiernan', ed. D. Murphy, in *The Bulletin of the New York Public Library* 71.10 and 72.1–2 (December 1967 and January/February 1968).

CRITICAL STUDIES AND COMMENTARY

H. Adams, *Lady Gregory* (Bucknell's Irish Writers Series, Lewisburg, Pa., 1973).

E. Coxhead, *Lady Gregory: A Literary Portrait* (London and New York, 1961; rev. edn. 1962).

A. Gregory, *Me and Nu: Childhood at Coole* (Gerrards Cross and New York, 1970).

ed. I. A. (Lady) Gregory, *Ideals in Ireland* (London, 1901).

A. Saddlemyer, *In Defence of Lady Gregory, Playwright* (Dublin and Chester Springs, Pa., 1966).

ed. C. Smythe, *Seventy Years 1852–1922: Being the Biography of Lady Gregory* (Gerrards Cross, 1974).

Edward Martyn (1859–1924)

TEXTS

The Dream Physician: A Play in Five Acts (Dublin and London, 1914; repr. with Seumas MacManus's *The Townland of Tamney* in DePaul University Irish Drama Series, Chicago, 1972).

Grangecolman: a Domestic Drama in Three Acts (Dublin, 1912).

'*The Heather Field*' and '*Maeve*' (London, 1899).

The Heather Field (DePaul University Irish Drama Series, Chicago, 1966).

Maeve [with Alice Milligan's *The Last Feast of the Fianna*] (DePaul University Irish Drama Series, Chicago, 1967).

The Place Hunters: A Political Comedy in One Act, in *The Leader*, Dublin, 26 July 1902.

Romulus and Remus, or The Makers of Delights: A Symbolist Extravaganza in One Act, in *The Irish People*, Christmas Supplement, 21 December 1907.

'*The Tale of a Town*' and '*An Enchanted Sea*' (London, 1902).

CRITICAL STUDIES AND COMMENTARY

M.-T. Courtney, *Edward Martyn and the Irish Theatre* (New York, 1956).

D. Gwynn, *Edward Martyn and the Irish Revival* (London, 1930).

Sean O'Casey (1884–1964)

TEXTS

The Collected Plays, 4 vols. (London, 1949–51).
Five One-Act Plays (London and New York, 1966).
Three Plays (London and New York, 1966).
Three More Plays (London and New York, 1966).
Behind the Green Curtains: Figuro in the Night: The Moon Shines on Kylenamoe (London, 1961).
The Bishop's Bonfire (London, 1955).
The Drums of Father Ned (London, 1960).
Kathleen Listens In and *Nannie's Night Out*, in *Feathers from the Green Crow*, ed. R. Hogan (London, 1963).
Autobiographies, 6 vols. (London, 1939–51; repr. in 2 vols., 1963).
Blasts and Benedictions: Articles and Stories, sel. R. Ayling (London, 1967).
ed. R. Hogan, *Feathers from the Green Crow: Sean O'Casey, 1905–1925* (London, 1963).
The Flying Wasp (London, 1937).
The Green Crow (New York, 1956).
ed. S. Rudin, 'O'Casey's Letters to George Jean Nathan', in *Irish Renaissance*, ed. R. Skelton and D. R. Clark (Dublin, 1965).
ed. B. Atkinson, *The Sean O'Casey Reader: Plays, Autobiographies, Opinions* (London, 1968).
Under a Coloured Cap (New York, 1963).
Windfalls (London, 1934).

CRITICAL STUDIES AND COMMENTARY

ed. R. Ayling, *O'Casey* (Modern Judgments Series, London, 1967).
S. Cowasjee, *Sean O'Casey: The Man Behind the Plays* (Edinburgh, 1963; New York, 1964).
G. Fallon, *Sean O'Casey, the Man I Knew* (London, 1965).
R. Hogan, *The Experiments of Sean O'Casey* (New York, 1960).
D. Krause, *Sean O'Casey: The Man and His Work* (London, 1960; New York, 1962).
——, *A Self-Portrait of the Artist as a Man: Sean O'Casey's Letters* (Dublin, 1968).
E. H. Mikhail, *Sean O'Casey: A Bibliography of Criticism* (London, 1971).
E. O'Casey, *Sean* (London, 1971).

Lennox Robinson (1886–1958)

TEXTS

Plays [*The Round Table*; *Crabbed Youth and Age*; *Portrait*; *The White Blackbird*; *The Big House*; *Give a Dog*—] (London, 1928).
More Plays [*All's Over, Then?*; *Church Street*] (New York, 1935).
Two Plays: 'Harvest' and 'The Clancy Name' (Dublin, 1911).
The Cross-roads: A Play in a Prologue and Two Acts (Abbey Theatre Series, Dublin, 1907).

The Dreamers: A Play in Three Acts (London, 1915).
Ever the Twain: A Comedy in Three Acts (London, 1930).
The Far-Off Hills: A Comedy in Three Acts (London, 1931; New York, 1932).
'Killycreggs in Twilight' and Other Plays [Is Life Worth Living?; Bird's Nest] (London, 1939).
The Lost Leader: A Play in Three Acts (Dublin, 1918; repr. Belfast, 1954).
Patriots: A Play in Three Acts (Dublin, 1912).
The Whiteheaded Boy: A Play in Three Acts (Dublin, 1918; London, 1925).

Curtain Up: An Autobiography (London, 1942).
I Sometimes Think (Dublin, 1956).
Pictures in a Theatre: A Conversation Piece (Dublin, 1946).
Towards an Appreciation of the Theatre (Dublin, 1945).

CRITICAL STUDIES AND COMMENTARY

M. J. O'Neill, *Lennox Robinson* (Twayne's English Authors Series, New York, 1964).

John Millington Synge (1871–1909)

TEXTS

ed. A. Price, *The Collected Works, vol. 2: Prose* (London, 1966).
   'Letters of John Millington Synge' [to Max Meyerfeld], *Yale Review* 13 (July 1924).
ed. A. Saddlemyer, *The Collected Works*, vols. 3 and 4: *Plays, Books One and Two* (London, 1968; repr. without notes or appendices in 1 vol. paperback, 1969).
ed. A. Saddlemyer, *Letters to Molly: J. M. Synge to Maire O'Neill* (Cambridge, Mass., and London, 1971).
ed. A. Saddlemyer, *Some Letters of John M. Synge to Lady Gregory and W. B. Yeats* (Dublin, 1971).
Some Unpublished Letters and Documents by J. M. Synge Formerly in the Possession of Mr. Lawrence Wilson of Montreal (Montreal, 1959).
ed. A. Saddlemyer, 'Synge to MacKenna: the Mature Years', in *Irish Renaissance*, ed. R. Skelton and D. R. Clark (Dublin, 1965).

CRITICAL STUDIES AND COMMENTARY

M. Bourgeois, *J. M. Synge and the Irish Theatre* (London and New York, 1913; repr. Studies in Irish Literature Series, New York, 1969).
ed. S. B. Bushrui, *Sunshine and the Moon's Delight: A Centenary Tribute to J. M. Synge 1871–1909* (Beirut and Gerrards Cross; New York, 1972).
ed. A. Carpenter, *My Uncle John: Edward Stephens's Life of J. M. Synge* (London, 1974).
D. Corkery, *Synge and Anglo-Irish Literature* (Dublin and Cork, 1931).
J. Flood, 'The Pre-Aran Writings of J. M. Synge', in *Eire–Ireland* 5.3 (Autumn 1970).
D. Gerstenberger, *John Millington Synge* (Twayne's English Authors Series, New York, 1964).

D. H. Greene and E. M. Stephens, *J. M. Synge, 1871–1909* (New York, 1959; paperback repr. 1961).

ed. M. Harmon, *J. M. Synge: Centenary Papers, 1971* (Dublin, 1972).

D. Johnston, *John Millington Synge* (Columbia Essays on Modern Writers, New York, 1965).

J. Kilroy, *The 'Playboy' Riots* (Irish Theatre Series, Dublin, 1971).

P. Levitt, *John Millington Synge: A Bibliography of Synge Criticism* (Dublin and New York, 1973).

J. Masefield, *John M. Synge: A Few Personal Recollections with Biographical Notes* (Churchtown, Ireland, 1915).

A. Price, *Synge and Anglo–Irish Drama* (London, 1961).

A. Saddlemyer, 'A Share in the Dignity of the World: J. M. Synge's Aesthetic Theory', in *The World of W. B. Yeats*, ed. R. Skelton and A. Saddlemyer (Victoria, B.C. and Dublin, 1965; rev. edn. Seattle, Wash., 1967).

——, *J. M. Synge and Modern Comedy* (Dublin, 1968).

R. Skelton, *J. M. Synge* (Bucknell's Irish Writers Series, Lewisburg, Pa., 1972).

——, *J. M. Synge and his World* (London, 1971).

——, *The Writings of J. M. Synge* (London, 1971).

S. Synge, *Letters to My Daughter: Memories of John Millington Synge* (Dublin and Cork, 1931).

The Synge Manuscripts in the Library of Trinity College Dublin (Dublin, 1971).

T. R. Whitaker, comp., *Twentieth-Century Interpretations of 'The Playboy of the Western World': A Collection of Critical Essays* (Englewood Cliffs, N.J., 1969).

Yeats Studies, Number Two, ed. R. O'Driscoll and L. Reynolds (Dublin and Toronto, Bealtaine, 1972).

William Butler Yeats (1865–1939)

TEXTS

The Collected Plays of W. B. Yeats (2nd edn., London, 1952; New York, 1953).

ed. R. K. Alspach assisted by C. Alspach, *The Variorum Edition of the Plays of W. B. Yeats* (New York, 1965; London, 1966).

ed. A. N. Jeffares, *Selected Plays of W. B. Yeats* (London, 1964).

Autobiographies (London and New York, 1927).

Essays and Introductions (London and New York, 1961).

Explorations, selected by Mrs. W. B. Yeats (London, 1962; New York, 1963).

On the Boiler (Dublin, 1939).

ed. J. P. Frayne, *Uncollected Prose*, vol. 1: *First Reviews and Articles 1886–1896* (New York, 1970).

ed. R. McHugh, *Ah, Sweet Dancer: W. B. Yeats Margot Ruddock: A Correspondence* (London and New York, 1970).

ed. C. Bax, *Florence Farr, Bernard Shaw and W. B. Yeats* [Letters] (Dublin, 1941; London, 1946).

ed. Allan Wade, *The Letters of W. B. Yeats* (London, 1954; New York, 1955).

ed. U. Bridge, *W. B. Yeats and T. Sturge Moore: Their Correspondence, 1901–1937* (London, 1953).

ed. R. McHugh, *W. B. Yeats: Letters to Katharine Tynan* (Dublin and New York, 1953).

ed. A. N. Jeffares, *Selected Criticism of W. B. Yeats* (London, 1964).

ed. A. N. Jeffares, *Selected Prose of W. B. Yeats* (London, 1964).

CRITICAL STUDIES AND COMMENTARY

C. B. Bradford, *Yeats at Work* (Carbondale, Ill., 1965).

. S. B. Bushrui, *Yeats's Verse-Plays: The Revisions 1900–1910* (Oxford, 1965).

D. R. Clark, *W. B. Yeats and the Theatre of Desolate Reality* (Dublin, 1965).

K. G. W. Cross and R. T. Dunlop, *A Bibliography of Yeats Criticism 1887–1965* (London, 1972).

E. Domville, *A Concordance to the Plays of W. B. Yeats*, 2 vols. (Ithaca, N.Y., 1972).

ed. D. Donoghue and R. Mulryne, *An Honoured Guest: New Essays on W. B. Yeats* (London and New York, 1965).

R. Ellmann, *Eminent Domain: Yeats among Wilde, Joyce, Pound, Eliot and Auden* (New York and London, 1967).

——, *The Identity of Yeats* (London and New York, 1954).

—— *Yeats: The Man and the Masks* (New York, 1948; London, 1949).

J. Hone, *W. B. Yeats, 1865–1939* (London and New York, 1943; 2nd edn., 1962).

H. Ishibashi, *Yeats and the Noh: Types of Japanese Beauty and Their Reflection in Yeats's Plays*, ed. A. Kerrigan (Yeats Centenary Papers, Dublin, 1965; Chester Springs, Pa., 1968).

A. N. Jeffares, *W. B. Yeats Man and Poet* (London and New Haven, Conn., 1949; rev. edn., 1962).

—— and K. G. W. Cross, ed., *In Excited Reverie: A Centenary Tribute, W. B. Yeats 1865–1939* (London and New York, 1965).

F. Kermode, *The Romantic Image* (London, 1957).

ed. D. E. S. Maxwell and S. B. Bushrui, *W. B. Yeats 1865–1939: Centenary Essays on the Art of W. B. Yeats* (Ibadan and Nigeria, 1965).

Modern Drama 8.3 (December 1964).

J. R. Moore, *Masks of Love and Death: Yeats as Dramatist* (Ithaca, N.Y., 1971).

V. Moore, *The Unicorn: W. B. Yeats's Search for Reality* (New York, 1954).

L. E. Nathan, *The Tragic Drama of William Butler Yeats: Figures in a Dance* (New York, 1965).

T. Parkinson, *W. B. Yeats: Self-Critic* (Berkeley, Calif., 1951).

G. B. Saul, *Prolegomena to the Study of Yeats's Plays* (Philadelphia, Pa., and London, 1958).

ed. M. Sidnell, G. P. Mayhew, and D. R. Clark, *Druidcraft: The Writing of 'The Shadowy Waters'* (Manuscripts of W. B. Yeats, Cambridge, Mass., London, and Dublin, 1971).

ed. R. Skelton and A. Saddlemyer, *The World of W. B. Yeats: Essays in Perspective* (Victoria, B.C., and Dublin, 1965; rev. edn., Seattle, Wash., 1967).

G. Steiner, *The Death of Tragedy* (London and New York, 1961).

P. Ure, *Yeats the Playwright: A Commentary on Character and Design in the Major Plays* (London and New York, 1963).

H. H. Vendler, *Yeats's 'Vision' and the Later Plays* (Cambridge, Mass., and London, 1963).

A. Wade, *A Bibliography of the Writings of W. B. Yeats* (3rd rev. edn. by R. K. Alspach, London, 1968).

T. R. Whitaker, *Swan and Shadow: Yeats's Dialogue with History* (Chapel Hill, N.C., 1964).

F. A. C. Wilson, *W. B. Yeats and Tradition* (London and New York, 1957).

——, *Yeats's Iconography* (London and New York, 1960).

Other Dramatists
AE (George William Russell) (1867–1935)

Deirdre: A Legend in Three Acts (Dublin, 1907; repr. DePaul University Irish Drama Series, Chicago, Ill., 1970).

Dion Boucicault (1820?–90)

ed. D. Krause, *The Dolmen Boucicault, The Complete Authentic Texts of 'The Colleen Bawn', 'Arrah-na-Pogue', 'The Shaughraun'* (Dublin, 1962).

William Boyle (1853–1923)

The Building Fund: A Play in Three Acts (Abbey Theatre Series, Dublin, 1905).
The Eloquent Dempsey: A Comedy in Three Acts (Dublin, 1907).
Family Failing: A Comedy in Three Acts (Dublin, 1912).
The Mineral Workers: A Play in Four Acts (Dublin, 1907).

Paul Vincent Carroll (1900–68)

Conspirators [revision of *The Coggerers*] (London, 1947).
Shadow and Substance (New York, 1937; London, 1938).
Things that are Caesar's (London, 1934).
We Have Ceased to Live, in *Journal of Irish Literature* 1.1 (January 1972).
The Wise Have Not Spoken (London, 1947; New York, 1954).

P. A. Doyle, *Paul Vincent Carroll* (Bucknell's Irish Writers Series, Lewisburg, Pa., 1971).

Austin Clarke (1896–1974)

Collected Plays (Dublin, 1963).
The Impuritans: A Play in One Act, in *Irish University Review* 1.1 (Autumn 1970; repr. Dublin, 1973).

The Visitation: A Play, in *Irish University Review* 4, 1 (Spring, 1974).
Two Interludes adapted from Cervantes: 'The Student from Salamanca' and 'The Silent Lover' (Dublin, 1968).
The Celtic Twilight and the Nineties (Tower Series of Anglo–Irish Studies, Dublin, 1969).
First Visit to England and Other Memories (Dublin and London, 1945).
Twice Round the Black Church (London, 1962).

L. Miller, 'The Books of Austin Clarke: A Checklist', in *A Tribute to Austin Clarke on his Seventieth Birthday*, ed. J. Montague and L. Miller (Dolmen Editions, Dublin, 1966).

Padraic Colum (1881–1972)

Three Plays [The Land; Thomas Muskerry; The Fiddler's House] (New York, 1925; Dublin, 1963).
Balloon (New York, 1929).
The Betrayal, in *One-Act Plays of Today*, Series 4, ed. J. W. Marriott (London, 1928).
Children of Lir and *Cloughoughter*, in *Journal of Irish Literature* 2.1 (January 1973).
The Desert: A Play in Three Acts (Dublin, 1912).
The Land: A Play in Three Acts (Abbey Theatre Series, Dublin, 1905).
The Miracle of the Corn: A Miracle Play in One Act (Dublin, 1907).
Mogu, the Wanderer, or The Desert: A Fantastic Comedy in Three Acts (Boston, Mass., 1917).
Moytura: A Play for Dancers (Dublin, 1963).
The Saxon Shillin', in *Lost Plays of the Irish Renaissance*, ed. R. Hogan and J. Kilroy (Newark, Del., 1970).
Swift's Pastoral: A One-Act Play, in *Poetry* 17 (January 1921).
Thomas Muskerry: A Play in Three Acts (Abbey Theatre Series, Dublin, 1910).

Z. R. Bowen, *Padraic Colum: A Biographical-Critical Introduction* (Carbondale, Ill., 1970).
——, 'Padraic Colum and Irish Drama', in *Eire–Ireland* 5.4 (Winter 1970).

St. John Ervine (1883–1971)

Four Irish Plays [Mixed Marriage; The Critics; Jane Clegg; The Orangemen] (Dublin, 1914).
Boyd's Shop: A Comedy (London, 1936).
Friends and Relations: A Comedy in Three Acts (London, 1947).
John Ferguson: A Play in Four Acts (Dublin, 1915).
The Magnanimous Lover: A Play in One Act (Dublin, 1912).
Mixed Marriage: A Play in Four Acts (Dublin, 1912).
Some Impressions of My Elders (London, 1923).

George Fitzmaurice (1885–1940)

Plays, 3 vols. (Dublin and Chester Springs, Pa., 1967–70).
Five Plays [*The Country Dressmaker*; *The Moonlighter*; *The Pie-Dish*; *The Magic Glasses*; *Dandy Dolls*] (Boston, Mass., 1917).
The Country Dressmaker: A Play in Three Acts (Abbey Theatre Series, Dublin, 1914).

H. K. Slaughter, *George Fitzmaurice and his Enchanted Land* (Irish Theatre Series, Dublin, 1972).

Brian Friel (1929–)

'*Crystal and Fox*' and '*The Mundy Scheme*' (New York and London, 1970).
Lovers [*Winners*; *Losers*] (New York, 1968; London, 1969).
The Loves of Cass McGuire (New York and London, 1966).
Philadelphia, Here I Come! (New York, 1965).

D. E. S. Maxwell, *Brian Friel* (Bucknell's Irish Writers Series, Lewisburg, Pa., 1971).

Denis Johnston (1901–)

Collected Plays, 2 vols. (London, 1960).

John B. Keane (1928–)

Hut 42 (Irish Play Series, Dixon, Calif., 1968).
Moll (Cork, 1972).
Sharon's Grave (Dublin, 1960).
Sive (Dublin, 1959).

Thomas Kilroy (1934–)

The Death and Resurrection of Mr. Roche: A Comedy in Three Acts (London and New York, 1969).

Christine, Countess of Longford (1900–)

The Earl of Straw (Dublin, 1944).
The Hill of Quirke (Dublin, 1958).
Lord Edward (Dublin, 1941).
Mr. Jiggins of Jigginstown, in *Plays of Changing Ireland*, ed. Curtis Canfield (New York, 1936).
Patrick Sarsfield (Dublin, 1943).
The United Brothers (Dublin, 1942).

Rutherford Mayne (Samuel Waddell) (1878–1967)

The Drone: A Play in Three Acts (Dublin, 1909).
The Drone and Other Plays [*The Turn of the Road*; *Red Turf*; *The Troth*] (Dublin, 1912).

The Troth: A Play in One Act (Dublin, 1909).
The Turn of the Road: A Play in Two Scenes and an Epilogue (Dublin, 1907).

George Moore (1852–1933)

The Bending of the Bough: A Play in Five Acts (London, 1900; repr. DePaul
  University Irish Drama Series, Chicago, 1969).
with W. B. Yeats, *Diarmuid and Grania*, in *Dublin Magazine*, April–June 1951.

J. Egleson Dunleavy, *George Moore* (Bucknell's Irish Writers Series,
  Lewisburg, Pa., 1973).

Thomas Cornelius Murray (1873–1959)

Aftermath: A Play in Three Acts (Dublin, 1922).
Autumn Fire: A Play in Three Acts (Boston, Mass., 1926; London, 1952).
Birthright: A Play in Two Acts (Dublin, 1911).
'Maurice Harte' and *'A Stag at Bay'* (London, 1934).
Michaelmas Eve: A Play in Three Acts (London, 1932).
'Spring' and *Other Plays* [*Sovereign Love*; *The Briery Gap*] (Dublin, 1917).

Seamus O'Kelly (1881–1918)

The Bribe: A Play in Three Acts (Dublin, 1914).
The Shuiler's Child (Dublin, 1909; repr. DePaul University Irish Drama
  Series, Chicago, Ill., 1971).
Three Plays [*The Matchmakers*; *The Home-Coming*; *The Stranger*] (Dublin,
  1912).

G. B. Saul, *Seamus O'Kelly* (Bucknell's Irish Writers Series, Lewisburg, Pa.,
  1971).

George Shiels (*George Morshiel*) (1886–1949)

Bedmates (Dublin, 1922).
The Passing Day: A Play in Six Scenes and The Jailbird: A Comedy in Three Acts
  (London, 1937).
'The Rugged Path' and *'The Summit'* (London, 1942).
Three Plays: Professor Tim, Paul Twyning, The New Gossoon (London, 1945).

Sam Thompson (1916–65)

Over the Bridge (Dublin and London, 1970).

Joseph Tomelty (1911–)

All Souls' Night (Belfast, 1955).
The End House (Dublin, 1962).
Is the Priest at Home? (Belfast, 1954).
Right Again, Barnum (Belfast, 1950).

16. ENGLISH DRAMA 1900–1945

ALLARDYCE NICOLL

IF we exclude from consideration a limited number of 'dramas' which in fact are nothing but long poems penned in dialogue form, we may reasonably assume that practically all playwrights have planned their works with at least some hope of theatrical production in mind. Nevertheless, another fact is equally important: from the time of classical Athens onwards many dramatic authors (and certainly the entire company of major writers) have composed their scenes with a double end in view: they have sought to appeal to audiences, but they have also thought of individual readers. An inescapable corollary follows: present-day students, when engaged in exploring the range of dramatic literature in past ages, must consider both the characteristics of the contemporary stage and the prevailing styles adopted by publishers in bringing plays before these individual readers.

With these thoughts in mind, we realize the peculiar interest which attaches to the study of early twentieth-century drama. In examining earlier periods, all but the most advanced researchers are compelled to use edited texts, whereas the students engaged in examining this later period must turn, in general, to the original printings; and almost at first glance these original printings demonstrate that a new spirit was then at work, a spirit of adventure, a self-confident faith in the possibility of creating a brave new play-world which its proponents did not hesitate to describe as 'modern'.

In order fully to appreciate what was happening during those years, it is, of course, essential to glance at least cursorily at the typical patterns of play-publishing which had become established during the middle years of the preceding century. At that time, although a few general publishers occasionally issued various 'literary' (and, in particular, 'poetic') dramas in the octavo style which had been familiar for well over a hundred years, the printing of plays tended ever more and more to be restricted to a number of firms specializing exclusively in theatrical texts. Thomas Hailes Lacy became a leader in this field, flourishing until his stock and style were taken over by Samuel French. These Lacy–French 'standard' and 'minor' plays were cheaply printed, issued in cheap coloured-paper wrappers, and cheaply priced. Even cheaper still were the thousand-odd melodramas, dramas, comedies, and farces sold at a penny each by the rival firm of John Dicks. Obviously, such texts were not intended for general reading: their chief appeal was to the teeming multitudes of 'dramatic spouters' active in that period, to the scores of minor provincial theatre managers, and to the leaders of small touring groups. Even a fairly well-known performer like Henry Neville bought a complete collection of Dicks's penny texts and, as his manuscript annotations indicate, read through them diligently to see what items in this large assemblage of 'free acting drama' might be considered suitable for revival. Professionals of this kind as well as secretaries of amateur societies wanted to know how many actors and actresses were needed for each piece, and therefore the catalogues issued both by Lacy-French and by Dicks have two columns following the play-titles, the first column headed with an 'M' (for 'male') and the second with an 'F' (for 'female'). Dicks's list thus begins ambitiously with:

	M.	F.
1. *Othello*	18	2
2. *The School for Scandal*	11	4

and, in less exalted but similar style, the Lacy–French list starts with more popular fare:

	M.	F.
1. *Abou Hassan*	6	7
2. *Accusing Spirit*	8	3

Lacy demonstrated at least part of his objectives when, in addition to his hundreds of dramas, he published several 'do-it-yourself' guides such as *The Amateur's Handbook to Home and Drawing Room Theatricals* and anthologies of 'pieces' such as *The Dramatic Reciter*: as his business expanded, his catalogues also came to include such items as 'might be needed by Amateurs', like 'Tableau Lights', 'Coloured Fire in Bulk', 'Mongolian' (described as 'in a paste, for Indians, Mullatoes, etc.'), 'Wigs', 'Beards', and 'Prepared Burnt Cork'.

The first faint signs of change came shortly after the year 1890, but clearly it was only after the start of the present century when a large new reading public arose to welcome 'modern' plays printed in attractive forms. The firm of Dicks still remained in being, but its sales were steadily declining, and soon it disappeared. Samuel French continued to hold, and of course still continues to hold, an important position in the realm of theatrical publishing, but texts issued by this firm during the present century have tended to be better printed, more attractively produced, and more highly priced than their predecessors. Particularly significant was its announcement in 1906 that it had been successful in the arranging of future publication of the plays of Henry Arthur Jones; these, they emphasized, would 'be printed and bound in a tasteful manner', and, although the stage-directions would provide 'all the necessary details for the complete production of each drama', all such directions would be placed 'discreetly' in the margin, so as not to interfere with 'the easy reading of the play in the study'. Still more significant is the way in which several general firms of distinction, following the early lead of Macmillan, Heinemann, and Constable, discovered that in the cultivation of dramatic literature profits and prestige could be gained, so that they hurried to have the new plays of their favoured 'house' authors presented in double format—unbound, with paper covers (for amateur and professional stage use), and cloth-bound, usually with some distinctive coloured dust-jackets (for readers and library shelves). Thus any student who becomes familiar with this territory may, at a glance and even without reading the titles, immediately recognize the writings of at least half a dozen prominent playwrights.

Quite clearly, the publishers largely aimed at appealing to the tastes of that new and distinctive race of ambitious amateurs who established so many play-producing societies during those years and whose enthusiasm led to the founding of the then-novel repertory theatres; and both the range and the interests of this section of the public are shown in another, related, development. In 1911 the Glasgow firm of Gowans and Gray launched an attractively printed series of *Repertory Plays*, and the gay, decorated 'parchment' covers of these booklets continued to appear well into the 1920s. A dozen years later, in 1923, Ernest Benn inaugurated another venture, the publication of single plays, many of them either unproduced on the stage or else the first essays of authors as yet little-known, under the general title of *Contemporary English Dramatists*: the readers of this series, which ran successfully for many years, were here able to peruse numerous 'experimental' plays which, in fact, never succeeded in reaching the stage, and they also had the privilege of being the first to scan the texts of the earliest dramatic essays written by a young theatrical aspirant named Noël Coward. Two years afterwards, Sidgwick and Jackson also broke relatively new ground by publishing two volumes containing a collection of recently performed dramas which had captured the attention of discerning playgoers;

and five years later still Victor Gollancz issued another volume similarly titled—and the welcome accorded to the effort was such as to encourage the firm to proceed with a set of annual collections, starting with *Famous Plays of 1931* and ending with *Famous Plays of 1938-1939*. Still another bright idea came to Faber and Faber, also eager to attract the new 'dramatic' reading public: in 1934 they issued a volume entitled *My Best Play*, consisting of 'An Anthology of Plays chosen by their own Authors'.

While many playwrights liked to see their stage pieces appear one by one, with the publication date usually agreeing with the date of the theatrical première, others preferred to allow the printing to wait until three, four, or five plays might make up a sizeable, and therefore shelf-worthy, volume—and of course there were at least a few who sought to get the best of both worlds by arranging to have their writings offered to the public in two forms—as single pieces and as parts of collective groupings. Some authors, in giving general titles to the volumes, adopted the simple device exemplified by A. A. Milne's *First Plays* (1919), *Three Plays* (1923), and so on: others, such as James Bridie (O. H. Mavor), favoured slightly variant but equally simple headings like '*A Sleeping Clergyman*' *and Other Plays* (1934); but some of their companions anxiously sought for captions of more adventuresome kind, and this trend was considerably influenced by a characteristic development of the century's early decades—the cult of what may be described as the 'ambitious', or the 'literary', or the 'artistic' one-act drama.

Such short pieces were clearly those best fitted for interpretation by the multiplying number of high-minded, earnest, and eager amateur acting societies, of the other societies sponsoring occasional productions by young professionals, of the new repertory theatres—while for the enthusiastic would-be dramatists who had not yet had the opportunity of becoming versed in theatrical skills they offered manifest advantages. Hundreds, indeed thousands, of these one-acts were issued separately, but obviously they were better suited for reading (besides being given a more 'significant' appearance) when half a dozen or more were gathered together in substantial volumes; and for such volumes simple general titles rarely seemed sufficiently attractive. Hence Lord Dunsany devised his evocative *Plays of Gods and Men* (1917) and *Plays of Near and Far* (1923); John Drinkwater's early pieces appeared as *Pawns* (1917); Clifford Bax had his *Antique Pageantry* (1921). Among the authors who concentrated chiefly upon the shorter dramatic pieces the once widely read and widely acted Laurence Housman saw his *Little Plays of St. Francis* (1922) expanded into three fairly fat volumes, while *Angels and Ministers* (1921), *Palace Plays* (1930), and *The Golden Sovereign* (1937) closely rivalled the Franciscan series in appeal. Any present-day students who may be tempted to dismiss these pieces with a supercilious smile will find that, if prejudices are set aside, there is still pleasure to be found in their simple, delicate, adroit style; and perhaps, when reference is made to the standard, comprehensive bibliography relating to the excitingly innovating activities of Gordon Craig, respect for Housman will be aroused when it is discovered that the section devoted to 'texts of plays produced by Gordon Craig' starts with the entry of that author's *Bethlehem* (1902), presented by amateurs, not in a playhouse but in the hall of the Imperial Institute, South Kensington, which became the administrative centre of the University of London.

Two particular deviations from the general pattern in play-printing deserve particular notice, each of them demonstrating, first, the intimate connection between stage presentation and book publication and, secondly, the manner in which the range of interested readers was extending beyond that of the enthusiastic amateurs. In 1905 the vast auditorium of Drury Lane was filled to capacity for Hall Caine's *The Bondman*, and eagerly this ambitious, albeit melodramatic, show was discussed in circles high and low. The result of this was that the energetic *Daily Mail* issued the text under the title of *The Bondman Play* in a manner absolutely without previous parallel: the substantial volume of 240 pages was printed on thick paper and embellished with numerous photographs of actors and scenes. The second example also concerns a Drury Lane production, presented to the public almost exactly twenty-six years later: Noël Coward's *Cavalcade* was seized upon by Heinemann, and their volume was still larger in format and adorned with even more photographs of players and episodes.

These 'special' publications were concerned with individual plays which had attracted an attention keener and greater than was usual, whereas the second kind of what might be styled 'publishing abnormalities' is associated with just three dramatists whose total contributions to the stage had won them particular esteem. From the time when, towards the close of the nineteenth century, Jones and Pinero began to have their works issued in separate volumes each provided with general headings reading 'The Plays of . . .', numerous popular playwrights saw their writings similarly presented: this, indeed, may be taken as the norm for those authors who were regarded as standing in the first rank. In addition to those, particular

interest attaches to a strictly limited group made up of authors
distinguished by having specially edited 'collected' volumes of their
works set before the public. In 1912 the *Dramatic Works* of St. John
Hankin appeared in three volumes, and in 1923 his plays, revised,
were again published as a collection, with an introduction by John
Drinkwater. Three volumes of Stanley Houghton's dramas, with an
introduction by Harold Brighouse, appeared in 1914. In 1921 Hugh
Walpole wrote an enthusiastic preface for the collected plays of
Hubert Henry Davies, issued in two volumes. Two volumes of John
Drinkwater's dramatic writings followed in 1925; and from 1931 to
1934 came six volumes of Somerset Maugham's plays.

Such volumes of 'collected plays' were, of course, no novelties:
they were simply the latest additions to the already lengthy series of
similar publications which went back to the early seventeenth
century; and they were to be followed by others down to the
present. Distinctive, however, and especially noteworthy were three
weighty books, which might almost be styled 'jumbo' editions, each
one containing the complete works of an author regarded with
extraordinary esteem. Although these can hardly be called 'folios', in
effect their origin is to be found in Ben Jonson's *Workes* of 1616 and
in Shakespeare's 'first folio' of 1623. Beaumont and Fletcher were to
be similarly honoured later in the seventeenth century, and a few
others from time to time joined the select company—but for the
most part these bulky folios soon gave way to more manageable
octavos or duodecimos. With these facts in our minds, we realize, as
we look at the fat, eight-hundred-page, *Plays of J. M. Barrie in One
Volume* (1928), that paradoxically it is an unconscious imitation of
an ancient style and yet is a complete innovation. The publishers,
Hodder and Stoughton, clearly found this a very profitable venture,
and its success must be regarded as responsible for the appearance
of the second 'jumbo' just one year later—an even bulkier volume
(more than 1,100 pages), *The Plays of John Galsworthy*, which em-
phatically testifies to that author's high position in the dramatic
hierarchy. The true theatrical colossus of the time, however, was
a third author, George Bernard Shaw, and it was entirely proper
that his 'jumbo' *Complete Works* (1931) should take shape as something larger, stronger, and more handsome than its companions.
Even although G.B.S., rightly, is graced with a separate essay in
the present book, reference may here appropriately be made to the
author's advice to his readers that they should carefully peruse the
entirety of the single-volume *Works* 'at least twice every year for ten
years or so'—carefully explaining that 'that is why this edition is so

substantially bound for you.' (This statement, it may be added, is absolutely correct: Barrie and Galsworthy are apt to split their bindings at the spine, whereas, even after hard usage, Shaw remains stiffly and steadily and jauntily erect.)

The publication of these three books between 1928 and 1931 also has a double significance. The emphasis placed by G.B.S. on 'reading' reminds us that they could not have come into being save at a time when an ever-increasing multitude of men and women had come to take delight in the perusal of plays: and all the three authors, each in his own way, deliberately sought to make appeal to this public. Barrie's first words are chatty in tone, taking shape as a few 'disquietening confessions': he underlines the fact that *Peter Pan*, although so well known on the stage, is now being printed for the first time; he professes to have 'no recollection of having written it', and, with mock modesty, he expresses his gratitude for having been admitted to the rehearsals; above all, he envelops the stage directions of all the plays in a strangely theatrical/non-theatrical style of commentary which is eminently 'readable'. Galsworthy has a similar aim, although his method is far different and although he shows a tendency to move from the mainly 'practical' stage directions of his earlier plays to the introduction of suggestive comment directed towards readers rather than producers. Everyone knows, of course, that Shaw's methods were, if idiosyncratically different in style, fundamentally similar. Thus these three bulky volumes, although separate and distinct, come together as a highly representative unit.

It has been said above that these 'jumbos' may be regarded as having a double significance, and their second import derives from the fact that all three appeared within the short period from 1928 to 1931— that is to say, after thirty years from the effective start of the 'modern' movement. This reminds us that the present-day students who apply themselves to examination of early twentieth-century drama have the interesting task of determining for themselves just how the dramatic trend which began in 1900 pursued its original course and precisely when it showed signs of changing its path. It is, of course, tempting to think of one consistent development extending from the century's start until the end of the war in 1945, and these, in fact, are the dating limits observed in this volume. Many arguments may be adduced for the acceptance of these limits, limits which are at least approximately supported in Ernest Reynolds's *Modern English Drama: A Survey of the Theatre from 1900* and in J. C. Trewin's *The Theatre since 1900*—although it should be observed that the range of both these surveys was determined by the time when each was written and published: the one appeared in 1949 and the other in 1951.

It would obviously not be proper to argue this question at length here, but it must be emphasized that any student engaged in exploring this area must ask himself a major question: 'What period am I concerned with? Is the drama of 1900–45 to be accepted as having a clear beginning and an equally clear end?' My own answer to the basic query appears, argued at length, in *English Drama, 1900–1930*, where I have sought to indicate the facts which appear to support my own belief that the end of the first 'modern' movement in the twentieth-century drama came around the year 1930, and to this I ought to add (1) my own belief that the choice of the year 1945 as an end-date is artificial, if convenient, and (2) that the second movement drew to its end during the middle 1950s. These, however, are merely personal opinions, and each individual student must make up his own mind on this basic question which offers to all a stimulating, if at times puzzling, theme of inquiry.

Students will, no doubt, be particularly interested in two aspects of the dramatic literature produced within this period. They will want to know which authors stood high in reputation among contemporary audiences, and they will seek to discover which of their plays have an enduring value. Their attention will concentrate upon dramas once famous which now mean nothing and upon other dramas once neglected which have at least some relevance for today. When the century opened, the names of four men were prominent in the minds of those interested in theatrical affairs, and within a year or two the name of a fifth was being mightily lauded. There was the contrasting pair of H. A. Jones and A. W. Pinero, there was a second contrasting pair of J. M. Barrie and G. B. Shaw, and there was the lone figure of Stephen Phillips. References to critical-biographical studies relating to the first pair appear in Chapter 13 of this volume, and, of course, Shaw has a chapter all to himself—for, as everyone knows, this 500-to-1 outsider soon edged his red beard ahead of his competitors and became acknowledged champion. The critical esteem in which Barrie was held is amply demonstrated by the number of books and articles devoted to examination of his work: during the 1920s no fewer than four studies of his writings made their appearance (by H. M. Walbrook, Thomas Moult, J. A. Hammerton, and F. J. H. Darton). At the close of the 1930s interest in him remained sufficiently strong to urge J. A. Roy and the theatre critic W. A. Darlington to add other studies of his work; and, despite the fact that many have sought to decry his 'sentimentalism', that interest even now has urged Janet Dunbar to add a further critical evaluation to those of her predecessors. If Barrie had and still has a high reputation, however, the blazing meteor that was Stephen Phillips soared high and crashed down with such startling suddenness that no critic had time to write an appreciation of his work: in hurriedly penned essays various ordinarily perceptive and cautious critics hailed him as a second Shakespeare and then fell silent; today, we can do no more than regard this episode as one of the theatre's not infrequent strange aberrations, and seek to puzzle it out.

Before the first decade of the century had ended, two younger competitors made their appearance—Somerset Maugham and John Galsworthy—and of course these are well known to all. Maugham's own *Summing Up* tells the story of his creative life; there is a Mander and Mitchenson 'theatrical companion' to his plays; and R. A. Cordell has a well-balanced critical survey of his contributions to the stage. No doubt Galsworthy now is far better known for his novels than for his dramas, but the latter are by no means forgotten: the story of his life is well told by H. V. Marrot and by D. R. Barker, and four critical studies of his dramatic writings—by R. H. Coats, J. Kroener, Victor Dupont, and A. C. Choudhuri—are devoted to analysis of his dramatic method and achievement. These two playwrights were followed during the 1920s by another oddly assorted pair—A. A. Milne and Noël Coward—the former continuing to make his contributions until the end of the thirties and the latter pursuing his extraordinary career into the forties, the fifties, and even the sixties. On Milne's stage work little has been written, but apart from another 'theatrical companion', Coward's writing is discussed by himself in *Present Indicative*; Patrick Braybooke has an entertaining record of his early career; and Sheridan Morley's biography brings the story down to the late sixties. The appearance of prominent pairs seems to be a dominating feature of this strange eventful history, since the early thirties saw the sudden flourishing of two other widely lauded dramatists, one of them a novelist, J. B. Priestley, who soared to popular fame with *The Good Companions*, and the other a Glasgow doctor, Osborne Henry Mavor, who first appeared, very obscurely, in his native city under the pseudonym of 'Mary Henderson', and whose later rapid rise, as 'James Bridie', from obscurity to fame was almost as sudden. Rex Podgson, Ivor Brown and, with particular concentration upon his dramatic work, Gareth Lloyd Evans have all applied themselves to critical appreciation of the former author; Bridie's work has been examined both by Winifred Bannister and by Helen Luyben.

Probably everyone, or nearly everyone, would concur in recognizing these dramatists as having been of supreme importance during the first part of the century. It must, however, be recognized that there are a few enigmatic and puzzling authors whose power and position are difficult to classify. Of these, typical is Harley Granville-Barker, whose creative plays are few but whose theatrical activities were many: his work clearly demands careful scrutiny, and students will find much to interest them in the critical studies of C. B. Purdom and Margery M. Morgan. And, in addition to such authors, it must be emphasized that those who restrict their reading to the plays of the 'major' playwrights mentioned above will certainly be missing much of importance. Some other authors, such as Frederick Lonsdale (concerning whom Frances Donaldson has written an intimately appreciative study), Terence Rattigan, and Emlyn Williams were closely associated with the 'major' group and their total dramatic output is of considerable significance. Others belonged to particular 'schools' and drew at least part of their strength from that fact: of these schools the most important was that to which was given the distinguishing descriptive epithet of 'Manchester', its particular triumphs being Stanley Houghton's *Hindle Wakes* (1912) and Harold Brighouse's *Hobson's Choice* (1915). Others are Alfred Sutro, significant both for his championing of Maeterlinck in England and for his own social-realistic writings, and Benn Levy, whose early contributions to the stage deserve attention. Others warrant attention because, like poor Stephen Phillips, they suddenly soared to fame and soon suffered equally sudden Phaethon-like falls: still others, like D. H. Lawrence, demand scrutiny because today they occasionally receive polite praise for their dramas whereas in their own times they had little or none: others, such as H. H. Davies, whom contemporaries hailed as possessing powers of endurance, need attention since there is always the possibility that now they may be thought to be unduly neglected; and there are still a few others whose plays may be considered overrated because of their authors' unquestioned brilliance in other areas of theatrical activity—the most outstanding figure of this kind being Granville-Barker. Brighouse's autobiography, *What I Have Had*, is relevant here.

In addition to such authors, this first part of the twentieth century welcomed numerous authors whose reputation (even although individually they may have been reasonably prolific) rests, in general, upon single writings—*The Tragedy of Nan* (1908: John Masefield), *Abraham Lincoln* (1918: John Drinkwater), *Outward Bound* (1923:

Vane Sutton-Vane), *Journey's End* (1929: R. C. Sherriff), *The Barretts of Wimpole Street* (1930: Rudolf Besier), *The Rose without a Thorn* (1932: Clifford Bax), *Richard of Bordeaux* (1932: Gordon Daviot)—or at most in just a couple of plays, for example Harley Granville-Barker's *The Voysey Inheritance* (1905) and *The Madras House* (1910). Of singular interest, too, are the continuous and diverse attempts made during these years to establish a truly effective poetic theatre. Stephen Phillips had, like numerous nineteenth-century authors, based his dialogue style upon Elizabethan models, but the chief 'creative' trend during the Edwardian and Georgian periods was directed towards discovering some other kind of poetic expression which might enable the dramatists to escape from what had by now become the outworn rhythms of the Shakespearian age. Gordon Bottomley, although never attaining to supreme success, was one of the most interesting among the earlier authors belonging to this group—striking out on an individual path both by his imaginative choice of theme in *King Lear's Wife* (1915) and *Gruach* (printed 1921; acted 1923), two dramas which take shape as what might be described as 'prologues' to *King Lear* and *Macbeth*, and, in his later choric plays, experimenting in fresh dramatic and stylistic patterns. In 1923 J. E. Flecker produced in *Hassan* a drama which has proved to possess enduring appeal; there are studies of Flecker by his nephew, John Sherwood, and by Douglas Goldring. During the following decade T. S. Eliot (also discussed in the following chapter) broke completely fresh ground with *Murder in the Cathedral* (1935) and *The Family Reunion* (1939); and we must remember that Christopher Fry, whose star shone so brightly after 1945, had been hailed before 1939 by at least a few discerning theatre-men for his earliest, tentative experiments in this kind.

Practically all these plays will, of necessity, have to be sought out in their original printed forms, either as separate texts or in one or other of the 'Collected Works' of individual playwrights. In 1929 J. W. Marriott prepared an anthology of *Great Modern British Plays* and in 1931 E. Bradlee Watson and Benfield Pressey edited two volumes of *Contemporary Drama: European–English and Irish–American Plays* (1931), but these are now out of print; and, as has been suggested above, even if they had been available, much would be lost by turning to their pages instead of to the pages of the original printings. There is an Everyman anthology of *Modern Plays*; otherwise the anthologies which will most assist students today are those presenting some of the shorter dramas of the time, particularly the various volumes of Marriott's *Best One-Act Plays*.

As yet there has been no detailed survey of dramatic writing for the entirety of the years 1900–45. My own volume, cited above, is restricted to the years 1900–30. Excellent, briefer, but chronologically more wide-ranging panoramic views are those by Ernest Reynolds and J. C. Trewin; W. A. Darlington's lively *Six Thousand and One Nights* (1960) surveys the field from 1920 on to the late 1950s. Nor should students neglect the earlier critical volumes written when these plays were still the latest 'modern' drama— P. P. Howe's *Dramatic Portraits* (1913), John Palmer's *The Future of the Theatre* (1913), Barrett H. Clark's *The British and American Drama of Today* (1915), Thomas H. Dickinson's *The Contemporary Drama of England* (1917), Ashley Dukes's *Modern Dramatists* (1911), Frank Vernon's *The Twentieth-Century Theatre* (1924), A. E. Morgan's *Tendencies of Modern English Drama* (1924), and Martin Ellehauge's *Striking Figures among Modern English Dramatists* (1931).

The present essay is, of course, concerned specifically with drama, not with theatre; but everyone knows that the appreciation and evaluation of dramatic literature demand that plays should be examined, discussed, and assessed with at least some attempt to place them within their proper theatrical habitat. This means not only that the reader should try to imagine the scenes taking shape in what W. A. Darlington has called the 'theatre of the mind', but also that an effort should be made imaginatively to reconstruct the playhouse world of the period when they were composed—not only the theatre forms, the scenery, the actors' styles, but also something far more elusive (and therefore often neglected), the nature of the audiences who witnessed these productions. It might well have been thought that, since the early decades of the twentieth century are not so very far removed from the present, this exercise of the imagination would have been less difficult than, let us say, the attempt mentally to reconstruct the effects which might have been created by a performance in Shakespeare's Globe theatre—the exact shape of which is unknown to us—at the beginning of the seventeenth century: but, in fact, the exercise must be seen as being much more difficult rather than less.

Shakespeare and his companions used only a few bare, limited stage directions, often doing no more than indicate the entries and the exits of characters, and, as a result, the modern reader is compelled to exercise his imagination to the full, conceiving in his fancy actions appropriate to the players' lines, making allowances for the non-realistic dramatic patterns, and, particularly, attempting to place the scenes within the strange circle of the Globe or within the equally strange ambience of the Blackfriars. By contrast, in reading these early twentieth-century plays and in observing that such-and-such a comedy had been originally performed at the Haymarket and that such-and-such a drama had appeared first at Drury Lane, we are aware that these theatres are virtually the same as those with which we are familiar today; and, because of that, we may well be unconsciously inclined to set aside consideration of the audience attitudes and behaviour prevailing within these well-known playhouses some fifty or sixty years ago; and, still further, since there is so little call for the exercise of our imagination and since so many of the stage directions are, as we have seen, carefully framed in nontheatrical terms, we may, unless we are very careful, incline to forget the playhouse entirely and to read the texts as though they belonged to the world of narrative fiction.

The student's first task (and it is not so much a task as a pleasure) should be to appreciate the peculiar, special position occupied by the earliest decades because of their sudden, almost inexplicable, growth of dramatic interest outside the professional magic of the metropolitan ring. The development of the 'repertories' is, of course, the best-known example of this new spirit, but almost equally important is the truly extraordinary multiplication of ambitious amateur, or professional, or amateur–professional, play-producing clubs in almost all areas of the British Isles—something which was responsible both for the creation of the British Drama League and for the preliminary work which eventually led to the launching of a National Theatre. Strangely, the only book devoted exclusively to an examination of this subject is the work of a German author, Harry Bergholtz, *Die Neugestaltung des modernen englischen Theaters, 1870–1930* (1933), and, since this volume was printed in a strictly limited edition of 150 copies, it is understandable that it should have remained almost entirely unknown—while obviously none but advanced researchers are likely to be able to consult it; another German historian critic, Heinz Kosok, has contributed to *Maske und Kothurn* (1968) an interesting survey of the 'repertory' movement in England and Scotland; since, in general, the significance of the play-producing societies has been ignored, I have introduced a condensed, but comprehensive, section on the subject into *English Drama, 1900–1930*. Almost always, the professional repertory theatres which proved so characteristic and important an element in early twentieth-century theatrical affairs arose directly from amateur societies active in various cities outside of the metropolis;

and fortunately this 'repertory' movement has been satisfactorily documented. Rex Podgson deals with the story of *Miss Horniman and the Gaiety Theatre, Manchester*, J. C. Trewin with *The Birmingham Repertory Theatre, 1913–1963*, and Grace Wyndham Goldie with *The Liverpool Repertory Theatre, 1911–1934*; although not presenting much detailed factual information, Cecil Chisholm's *Repertory: An Outline of the Modern Theatre Movement* is valuable for its reflection of the eager aspirations which animated those active in that area. Desmond MacCarthy's *The Court Theatre 1904–1907: A Commentary and a Criticism* (1907) provides a detailed record of what was achieved by the 'Vedrenne–Barker' seasons—and mention of Harley Granville Barker (who later became Harley Granville-Barker) reminds us of the way in which this thoughtful dramatist–director strove to promote the idea of a 'national theatre': collaborating with William Archer he produced in 1904 a privately printed set of 'Schemes and Estimates', and these formed the main substance of *A National Theatre* (1930); with this volume may be associated Geoffrey Whitworth's *The Making of a National Theatre* (1951), and the general atmosphere inspiring such endeavours is well reflected in St. John Ervine's *The Organised Theatre: A Plea in Civics* (1924), and in *The Other Theatre* (1947), by Norman Marshall.

Factual information concerning the London stages is presented in *The Theatres of London* (1963) by Raymond Mander and Joe Mitchenson and in Diana Howard's *London Theatres and Music Halls 1850–1950* (1970): for students, the latter may prove particularly useful because, in addition to its great range of theatrical records, it cites numerous books and articles likely to aid those who wish to pursue further particular research investigations. It need hardly be said that the scanning of current theatrical criticism is of the greatest service to those who are endeavouring to get the 'feel' of any period of dramatic activity, and fortunately many of the reviewers active between 1900 and 1945 displayed such incisive judgement, perceptive vision, and lively style as to make their writings as readable today as they were forty, fifty, sixty years ago; fortunately, too, several of these surveyors of the contemporary stage issued collected volumes of at least some among their essays. The names and titles are too numerous to list here, but a brief indication of the principal periodical critics, with their affiliations and with some references to their collected volumes, is provided in my *English Drama, 1900–1930*. Many of the more significant metropolitan playhouses have their own 'biographies'—as, for example, Barry Duncan's *Strange and Complete History* of the St. James's Theatre and W. Macqueen-

Pope's *Haymarket: Theatre of Perfection*—while the numerous biographies of prominent actors associated with these playhouses (extending from general studies, such as Hesketh Pearson's *The Last Actor-Managers*, to particular studies, which may be exemplified by the same author's *Beerbohm Tree: His Life and Laughter*, Daphne du Maurier's *Gerald: A Portrait*, and Cyril Maude's own *Behind the Scenes with Cyril Maude*, not only provide delightful reading but also are indispensable for any who now wish to travel back in imagination to a theatrical realm which, even although it is the basis of our own, exhibits so many features now strange to us.

That last statement may be regarded as indicating what is the most fascinating aspect of this subject. Barrie, Shaw, and Coward are gone, but Priestley and Rattigan, happily, are still present: Beerbohm Tree, du Maurier, and Maude are no longer delighting audiences, but still powerful is the spirit of those many actors and actresses, headed by such distinguished performers as Sir John Gielgud, Sir Ralph Richardson, Lord Olivier, Dame Peggy Ashcroft, Dame Sybil Thorndike, and Dame Edith Evans, who enrich the stages of the 'seventies with the penetration, delicacy, and expertise which they learned during the earlier years of this century. If we seek for symbols, we do not have to search far or long: Sir John Gielgud and Sir Ralph Richardson first won fame at the Old Vic when that theatre was valiantly struggling, under the devoted direction of Lilian Baylis, to emerge from its 'coffee-house' chrysalis and unfold its richly coloured Shakespearian wings: Dame Edith Evans made her earliest appearance under the tutelage of William Poel, whose activities, excellently narrated by Robert Speaight in *William Poel and the Elizabethan Revival*, might well seem to many students to belong to a distant historical past, while her first important role was that of the heroine in *Troilus and Cressida*—a play which, in 1912, it was the peculiar privilege of the early 'modern' theatre to discover.

In view of the anomalous position of this subject, it may prove helpful to add a few notes concerning some of the principal reference works relevant to the period. Frequently, students engaged in investigating the drama are confronted by play-titles without any indication of the authors' names, or by the names of authors without any citation of their writings, or by allusions to performances without any precise dates. If these plays, playwrights, or performances come before the year 1900, then students are likely to be able to find the information they seek without any great trouble; but the situation is entirely different when we proceed beyond the beginning of our own century—when the required facts may have to be sought for in several different sources of information. Three periodical publications should be borne in mind: (a) *The Era Annual,* which started its life as *The Era Almanack* in 1868, was, as its title indicates, a publication sponsored by the well-known theatrical journal called *The Era*: each issue contains particulars relating to places and performance-dates of new plays 'in London and the Provinces' during the preceding twelve months; but unfortunately this annual ceased publication in 1919; (b) *'The Stage' Year Book,* produced by the other well-known theatrical journal, was first issued in 1908; publication was temporarily discontinued in 1928; it started afresh in 1949, but the last volume appeared in 1969: here also information is provided concerning performances of new plays, and most of the volumes contain interesting articles on the theatrical activities of the time; (c) *Who's Who in the Theatre* was launched under the editorship of John Parker in 1912 and the fifteenth edition has now appeared (1972): in the fourth edition (1922) a new feature was introduced under the general heading of 'London Playbills'—lists of new plays presented in the metropolis, and the latest edition has a cumulative index to all the productions thus recorded from 1921 to 1965. When facts are being sought concerning performances (dates, theatres, actors), these are the principal sources to keep in mind, but advanced students should also be prepared to consult files of *The Era* and *The Stage* or to explore the rich assemblage of playbill material preserved in the Gabrielle Enthoven Collection at the Victoria and Albert Museum. Such students may be well advised to join The Society for Theatre Research, which both in its sponsored lectures and in its periodical publication, *Theatre Notebook,* has brought to notice much interesting material relating to the drama and stage since 1900.

Students concerned with the drama before 1900 have at their service comprehensive lists (for the earlier period complete, for the later almost complete, but, because of the increasing number of dramatic writings and the growing complexity of the subject, constantly calling for divers additions and adjustments), but whether there can ever be compiled corresponding statistical surveys for the twentieth century seems most problematical. The difficulties involved may be exemplified by the 'Hand-List of Plays' which forms part of my *English Drama, 1900-1930*: although this embraces only thirty years, although deliberately several entire categories of dramatic texts have been excluded, although the information is presented in a condensed form, and although the catalogue has been

printed in small type, it still occupies more than five hundred pages.
No similar list is available for the years between 1930 and 1945. For
facts regarding publication of at least some of the plays written between 1930 and 1945 reference may be made to *The Player's Library*
and its supplements—but unfortunately, although publishers' names
are listed, no dates are indicated in these volumes, and of course it
must be borne in mind that the volumes themselves are primarily
designed only as a catalogue of the British Drama League library,
a collection certainly large but by no means complete. And still
another note may be added here for advanced students: since the
abolition of the Lord Chamberlain's 'censorship', the enormous
collection of manuscript and typewritten texts originally deposited
at his Office in St. James's Palace has been removed to the British
Museum, dramatic treasure trove indeed for future researchers.

REFERENCES

REFERENCE WORKS

The Era (weekly publication from 1838 to 1939).
   (This periodical originally specialized in sporting events but later became
   identified with theatrical affairs.)
The Era Almanack (annual volumes, with a later change in title to *The Era
   Annual*, from 1868 to 1919).
The Player's Library: The Catalogue of the British Drama League (London, 1950;
   supplements, 1951, 1956).
The Stage (various periodicals of this title appeared, and then vanished,
   during the nineteenth century; the present *Stage* extends from 1881
   onwards).
'*The Stage' Year Book* (annual volumes from 1908 to 1920, a composite
   volume for 1921–5, annual volumes from 1926 to 1928, and from 1949
   to 1969).
Who's Who in the Theatre
   (The origin of this well-known and indispensable series may be traced to
   The Green Room Book and Who's Who on the Stage, a volume published in
   1907. With a general heading of 'The New Dramatic List', the first
   volume of the series itself appeared in 1912 as *Who's Who in the Theatre:
   A Biographical Record of the Contemporary Stage*, compiled and edited by John
   Parker. The following volumes up to the 'Tenth Edition', published in
   1947, are particularly relevant to the period covered by this essay, but it
   should be particularly noted that the 'Fourteenth and Jubilee Edition',
   edited by Freda Gaye, published in 1967, contains a most useful general
   index to performances listed between 1921 and 1960: this is included also
   in the latest 'fifteenth' edition of 1972.)

GENERAL CRITICAL STUDIES

B. H. Clark, *The British and American Drama of Today; Outlines for their Study* (New York, 1915).

W. A. Darlington, *Six Thousand and One Nights: Forty Years a Critic* (London, 1960).

T. H. Dickinson, *The Contemporary Drama of England* (Boston, Mass., 1917).

A. Dukes, *Modern Dramatists* (London, 1911).

M. Ellehauge, *Striking Figures among Modern English Dramatists* (Copenhagen, 1931).

P. P. Howe, *Dramatic Portraits* (London, 1913).

A. E. Morgan, *Tendencies of Modern English Drama* (London, 1924).

A. Nicoll, *English Drama, 1900–1930: The Beginnings of the Modern Period* (Cambridge, 1973).

J. Palmer, *The Future of the Theatre* (London, 1913).

E. Reynolds, *Modern English Drama: A Survey of the Theatre from 1900* (London, 1949).

J. C. Trewin, *The Theatre since 1900* (London, 1951).

F. Vernon, *The Twentieth-Century Theatre* (London, 1924).

BACKGROUND STUDIES

H. Bergholtz, *Die Neugestaltung des modernen englischen Theaters, 1870–1930* (Berlin, 1933).

C. Chisholm, *Repertory: An Outline of the Modern Theatre Movement* (London, 1934).

D. du Maurier, *Gerald: A Portrait* (London, 1934).

B. Duncan, *The St. James's Theatre: Its Strange and Complete History 1835–1957* (London, 1964).

St. J. G. Ervine, *The Organised Theatre: A Plea in Civics* (London, 1924).

G. W. Goldie, *The Liverpool Repertory Theatre, 1911–1934* (Liverpool, 1935).

H. Granville-Barker, *A National Theatre* (London, 1930).

D. Howard, *London Theatres and Music Halls 1850–1950* (London, 1970).

H. Kosok, 'Die Anfänge der modernen Repertoiretheaterbewegung in England und Schottland', *Maske und Kothurn* 14 (1968).

D. MacCarthy, *The Court Theatre 1904–1907: A Commentary and a Criticism* (London, 1907).

W. Macqueen-Pope, *Haymarket: Theatre of Perfection* (London, 1948).

R. Mander and J. Mitchenson, *The Theatres of London* (London, 1963).

N. Marshall, *The Other Theatre* (London, 1947).

C. Maude, *Behind the Scenes with Cyril Maude* (London, 1927).

H. Pearson, *Beerbohm Tree: His Life and Laughter* (London, 1956).

——, *The Last Actor-Managers* (London, 1950).

R. Podgson, *Miss Horniman and the Gaiety Theatre, Manchester* (London, 1952).

R. Speaight, *William Poel and the Elizabethan Revival* (London, 1954).

J. C. Trewin, *The Birmingham Repertory Theatre, 1913–1963* (London, 1963).

G. Whitworth, *The Making of a National Theatre* (London, 1951).

ANTHOLOGIES OF PLAYS

ed. J. W. Marriott, *Great Modern British Plays* (London, 1929).
——, *One-Act Plays of To-day* (London, 1924).
——, *The Best One-Act Plays of 1931* (London, 1932); continued as an
  annual series to *The Best One-Act Plays of 1944–45* (London, 1946).
Modern Plays (Sherriff's *Journey's End*, Maugham's *For Services Rendered*,
  Coward's *Hay Fever*, Milne's *Dover Road*, Bennett and Knoblock's
  Milestones; Everyman's Library, London, 1956).
ed. E. B. Watson and B. Pressey, *Contemporary Drama: European–English and
  Irish–American Plays*, 2 vols. (New York, 1931).

Individual Dramatists

Sir James M. Barrie (1860–1937)

The Plays of J. M. Barrie in One Volume (London, 1928).
ed. A. E. Wilson, *Plays* (London, 1942).

W. A. C. Darlington, *J. M. Barrie* (London, 1938).
F. J. H. Darton, *J. M. Barrie* (London, 1929).
J. Dunbar, *J. M. Barrie: The Man behind the Image* (London, 1970).
J. A. Hammerton, *Barrie: The Story of a Genius* (London, 1929).
T. Moult, *Barrie* (London, 1928).
J. A. Roy, *J. M. Barrie* (London, 1937).
H. M. Walbrook, *J. M. Barrie and the Theatre* (London, 1922).

Clifford Bax (1886–1962)

Valiant Ladies: Three New Plays (London, 1931; includes *The Venetian*, *The
  Rose Without a Thorn*, and *The Immortal Lady*).

Rudolf Besier (1878–1942)

The Barretts of Wimpole Street (London, 1930).

Gordon Bottomley (1874–1948)

ed. C. C. Abbott, *Poems and Plays* (London, 1953).

James Bridie (1888–1951)

'*The Anatomist*' and Other Plays (London, 1931).
'*A Sleeping Clergyman*' and Other Plays (London, 1934).

W. Bannister, *James Bridie and His Theatre* (London, 1955).
H. Luyben, *James Bridie, Clown and Philosopher* (Pennsylvania University
  Press, Pa., 1965).

Harold Brighouse (1882–1958)

Hobson's Choice (London, 1916; ed. E. R. Wood, London, 1964).
What I Have Had: Chapters in Autobiography (London, 1953).

Sir Noël Coward (1899–1973)

Play Parade, 6 vols. (London, 1934–62).

P. Braybrooke, *The Amazing Mr Noël Coward* (London, 1933).
N. Coward, *Present Indicative* (London, 1937).
R. Mander and J. Mitchenson, *A Theatrical Companion to Coward* (London, 1957).
S. Morley, *A Talent to Amuse: A Biography of Noël Coward* (London, 1969; includes a bibliography).

Hubert Henry Davies (1876–1917)

Plays, 2 vols. (London, 1921).

Gordon Daviot (1896–1952)

Plays, 3 vols. (London, 1953–4).

John Drinkwater (1882–1937)

Collected Plays, 2 vols. (London, 1925).

Lord Dunsany (1878–1957)

Plays of Gods and Men (London, 1917).
Plays of Near and Far (New York, 1923).

Thomas Stearns Eliot (1888–1965)

Collected Plays (London, 1962).

E. M. Browne, *The Making of T. S. Eliot's Plays* (London, 1969).
C. H. Smith, *T. S. Eliot's Dramatic Theory and Practice, from 'Sweeney Agonistes' to 'The Elder Statesman'* (Princeton, N.J., 1963).

James Elroy Flecker (1884–1915)

Hassan (London, 1922; acting edn. with introduction by B. Dean, London, 1966).
D. Goldring, *James Elroy Flecker* (London, 1922).
J. Sherwood, *No Golden Journey* (London, 1973).

John Galsworthy (1867–1933)

The Plays of John Galsworthy (London, 1929).

D. R. Barker, *The Man of Principle* (London, 1963).
A. C. Choudhuri, *Galsworthy's Plays. A Critical Survey* (Bombay, 1961).

R. H. Coats, *John Galsworthy as a Dramatic Artist* (London, 1926).
V. Dupont, *John Galsworthy: The Dramatic Artist* (Toulouse and Montpellier, 1946).
J. Kroener, *Die Technik realistischen Dramas bei Ibsen und Galsworthy* (Leipzig, 1935).
H. V. Marrot, *The Life and Letters of John Galsworthy* (London, 1935).

Harley Granville-Barker (1877–1946)

Collected Plays (London, 1967–).
M. M. Morgan, *A Drama of Political Man: A Study in the Plays of Harley Granville-Barker* (London, 1961).
C. B. Purdom, *Harley Granville-Barker* (London, 1955).

St. John Hankin (1869–1909)

The Dramatic Works, 3 vols. (London, 1912; rev. in 2 vols., London, 1923).

William Stanley Houghton (1881–1913)

ed. H. Brighouse, *The Works of Stanley Houghton*, 3 vols. (London, 1914).

Laurence Housman (1865–1959)

Angels and Ministers (London, 1921).
Little Plays of St. Francis, 3 vols. (London, 1935).
Victoria Regina (London, 1934; includes *Angels and Ministers* (1921), and *Palace Plays* (1930)).

David Herbert Lawrence (1885–1930)

The Complete Plays of D. H. Lawrence (London, 1965).
Lawrence: Three Plays, Introduction by R. Williams (Harmondsworth, 1969).

Benn Levy (1900–74)

Mrs. Moonlight (London, 1929).
The Devil (London, 1930).

Frederick Lonsdale (1881–1954)

The Last of Mrs Cheyney (London, 1925).
On Approval (London, 1927).

F. Donaldson, *Freddy Lonsdale* (London, 1957).

John Masefield (1878–1967)

'*The Tragedy of Nan*' *and Other Plays* (London, 1909).
The Poems and Plays of Masefield, 2 vols. (New York, 1918).

William Somerset Maugham (1874–1965)

Plays by W. Somerset Maugham, 6 vols. (London, 1931–4; repr. as *Collected Plays*, 3 vols., London, 1952).

R. A. Cordell, *W. Somerset Maugham* (London, 1937).
R. Mander and J. Mitchenson, *A Theatrical Companion to Somerset Maugham* (London, 1955).
W. S. Maugham, *The Summing Up* (London, 1938).

Alan Alexander Milne (1882–1956)

Mr Pim Passes By; in *Second Plays* (London, 1923).
The Dover Road; in *Three Plays* (London, 1923).

Stephen Phillips (1864–1915)

Herod (London, 1900).
Paolo and Francesca (London, 1900).

John Boynton Priestley (1894–)

The Plays, 3 vols. (London, 1948–50).

I. Brown, *J. B. Priestley* (London, 1957).
G. L. Evans, *J. B. Priestley—the Dramatist* (London, 1964).
R. Podgson, *J. B. Priestley and the Theatre* (Drama Study Books, no. 2, London, 1947).

Terence Rattigan (1911–)

The Collected Plays of Terence Rattigan (London, 1953–).

Robert Cedric Sherriff (1896–)

Journey's End (London, 1929; see also 'Anthologies of Plays', p. 286).

Alfred Sutro (1863–1933)

The Walls of Jericho (London, 1904).
John Glayde's Honour (London, 1907).

Vane Sutton-Vane (1888–1963)

Outward Bound (London, 1924).

Emlyn Williams (1905–)

The Collected Plays (London, 1961–).

George: An Early Autobiography (London, 1961).
Emlyn: An Early Autobiography (1927–1935) (London, 1973).

17. ENGLISH DRAMA SINCE 1945

JOHN RUSSELL BROWN

M OST accounts of British drama since the Second World War speak
of the London productions of Samuel Beckett's *Waiting for Godot* and
John Osborne's *Look Back in Anger*, in 1955 and 1957 respectively, as
events that made the English theatre, once again, the mirror of its
age. Three books that appeared between 1960 and 1962 were concerned with the newly produced plays and were influential in
establishing this view: Laurence Kitchin's *Mid-Century Drama*,
Martin Esslin's *The Theatre of the Absurd*, and John Russell Taylor's
Anger and After. Kitchin was the drama critic of the London *Times*,
and his book, which includes interviews and reviews, places new
plays in a context of production, fashion, personalities, and theory:
it was a strong stimulus to the current debate about emerging talents
and change in theatre practice. Esslin's book has a European perspective and a basic interest in philosophy and meaning: it considers English writers, especially Harold Pinter and Samuel Beckett,
as pioneers of a new sensibility. *Anger and After* is specifically 'a guide
to the new British drama'; there are chapters on plays first produced
at the Royal Court Theatre, London, at Joan Littlewood's Theatre
Workshop, at theatres in the provinces, and on radio and television.
Taylor tells the story of how these plays came to be written and performed, as well as giving his own impressions of them; this book
is in the best sense journalistic, being both informative and indispensable. Both Kitchin and Taylor subsequently published sequels,
Drama in the Sixties and *The Second Wave*.

There are inherent difficulties about writing criticism of drama
hard at the heels of its first performance, and it is not surprising that
some of the more penetrating and considered accounts can be
found in books which bring together specially commissioned articles
by various hands. *Experimental Drama* (1963), edited by W. A.
Armstrong, and *Contemporary Theatre* (1962), edited by J. R. Brown
and B. Harris, both attempt a longer perspective in time than the
books hitherto mentioned, the former including an informative
chapter by the editor on theatre management and its influence on
dramatists. Two periodicals devoted special issues to new British

drama and both would repay separate publication: one was the *Tulane Drama Review* in 1966, and the other *The Twentieth Century* in 1961, edited by Richard Findlater. There have also been volumes of studies previously published in periodicals and books; the widest in scope are the Twentieth Century Views collection, edited by J. R. Brown and called *Modern British Dramatists* (1968), and the Grove Press *New British Drama* (1964), edited by H. Popkin. Two books edited by Charles Marowitz and others—*Theatre at Work* (1967) and *The Encore Reader* (1965)—contain interviews with dramatists as well as accounts of plays at the time of their first performance. There are two collections of interviews that include a good proportion of British writers: J. F. McCrindle's *Behind the Scenes* (1971), and W. Wager's *The Playwrights Speak* (1967).

After the excitements of special reports from a widespread and rather confusing battlefield, those accounts in which recent English drama takes its place in formal histories of twentieth-century drama or in accounts of European drama since Ibsen strike a calmer and usually less enthusiastic note. Of the histories and surveys, the best are Bamber Gascoigne's *Twentieth Century Drama*, Frederick Lumley's *New Trends in 20th Century Drama*, and Allan Lewis's *The Contemporary Theatre*. Raymond Williams's *From Ibsen to Eliot*, Ruby Cohn's *Currents in Contemporary Drama*, and Ronald Gaskell's *Drama and Reality* deal with only a few British writers, but their assessments of twentieth-century theatre provide conceptual frameworks within which intentions and achievements of other writers may be judged. Allardyce Nicoll's *English Drama: A Modern Viewpoint* considers post-war plays together with those plays from other ages which have survived in current repertory; he makes unfashionable and con-sidered judgements. John Russell Brown's *Theatre Language* (1972) studies the ways in which Harold Pinter, John Osborne, Arnold Wesker, and John Arden have used the resources of theatrical performance.

TEXTS

Few dramatists in this period have published their collected plays, but very many plays have been published, often in different versions. Beckett's plays are considered in Chapter 15, but here it is relevant to notice that the English text of *Waiting for Godot* was first published in England in 1956, but also appeared in New York with those parts of the text restored that had been cut in performance in London in compliance with the Lord Chamberlain's censoring instructions; the authoritative text was not published in England until 1965. Harold

Pinter's *The Caretaker* was published in two versions, in 1960 and 1962, the second representing the author's revisions subsequent to the first stage production. Pinter's *The Dwarfs* has been published in one radio version and two stage versions. The published text of T. S. Eliot's *The Elder Statesman* represents the first production, but some writers on Eliot have consulted an earlier version. One episode of his *Sweeney Agonistes* was delayed for posthumous performance and publication. Now that censorship has been ended, more and more texts may be reissued with the Lord Chamberlain's cuts restored.

Scholarship and computers are unlikely to catch up with the bewildering textual problems which this multiple publication involves until the end of the century. At present a bibliographer can do little more than warn that texts may differ from issue to issue, as well as from edition to edition, and to note the few authoritative collected editions that are available.

Some play-texts may not be found in library catalogues under authors' names. This can happen easily when they are published in periodicals, and the files of *Plays and Players* (London), *Gambit* (London), and *Plays of the Year*, edited by J. C. Trewin (London), should certainly be consulted. The series of paperback volumes called *New English Dramatists* and published by Penguin Books (Harmondsworth) sometimes escapes being listed or catalogued under the names of the various dramatists whose works appear within a single volume; occasionally these books are listed under the name of the critic introducing a particular volume.

DRAMATISTS

Only a very few of the dramatists working in the English Theatre since 1945 have received independent critical attention beyond reviews in periodical publications as their plays are first performed or published. Brief factual information can be found, however, in the various issues of *Who's Who in the Theatre*. Moreover all dramatists living in 1972 and whose work had then been seen in professional performance on more than a few occasions are the subjects of individual biographical, bibliographical, and critical entries in the dictionary, *Contemporary Dramatists*, edited by James Vinson.

Among the English dramatists of the late forties, T. S. Eliot has received by far the greatest and most sustained critical attention, and his collected plays appeared in 1962. A bibliography by D. Gallup covers Eliot's critical writings and poems, as well as the plays, as do many of the most perceptive critical and scholarly writings. Helen Gardner's *The Art of T. S. Eliot* is probably the best general account of the poet, and G. Smith's *T. S. Eliot's Poetry and Plays* the best guide to the sources and influences of all Eliot's creative works. Denis Donoghue's *The Third Voice* and Ronald Peacock's *The Poet in the Theatre* consider Eliot's dramatic poetry; but any consideration of this subject should include the study of the dramatist's own critical writings, in particular the lectures entitled 'Poetry and Drama' and 'The Three Voices of Poetry' which are republished in *On Poetry and Poets* (1957). Among the studies of the plays themselves, E. Martin Browne, the director of their first performances, has written an inside account of *The Making of T. S. Eliot's Plays* (1969); books by D. E. Jones and Carol H. Smith are to be recommended.

Christopher Fry's first published play appeared in 1939, *The Boy with a Cart*, but his greatest success, with *The Lady's Not for Burning* and *Venus Observed*, was immediately after the war. Then he seemed to join with T. S. Eliot in heralding a return to poetic drama in the contemporary theatre. His comments on his art, *An Experience of Critics* (1952), record something of the changing esteem of journalism and, with more than usual finesse, his own sense of the times and of a dramatist's tasks. Derek Sandford's *Christopher Fry: An Appreciation* (1951) assesses his achievement in mid-career; a revised edition appeared in 1962.

Noël Coward, Terence Rattigan, and J. B. Priestley were dramatists of established reputation in 1945 and some postwar plays are included in their collected editions. Sheridan Morley has written a biography covering the whole of Coward's career, as author, actor, entertainer, and wit, called *A Talent to Amuse*, and Gareth Lloyd Evans has studied Priestley's plays in *J. B. Priestley—the Dramatist*, a book that examines individual plays with care and also clearly marks Priestley's progress in the theatre. The novelist, Graham Greene, had his first play performed in the West End in 1953 and his dramatic writing has been considered as part of his long career as a writer in general studies, such as that by John Atkins.

The plays of Samuel Beckett, an Irishman living in France and usually writing in French before making his own translations into English, have a questionable validity as part of English drama. They are considered in the context of Irish drama in Chapter 15. But his influence on younger English writers is obvious and sustained, and no bibliography of this period would be complete without a selection from the large quantities of exegesis, philosophizing, and criticism that have followed his progress as a creative writer. Fortunately bibliographies are available, the most useful by Federman and Fletcher, and some books give both a balanced view and special insights. Frederick J. Hoffman's *Samuel Beckett: The Language of Self* relates *Waiting for Godot* to the novels that preceded it and Beckett's concept of the self with those of Dostoevsky, Kafka, and others. Books on Beckett by Hugh Kenner and Ruby Cohn, subtitled *A Critical Study* and *The Comic Gamut* respectively, are probably the most astute and balanced accounts of his art: on the plays, Professor Cohn is the more authoritative and suggestive. John Fletcher, who had earlier written a book on the novels, joined with the dramatist John Spurling to write *Beckett: A Study of His Plays* which was published in 1972; not only does this cover all the dramatic output, but it is also concerned with Beckett's interest in, and influence on, the theatre in general. Anthologies of criticism serve a special purpose for a writer who has attracted so much attention, and the collection by Martin Esslin (whose *Theatre of the Absurd* included a highly influential and pioneer study of Beckett's early plays) is especially useful. This book included *Three Dialogues* by Beckett and Georges Duthuit, in which the playwright examines the 'expressive act' of three painters and, by implication, comments on his own.

Of the dramatists born just before the Second World War and seeing their first plays produced in the fifties, John Osborne and Harold Pinter have each attracted several full-scale critical studies, as well as shorter monographs and 'study aids'. Simon Trussler's *The Plays of John Osborne* and Martin Esslin's *The Peopled Wound: the Work of Harold Pinter* are the best of these, Trussler's book being remarkable for maintaining a full theatrical context for criticism and Esslin's for its sustained attention to philosophical implication and its authoritative and perceptive account of Pinter's whole career in the theatre—biographical information was supplied or verified by the dramatist. On Pinter's plays Lois Gordon's *Stratagems to Uncover Nakedness* is good on dramatic structure; and Walter Ker's brief *Harold Pinter* is alert and lively. Other dramatists of the same generation have not attracted such sustained critical interest as these two, but there are considered studies of Arnold Wesker by Glenda Leeming and Simon Trussler, of John Arden by Albert Hunt, and of John Whiting by Simon Trussler. Wesker has also been the subject of a collection of documentary materials edited by M. Marland and published by The Times Education Services; he has himself published two volumes of critical and political essays.

The Contemporary Dramatists Series by Ronald Hayman is valuable in providing short (and inexpensive) introductory accounts of writers who have not been the subject of more extended studies: his volumes on Robert Bolt, John Whiting, and John Arden are especially recommended. Since it commenced publication early in 1971, *Theatre Quarterly* has sometimes featured individual dramatists, such as the critical essay, the interview, and the production log for *Lear* in Volume 2 No. 5 of January–March 1972 that together provide a useful basis for the study of Edward Bond. But such special issues are bound to be limited in scope, and any study of Bond at this stage of his career would also benefit from reference to the special issue of *Gambit* that appeared a short time before.

For most dramatists working in the English Theatre since 1945 a student must search newspapers and periodicals for criticism and biographical information. Nor should he neglect the interviews, reviews, articles, essays, letters, and poems by the dramatists themselves which are published in many different forms. A successful dramatist is today pursued by publishers, journalists, interviewers, critics, and students as never before; some like Beckett and Pinter resist these attentions, others use them occasionally for their own purposes, and others talk and write freely. The interest of such material may be gauged by reference to John Whiting's account of *The Art of the Dramatist* and his published theatre reviews, to Harold Pinter's volume of collected *Poems* which includes a commentary on his play, *The Birthday Party*, in the verses entitled 'A View of the Party', and to Ann Jellicoe's candid and revealing lecture given in the University of Cambridge in 1967, entitled *Some Unconscious Influences in the Theatre*.

REFERENCES

GENERAL

ed. W. A. Armstrong, *Experimental Drama* (London, 1963).
ed. J. R. Brown, *Modern British Dramatists: A Collection of Critical Essays* (Twentieth Century Views, Englewood Cliffs, N.J., 1968).
J. R. Brown, *Theatre Language: A Study of Arden, Osborne, Pinter and Wesker* (London, 1972).
ed. J. R. Brown and B. Harris, *Contemporary Theatre* (Stratford-upon-Avon Studies 4, London, 1962).
R. Cohn, *Currents in Contemporary Drama* (Bloomington, Ind., 1969).
M. Esslin, *The Theatre of the Absurd* (London, 1961).
B. Gascoigne, *Twentieth Century Drama* (London, 1962; rev. edn., 1967).

R. Gaskell, *Drama and Reality: The European Theatre Since Ibsen* (London, 1972).

L. Kitchin, *Drama in the Sixties: Form and Interpretation* (London, 1966).

——, *Mid-Century Drama* (London, 1960; rev. edn., 1962).

A. Lewis, *The Contemporary Theatre: The Significant Playwrights of Our Time* (New York, 1962; rev. edn., 1971).

F. Lumley, *New Trends in 20th Century Drama: A Survey since Ibsen and Shaw* (London, 1956; rev. edn., 1967).

ed. J. F. McCrindle, *Behind the Scenes: Theatre and Film Interviews from the Transatlantic Review* (New York, 1971).

ed. C. Marowitz, T. Milne, and O. Hale, *The Encore Reader* (London, 1965).

ed. C. Marowitz and S. Trussler, *Theatre at Work* (London, 1967).

A. Nicoll, *English Drama: A Modern Viewpoint* (London, 1968).

ed. H. Popkin, *The New British Drama* (New York, 1964).

J. R. Taylor, *Anger and After: A Guide to the New British Drama* (London, 1962; rev. edn., 1969).

—— *The Second Wave: British Drama for the Seventies* (London, 1971).

Tulane Drama Review 11.2 (New York, 1966).

The Twentieth Century 169, no. 1008 (London 1961).

ed. W. Wager, *The Playwrights Speak* (New York, 1967).

R. Williams, *From Ibsen to Eliot* (London, 1952; rev. edn., 1958).

INDIVIDUAL DRAMATISTS

ed. J. Parker, *et al.*, *Who's Who in the Theatre: A Biographical Record of the Contemporary Stage* (London, 1912, etc.).

ed. J. Vinson, *Contemporary Dramatists* (London and Chicago, Ill., 1973).

John Arden (1930–)

R. Hayman, *John Arden* (Contemporary Playwrights Series, London, 1968).

A. Hunt, *Arden: A Study of His Plays* (London, 1973).

Samuel Beckett (1906–)

R. Federman and J. Fletcher, *Samuel Beckett: His Works and His Critics. An Essay in Bibliography* (Berkeley, Calif., 1970).

R. Cohn, *Samuel Beckett: The Comic Gamut* (New Brunswick, N.J., 1962).

ed. M. Esslin, *Samuel Beckett: A Collection of Critical Essays* (Twentieth Century Views, Englewood Cliffs, N.J., 1965).

J. Fletcher and J. Spurling, *Beckett: A Study of His Plays* (London, 1972).

F. J. Hoffman, *Samuel Beckett: The Language of Self* (Carbondale, Ill., 1962).

H. Kenner, *Samuel Beckett: A Critical Study* (New York, 1961).

Robert Bolt (1924–)

R. Hayman, *Robert Bolt* (Contemporary Playwrights Series, London, 1969).

Edward Bond (1934–)
Theatre Quarterly 2, No. 5 (London, 1972).
Gambit 5, No. 17 (London, 1970).

Sir Noël Coward (1899–1973)
Play Parade, 6 vols. (London, 1934–62).

S. Morley, *A Talent to Amuse: A Biography of Noël Coward* (London, 1969).

Thomas Stearns Eliot (1888–1965)
Collected Plays (London, 1962).
On Poetry and Poets (London, 1957).

E. M. Browne, *The Making of T. S. Eliot's Plays* (London, 1969).
D. Donoghue, *The Third Voice; Modern British and American Verse Drama* (Princeton, N.J., 1959).
D. Gallup, *T. S. Eliot: A Bibliography* (New York, rev. edn., 1969).
H. Gardner, *The Art of T. S. Eliot* (London, 1949).
D. E. Jones, *The Plays of T. S. Eliot* (London, 1960).
R. Peacock, *The Poet in the Theatre* (London, 1946; rev. edn., 1960).
C. H. Smith, *T. S. Eliot's Dramatic Theory and Practice* (Princeton, N.J., 1963).
G. Smith, *T. S. Eliot's Poetry and Plays* (Chicago, Ill., 1956).

Christopher Fry (1907–)
An Experience of Critics (London, 1952).

D. Sandford, *Christopher Fry: An Appreciation* (London, 1951; rev. edn., 1962).

Graham Greene (1904–)
J. Atkins, *Graham Greene* (London, rev. edn., 1966).

Ann Jellicoe (1927–)
Some Unconscious Influences in the Theatre (Judith Wilson Lecture, Cambridge, 1967).

John Osborne (1929–)
Simon Trussler, *The Plays of John Osborne: An Assessment* (London, 1969).

Harold Pinter (1930–)
Poems (London, 2nd edn., 1971).
M. Esslin, *The Peopled Wound: The Work of Harold Pinter* (London, 1970).

Lois G. Gordon, *Stratagems to Uncover Nakedness: The Dramas of Harold Pinter* (Columbia, Mo., 1969).
W. Ker, *Harold Pinter* (New York, 1967).

John Boynton Priestley (1894–)
The Plays (3 vols., London, 1948–50).

G. L. Evans, *J. B. Priestley—the Dramatist* (London, 1964).

Terence Rattigan (1911–)
Collected Plays, 3 vols. (London, 1953–64).

Arnold Wesker (1932–)
Fears of Fragmentation (London, 1970).
Six Sundays in January (London, 1971).

G. Leeming and S. Trussler, *The Plays of Arnold Wesker: An Assessment* (London, 1971).
ed. M. Marland, *Arnold Wesker* (Times Authors series, London, 1970).

John Whiting (1917–63)
ed. R. Hayman, *The Collected Plays*, 2 vols. (London, 1969).
——, *The Art of the Dramatist* (London, 1970).
John Whiting on Theatre (London, 1966).

R. Hayman, *John Whiting* (Contemporary Playwrights Series, London, 1969).
S. Trussler, *The Plays of John Whiting: An Assessment* (London, 1972).

NOTES ON THE CONTRIBUTORS

John Bamborough is the Principal of Linacre College, Oxford, and editor of *The Review of English Studies*. His publications include *Ben Jonson* (1970) and the New English Classics edition of *Volpone* (1963).

John Barnard is Senior Lecturer in English at the University of Leeds. He has edited Congreve's *The Way of the World* (1972), the Penguin *Works of John Keats* (1973), and the Critical Heritage *Pope* (1973).

Michael Booth is Professor of Drama at Warwick University and the editor of *Eighteenth-Century Tragedy* (1965) and *The Magistrate and Other Plays* (1974). He is publishing a five-volume edition of *English Plays of the Nineteenth Century* (1969–76).

John Russell Brown is Professor of English at the University of Sussex and an Associate Director of the National Theatre. He has edited several plays by Shakespeare and Webster and is the co-editor of volumes of Stratford-upon-Avon Studies on Elizabethan, Jacobean, and contemporary drama. Among his books on modern drama are *Effective Theatre* (1969), and *Modern British Dramatists* in the Twentieth-Century Views series (1968).

T. W. Craik is Professor of English at the University of Dundee. He is the author of *The Tudor Interlude* (1958) and *The Comic Tales of Chaucer* (1964), and has edited plays by Massinger for the New Mermaids series.

H. Neville Davies is a Fellow of the Shakespeare Institute and Lecturer in English at the University of Birmingham. His publications include contributions to *Silent Poetry* (1970), edited by A. Fowler, and *Fair Forms* (1975), edited by M.-S. Røstvig.

Inga-Stina Ewbank is Professor of English at Bedford College, London University, and the author of *Their Proper Sphere* (1966), a study of the Brontë sisters. She has published articles and critical essays on Elizabethan and Jacobean dramatists and on Ibsen.

Kathleen M. Lea, Emeritus Fellow and former Vice-Principal of Lady Margaret Hall, Oxford, is the author of *Italian Popular Comedy* (1934), and Secretary of the Malone Society.

John Leyerle, Director of the Centre for Medieval Studies at the University of Toronto, has published essays on medieval literature.

Margery M. Morgan is Reader in English at the University of Lancaster. Her publications include *A Drama of Political Man: A Study in the Plays of Harley Granville Barker* (1961) and *The Shavian Playground* (1972).

Allardyce Nicoll, Professor Emeritus of English Language and Literature at the University of Birmingham, has held Professorships at the Universities of London and Yale, and was for ten years the Director of the Shakespeare Institute in Stratford-upon-Avon. Among his numerous publications are *The English Theatre* (1936), *A History of the English Drama 1660–1900* (1952–9), *Theatre and Dramatic Theory* (1963), and *English Drama: A Modern Viewpoint* (1968).

David J. Palmer is Senior Lecturer in English at the University of Hull. He has edited two plays by Shakespeare and is the author of *The Rise of English Studies* (1965) and a number of studies on Shakespeare and other dramatists.

Cecil J. L. Price is Professor of English at University College, Swansea, and the author of *The English Theatre in Wales* (1948) and *Theatre in the Age of Garrick* (1973). He has edited *The Letters of Richard Brinsley Sheridan* (1966) and *The Dramatic Works of Richard Brinsley Sheridan* (1973).

Ann Saddlemyer is Professor of English and Director of the Graduate Centre for the Study of Drama at the University of Toronto. She has edited *The Plays of J. M. Synge* (1969), *The Plays of Lady Augusta Gregory* (1971), and *Letters to Molly: John Millington Synge to Maire O'Neill* (1971), and is the author of *In Defence of Lady Gregory, Playwright* (1966).

S. Schoenbaum is Franklyn Bliss Snyder Professor of English Literature at Northwestern University, Illinois, and the author of *Shakespeare's Lives* (1970) and *Shakespeare: A Documentary Life* (1975). He is the joint editor of *A New Companion to Shakespeare Studies* (1971), and has written extensively on Jacobean drama.

Michael J. Taylor is Associate Professor of English at the University of New Brunswick and has published critical essays on Shakespeare and his contemporaries.

Peter Thomson is Professor of Drama at Exeter University and co-editor (with Kenneth Richards) of *Nineteenth-Century British Theatre* (1971) and *The Eighteenth-Century English Stage* (1972).

THE EDITOR

Stanley Wells is Reader in English and Fellow of the Shakespeare Institute of the University of Birmingham. He is a Governor of the Royal Shakespeare Theatre and Director of their Summer School. He is the author of *Literature and Drama: with Special Reference to Shakespeare and his Contemporaries* (1970) and of a number of studies of Shakespeare and the theatre. He is Associate Editor of the New Penguin Shakespeare, for which he has edited several volumes.

INDEX OF DRAMATISTS AND ANONYMOUS PLAYS

Addison, Joseph, 204, 207
Albery, James, 214, 228
Arden, John, 291, 294–6
Bale, John, 33, 39
Barrie, Sir James M., 273, 275–6, 286
Bax, Clifford, 278, 286
Beaumont, Francis, 100–3, 108–10, 136, 146
Beckett, Samuel, 253–4, 256–8, 290, 291, 293–4, 296
Behan, Brendan, 253, 258
Behn, Aphra, 179, 191
Besier, Rudolf, 278, 286
Bolt, Robert, 295, 296
Bond, Edward, 295, 297
Bottomley, Gordon, 278, 286
Boucicault, Dion, 214, 218, 228, 248, 264
Boyle, William, 252, 264
Bridie, James, 276, 286
Brighouse, Harold, 277, 286
Browne, William, 136, 144
Campion, Thomas, 136, 142, 146
Carew, Thomas, 136, 142, 144, 146
Carroll, Paul Vincent, 253, 264
Chapman, George, 61–4, 67–8, 136, 141–2, 146, 149
Chester Plays, 23, 24, 27
Cibber, Colley, 179, 186, 191, 204–5, 208
Clarke, Austin, 253, 264–5
Cokayne, Aston, 136, 146
Colman, George, the Elder, 204–6, 208
Colman, George, the Younger, 218, 220, 228
Colum, Padraic, 252, 265
Congreve, William, 174, 176–8, 183–6, 190, 195–7
Coventry Plays, 25, 27
Coward, Sir Noël, 272, 276, 287, 293, 297
Crowne, John, 179, 191

Cumberland, Richard, 204–5, 208
Daniel, Samuel, 136, 140, 146
Davenant, William, 136, 138, 142, 144–6, 150–5, 166–9
Davies, Hubert Henry, 273, 277, 287
Daviot, Gordon, 278, 287
Dekker, Thomas, 106–8, 112
Dibdin, Charles, the Younger, 218, 228
Drinkwater, John, 273, 277, 287
Dryden, John, 151–72
Duffett, Thomas, 152, 154, 167, 171
Eliot, T. S., 278, 287, 292–3, 297
Ervine, St. John, 254, 265
Etherege, George, 175–6, 180–1, 193
Everyman, 25, 27, 29
Farquhar, George, 187–8, 198
Fielding, Henry, 204–6, 208
Fitzball, Edward, 218, 228
Fitzmaurice, George, 252, 266
Flecker, James Elroy, 278, 287
Fletcher, John, 100–3, 108–10
Foote, Samuel, 206, 208
Ford, John, 113–19, 123–6, 127–8, 131–3
Friel, Brian, 254, 266
Fry, Christopher, 278, 293, 297
Galsworthy, John, 273, 276, 287
Garrick, David, 152, 204–6, 209
Gay, John, 200–1, 209
Gesta Grayorum, 139, 146
Gilbert, Sir William Schwenk, 214, 218, 222–4, 228–9
Goldsmith, Oliver, 201, 210
Granville-Barker, Harley, 277–8, 281, 288
Greene, Graham, 293, 297
Greene, Robert, 29, 33, 35, 40
Gregory, Lady Isabella Augusta, 248, 251, 258–9
Hankin, St. John, 273, 288
Heywood, John, 30, 33, 39
Heywood, Thomas, 104–6, 110–12

Holcroft, Thomas, 205, 211
Home, John, 204, 207
Houghton, Stanley, 273, 277, 288
Housman, Laurence, 271–2, 288
Jellicoe, Ann, 295, 297
Johnston, Denis, 253, 266
Jones, Henry Arthur, 213–14, 218, 225, 229, 270
Jonson, Ben, 54–61, 65–7, 136, 138, 140–9
Keane, John B., 253, 266
Kilroy, Thomas, 253, 266
Knowles, Sheridan, 218, 229
Kyd, Thomas, 29, 33–5, 40
Lawrence, D. H., 277, 288
Lee, Nathaniel, 163–9, 172
Levy, Benn, 277, 288
Lewes, George Henry, 220
Lillo, George, 204–5, 211
Longford, Christine, Countess of, 253, 266
Lonsdale, Frederick, 277, 288
Lyly, John, 29, 33, 34, 39
Lyndsay, Sir David, 33, 39
Macklin, Charles, 206, 211
Marlowe, Christopher, 35, 42–53
Marston, John, 69–76, 92–4, 136
Marston, John Westland, 221
Martyn, Edward, 252, 259
Masefield, John, 277, 288
Masque of Flowers, 146
Massinger, Philip, 69, 86–92, 97–9
Maugham, William Somerset, 273, 276, 289
Mayne, Rutherford, 254, 266
Medwall, Henry, 29–30
Middleton, Thomas, 69, 76–86, 94–7, 122, 146
Milne, A. A., 276, 289
Milton, John, 144
Montague, William, 136, 146
Moore, George, 248, 267
Murray, Thomas Cornelius, 252, 267
Mystery cycles:
  Chester, 23, 24, 27
  Coventry, 25, 27
  Towneley (Wakefield), 24, 27
  York, 24, 27
Nabbes, Thomas, 136, 146
Norton, Thomas, Earl of Dorset, 30
O'Casey, Sean, 252–3, 260

O'Kelly, Seamus, 252, 267
Osborne, John, 290, 291, 294, 297
Otway, Thomas, 164–8, 172
Peele, George, 29, 33, 35, 39–40, 41
Phillips, Stephen, 276, 289
Pinero, Arthur Wing, 213–14, 225, 229
Pinter, Harold, 290–5, 297
Planché, James Robinson, 218, 222–3, 230
Priestley, John Boynton, 276, 289, 293, 298
Proteus and the Adamantine Rock, 139, 146
Quem quaeritis?, 21
Rastell, John, 30
Rattigan, Sir Terence, 277, 289, 293, 298
Reade, Charles, 223, 230
Redford, John, 30
Robertson, Thomas William, 217, 218, 223, 230
Robinson, Lennox, 252, 260–1
Rowe, Nicholas, 205, 211
Russell, George William ('A.E.'), 252, 264
Sackville, Thomas, 30
Settle, Elkanah, 154
Shadwell, Thomas, 152, 154, 181–2, 193–4
Shaw, George Bernard, 231–47, 273–4
Sheridan, Richard Brinsley, 201–3, 204, 211–12
Sherriff, R. C., 278, 289
Shiels, George, 254, 267
Shirley, James, 136, 138, 144, 146, 148
Skelton, John, 33, 39
Steele, Richard, 204–5, 212
Stephen, George, 221
Suckling, Sir John, 179, 192
Sutro, Alfred, 277, 289
Sutton-Vane, Vane, 278, 289
Synge, John Millington, 250, 261–2
Taylor, Tom, 222, 230
Thompson, Sam, 254, 267
Tomelty, Joseph, 254, 267
Tourneur, Cyril, 113–19, 121–3, 127–8, 130–1
Towneley (Wakefield) Plays, 24, 27
Townshend, Aurelian, 136, 146
Udall, Nicholas, 33, 39
Vanbrugh, Sir John, 186–7, 197

Villiers, George, Duke of Buckingham, 154, 167, 179, 191
Wager, William, 29–30, 33, 39
Wakefield Plays, 24, 27
Webster, John, 113–21, 127–30
Wesker, Arnold, 291, 294, 298
Whiting, John, 294, 295, 298

Wilde, Oscar, 214, 218, 220, 224–5, 230
Williams, Emlyn, 277, 289
Wycherley, William, 174, 176–8, 182–3, 194–5
Yeats, William Butler, 248–51, 262–4
York Plays, 24, 27

95644